# Meditations
## by
# John Baptist de La Salle

**Frontispiece**: An engraving by Joffroy of a portrait made of De La Salle in his coffin. See **Iconographie**, by Joseph Cornet, FSC, and Emile Rousset, FSC, *Cahiers lasalliens 49*, 1989, Presses de Gedit, Belgium. This is the frontispiece of the original edition of both volumes of De La Salle's meditations.

# Meditations
# by
# John Baptist de La Salle

Translated by Richard Arnandez, FSC, and
Augustine Loes, FSC

Edited by Augustine Loes, FSC, and
Francis Huether, FSC

1994, reprinted 2007
Lasallian Publications

This volume is a translation of two works by John Baptist de La Salle, *Méditations pour les Dimanches et les principales Fêtes de l'année* (*Meditations for the Sundays and the Principal Feasts of the Year*) [1731?] and *Méditations pour le Temps de la Retraite* (*Meditations for the Time of Retreat*) [1730?].

———— ✦ ————

*Meditations by John Baptist de La Salle*
is volume 4 of Lasallian Sources:
The Complete Works of Saint John Baptist de La Salle

Copyright © 1994 by Christian Brothers Conference
All rights reserved

Printed in the United States of America

Library Congress catalog card number 94-070440
ISBN 0-944808-11-5 (hardbound)
ISBN 0-944808-12-3 (paperback)

**Cover**: Church of Saint Remigius in Reims, where De La Salle often spent nights in prayer when he was beginning the work of the Christian Schools.

Brother Richard Arnandez, FSC, was born in New Iberia, Louisiana. From 1933 to 1936, he taught in the boarding school of the Christian Brothers in Passy-Froyennes, Belgium. He holds a Bachelor's degree from Manhattan College and a *Licence ès Lettres* from the University of Lille, France. After a number of years as teacher and administrator, Brother Richard was appointed Provincial of the New Orleans–Santa Fe Province. From 1969 to 1972 he served in Rome as the Secretary General and the Vice-Procurator General of the Congregation. He is the author of several books and journal articles and a professional translator.

Brother Augustine Loes, FSC, did his undergraduate studies at the Catholic University of America and holds a Master's degree in classics from Fordham University and in clinical psychology from Catholic University. He has taught in several secondary schools of the New York District and administered schools, child care institutions, a training college for young Brothers, and a retirement home for aged and infirm Brothers. He served for several years as Provincial of his New York Province. Currently he works as editor and translator for Lasallian Publications.

Brother Francis Huether, FSC, is a native of New York City, although for many years he has worked in the Chicago area. In his sixty-plus years as a Christian Brother, he has been teacher, administrator, comptroller, and supervisor of schools. In 1972 he helped establish the national (later regional) education office of the Christian Brothers Conference, and he served as its first secretary for over fifteen years. The Huether Workshop of Lasallian educators is named in his honor. Bother Francis holds Bachelor's and Master's degrees in German from The Catholic University of America and has studied at Fordham, Columbia, Canisius, and Rhode Island College. Presently he is copy editor for Lasallian Publications.

# Lasallian Publications

Sponsored by the Regional Conference of Christian Brothers of the United States and Toronto, Lasallian Publications will produce 30 volumes on the life, writings, and work of John Baptist de La Salle (1651–1719), founder of the Brothers of the Christian Schools, and on the early history of the Brothers. These volumes will be presented in two series.

✦ **Lasallian Sources**, in 9 volumes, consists of new English translations and editions of all the writings of John Baptist de La Salle.

✦ **Lasallian Resources** consists of the three early biographies of John Baptist de La Salle, four thematic studies based on documents contemporary with the foundation of the Brothers of the Christian Schools, and translations and editions of current Lasallian studies.

## Volumes Already Published in This Series

### Lasallian Sources

> *The Letters of John Baptist de La Salle.* Translated and edited by Colman Molloy, FSC, and Augustine Loes, FSC (1988).
>
> *Collection of Various Short Treatises.* Translated by W. J. Battersby, FSC, and edited by Daniel Burke, FSC (1993).
>
> *The Rules of Christian Decorum and Civility.* Translated by Richard Arnandez, FSC, and edited by Gregory Wright, FSC (1985).

### Lasallian Resources

#### Early Biographies
> *The Life of John Baptist de La Salle.* Canon John Baptist Blain. Translated by Richard Arnandez, FSC (1985).

#### Early Documents
> *John Baptist de La Salle: The Formative Years.* Luke Salm, FSC (1989).

#### Current Lasallian Studies
> *John Baptist de La Salle and Special Education: A Study of Saint Yon.* Othmar Würth, FSC. Translated by Augustine Loes, FSC. Adapted by Francis Huether, FSC. Edited by Bonaventure Miner, FSC (1988).
>
> *So Favored by Grace: Education in the Time of John Baptist de La Salle.* Edited by Lawrence J. Colhocker, FSC (1991).

# Contents

## Part Two: Meditations for the Principal Feasts of the Year

### January

## February

## March

## April

## May

## June

## July

## August

## September

## October

## November

## December

## Six Additional Meditations for Certain Feasts That Occur During the Year

## Part Three: Meditations for the Time of Retreat

## Appendices

# Editors' Note

De La Salle's style of writing, especially in his meditations, has been described as austere. It is, in fact, a very simple style, probably because he composed the meditations for public reading to the Brothers in preparation for the prayer they would make privately together following the community vocal prayers. In translating the meditations, an effort has been made to preserve this simplicity.

Two examples are worth noting. Often De La Salle will repeat the same word two or three times in a sentence or in successive sentences; a translator would be inclined to use synonyms to avoid the repetition. Similarly, De La Salle has favorite adjectives and adverbs, such as *bien, fort, grand,* and *beaucoup,* which he uses uniformly; in English the adjective or the adverb would vary according to the noun or the verb that is being modified. The present translation has kept to De La Salle's usage as far as possible, out of respect for the author's style and the classical status of his work.

Another aspect of De La Salle's style is his use of long sentences, not uncharacteristic of his time, often including several participial clauses; in English today such sentences would be broken up into several shorter sentences. (Such a long sentence is preserved in the translation, in Appendix A, of the original introduction of the first volume of meditations, probably written by Brother Timothée, second Superior General.) The present translation has tried to preserve some of the long sentences, sometimes by changing the participial clauses into dependent clauses. In other instances the long sentences have been broken into shorter ones for easier reading.

Two goals have been sought throughout the translation: to keep as close as possible to the language as well as the thought of De La Salle and to write in a way that makes for fluent reading. A Glossary is presented in Appendix B to explain how individual French words have been translated and to comment on certain expressions that are typical of De La Salle and the spirituality of his time.

In his meditations De La Salle uses the Scriptures more by memory, allusion, and paraphrase than by direct quotation. This translation has been made accordingly; modern English translations have only occasionally been consulted for a word or phrase. (See MDF 92.3.)

The numbering of the meditations for the Sundays and feasts does not follow completely the sequence of the original edition, which is kept in this present edition, but follows the numeration of the edition of 1882. For the sake of uniformity in making references, the numbering of the 1882 edition has been accepted as the standard numbering for all editions. In the 1882 edition, the sequence of the meditations was changed to follow the liturgical year for feast days, instead of the calendar year as in the original. Also, six meditations in the *Additions* of the original volume were placed in the body of the text; putting them back in the *Additions* has put their numbering out of order.

This present edition includes the meditations written by De La Salle for the time of retreat, which originally appeared as a separate volume. They have been included here in order to make all of De La Salle's meditations available in one volume.

Biographical and related notes have been added to the meditations for feasts, often borrowing material from the notes prepared by Battersby for his edition of the meditations in 1953.

# Acknowledgments

Several Brothers have collaborated on this new translation of the meditations written by De La Salle. The major work, of course, was accomplished by Richard Arnandez, who did the translation of the meditations for the Sundays and feasts of the year. Augustine Loes reworked his 1975 translation of Meditations for the Time of Retreat. Joseph Schmidt, Francis Huether, Lawrence Oelschlegel, and Augustine Loes collaborated on the editing, with the final decisions shared by Huether and Loes. A team of Brothers from De La Salle Hall, Lincroft, New Jersey, collaborated on the proofreading of the manuscript: Michael Finnegan, Benedict Ginane, Bernard McKenna, Henry McGrath, Daniel O'Brien, Austin O'Malley, and Gregory Quinn, assisted by Mr. Robert Quinn (no relative). So it happened that a certain balance of ethos was assured in the undertaking! Subsequently, Brothers Floyd Warwick and Jack Curran made additional corrections while following Buttimer III in the summer of 1993. The editors are likewise greatly indebted to Mrs. Carol Hamm of the Christian Brothers Conference office and Mr. Leonard Heinzmann of Queen of Peace High School, North Arlington, New Jersey, for their invaluable assistance in the computer processing of the manuscript.

# Abbreviations

**AMG**  Archives, Generalate of the Brothers of the Christian Schools, Rome, Italy

**CIA**  *Circulaires instructives et administratives* of the Institute of the Brothers of the Christian Schools

**CL**  *Cahiers lasalliens*

**MDF**  *Méditations pour les Dimanches et les principales Fêtes de l'année* (CL 12)

**MTR**  *Méditations pour le Temps de la Retraite* (CL 13)

**R**  *Recueil de différents petits traités à l'usage des Frères des Ecoles Chrétiennes*

**RC**  *Règles communes des Frères des Ecoles Chrétiennes*

# Introduction

The Second Vatican Council urged religious institutes to become familiar with and preserve the spirit and goals of their founders as well as the history and traditions of their communities.[1] This invitation has inspired a great deal of research into the original writings of John Baptist de La Salle that gave direction to the spiritual journey of his first disciples. The same invitation has also encouraged research and study to throw light on the specific spiritual insights that gave direction to the Founder in the decisions he made throughout his own life.

Following Vatican II and in the course of the adapted renewal that it proposed, it has also been necessary to read the signs of the times. In a world that is constantly evolving, how can community discernment and recourse to the Holy Spirit rediscover the dynamism and the relevance of the original spirit of the Institute? The lack of new members, the aging of those in the work, the takeover of the schools by the state or by lay colleagues, have undermined the previous feeling of security. A new era has begun without warning. All of a sudden, it seems, a new path must be found or created by the religious community. It is a task that calls for continual work. As Pope Paul VI declared, "The adapted renewal cannot be effected once and for all time; it must be undertaken ceaselessly by the fervor of individual religious and well-planned efforts of chapters and superiors."[2]

It is now 300 years since De La Salle took the initiative and set out on a new way of life. He saw that the children of the working class and the poor were almost totally neglected, without training or education; he formed a body of teachers and organized schools with a program that assured effective teaching. A *Mémoire* submitted to the town council of Rouen in 1721 describes this original work of De La Salle.

> This Institute was started in the year 1680 by M. De La Salle, Canon of Reims, a man filled with great compassion for the large

number of children of the poor and the working class whose fathers and mothers were unable to teach them the truths of religion, partly because they were not educated themselves, partly because they had to go to work every day to earn their livelihood and leave their unfortunate children to fend for themselves. De La Salle developed a plan to establish schools where the children of the poor and the working class would receive free lessons in reading, writing, and arithmetic, and a Christian education through catechetical instruction and other daily training suited to form good Christians. To do this he formed a group of unmarried young men who, although willing to become teachers for young people and to live an obscure life, were largely unable to do so for lack of opportunity.[3]

What was the secret of this priest from Reims that explains the perduring success his Institute has had, a success without precedent in history? To understand the charism that inspired him—not just to retrace the story of his life but, rather, to set forth as clearly as possible the vital force behind his apostolic activity—his disciples have since 1956 been in the process of discovering the answer to this question by studying his writings and the decisions he made at the important junctures of his life.

De La Salle is recognized as having a prominent place among the leaders of elementary education in his day, but as a teacher of spirituality, he has for too long been overlooked in the Church.[4] This has happened because his spiritual writings have been circulated almost exclusively among the members of the Institute he founded. Yet it is altogether fitting that he be given his place among the spirituality traditions of Saint Francis de Sales, Pierre de Bérulle, Charles de Condren, Jean-Jacques Olier, Saint Vincent de Paul, and Saint John Eudes.[5]

Modern Lasallian study was initiated with the decision of the General Chapter of 1956 to create the *Monumenta Lasalliana* of the *Cahiers lasalliens* [CL], a series which now includes facsimiles of all the first editions of the pedagogical and spiritual writings of the Founder, John Baptist de La Salle, and more than 40 other volumes of original research.[6] The Institute's expansion outside of France in the nineteenth century led to English and Spanish translations of most of De La Salle's writings. This volume is a new English translation of two of his works, *Meditations for Sundays and the Principal Feasts* (MDF) and *Meditations for the Time of Retreat* (MTR).

Since 1959 two exhaustive studies of MTR have been completed;[7] however, MDF is hardly known outside of the Institute. It would indeed be true to say that very few Brothers have profited from the thought of their Founder as it is found in these meditations. Yet this legacy of De La Salle conveys a spiritual doctrine that is especially suited for people engaged in the Christian education of youth. His meditations are concerned with the everyday life of teachers and with their religious formation, without separating their personal consecration to God from an apostolic ministry immersed in the daily problems of a demanding work. Recently a study of the sources of *Meditations for the Principal Feasts* was published in an effort to stimulate a return to these texts, which are so replete with authentic Lasallian spirituality.[8]

Appendix C sets forth briefly the arrangement and the content of the texts of MDF and MTR, the various editions published through the years, and the sources of some of the texts in the light of published research during the past 30 years.

This introduction will have four parts, first, in order to appreciate the spirituality of seventeenth-century France, a description of the state of religious practice at the end of the sixteenth century; second, a brief summary of De La Salle's contact with the French School of spirituality; third, a selection of passages from De La Salle's meditations to show how he made use of the principal themes of that spirituality, and fourth, how he developed an original spirituality for the community of Brothers he established, which is pertinent to all Christian teachers today.

# I

# Religious Practice in France at the End of the Sixteenth Century

Before illustrating the spirituality of De La Salle with selections from his meditations, it seems advantageous to describe the state of religion in France at the end of the sixteenth century, in order to understand better the spirituality of the seventeenth century, which was in large part a reaction to that condition. This will also help understand better the spirituality of the Founder.

"To speak of the decadence of religion in France at the end of the sixteenth century has become commonplace, both for historians and biographers."[9] After 40 years of civil war, the social structure was riddled with the worst disorders, and the practice of religion had become increasingly abandoned. At all levels of the Catholic hierarchy, made up of men from the upper class, there was every sort of intrigue and complicity to maintain privilege and gain promotions to higher status and greater financial benefit.

To understand this behavior and the greed that also possessed the noble and bourgeois classes, it is necessary to know that for many years numerous families had taken advantage of the connection between politics and religion to improve their financial and social position, which originally had been won with great effort. The sense of honor and of ancestral tradition forbade any return to the past. Everyone understood clearly that the one sure way to add to the glory of the family name and to strengthen its position in the social order was through the power of money.

The Church was rich at this time, and France was rich, very rich. Church wealth was equal to more than one-third of the total wealth of the entire nation, and this ratio was continually increasing in favor of the Church.[10] To secure an appointment in this ecclesiastical organism was sure to be rewarding, so applicants were always at hand.

The financial power of the Church could have created serious problems for the unstable government of the monarchy if the Concordat of 1516, in exchange for certain royal privileges granted to the clergy, had not given the king control of a large number of Church positions that provided those who held title to them with considerable financial benefit. The king had, in effect, a kind of treasury of bonuses to distribute under the guise of rewards for good servants of the state.

By the system of *commendam,* the king would assign ownership of abbeys, parishes, and even bishoprics to people who were ineligible according to Church law. Such titulars could be secular priests, members of the laity, women, even young children, who would receive the tonsure to make them technically qualified for the benefits. Sully, a Protestant and friend of Henry IV, was given four abbeys. A deputy chosen by the titular would then carry out the function in return for a small part of the revenue. More often than not, the titular never appeared in the assigned diocese or monastery. This system naturally led to an almost complete separation of the spiritual responsibility from the financial revenue attached to it.

In convents the abbesses and prioresses were elected in most cases and lived in their convents. Nevertheless, the king could suspend the election and name whomever he pleased. In this way the Abbess of Maubuisson, who had been elected in good and proper form, was deposed by Henry IV in favor of Angélique d'Estrée, sister of his mistress, the beautiful Gabrielle. It was customary to choose titulars of 15 to 18 years of age; Jacqueline Arnauld, the future Mother Angélique, was Abbess of Port Royal at the age of eleven.

When families had one of their members receive such an honor, they did all they could not to lose it. Every means was appropriate, even the most fraudulent. In this way a worldly clergy was created, people incapable of performing worthy priestly functions, whose main preoccupation was to increase their revenue.

Most bishops were members of the king's court, literary or military personalities, diplomats, or financiers. Many of the candidates for the priesthood were much more interested in the chance to make money than in the opportunity to serve as priests; ordination was often conferred simply for the asking. The ignorance of the priests, especially in the rural areas, was shameful. Many of them were given over to wine, lust, and witchcraft. Teaching the people the faith was not high on the list of their activities.

Religious priests were not much better. Religious houses for men and women were often a refuge for boys whom their families wanted to disown or girls who had no dowry. Most of the monks never made a novitiate, and in a number of abbeys, military service replaced the practice of prayer for many of their members. This situation did not seem to bother the titulars who had been assigned; in fact, any effort to reform the situation would probably have had a negative effect on their revenue.

In the face of this less than fervent clergy, it is not hard to imagine the religious spirit that characterized the Christian people and the religious life of France at the end of the sixteenth century. The structure was there. Bishops and priests held their positions. Churches gathered in the faithful. Monasteries housed the monks; convents, the nuns. The people came together mostly for display. But all these externals had little or no religious substance. The separation of the revenues of the Church from the spiritual responsibilities produced a similar separation of external appearances from personal morality. A person could easily claim to be a Christian and even a priest, but that could be no guarantee of any personal commitment. The performance of the external acts of religion was most often a social and political duty, not an expression of profound faith.

This, then, was the situation in France at the end of the sixteenth century: a true and profound interior spirit was not generally considered fundamental to the Christian life. The task, therefore, of spiritual leaders and their followers was to bring to life this essential element of Christianity.

The outstanding religious event of the sixteenth century was undoubtedly the Council of Trent (1545–1563), with the great movement for reform that it planned for the whole Catholic Church. The Fathers of the Council placed the execution of their decisions in the hands of the bishops. But, as noted, the bishops of France, with few exceptions, were in a poor condition to make any significant changes. Their feeling was that such a reform was an untimely interference by a foreign authority in the functioning of a system that belonged to the king. This is the principal reason for the delay in following the directives of the Council.

Nonetheless the situation in France was not entirely bleak. There were some points of light, shining and giving promise for a bright future. A few austere religious orders remained untouched by the general moral decline of the times, and faithful Christians turned to them. Among these orders were the Capuchins, established in France in 1573, who were fervent observers of the Rule of Saint Francis. Their heroic life and their mysticism attracted people of all ranks and nurtured their devotion.

The Carthusians, a cloistered and contemplative order, were venerated for their special way of life, their mortification, silence, and solitude. Their religious spirit and the originality of their monastic practices also drew the elite of France to join them.

The Jesuits came to France in 1552. Through their distinguished *collèges* they developed a growing influence among the aristocracy and bourgeoisie. Their theologians and spiritual writers had a strong influence on the religious thought of the seventeenth century.

The example of the religious orders of men was soon followed by congregations of women who were equally fervent. Madame Acarie (1566–1618) led a community of outstanding religious and invited the reformed Carmelites of Teresa of Jesus to come from Spain. Through the efforts of Pierre de Bérulle (1575–1629), seven Spanish religious founded the first French Carmel in 1604. Several other contemplative congregations soon followed.[11] Congregations of the active life were founded about the same time and developed rapidly: the Ursulines (1596), the Daughters of Notre Dame (1607), and the Religious of Notre Dame of Lorraine (1618), founded by Peter Fourier (1565–1640) and Alix Le Clerc (1576–1622).

A list of the books printed during the sixteenth century testifies that devotional writing of all sorts was abundant.[12] It is, therefore, possible to give a fairly clear picture of the kind of reading that was done by the literate, pious people of the time. Unfortunately, there was an almost complete lack of original French works, and the literary and spiritual quality was poor. Most of the good books available were translations into French of Latin translations by the Carthusians of Cologne of books by German or Flemish writers.[13] There were also translations of the Spanish books of Louis of Granada (d. 1588), Teresa of Jesus (d. 1582), John of the Cross (d. 1591), Peter of Alcantara

(d. 1562), and Louis du Pont (d. 1624). From Italy came the spiritual writings and the biography of Saint Catherine of Genoa (d. 1510), published by the Carthusians of Bourgfontaine through numerous editions. A collection of the meditations of Matthias Bellintani (d. 1611), *The Practice of Prayer or Contemplation*, was popular at the beginning of the seventeenth century.

Nevertheless, the need for a basic reform was great, and great spiritual leaders in France responded with the development of a spirituality that has won for seventeenth-century France the titles, "the golden age of spirituality"[14] and "the great age of the soul."[15] Outstanding among those leaders were Saint Francis de Sales (1567–1622), author of *Introduction to the Devout Life* and *Treatise on the Love of God*; Pierre de Bérulle, often referred to as the Founder of the French School of spirituality; Charles de Condren (1588–1641), successor to Bérulle as Superior of the French Oratory; Jean-Jacques Olier (1628–1657), Founder of the Sulpicians, and John Eudes (1601–1680), Founder of the Congregation of Jesus and Mary. Each of these leaders called for a reformed and pious clergy and thus had an influence on John Baptist de La Salle, but De La Salle eventually developed an original spirituality for the Brothers of the Christian Schools and, indeed, for all Christian educators.

# II

## John Baptist de La Salle and the French School

In 1651, when John Baptist de La Salle was born, the chief representatives of the French School of spirituality, Bérulle and Condren, were dead; their two most faithful disciples, Jean-Jacques Olier and John Eudes, were still living. Olier had six more years to live and would spend them in ill health, retired from his work as pastor of Saint Sulpice and devoted to the revision of his writings on the essence of the Christian life. Eudes would live almost 30 years longer, ardently promoting devotion to the hearts of Jesus and Mary while carrying on a rough battle against the untiring opposition of those opposed to his spirituality and practices.

At what moment in his life was the young John Baptist put in contact with the spirituality of the French School? He had occasion at an early age to meet with several devout priests reputed for their knowledge and wisdom. Among them was the Canon Pierre Dozet,

Vicar General, Chancellor of the University of Reims, and relative of the La Salle family, who encouraged John Baptist to receive the tonsure when he was not yet eleven years old. A few years later, in 1661, Canon Dozet resigned his canonry in favor of his young cousin. Such events indicated that as a youth, De La Salle was already aspiring to the priesthood and had the intellectual and moral predispositions for such a state in life.

His parents could afford to have John Baptist attend excellent schools, the Collège des Bons Enfants and the School of Theology of the University of Reims. In 1670 he was admitted to the Sorbonne in Paris to study for a doctorate in theology. Here he met with the disciples of Olier at the seminary of Saint Sulpice and for a year and a half had the benefit of Sulpician formation under the spiritual direction of Louis Tronson and François Leschassier. He could not have found a better way to become familiar with the spirituality of that time.

The death of his mother in 1671 and that of his father nine months later, in 1672, put a premature end to De La Salle's stay in Paris. He had then to take responsibility for the care of his four brothers and two sisters, as well as the family estate. Nonetheless, he managed to continue his studies for the doctorate in theology and ordination to the priesthood. A close relationship with Canon Nicolas Roland, founder of a congregation of women dedicated to the education of young girls, and a chance meeting with Adrien Nyel, a layman devoted to the education of poor boys, led John Baptist to be involved in the establishment of schools and the training of teachers for the Christian education of the poor. In the process he saw the urgent need to provide spiritual formation and pedagogical guidance to these teachers, recognizing as he did the great importance of the schools.

Eventually, John Baptist was led to give up the wealth and social prestige of his canonry and to use his share of the family estate to buy food for the poor people of Reims in a time of famine. This was a major conversion for John Baptist: he was stepping out of one world and into another that was diametrically opposed. With patience he gradually assembled a group of young men who were willing for the glory of God to commit themselves completely to the human and spiritual education of poor children. The program organized by De La Salle had a tremendous impact on the primary school in France. He divided the large class of children into small groups according to their level of learning, adapted an earlier simultaneous method of teaching groups, rather than instructing each student one at a time, and taught children to read the mother tongue, French, instead of Latin, the usual practice at that time. In addition the method of discipline and order established in the classes and in the school brought about extraordinary educational results in a short time.

De La Salle envisioned the spiritual and moral formation of children through the school. He knew that to achieve this result, the teachers would be the major force. He prepared the Brothers for their encounter with the students by making them aware of the presence and action of God in their own life and the dignity and importance of the mission that God had entrusted to them:

> Adore God's fatherly Providence in your regard. He withdrew you from the world in order to prepare you to acquire the virtues you need to do your work well and to educate a great number of children in the Christian spirit. (MDF 131.1)

For De La Salle the spiritual formation of the teachers was uppermost in preparing them for their work with the children. To achieve this formation, he wrote rules to guide them and meditations to teach them the principal themes of spirituality for a Christian educator. Initially inspired by Bérulle, Condren, and their disciples, he gradually developed an original adaptation that established him as a master of Christian spirituality.

# III

## Themes from the French School in De La Salle's Meditations

Rayez has remarked that De La Salle took whatever was good for his purpose wherever he found it and was "extraordinarily attuned to the spiritual influences of people and writings that were available at the end of the seventeenth century."[16] The themes De La Salle developed were already present in the writings of the French School of spirituality and other spiritual leaders of his time. His genius was to adapt these themes to a spirituality for Christian teachers.

Four themes have been selected to show the influence of the French School upon De La Salle and to reflect his own creativity. These themes are theocentrism, christocentrism, the action of the Holy Spirit, and the human person before God. After examining them, we will show how De La Salle personalized them in his own spirituality, as developed in the meditations.

## Theocentrism

When Bérulle speaks of God, he insists on the majesty (*grandeur*) and the holiness of God, which he worships in the admirable unity of nature and adores in the Trinity of Persons. Whether he contemplates God in the absolute quality of the divine essence or imagines God deliberating in council with creatures, for Bérulle there is nothing great except God. This is how Bérulle and his followers define a major and primary basis for their spirituality, theocentrism. This was a reaction to the neglect of God in sixteenth-century France and to the humanism that pervaded much of whatever spirituality did exist; it was also a response to the appeal for reform by the Council of Trent.

In his meditations De La Salle presents God as infinitely superior to all created things:

> To whom ought we to give ourselves if not to the One from whom we have received everything, who alone is our Lord and our Father, and who, as Saint Paul says, has given being to all things and has made us only for himself?" (MDF 90.2)

For Bérulle there was nothing more natural than for a creature to offer God the homage of adoration and of abandonment to the divine will. Condren and Olier use the term "sacrifice-adoration" to express this submission to the divinity. Because the creature is nothing before God, it can only glorify God by self-destruction, by the sacrifice of its being after the example of the Incarnate Word, in particular by the deprivation of personhood in the humanity of Jesus, as well as by the sacrifice of the Cross.

Lasallian spirituality is closer in this to Bérulle than to Condren. When De La Salle describes the attitude of the Virgin Mary before the work that God accomplished in her, he expresses his own feeling of how a person properly responds to the generosity of God:

> By a special privilege, she already enjoyed the use of reason [at the moment of her birth] and made use of it to adore God and to thank him for all his goodness. From that time on, she consecrated herself entirely to God to live and to act only for him during the rest of her life.
>
> She professed her nothingness profoundly in the depths of her soul, acknowledging that she owed everything to God. She admired interiorly what God had done in her, saying to herself what she later declared in her Canticle, God has done great things in me. (MDF 163.3)

## Christocentrism

Bérullian spirituality places the mystery of the Incarnation at the center of the Christian life. A person contemplating the Incarnate Word contemplates the Father, of whom the Son is the perfect image. This is the work of the Holy Spirit, bond of love and unity among the Divine Persons and source of the creativity in the Incarnation of the Word. By his sanctifying action, the Son returns to the Father as origin and source of everything, all that is achieved in the work of God. This is the basis for the divine pattern (*exemplarisme*), an intuition dear to Bérulle.

By considering the states and the mysteries of the life of Jesus, a person achieves an intimate union with him who is "the perfect servant, the perfect religious of God, the perfect adorer of the Father." Several expressions of Saint Paul on this theme can be found again and again in Bérulle's writings: "It is no longer I who live, but Jesus who lives in me" (Gal 2:20); "Have this mind in you which was also in Christ" (Ph 2:5); "May Christ dwell by faith in your hearts" (Eph 3:17). In the French School, this is the summit of the whole life of a Christian.

Lasallian spirituality develops its fundamental orientation from this Christocentrism. Sharing in the mystery of Christ and uniting with him are at the heart of De La Salle's meditations for his disciples:

> Attach yourselves only to Jesus Christ, his doctrine, and his holy maxims, because he has done you the honor of choosing you in preference to a great number of others to announce these truths to children, whom he loves so specially. (MDF 167.2; see also 59.2, 102.2)

In this spirit De La Salle made the phrase, Live Jesus in our hearts, forever! the greeting of the Brothers whenever they wished to begin a conversation and also at the beginning and the end of their principal actions.[17]

## The Action of the Holy Spirit

The Spirit of love and unity holds an important place in the spirituality of the French School. Bérulle writes, "I desire that the Spirit of Jesus Christ be the Spirit of my spirit and the life of my life." Olier encourages his disciples to give themselves completely over to the Spirit and to allow him to act in them. Eudes advises, "Have a great care to give yourself to the Holy Spirit of Jesus, so that he will find you without attachment to your own spirit, . . . will have full power and freedom to act in you according to his desire, . . . and will guide you in the way that pleases him."

Lasallian spirituality gives a central role to the Holy Spirit; it is the soul of the entire life of the Brother:

> You need the fullness of the Spirit of God in your state, for you ought to live and be guided entirely by the spirit and the light of faith; only the Spirit of God can give you this disposition. (MDF 43.2)
>
> You carry out a work that requires you to touch hearts, but this you cannot do except by the Spirit of God. Pray to him to give you today the same grace that he gave to the holy Apostles. Ask him that after filling you with his Holy Spirit to sanctify you, he will also communicate himself to you to procure the salvation of others. (MDF 43.3; see also 43.2)

### The human person before God

The nothingness and the weakness of the sinner are confronted by the majesty (*grandeur*) and holiness of God. This emphasis on the nothingness and the sinfulness of the human person is a fundamental characteristic of the French School of spirituality. The pessimism of Bérulle regarding the sinful human condition, and even more the pessimism of Condren and Olier, reflects clearly a Platonic vision of God. Condren writes that God is ". . . so great, so pure, so living within himself, so separated from a creature, and the creature so unworthy, that if God only looks at a creature, it would be destroyed and consumed in his presence because of his great holiness."[18]

De La Salle does not accept this dark view of the creature before God, but he does insist on the need to recognize "the dependence we have on God and how undeserving we are of enjoying the benefits and happiness of his holy presence."[19] When he uses the expressions "annihilation" and "nothingness," which are so much a part of the vocabulary of the French School when speaking of creatures, his teaching never encourages the self-destruction of the person in order to give honor to God. De La Salle writes, "All creatures . . . must abase themselves and acknowledge their nothingness before God in the sight of his glory and majesty" (MDF 169.1), but he insists only that this ought to lead a person to "a feeling of adoration at the thought of God's presence" (MDF 90.1).

Unlike the French school, De La Salle uses the word "destruction" almost solely in reference to sin.[20] Instead, he uses expressions such as "strip yourself" and "empty yourself" in order to give place entirely to God and his Spirit.

> Because you cannot seek anything but God there [in solitude],
> your first thought is to empty your heart of all created things in
> order to be able to fill it entirely with God. (MDF 180.2)

The feast of the martyrdom of Saint Bartholomew gives De La Salle an
opportunity to show how far this stripping of self and this possession
by God can go:

> This saint endured [the torment of being flayed alive] with such
> patience that he seemed to be dead and no longer have feeling,
> for he was so filled with the Spirit of God that the interior feel-
> ings that enlivened his soul continually raised him to God and
> seemed to deprive his body of the feeling natural to it. (MDF
> 159.3)

To achieve this stripping of self, or annihilation, asceticism is
needed. For Bérulle the practice of mortification does not aim at the
destruction of the creature, which belongs to God, for this would be
an offense against the Creator; rather, mortification aims at the use of
the creature (human nature), because sin is the abuse of human nature. Condren and Olier, however, take the absolute position without
qualification that the creature is nothing and sinful; therefore, they see
no solution to the human condition other than the destruction and annihilation of the creature, and this they see exemplified in the annihilation of the human person of the Incarnate Word.

Lasallian spirituality follows more the asceticism of Bérulle than
that of Condren and Olier. Though his recommendations to his disciples and his own personal practices of mortification of the senses are
rigorous, in his writings De La Salle puts the emphasis on fidelity to
the duties of state, observance of the daily spiritual exercises, attention
to little things, in a word, on the mortification of the spirit and mind.
There is no corporal mortification prescribed in the Rule of the Brothers. Instead De La Salle urges his disciples to accept, and even love,
the sufferings of the day in imitation of their teacher, Jesus Christ, and
in living the Pascal Mystery, or simply as a condition of the Christian
life:

> You have to suffer a constant martyrdom that is no less violent
> for the spirit than Saint Bartholomew's was for his body. You
> must, so to speak, tear off your own skin, which Saint Paul calls
> the old man, in order to be clothed with the Spirit of Jesus Christ,
> which is, according to the same Apostle, the new man. Let this,
> then, be your effort throughout your life, so that you may truly
> become disciples of Jesus Christ and imitators of this holy Apostle
> in his martyrdom. (MDF 159.3; see also 89.2, 152.3)

De La Salle does use Condren's idea of destruction of the spirit (mind) when he writes about obedience, a topic that will be treated below.

# IV

## John Baptist de La Salle's Originality

Unquestionably the spirituality of De La Salle was influenced by the major themes of the French School, as well as the spirit of reform created by the Council of Trent (1545–1563), of which the French School was certainly a part. Although these elements did give him his general orientation and guide him on his own spiritual journey, John Baptist nonetheless formed a spirituality of his own out of his personal experiences and the need to adapt his teaching to the particular circumstances he encountered. De La Salle gave to the Church a spirituality that is altogether original, one that is uniquely suited for people who are dedicated to the Christian education of children, especially of the working class and the poor.

By studying the human and spiritual development of De La Salle when he was a young priest, it is possible to gain an insight into the principal characteristics of his own spiritual life. His first biographers describe various influences that guided him during his years of study in Paris and Reims and the doubts he experienced in choosing a suitable apostolic service. In all these experiences, he focused on doing the will of God, and he searched for this will in the events of his life as well as in the whole context of his human existence. He was a man of God, imbued with faith and zeal for God's glory, trained and guided by a solid theological foundation. Out of this wealth as a person, he designed for himself and then for his disciples a spiritual doctrine adapted to their role as Christian educators in the service of the poor, encouraging them by his example even more than by his words.

The French School developed its spirituality largely for the clergy. De La Salle's spirituality was addressed specifically to a group of men who were not clerics, the Brothers of the Christian Schools. De La Salle gave up his social status, his family, his canonry, and his inherited wealth to establish the community and to devote all his time and effort to the formation of its members. His writing was aimed at this purpose, to confirm the Brothers in the spirit of their vocation and their profession as teachers. Originally, these men were uncultured and uneducated (De La Salle ranked them below his valet); under their Founder's guidance, they underwent a conversion at which he labored for a period of forty years.

Early in his association with the teachers, De La Salle put himself at their level, lived their life, learned firsthand their problems and their weaknesses, and encouraged and supported their efforts day by day. Gradually, he helped them appreciate the importance and the greatness of their work, and he engaged them in a style of life open to the demands that come from the call of God. He gave them a spirituality for the educational activity that they were carrying on with poor children. Rather than turn the teachers' focus away from their daily work, the interior life that he developed led them to be aware that school is the place in which to meet God in the concrete events of their personal experience.

The following themes of Lasallian spirituality for teachers are the principal elements developed by De La Salle in collaboration with the Brothers.

### You are called by God

God's providential act was revealed to De La Salle in the action of those who joined him with the desire to conduct schools in the service of the poor. This was not simply the result of some accident, because for them there was little or no other employment. He was convinced through faith that the Lord Jesus had come into their life and that each one of them had received a personal call to come follow him. He constantly reminded his Brothers of this call:

> Adore God's fatherly Providence in your regard. He withdrew you from the world in order to prepare you to acquire the virtues you need to do your work well and to educate a great number of children in the Christian spirit. (MDF 131.1; see also MTR 193.3)

In their response to this call of God, the Brothers had experienced a divine event in their personal history. This specific intervention by God is often noted in De La Salle's meditations, as when he describes the conversion of Saint Paul:

> How fortunate this saint was to be forestalled by grace and changed in an instant from a persecutor to an Apostle and a preacher of the Gospel!
>
> Rejoice with the saint over the special favor he received from God, and thank God for the grace he has given you in withdrawing you from the world and calling you to such a holy work of instructing children and leading them to piety. (MDF 99.1)

### Called to do God's work

Awareness of this special favor given to the Brothers was very gratifying and was meant to move them deeply with the sense of God's presence in their life. But De La Salle calls the Brothers to realize that this grace was not intended to be jealously treasured for themselves alone. The good news of salvation, which gave them joy and transformed their life, must be passed on to the poor and abandoned youths entrusted to their care. When De La Salle speaks of the choice God has made of each Brother, he always joins to this choice the purpose that God has in mind:

> It is God who has called you, who has destined you for this work, and who has sent you to work in his vineyard. Do this, then, with all the affection of your heart, working entirely for him. (MTR 201.1; see also MDF 87.2, 99.2)

### As co-workers with God

For De La Salle, to work in the vineyard means to be partners with God to help in his work of announcing the Gospel of his Son:

> Because God in his mercy has given you such a ministry, do not falsify his word, but gain glory before him by unveiling his truth to those whom you are charged to instruct. Let this be your whole effort in the instruction you give them, looking upon yourselves as the *ministers of God and the dispensers of his mysteries.* (MTR 193.1, emphasis added; see also MDF 3.2, 166.3, MTR 205.1)

To work in this vineyard also means to be co-workers with Jesus Christ in the work of saving children:

> Because you are obliged to help your disciples save themselves, you must engage them to unite all their actions to those of Jesus Christ, our Lord, so that their actions, made holy by his merits and his consecration, are able to be pleasing to God and a means of salvation for them. (MTR 195.1; see also 196)

For anyone who wishes to accomplish a work that is true and effective, it is most important to be like a branch attached to a vine:

> Jesus Christ wants you to understand from this comparison that the more your work for the good of your disciples is given life by him and draws its power from him, the more it will produce good in them. (MTR 195.3)

In their mission to youth, De La Salle does not hesitate to call his Brothers ambassadors and ministers of Jesus Christ. (MTR 195.2, 201, 205.1)

### Especially for the poor

Lasallian spirituality puts an emphasis on the service of the poor in the Brothers' ministry as ambassadors of Jesus Christ. The Christian Schools were founded for those who could not pay for the education of their children, and this included most of the artisans and the working class of the time. In *Meditations for the Time of Retreat,* De La Salle asks the Brothers to study the signs of their times and to realize that poor children are being deprived of education. Then he adds,

> God has had the goodness to remedy so great a misfortune by the establishment of the Christian Schools, where the teaching is offered free of charge and entirely for the glory of God. (MTR 194.1; see also 193.2, 3, MDF 37.3, 132.2, 189.1, RC 1.5 and 6)

To proclaim the Gospel to poor children effectively, De La Salle saw the necessity in all education, especially in the education of the disadvantaged, for an affective bonding between the teacher and the students. For him this is an integral part of the spirituality of the teacher, based as it is on the spirit of faith:

> Every day, you have poor children to instruct. Love them tenderly, as this saint [Cyprian] did, following in this the example of Jesus Christ. . . . These poor children are also the ones whom God has entrusted to you and to whom you are obliged to proclaim the truths of the holy Gospel. (MDF 166.2; see also 80.3, 101.3, 133.3, 150.1, 173.1)

### In the service of the Church

To work in God's vineyard also means to place yourself in the service of the Church and to hold in the Church a role of the highest importance, similar to that of the Apostles, of priests, and even of bishops:

> You must, then, look upon your work, which has been entrusted to you by pastors and by fathers and mothers, as one of the most important and necessary services in the Church. (MTR 199.1; see also MDF 102.1, 145.3, MTR 193.3, 200.1)

In his meditation on Saint Marcellinus, bishop of Paris, De La Salle compares the apostolic responsibility of the Brothers to that of this saint:

In some sense it can be said that each of you is a bishop, that is, the vigilant guardian of the flock that God has entrusted to you. (MDF 186.3)

### For building the body of Christ

To teach the truths of Christianity to children and to form them in the practice of religion are the main duties of the Brothers, with the intention of "building up the body of Christ which is his Church" (MTR 205.3). This doctrine of the incorporation of all the members of the Church into Jesus Christ occurs frequently in De La Salle's writings. In this he joins the teaching of the leaders of the French School of spirituality, who revived this theological truth which had lost "some of its force and influence in the work of scholasticism."[21] The meditation, "Commemoration of the Souls in Purgatory," especially carries the thought of De La Salle on this doctrine:

> We are united with these holy souls by an external union, because we are all members of the Church and of Jesus Christ. We are also united with them in Jesus Christ through sanctifying grace, which we share with them. (MDF 185.2)

### Through the action of the Holy Spirit

The Church, as a communion of believers, is also "the sanctuary where God dwells through his Holy Spirit" (MTR 199.3, 205.3). Since the day of Pentecost, this Spirit of God has been among us to bring "a new law, the law of grace and love" (MDF 43.1). De La Salle urges the Brothers to allow the Holy Spirit to live in them "to make it possible for you to live and to act only by the Spirit's action in you" (MDF 43.1). It is further necessary to ask the Holy Spirit for the grace to touch the hearts of those entrusted to them and to obtain their salvation (MDF 43.3, MTR 195.3, and 196.3). In De La Salle's writing, the role of the Holy Spirit holds a central position.

The mystery of the Trinity and the work of salvation are fundamental to the mission of the Brother: called by God the Father in his providential care for his children, the Brother is given a task which unites him with Jesus Christ in his work of saving children, building up the Church as the city of God and the Body of Christ, and revealing to the heirs of God's kingdom the mystery of the living God through the action of the Holy Spirit. But although he did indeed borrow from the Trinitarian themes of the French School, De La Salle created from them an original spirituality for the Christian educator.

When we consider how De La Salle develops the theme of the human person before God, we see that he emphasizes several characteristics of this relationship to amplify the spirituality suitable for the special ministry of the teacher.

### In the spirit of faith

The personal experience of the Brother in his call and mission is an experience of faith.[22] De La Salle stresses this and makes the spirit of faith one of the vital signs of the young society of the Brothers of the Christian Schools:

> The spirit of this Institute is, first, a spirit of faith, which ought to induce those who compose it not to look upon anything but with the eyes of faith, not to do anything but in view of God, and to attribute everything to God. (RC 2.2 in CL 25:18)

To know God and his envoy, Jesus Christ, is for De La Salle the foundation of the Christian life. This knowledge is possible only by the light of faith. De La Salle describes the effect that faith has as the result of a personal experience with Jesus Christ:

> Jesus Christ, entering a soul, raises it so far above all human sentiments, through the faith that enlivens it, that it sees nothing except by the light of faith. No matter what anyone does to such a soul, nothing can disturb its constancy, make it abandon God's service, or even diminish in the least degree the ardor it feels for God, because the darkness that previously blinded its spirit is changed into an admirable light. As a result, the soul no longer sees anything except by the eyes of faith.
>
> Do you feel that you have this disposition? Pray to the risen Christ to give it to you. (MDF 32.2; see also MTR 193.1, MDF 96.1, 139.2)

Elsewhere he adds:

> Your faith must be a light that guides you in all things and a shining beacon to lead to heaven those you instruct. (MDF 178.1)
>
> Do you have such faith that you are able to touch the hearts of your students and to inspire them with the Christian spirit? This is the greatest miracle you can perform and the one that God asks of you, for this is the purpose of your work. (MDF 139.3)

### In the spirit of zeal

It is characteristic of Lasallian spirituality that faith is never separated from zeal, which is the manifestation of faith:

The spirit of this Institute consists, secondly, in an ardent zeal for the instruction of children and for bringing them up in the fear of God. (RC 2.9 in CL 25:20)

Thus, in the meditation on Saint Stephen, the first martyr, De La Salle presents the confrontation by Stephen of the Jews who disputed with him as typical of the relation between faith and zeal:

Was he [Stephen] not, in fact, inspired by this spirit when he spoke with such great zeal to the Jews and when several of them who disputed with him could not resist the Holy Spirit, who was in him and inspiring his zeal?

You ought to make known by your conduct, as he [Stephen] did, that you are true disciples of Jesus Christ, having only God in view in all your actions and announcing, with as much boldness and intrepidity as he did, the maxims of the holy Gospel. In all this what must strengthen your zeal as well as your faith is the fact that you announce these truths in your position as ministers of God. (MDF 87.1)

In this meditation De La Salle shows that faith serves as a guide and an enlightenment in the life of the deacon Stephen, who always guided himself and acted by the spirit of faith. These same expressions are used in *Recueil*: "The just, that is, true Christians, live by faith, because they are guided by and their actions are performed with views and motives of faith" (R 71 in CL 15:38).

Lasallian spirituality teaches that faith is especially guided and ruled in everything by the words and thoughts that come from the Scriptures. Saint Stephen is inspired precisely by biblical texts when he explains to his listeners all the benefits that God had bestowed upon their ancestors.

In Lasallian spirituality the action of the Holy Spirit is the essential and effective element in the effort of the Brothers to convert the heart and spirit of their students. The Holy Spirit lives at the still point of their being and prays in each of them (MDF 62.3). The Holy Spirit opens their minds and helps them understand and appreciate the mind of Christ (MDF 191.2). The Holy Spirit gives the vigor and power to proclaim the Gospel and touches hearts (MDF 43.3).

De La Salle spells out some of the effects of the faith of Saint Stephen: the power of the Holy Spirit living in him, his courage to denounce evil conduct at the risk of persecution and even death, his pardoning those who were attacking him, his joy anticipating the happiness of heaven.

### By living the interior life

De La Salle encourages the Brothers to live in a constant search for the living God, for his will in their life, for the reign of God that is yet to come. He calls them to recognize each day the intervention of the Lord in their life and by an interior effort to live with an awareness of the presence of God. This interior effort is essential to the purpose of the Institute, that is, the work of evangelization.

### Based on asceticism

The primary means to achieve this interiority is separation from the world and renunciation of its spirit, all of which De La Salle found incompatible with the search for God.

> The more he finds their hearts empty of the things of the world, the more he makes himself known to them and fills them with his Spirit. (MDF 171.1; see also 174.1)

The rigor of De La Salle's commitment to control and mortify his body and his mind seems extreme today. Rayez writes, "Even to the end of his life, the ideal that De La Salle sought was solitude, a hidden life, genuine poverty, and austerity."[23] He did not require his disciples to practice this ideal, but he did strongly urge them to have complete control of their senses, "allowing them only what is absolutely necessary for them" (MDF 80.1).

> If you give in to them, it will be quite difficult for you to control them later. Therefore, watch over them constantly, because no one can be sensual and Christian at the same time. (MDF 95.2)

De La Salle insists on the importance of both external and internal silence in order to become interior.

> We learn to speak to God only by listening to him, for to know how to speak to God and to converse with him can only come from God, who has his own language, which is special to him and which he shares only with his friends and confidants, to whom he gives the happiness of frequently conversing with him. (MDF 64.2; see also 135.1)

Recollection in order to "live in the depth of the soul" is a means to facilitate attention and docility to the movement of the Spirit. Following the spiritual writers of the seventeenth century, De La Salle emphasizes the importance of fidelity to the inspirations of the Holy Spirit.

When he studies the lives of the saints, he contemplates the intervening and effective action of the Spirit of God in them and the way they become aware of and carry out his will:

> [Saint Norbert] was specially favored by grace and felt himself touched by an extraordinary movement of the Spirit of God. Leaving the [emperor's] court, he withdrew entirely from the world to enter the ecclesiastical state. (MDF 132.1; see also 100.1, 118.1, 123.1, 143.1, 159.1, 161.2, 167.1, 174.2, 177.1)

### By attention to the presence of God

Attention to the presence of God is an important element in Lasallian spirituality. "It is the soul and the support of the interior life" (R 119 in CL 15:62). This encounter with the "intimate guest of the soul, who takes possession of the soul and is in turn possessed by the soul"[24] is the whole purpose of the effort to become interior, to be centered, and to become aware of the direction that life is taking.

De La Salle teaches the Brothers that they are loved by God with an intervening love and that the best way to respond to this love is to have all thoughts tend only to God and be entirely directed to him. "Nothing shows better that we love another person than when we cannot help thinking about that person" (MDF 70.3).

The importance that De La Salle places on the presence of God is shown by the place he gives it in *Méthode d'oraison,* which he composed for the Brothers. Almost half of this treatise deals with the topic. De La Salle says that the entire time of prayer can profitably be applied to the presence of God without any other subject for consideration:

> We must ensure that our mind remains filled with the thought of God's presence as long as possible, and we must not go on to any other subject until we cannot pay attention any longer.[25]

In his meditations De La Salle speaks of the benefits a person derives from union with God: "happiness anticipated in this life" (MDF 179.3). "It is also of great use to you in your work, because this work concerns God and aims at winning souls for him. It is, therefore, a matter of great consequence not to lose sight of God in your work" (MDF, *ibid.*; see also 67.1, 90.1, 95.1). At every hour and half hour in school, the work of teacher and students would stop when the boy assigned rang the bell and the prayer monitor announced, "Let us remember that we are in the holy presence of God" (CL 24:76, 209).

## With total abandonment to God

By attending to the presence and action of God, the Brother becomes aware of the fidelity of the One who chose him to do his work. Total abandonment to the guidance of the Spirit of God becomes, then, the surest way to realize the plan that God has for him. This is another dominant trait of Lasallian spirituality. De La Salle lived this trust in submission to God so thoroughly that it could be said that he "is one of the best representatives of the doctrine of abandonment to God in the seventeenth and eighteenth centuries."[26]

It was very early in De La Salle's association with the Brothers that the element of abandonment became strong in his spiritual life, perhaps as early as 1682, when the teachers expressed concern about their future and confronted him with the fact that he could speak easily about trust in divine Providence, since he was a wealthy man. This confrontation was for De La Salle a moment of profound conversion, to enter fully into the life of his poor teachers, to become one with them in their poverty, and in his own life[27] to embrace the practice of total abandonment to Providence.

He understood that this abandonment to God, inspired and sustained by a living spirit of faith, is an effective element in an apostolic spirituality:

> It is difficult to realize how much good a detached person is able to do in the Church. The reason for this is that detachment shows a deep faith. A person who abandons himself to the Providence of God is like a sailor who puts out to sea without sails or oars. (MDF 134.1)

The time of prayer is a special moment for surrendering to a total abandonment to God by faithful attention and response to the inspiration of the Holy Spirit:

> Do you abandon yourselves entirely to this divine Spirit, so that he may ask of God all you need to have for the good of your own soul and for those in your care and so that you may act only by him? (MDF 62.2)

It is especially in the experience of dryness, when the absence of God becomes difficult to endure, that a person must wait in patience:

> In your times of trouble, when you have had recourse to those who are appointed to guide you and they have been unable to provide a suitable remedy for your difficulty, God wants you, then, to remain completely abandoned to his guidance, awaiting from him alone and from his goodness all the help you need. (MDF 20.2)

De La Salle encourages the Brother to imitate Jesus Christ when he abandoned himself to suffering and death in accord with the will of his Father:

> Adore these different dispositions of Jesus Christ, which were conformable to the plans God had for him. As he said, the will of his Father was his nourishment, that is, the rule and, as it were, the soul of his conduct.

> Strive after the example of your divine master, Jesus Christ, to want only what God wants, when he wants it, and in the way he wants it. (MDF 24.1)

### In association

To provide a Christian education for the children of the poor and the working class, De La Salle planned to create a society of Brothers who would consecrate themselves by vow to announce the Gospel and at the same time provide in association a solid education in the fields of human learning and culture. Beginning in 1684, the teachers assembled with De La Salle expressed this identity in the title they gave to themselves, Brothers of the Christian Schools. This name included at the same time both the mystical and the social nature of their Gospel mission.

The formula of vows pronounced by a dozen Brothers with De La Salle in 1694 defines the character and the meaning of the Lasallian community. It pays supreme homage to the "infinite and adorable majesty" of the living God, who has taken hold of the Brothers and called them to him in the service of youth:

> Most Holy Trinity, Father, Son, and Holy Spirit, prostrate with the most profound respect before your infinite and adorable majesty, I consecrate myself entirely to you to procure your glory as far as I will be able and as you will require of me. (RC 116, CL 25:140)

As the formula of vows continues, it shows that the commitment of the Brothers is made only in community and that this community has no existence other than rooted in God and united with the poor:

> For this purpose, I promise and vow to unite myself and to remain in Society with [each of the other Brothers is named] to keep together and by association gratuitous schools wherever they may be . . . and to do anything in the said Society at which I will be employed, whether by the body of the Society or by the superiors who will have the government thereof.

This Lasallian community does not exist without a tension between its transcendent dynamic and its involvement in everyday life,
a sort of mystical realism: "It is born, becomes an organism, and establishes its identity and purpose in a movement coming from God
that takes hold of each Brother to commit him to the service of the
poor for the glory of God."[28]

### With obedience and the faithful observance of the Rule

De La Salle based the life of the community on two foundations,
obedience and faithful observance of the Rule. He took every occasion to insist on the importance of obedience in a religious house:

> Obedience is the principal and the most necessary virtue for reli-
> gious people and all people living in community. (No. 40, CL 15:
> 23)

In his meditations De La Salle cites Saints Bonaventure, Teresa,
Cassian, Bernard, Thomas Aquinas, and Ignatius of Loyola in order to
confirm the necessity of obedience (MDF 7.2, 3). It is especially to the
Brother Director as representing God that the Brother owes an entire
obedience. "You ought to do nothing and to be involved in nothing
except on the advice of your superiors" (MDF 107.2).

Faithful observance of the Rule, the second foundation of community, is no less demanding. It is striking to note how very precise
and minute the details are that the Brother is called upon to observe
in the most ordinary actions of the day: leaving everything at the first
sound of the bell, closing the doors without making any noise, teaching catechism for all the time assigned, observing silence and reserve
in the streets. "He who is faithful in little things will also be in those
that are great," says the Lord (MDF 92.1). De La Salle quotes Saint
Bonaventure:

> In [religious life] there is nothing small if everything practiced
> there is considered with the eyes of faith. (MDF 142.3)

The rigor of De La Salle's teaching on obedience and the observance of the Rule becomes more understandable when considered in
the social context of his age. There are even more rigorous texts on
these topics among his contemporaries. However, it can also be said
that this teaching on obedience reflects certain truths of the Gospel
that are still meaningful and significant in today's world.

It must be remembered that the various prescriptions of the Rule
were not imposed arbitrarily upon the Brothers. They collaborated

with the Founder in formulating the Rule for their community after living it for several years. They themselves came to the conclusion, after much experience, that obedience and fidelity to the Rule were necessary to maintain the strong, cohesive spirit and discipline needed for the success of their project of schools for the poor. These virtues gave the Brothers staying power when they were faced with an opposition that seemed to come from all sides, often when they were without support from those whom they were serving.

The members of the young community under the leadership of their Father and Founder were deeply aware that God was calling them to do his work, and they took heart from De La Salle's own courageous abandonment to the Providence of God and from sharing with him a radical obedience to the Gospel. For De La Salle's teaching on obedience to superiors was based on an interior participation in the mysteries of the obedience of Jesus Christ to his Father:

> We ought to obey them only because, according to the expression of Saint Paul, they are laboring for the perfection of the saints and the building up of the Body of Jesus Christ, who is our Head. (MDF 72.2)

De La Salle encourages the Brothers to reflect on the inner meaning of the various prescriptions of the Rule.

> To acquire a complete fidelity to the Rule, never limit your view of the practices of community to their mere external matter, but focus only on the relation that they have to God's will, which is the same for all of them, whatever they may be. (R 161 in CL 15:83)

De La Salle takes for his model the common life of the first Christians, and urges the Brothers to a union of mind and heart that ought to unite all the members:

> Deepen within you the conviction that in community you ought to live anew the spirit of the first Christians, who were all of one heart and one mind. (MDF 113.2)

Without this union and love, community life loses its very reason for being and becomes a kind of hell (MDF 65.1).

De La Salle is not unmindful of the problems of living in community, and in several meditations he stresses the need for the Brothers to bear one another's burdens. "The way to maintain union in a community, in spite of all these different personalities, is to bear up charitably with the defects of one another" (MDF 74.1).

For De La Salle, the community that is firmly united is an image of the mystery of the love that is in the Most Holy Trinity and participates in its unity, a union that resembles "the union among the three Divine Persons" (MDF 39.3).

### Union of religious vocation and professional work

The genius of De La Salle's charism and of Lasallian spirituality lies in awareness of the union between the mission of teachers to announce the Gospel of Jesus Christ and the professional work of teachers in the total education of their students. The Brothers learned this from De La Salle: to rely entirely on God by living in frequent remembrance of his presence, but still to keep in mind that the whole purpose of their call and the profound reason for their association together, is to conduct an excellent school as the medium for communicating the Christian spirit:

> Rest assured that you will never achieve your salvation more certainly and acquire greater perfection than by fulfilling well the duties of your state, provided you do so with the view of accomplishing the will of God. (No. 184-iv, CL 15:95)

In his letters to the Brothers, De La Salle several times speaks of his desire that the school be well conducted: "Take care that your school runs well."[29] He wants the students to make good progress in reading and writing; he sees the need for order, discipline, and silence in class; he urges the teachers to love their students *tenderly* in order to encourage them, in turn, to love the teachers and their school and be led thereby to the love of God. This is why he sees the need for professional competence and the value of community as a means to promote continually the professional growth of its members. Together with the Brothers, De La Salle composed a manual, "Conduct of the Christian Schools" (*Conduite des Écoles chrétiennes,* CL 24), based on their experience and containing in great detail all the pedagogical methods needed to assure the successful operation of their schools.

The Brothers regarded their students as citizens of both their country and heaven. This was no fantasy for De La Salle. In his meditation on Saint Louis, King of France, he encourages the Brothers:

> In your work you ought to unite zeal for the good of the Church with zeal for the good of the state, of which your disciples are beginning to be, and one day ought to be, perfect members. You will procure the good of the Church by making them true Christians and docile to the truths of faith and the maxims of the holy Gospel. You will procure the good of the state by teaching them

how to read and write and everything else that pertains to your ministry with regard to exterior things. But piety must be joined to exterior things; otherwise, your work would be of little use. (MDF 160.3)

This concern for the eternal salvation and for the temporal well-being of the students is a specific trait of Lasallian spirituality and pedagogy. The authors of *Annoncer L'Evangile Aux Pauvres*[30] give a good name for this in the expression "mystical realism." The aim of De La Salle is to have his disciples unite closely the spirit of faith and of zeal, the practice of interior prayer, and the ministry of education.

Jean-Guy Rodrigue, FSC
Generalate, Rome

This introduction is condensed from an article written by Brother Jean-Guy on the influence of the French School of spirituality on De La Salle, which will be published in a book concerning the spiritual influences on the Founder of the Brothers of the Christian Schools.

---

1. *Perfectae Caritatis*, 2b.

2. Paul VI, *Motu proprio Ecclesiae sanctae*, August 6, 1966.

3. The original of *Mémoire rouennais* is found in the city archives of Rouen, file 281, dossier 3. The archives of the Generalate has a modern copy without reference (AMG, CA 101/1, D3). The entire text is reproduced in CL 11, pp. 128–130.

4. There is no mention of De La Salle as a spiritual writer in the distinguished work of Henri Bremond, the *Histoire littéraire du sentiment religieux en France depuis la fin des guerres de religion jusqu'à nos jour*, Bloud et Gay, 1916–1933. In 1952 A. Rayez S.J., Director of the *Dictionnaire de Spiritualité*, wrote, "[De La Salle's] pedagogy is known worldwide, but his interior life, the path he followed under the guidance of grace, and the spiritual doctrine he slowly developed for his disciples and for Christian educators are hardly known at all." (*Études lasalliennes*, in *Revue d'ascétique et de mystique*. RAM, No. 109, January-February, p. 20.)

5. After reviewing the various works that treat of the spiritual doctrine of De La Salle, Rayez concluded, "We are still at a loss to appreciate the place of the saint in the history of spirituality. . . . We must state that we do not have yet a definitive work on Lasallian spirituality. . . . There are two reasons for this lack: the sources of his spirituality have not been thoroughly researched, and there is no complete critical edition of his writings. (op. cit. in RAM, 109, pp. 20, 28). Since then the critical edition has not been completely realized, but some research on the sources has been done on MTR (CL 1, 45, 46), on the *Recueil des petits traités* (CL 16), and on *Méditations sur les principales fêtes* (CL 47). These studies have produced some results; in 1974, *Dictionnaire de Spiritualité* (vol. viii, col. 802–821) printed a substantial article on the life, the work, and the spiritual doctrine of the Founder, and in a recent study on the spiritual writers

of the seventeenth century, R. Deville refers to De La Salle (*L'École française de Spiritualité*, Paris, Desclée, 1987, pp. 125–137, coll. *Bibliothèque d'histoire du Christianisme*, No. 11).

6. Volumes 12 to 25 of the *Cahiers lasalliens* (CL) present the first edition of all the educational and spiritual writings of De La Salle, or the earliest printed editions available.

7. M. Sauvage, FSC, *Les citations néotestamentaires dans les Méditations pour le Temps de la Retraite*, Rome, 1959 (CL 1), Miguel Campos, FSC, *L'Itinéraire évangélique de saint Jean-Baptiste de La Salle et le recours à l'Ecriture dans ses Méditations pour le Temps de la Retraite*, Rome, 1974, 2 Vols. (CL 45 & 46), also Sauvage, *Catéchèse et laïcat*, Paris, Ligel, 1962, 557 pp. and L. Varela, FSC, *Biblia y Espiritualidad en San Juan B. de La Salle*, Tejares-Salamanca, 1966, 362 pp. in *Sinite* 10).

8. Jean-Guy Rodrigue, FSC, *Contribution à l'étude des sources des Méditations sur les principales festes de l'année*, Rome, 1988 (CL 47).

9. L. Cognet, *Les origines de la Spiritualité française au XVIIe siècle*, Paris, Vieux Colombier, Sept. 1949, 105 pp. (Revue *Culture Catholique* 4), p. 5.

10. Cf. "Mémoire" written by Richelieu in 1625.

11. Among many others, the *Feuillantines*, the feminine branch of the Capuchins, and the Visitation Sisters founded by Saint Francis de Sales.

12. Cf. J. Dagens, *Bibliographie chronologique de la littérature de piété et de ses sources (1501–1601)*, Paris, 1952. Also L. Cognet, *La spiritualité moderne, I. L'essor: 1500–1650*, Paris, Aubier, 1966, 511 pp. (*Coll. Histoire de la spiritualité chrétienne* III), p. 237.

13. Among these, Pseudo-Denys (sixth century), *Théologie mystique*; Tauler, *Institutiones*; Ruysbroeck (1381), *L'ornement des noces*; Harphius (Henri de Herp, 1477), *Théologie mystique*; Louis de Blois (1556), *Régle de vie spirituelle, L'Institution spirituelle*, and *Miroir de l'âme*; *La Perle évangélique*, an anonymous work that was the beginning of Bérulle's conversion to Christocentrism (Cf. J. Huijben, in *S.V.S.*, May 1931, pp. 94–122).

14. A. Rayez, article *Française (École)*, in *Dictionnaire de Spiritualité (DS)*, t. V, col. 783–784.

15. Daniel-Rops, *Histoire de l'Église du Christ*, Vol. V; I. *Le grand siècle des âmes*,. Paris, Fayard, 1958.

16. A Rayez, SJ, *Études lasalliennes*, in RAM, 109, January-March, 1952, p. 56.

17. See the article by Antonio Temprado in LASALLIANA, 17–1–A–67, on this Lasallian greeting.

18. Condren, Charles de, *Idée du Sacerdoce et du sacrifice de Jésus Christ.*

19. Sauvage, Michel, FSC, Campos, Miguel, FSC, *Explication de la Méthode d'oraison, Présentation du texte de 1739, Instrument de travail*, Rome, 1989, CL 50, pp. 341–343, 423–426, 476–479, 510–511.

20. *Vocabulaire lasallien*, Paris, 1984–1988. 2, pp. 108–109.

21. Mersch, E., SJ, *Le corps mystique du Christ, Étude de théologie historique*, Paris, Desclée de Brouwer, 1936, 2, pp. 301 ff.

22. Sauvage, Campos, *Jean-Baptiste de La Salle, Annoncer l'Evangile aux pauvres*, Paris, Beauchesne, 1977, p. 79. Part of this work has been translated by Matthew J. O'Connell under the title of *Saint John Baptist de La Salle, Announcing the Gospel to the Poor*, published by the Christian Brothers National Office, Romeoville, IL 60441, 1981.

23. A. Rayez, SJ, *La spiritualité d'abandon chez saint Jean-Baptiste de La Salle*, in RAM, 121, January-March, 1955, p. 48.

24. Sauvage, Campos, *Annoncer L'Evangile*. . . , p. 154; cf. CL 50, pp. 224–259.
25. CL 14, p. 35; cf. CL 50, p. 313.
26. A. Rayez, SJ, *La spiritualité d'abandon*. . . , p. 47.
27. Sauvage, Campos, *op. cit.*, pp. 52–56.
28. *Idem*, p. 359.
29. *The Letters of John Baptist de La Salle*, translated by Brother Colman Molloy, FSC, Lasallian Publications, Romeoville, IL 60441, 8.18, 16.3, 42.12, 44.20, 62.5.
30. Sauvage, Campos, *op. cit.*, pp. 322–327.

# PART ONE

———— ✦ ————

# Meditations
# for All the Sundays of the Year

# First Sunday of Advent

## GOSPEL: SAINT LUKE 21:25-33

*The Last Judgment*

### 1.1 First Point

Speaking of the Last Judgment in today's Gospel, Jesus Christ says that all people will see the Son of Man coming on a cloud with great power and majesty.[1] The regal aspect in which Jesus Christ will appear and the great power he will display when he comes to judge the world ought to make us fear his coming. This is what Saint Jerome says, commenting on these words of the Prophet Malachy: Who can think of the day of his coming?[2] If no one dares think of the day of the Last Judgment, because of the majesty and power of him who will be the judge, who will be able to endure the strictness of his judgment? This will be all the more difficult, he adds, because the One who will act as witness will also be the One who will judge; this is what ought to lead us to dread this judgment all the more.

As the same saint says elsewhere, *the very severity of the Judge who will render to all of us according to our works*[3] will be such that those present will not dare to look him in the face. Then, says Saint Ephrem, there will be a minute and terrible scrutiny of our actions, and even of our thoughts, when each of us appears before this Judge's tribunal. He will make known to the whole world all the thoughts of all, their words and their deeds, all of which were entirely hidden in this life because they were performed in darkness.[4]

So that we, says Saint Augustine, will not endure a terrible and crushing sentence when we appear before the tribunal of this inexorable Judge who will judge us for eternity, let us constantly strive to free ourselves of our defects, for we cannot know either the day or the hour[5] when we will die. Those whose life span is so uncertain must not delay to take the steps needed to insure their salvation.

### 1.2 Second Point

It is not only the wicked who need to be afraid of the Last Judgment because of the evil life they have led. It will be a harrowing experience for the good as well as the wicked, says Saint Augustine. For, asserts Saint Jerome, there will be few, in fact there will be none, in that general gathering who will not deserve to be reproved with severity and anger by the Judge. This is why, he adds, there is no soul that does not fear God's judgment, for *the stars themselves,* meaning the saints, will not be pure in his presence.[6] It will be very difficult, this holy doctor continues, to find anyone pure and irreproachable enough to appear before this Judge with assurance and dare to say, who will convict me of sin?[7] Because of this, says Saint Ephrem, all creatures will be penetrated with fear, and all the legions of holy angels will shudder[8] on the great day of the Lord's vengeance.

The main reason why the just themselves will fear while awaiting the Last Judgment is that we will have to give an account not only of the idle words we have spoken,[9] as Jesus Christ says in the Gospel, but even of the good works we have performed, according to what God declares through the Royal Prophet: I will judge justices,[10] meaning all the good that we have accomplished during our life. He will probe it to see if it was truly good and whether anything defective can be found in it. Who of us, then, will not fear God's judgment?

### 1.3 Third Point

How could we not fear God's judgments, since the greatest saints, despite their eminent holiness, did not fail to dread them? Job, whom God defended against those who reproached him falsely, says to God: I trembled at every action I performed, knowing that you do not pardon the one who sins;[11] and again, What will I do when God will arise to judge me, and when he demands an account of my life, what will I answer him?[12] After relating in considerable detail his manner of living, so upright and so free from sin, he adds that he always dreaded the judgment of God and that this fear had always penetrated him like a heavy burden.[13]

Saint Hilarion, bowed down beneath the weight of years and austerities, was seized with terror at the hour of his death. Saint Jerome, who had grown grey in solitude and in all sorts of penitential exercises, declares that he had restricted himself in this way and had condemned himself to a sort of prison out of fear of the Last Judgment. He tells us elsewhere that being, as he was, completely filled with sin, he hid himself day and night, fearing that he might hear the words, "Jerome, come forth!" and that he would then be forced to pay the last penny.[14]

Saint Ephrem, who led a solitary life from his childhood and who was so pure, so penitent, and so filled with the Spirit of God, says that his heart trembled and his whole body shook every time he reflected that all our thoughts, words, and actions will be made manifest on Judgment Day. Acknowledging that he was still guilty, he constantly feared to be judged in strict rigor, knowing that he had no excuse for his negligence.

If such great saints felt so much fear when considering this terrible day, what feelings of dread ought we not to experience, we who show such little fervor in God's service and who fulfill our duties so negligently?

---

| | | |
|---|---|---|
| 1. Lk 21:27 | 6. Jb 15:15 | 11. Jb 9:28 |
| 2. Mal 3:2 | 7. Jn 8:46 | 12. Jb 31:14 |
| 3. Rom 2:6 | 8. Mk 13:25 | 13. Jb 31:23 |
| 4. Lk 12:2–3 | 9. Mt 12:36 | 14. Mt 5:26 |
| 5. Mt 25:13 | 10. Ps 75:3 | |

# Second Sunday of Advent

## GOSPEL: SAINT MATTHEW 11:2-10

(Notice: Advent being a season established by the Church to prepare the faithful to celebrate properly our Lord's coming into this world and to draw him into their hearts so that they may no longer live save by his Spirit, it would be very proper for us today and on the following Sundays to apply ourselves to prayer in order to prepare our hearts to receive our Lord, all the more because the Gospels of these three Sundays provide us with an opportunity to do this and urge us to do so.)

*You must prepare your own hearts and the hearts of those you are charged to instruct to receive our Lord and his holy maxims.*

### 2.1 First Point

Today's Gospel informs us that Saint John the Baptist, while in prison where he had been thrown by Herod's command, sent two of his disciples to Jesus Christ to ask him whether he is the Messiah. This gave Jesus Christ the opportunity to praise Saint John before the people; he ended by saying that John is the man of whom it was written: I am sending my angel before you, to prepare for you the path where you will walk.[1]

You too, as well as Saint John, are angels sent by God to prepare a path for him, so that he can enter your heart and the hearts of your disciples. For this purpose you need to do two things: first, you must resemble the angels by your interior and exterior purity. Like the angels, you must be entirely detached from your body and from the pleasures of the senses, so that nothing seems to be left in you but your soul, which you are concerned about exclusively and which is the only object of your care.

For you are destined by God to apply yourselves, like the holy angels, only to what refers to his service and to the care of souls. In you, as Saint Paul says, the outer man must decay, so that the inner man may be renewed day by day.[2] You must become like the angels and like them, as the same Apostle says, not consider things that are visible but only those that are invisible, for, he continues, the former are temporary and pass away, whereas the latter are eternal[3] and will be forever the object of our affection.

### 2.2 Second Point

Jesus Christ highly praises Saint John in the Gospel of this day. He says that John lived in the desert and was no reed shaken by the wind,[4] because he always continued the life of penance he had begun. He says that John wore no soft garments,[5] for as we read in Saint Matthew, he was clothed in camel's hair and wore a leather belt around his waist.[6] Jesus Christ further adds that Saint John ate no bread and drank no wine;[7] in fact, as we learn from Saint Matthew, he lived only on locusts and wild honey.[8] Jesus Christ then declared that there has never been a Prophet greater than John the Baptist.[9]

Why, do you think, did Jesus Christ praise Saint John so highly? It was to lead the people to accept his teaching and to make them understand that what John had said about himself was true: that Saint John had been sent to prepare their hearts to receive Jesus Christ and to profit by his teachings. This saint, who was Christ's precursor, began by living a life of seclusion, prayer, and penance to practice what he wanted to teach others and thus to dispose his own heart to receive the fullness of the Spirit of God in order to make himself fit to carry out his ministry properly.

Because you have to prepare the hearts of others for the coming of Jesus Christ, you must first of all dispose your own hearts to be entirely filled with zeal in order to render your words effective in those whom you instruct.

### 2.3 Third Point

After having prepared himself interiorly to preach to the Jewish people and in order to make them ready to receive Jesus Christ, Saint John proposed to them six ways to prepare a path and an entry into their hearts for Jesus Christ. **First,** he required of them a true horror for sin, reproaching them with being a generation of vipers.[10] **Second,** he urged them to fear the Last Judgment, assuring them that at that moment their sins would be closely scrutinized and strictly judged. Flee, he urged them, from the wrath to come.[11] Every tree that does not bear good fruit will be cut down and thrown into the fire.[12] **Third,** to help them escape the rigor of that judgment, he incited them to do penance by the words: Bring forth worthy fruits of penance.[13] **Fourth,** he did not want them to be satisfied with lamenting their sins and doing penance for them; he wanted them to do good works, without which their penances would be of no avail. This he pointed out to them by these words: Every tree that does not bring forth good fruit will be cut down and thrown into the fire.[14] **Fifth,** he declared that it was not enough for them to claim Abraham as their father, that they had no right to glorify themselves on that account unless they acted as Abraham did. Do not say, he told them, we have Abraham for our father.[15] **Sixth,** he gave them to understand that they could not be saved, whatever good deeds they might perform, unless they practiced the good works proper and becoming to their state of life. For this reason he pointed out to the wealthy their obligation of giving alms;[16] he told the publicans not to exact anything beyond what was due,[17] and he enjoined on the soldiers to be content with their pay.[18]

Take these counsels to heart, and follow them carefully; pass them on to your disciples and see to it that they practice them.

---

| | | |
|---|---|---|
| 1. Mal 3:1 | 7. Lk 7:33 | 13. Lk 3:8 |
| 2. 2 Cor 4:16 | 8. Mt 3:4 | 14. Lk 3:9 |
| 3. 2 Cor 4:18 | 9. Mt 11:11 | 15. Lk 3:8 |
| 4. Mt 11:7 | 10. Lk 3:7 | 16. Lk 3:11 |
| 5. Mt 11:8 | 11. Lk 3:7 | 17. Lk 3:13 |
| 6. Mt 3:4 | 12. Lk 3:9 | 18. Lk 3:14 |

# Third Sunday of Advent

## GOSPEL: SAINT JOHN 1:19–28

*Those who teach others are merely the voice that prepares hearts; it belongs to God to prepare them by his grace to receive him.*

### 3.1 First Point

The Jews sent priests and Levites from Jerusalem to ask Saint John who he was: the Christ, Elijah, or a Prophet.[1] Saint John told them he was none of these, but he declared, I am the voice of one crying in the desert: make straight the way of the Lord.[2] Saint John wished to leave to Jesus Christ all the honor of converting souls, the task at which he labored so constantly. He said, therefore, that he was only a voice crying out in the desert.[3] He thus showed that the substance of the doctrine he taught was not his own and that it was indeed the word of God which he preached; as for himself, he was only the voice which proclaimed it. In the same way that a voice is a sound that strikes the ear and makes it possible for a word to be heard, so it was that Saint John prepared the Jews to receive Jesus Christ.

The same thing is true of those who instruct others. They are only the voice of the One who disposes hearts to accept Jesus Christ and his holy teaching. The one who disposes them, according to Saint Paul, can only be God,[4] who imparts to human beings the gift of speaking of him. According to the same Apostle, when you speak all the tongues, both angelic and human, if you lack charity,[5] or rather, if it is not God who makes you speak and who uses your voice to reveal himself and his sacred mysteries, you are nothing but sounding brass and tinkling cymbals.[6] All you say will produce no good effect and will not be capable of bringing about any good results.

Let us, then, humble ourselves by considering that we are nothing but a voice and that of ourselves we cannot say anything that will do the least good for souls or make any impression on them. For we are a mere voice, only a sound, which becomes nothing once it has echoed through the air.

### 3.2 Second Point

Those who teach are only God's voice. The word that makes God known to those whom they instruct must come from him; it is God who speaks in teachers when they explain him and what is related to him. This is why Saint Peter says, If any speak, let it always be clear that God is speaking by their mouth; if any fulfill a ministry, let them do so as acting only by the power God communicates to them, so that in all things God may be glorified through Jesus Christ.[7]

Saint Peter also says on the subject of the truth he was preaching, I will never give up warning you of these things, even though you already know the truth about them, and it is established in you.[8] He adds, We have the word of the Prophets, which is firmly established and to which you do well to be attached, for it is like a lamp shining in a dark place until the day dawns and the morning star rises in our hearts. It was not through human will that in times past prophecy was uttered; rather, it was by the movement of the Holy Spirit that these prophets of God spoke.[9]

It is also by the movement of the Spirit of God that all those who today proclaim his kingdom continue to speak. But if God makes use of people to announce the truths of Christianity to others and to prepare their hearts to be docile to these truths, it is God alone, as the Wise Man says, who must guide their steps[10] and impart to their hearts the docility they need in order to welcome these holy truths that he is making known to them.

Do not be content, therefore, to read and to learn from others what you must teach your students. Pray God to impress all these truths so firmly in you that you will have no occasion to be or to consider that you are anything, as Saint Paul says, but the ministers of God and the dispensers of his mysteries.[11]

### 3.3 Third Point

Saint Zechariah, the father of Saint John the Baptist, says, in the canticle he sang at the birth of his son, that the reason why Saint John is to walk before Jesus Christ and to prepare the way for him is to bring to his people the knowledge of salvation.[12] But this knowledge is not enough; it is necessary for God, through Jesus Christ, our Lord, to show us the path we must follow and to inspire us to walk in the footsteps of his Son.

Although in this life we sigh under the weight of our bodies and long to be free of this burden,[13] it is God who created us for this very purpose and who gave us his Holy Spirit as a pledge.[14] It is, then, up to God to direct our path straight toward heaven, so that we may surely arrive there. For this reason, it was as the Son of God that Jesus Christ became the Author of our eternal salvation.[15] Salvation, as the Prophet says, comes from God;[16] perfection likewise comes from him. As Saint James assures us, every excellent grace and perfect gift come from on high and descend from the Father of lights.[17]

Beg God, therefore, to lead you on the way to heaven by the path he has traced out for you. Ask him to help you embrace the perfection of your state, because he is the one who brought you into it and who consequently desired, and still desires, that you find in it the way and the means to be sanctified.

---

| | | |
|---|---|---|
| 1. Jn 1:19–21 | 7. 1 Pt 4:11 | 13. 2 Cor 5:2 |
| 2. Jn 1:23 | 8. 2 Pt 1:12 | 14. 2 Cor 5:5 |
| 3. Jn 1:23 | 9. 2 Pt 1:19–21 | 15. Heb 5:9 |
| 4. 1 Cor 3:5–6 | 10. Prv 16:9 | 16. Ps 37:39 |
| 5. 1 Cor 13:1 | 11. 1 Cor 4:1 | 17. Jas 1:17 |
| 6. 1 Cor 13:1 | 12. Lk 1:76–77 | |

# Fourth Sunday of Advent

## GOSPEL: SAINT LUKE 3:1-6

*By penance and freedom from sin, we prepare ourselves to receive Jesus Christ.*

### 4.1 First Point

According to today's Gospel, Saint John went about all the country adjoining the Jordan, preaching the baptism of penance for the remission of sins,[1] in order to prepare the Jews for the coming of our Lord. By doing this, Saint John makes known to us that the principal dispositions we must bring to the reception of our Lord are penance and separation from all sin. We must, then, give our greatest effort to this, because penance washes and purifies a soul of the sins that sully it.

Saint Leo calls penance simply a baptism; Saint Gregory of Nazianzen calls it a painful baptism; Saint Ambrose says that David spoke of this baptism when he tells us that he wore himself out sighing and wailing, drenched his couch nightly with his tears, and soaked his pillow with his weeping.[2]

We too ought to be able to say the same thing as David, because we need penance no less than he did if we wish to draw Jesus Christ to us. This is why, as the Gloss says, each of you must expiate the sins of your past by penance, so that you may once again draw near to the salvation you have lost and recover the facility of returning to God, from whom you have strayed. This is why God declared, by one of the Prophets, be converted to me by fasting, weeping, and mourning.[3] For they are the surest means of finding God when we have lost him, the means that contribute most to obtaining for us that purity of heart which David so ardently begged from the Lord. It was also with this in mind that he asked God, Wash me yet more from my iniquities, and purify me from my sins.[4]

This penitent king was fully persuaded that the stains of a sinful soul will not be washed away except by the tears that flow from a humble and contrite heart. Let us frequently beg God for the grace to cleanse ourselves so perfectly that no trace of our sins will remain, and on our part, let us contribute to this by the penance we perform for our sins.

## 4.2  Second Point

It is said of Saint John that he preached penance for the remission of sins,[5] because it is penance that procures the remission of sins for those who have offended God. Saint Peter said to the Jews in the Acts of the Apostles, Do penance, and be converted, so that your sins may be forgiven.[6] For such is the specific end of this virtue; it alone can appease the heart of God irritated against sinners. God tells us this in Ezechiel, saying that if the wicked man does penance for all the sins he has committed, keeps all my precepts, and acts according to equity and justice, I will no longer remember all his iniquities, and they will no more be imputed to him.[7] Saint Peter, preaching to the Jewish people to make known to them the truths of the Gospel, told them, Do penance to obtain the remission of your sins.[8]

It was also by means of this same virtue that the Ninevites, who had outraged heaven by their disorderly conduct, induced God to revoke the sentence he had pronounced against them to destroy their city.[9] This they could not do except by a conversion of their hearts, following the preaching of Jonas and the invitation of their king. To avert the calamity that threatened them, there was no other recourse for them, says Saint Ambrose, than to fast continually and cover themselves with sackcloth and ashes to appease the anger of God.

By the same method, you too will obtain the remission of all the sins you committed in the world and all those you still commit every day in God's house. For, as Saint Jerome observes, every day God still addresses to people the same threats he addressed to the Ninevites, so that just as these menaces frightened those sinful people, they may in the same way convince people who are living now to do penance. Let us, then, profit by such an admirable example.

## 4.3  Third Point

As the Prophet Ezechiel informs us, penance not only obtains for us the remission of our sins but also preserves us from sin, which is the greatest blessing we can enjoy in this world. For after saying that if the wicked man does penance for all his sins, God will no longer remember them, he adds that man will live by practicing the works of justice, and he will not die.[10] This is why Saint Peter comforts us so much when he tells us that the Lord, on the day of his coming, will find in peace of soul those who have brought forth a worthy harvest of penance,[11] because he will find them free from sin. By this means, remarks Theodoret, they will have made their salvation certain. As the Church sings, it was by this means that Saint John the Baptist was able to preserve himself free from the slightest sins.

In the same way you will return to the grace of our Lord and, according to Saint Peter, you will receive the gift of the Holy Spirit,[12] who will make you firm in goodness, thanks to his dwelling in you. This Holy Spirit is the Spirit of Jesus Christ. Beg him to establish your heart so firmly in good that on the day of his coming, as Saint Peter says, you may be found pure and irreproachable in his eyes.[13] Take care that when he comes, he will not address to you the same reproach that Saint John in the Apocalypse made to a bishop, telling you that you have fallen away from your first charity.[14] If he upbraids you with this now, *remember the state from which you have fallen,* as this bishop was enjoined to do. Do penance, and return to the practice of your first works.[15]

1. Lk 3:3
2. Ps 6:7
3. Jl 2:12
4. Ps 51:4
5. Lk 3:3

6. Acts 3:19
7. Ez 18:21–22; 33:16
8. Acts 2:38
9. Jon 3:1–10
10. Ez 18:21–22

11. 2 Pt 3:14
12. Acts 2:38
13. 2 Pt 3:14
14. Rev 2:4
15. Rev 2:5

# Sunday in the Octave of Christmas

## GOSPEL: LUKE 2:33-40

*We must not contradict the truths, the precepts, or the counsels of the Gospel.*

### 5.1 First Point

Today's Gospel relates that Saint Simeon, after blessing Jesus' father and mother in the Temple, told Mary, his mother, that this Child had come for the fall and for the resurrection of many in Israel.[1] Many would profit by his death, while many others, lacking fidelity to the grace that the Redeemer would merit for them, would make of this very grace the occasion of their damnation. This saintly old man then added that Jesus Christ would be a sign of contradiction for all people.[2] Indeed, there were many who contradicted his conduct during his life.

Even among Christians there are still many who every day contradict his teaching and his maxims. Some show little respect for the decisions of the Church. Others, at times, presume to argue about predestination and grace—topics on which those who are not learned must never utter a single word, because these matters are beyond their understanding. If someone raises such subjects with you, your reply ought simply to be a general statement, I believe what the Church believes.

Let us do the same concerning a number of other questions relating to doctrine that our minds simply cannot fully grasp. We must remember the words of the Wise Man in Ecclesiasticus: Be not concerned over things that are above you.[3] Let us leave to the learned all these learned disputes; let us leave to them the task of refuting heresies and silencing heretics.

Let us teach only the common doctrine of Jesus Christ and make it our practice to abide in all things by what the Church teaches to the faithful in the catechisms approved by her, that is, those composed or adopted by the bishops who are united to the Vicar of Jesus Christ. Let us never take the liberty of dogmatizing on religious controversies.

### 5.2 Second Point

There is no less danger in contradicting the moral teachings of Jesus Christ than in rejecting his doctrine, for usually what causes the loss of faith is disorder in moral behavior. Jesus did not come so much to teach us the holy truths of Christian morality as to engage us to practice them faithfully. Still, it is common enough to see Christians, and even members of religious communities, who do not accept these practical truths and who contradict them in their hearts, sometimes even in their external conduct, as when someone tells them that on Judgment Day they will have to account for a useless word;[4] that we must pray without ceasing;[5] that we must enter heaven through the narrow gate;[6] that Jesus Christ has said, Unless you do penance, you will all likewise perish;[7] consequently, that it is an indispensable obligation to put these maxims into practice if we wish to be saved; that there is a command addressed to them to love their enemies, to do good to those who hate them, to pray to God for those who persecute them and calumniate them, so that they may be truly the children of their Father who is in heaven, who makes his sun rise on the good and the wicked alike.[8]

How many are there who believe that these teachings are merely counsels of perfection? Yet Jesus Christ taught that they are necessary practices and the way to achieve salvation. Take care not to fall into this gross error, which might lead you astray from the true path to heaven.

### 5.3 Third Point

It is not enough for us to avoid contradicting the moral precepts of the Gospel. Saint Paul says that he will show us an even more perfect, more excellent way[9] to which Jesus Christ calls us, which he has illustrated for us by his own example. If anyone wishes to follow me, says our Lord, let him renounce himself[10]—that is, let him renounce his own spirit and his own will—*let him carry his cross daily and follow me*. Who, indeed, does not contradict this divine saying of Jesus Christ, our Master, if not in word at least in heart?

How many would agree with this thought of Saint Bernard, that light and frivolous words in the mouth of a secular person may be only playful chatter, but in the mouth of a person consecrated to God, they are blasphemies? How many take to heart the words of Saint Dorotheus: "Let us be faithful in the slightest matters, lest they lead to regrettable consequences and unfortunate results"? To how many do not these words of Jesus Christ seem harsh? Blessed are the poor in spirit;[11] it is harder for a rich man to enter heaven than for a camel to pass through a needle's eye.[12]

For us, let us probe the depths of our hearts. Are they truly penetrated with what Jesus Christ said: Blessed will you be when people falsely say all sorts of evil against you?[13] How many there are who violate rules on many points, as though they were obliged to observe only the rules that they find convenient. Such people soon fall into disorderly living, for as Saint Dorotheus remarks, as soon as we begin to say, "What does it matter if I say this word? What harm is there if I eat this morsel? What crime do I commit in doing this or that?", we end up smothering all remorse of conscience, even on the most essential points.

Let us fear that we will be lost if we attach ourselves to maxims that lead to laxity, for we are people whom God has called to live according to the perfection of the Gospel.

---

1. Lk 2:34
2. Ibid.
3. Sir 3:22
4. Mt 12:36
5. Lk 18:1
6. Mt 7:13
7. Lk 13:5
8. Mt 5:44–45
9. 1 Cor 12:31
10. Lk 9:23
11. Mt 5:3
12. Mt 19:23–24
13. Mt 5:11

# Sunday Between the Circumcision of Our Lord and Savior, Jesus Christ, and the Epiphany or for the Eve of the Feast of the Kings

## GOSPEL: SAINT MATTHEW 2:13-15

*The love for seclusion, following the example of Jesus Christ, who lived hidden and unknown in Egypt*

### 6.1 First Point

Having been warned by an angel to bring the Child Jesus to Egypt, because Herod was searching for him to put him to death, Joseph without delay left with the most Blessed Virgin.[1] He felt secure in Judea, because this was the kingdom where the people of God lived; this is why he would have been unwilling to leave this country to go and live among strangers, except that God ordered it. His attitude was the same as that of Jesus Christ, who declares in the Gospel that he came into this world not to do his own will but only that of God, his Father.[2] This is how we ought to act when we must adopt some line of conduct or leave off doing something we have begun.

God has brought you into a secluded and holy place, his own house, where he brings together those he has chosen to belong to him. If you leave, it ought to be only because God wants you to do so and commands you, so that you may preserve the life of Jesus Christ in the hearts of those entrusted to your care or for some other necessity. The separation that ought to exist between you and people who are not part of your life must make you fear to leave your place of seclusion and to abandon the company of your Brothers, the place God has assigned you for your usual residence.

### 6.2 Second Point

Saint Joseph, the Blessed Virgin, and the Child Jesus remained so unknown in Egypt that there is nothing to prove that anyone ever heard of them there. The Gospel tells us nothing about them or about what they did during their entire sojourn in that country. We find no account that tells of this, because they lived so obscurely that nobody knew they were there. This humble and secret life was most highly prized by the Holy Family, and it was also what the Eternal Father had decreed for Jesus Christ until the time came for him to give himself to the preaching of his Gospel and to the conversion of souls, the primary purpose of his coming. His long hidden life was a preparation for his apostolic life.

When you are obliged to leave your place of seclusion to be active in the world, you too must behave in such a manner that no one will know who you are and that the very ones you teach will not even know your name. In your classroom be concerned only about how to fulfill your ministry in all that God requires of you for your disciples and to do all you can to procure for them the Christian spirit by acting this way. Following the example of the Holy Family, you will not make people talk about you; you will be mere passersby, solely concerned with doing God's work and causing Jesus to live in the souls of those who do not recognize him.

### 6.3 Third Point

*Right after Herod died, an angel told Saint Joseph to go back to Judea to settle there* and to remain there permanently with the Blessed Virgin and the Child Jesus. This summons was all he needed. So prompt was he in carrying out what God wanted of him that he got up at once and, taking the mother and the Child, departed in all haste.[3] What an admirable fidelity to God's orders Saint Joseph displays here!

Be faithful to follow the example of this great saint and to do all God wants of you, considering that it is by his orders that you must be guided in all you do. Be prompt to leave everything as soon as the bell rings to call you to some other exercise; let nothing keep you back. When you have finished what is required by your ministry, be careful not to delay or stop to do anything else. Return home as quickly as you can. The same God who had sent you out to do your work now calls you back. What more do you need? You must make it clear on all occasions that you depend on God and that at the slightest sign you are quite prepared to go wherever he calls you.

---

1. Mt 2:13–14         2. Jn 6:38         3. Mt 2:19–21

# The Sunday After the Feast of the Kings

## GOSPEL: SAINT LUKE 2:40-52

*The necessity of obedience*

### 7.1 First Point

Today's Gospel relates that Saint Joseph and the most Blessed Virgin went to Jerusalem with Jesus, then twelve years of age, to celebrate the feast of the Passover and that when they returned after the days of the festivity were completed, Jesus remained behind in Jerusalem. His parents came back looking for him; when they found him in the midst of the teachers, they brought him back with them to Nazareth, where he was subject to them,[1] as Saint Luke tells us. The Gospel gives us no more information about his life in Nazareth up to the time when he left to preach the Kingdom of God. What an admirable lesson for all those responsible for teaching Christian truth to others! Jesus Christ made himself ready by submission and obedience to carry out the great task of the redemption and conversion of souls, because he knew that nothing can ensure the success of this mission more certainly and more effectively than preparing himself for it by a long practice of a humble and submissive life. This is why, in the early Church, especially in the East, it was customary to choose as bishops people who had lived for a long time under obedience.

You whom God has called to a ministry that requires you to labor for the salvation of souls must prepare by the practice of obedience over a long period of time to be worthy of so holy a role and to be able to achieve great good in your exercise of it. The more faithful you are to the grace of Jesus Christ, who wishes to see you become perfect in this virtue of obedience, the more will God bless your efforts, because whoever obeys his superior obeys God.[2]

### 7.2 Second Point

What will encourage you more to exact obedience is that the first end we ought to have had in coming into this community is to obey those in charge, because, as Saint Bonaventure so rightly says, obedience is the foundation of communities, without which they fall into ruin. Saint Teresa also observes very correctly that a community cannot survive without obedience and does not even deserve the name community if this virtue is not observed in it, even if all the other virtues are practiced there to an eminent degree. Such was the case of those cenobites who, as Cassian relates, were living without any bonds of obedience and were judged for that reason by the ancient Fathers of the desert to be a monstrosity, not a community.

The practice of obedience was also the first injunction given to Abbot Postumus by the angel who taught him by God's command: the first rule to be observed by those who wish to live in community is to obey those appointed to guide them.

Reason demonstrates the necessity of obedience in a religious society, obedience being the virtue that establishes order, union, peace, and tranquillity among those who belong to it. Indeed, without obedience each one would act as he saw fit; trouble, disorder, and chaos could not fail to enter and thereby subvert the community from top to bottom. For, says Saint James, every house where there is division will fall into ruin.[3]

Because obedience is the most necessary of all the virtues required for life in a community, it ought to be the one you must cultivate most particularly, because without it we cannot for long sustain ourselves in our state.

### 7.3  Third Point

For every state, says Saint Thomas, there is a particular grace special to it; consequently, it is a necessary virtue for all those who belong to that state, if they wish to sanctify themselves and to find salvation there. For each one of you, this grace is the grace of obedience, because obedience ought to be the characteristic of people living in community. It ought to distinguish them from people living in the world and enjoying their full liberty. This is why Saint Lawrence Justinian says that whoever wishes to enter a religious society must, first of all, renounce his own will. Saint Bernard, to make us understand that this renunciation sanctifies, says that this is what Jesus Christ meant when he gave us in the Gospel the first means of reaching perfection, namely, to deny ourselves.[4] Saint Vincent Ferrer says that Jesus Christ will never give his grace to anyone in religious life who refuses to be governed by the superior.

Because we cannot be saved without the grace proper to our state and because the special grace needed by a person living in community is obedience, you ought to make every effort to possess it as nearly perfectly as possible. It is true that there are other virtues that you need to practice in order to fulfill your duty, being involved as you are in exterior work, but be quite convinced that you will never carry out your duty in an adequate manner unless you possess perfectly the virtue of obedience. This is why you ought to apply to you the words of Pope Saint Gregory, in his Dialogues, that the first and principal virtue you ought to claim for your practice is obedience, because it will be in you the source of all the others and also of your sanctification.

---

1. Lk 2:42–46, 51    3. Mk 3:25    4. Lk 9:23
2. Lk 10:16

# Second Sunday After the Feast of the Kings

## GOSPEL: SAINT JOHN 2:1–11

*Exact obedience*

### 8.1 First Point

Today's Gospel relates that Jesus Christ, having been invited to a wedding feast along with Mary, his mother, and his disciples and with the wine running short, Jesus changed water into wine at the plea of the Blessed Virgin, his mother, who told the table servants to do all that her Son would command them.[1] She knew that the best attitude they could display on their part to induce Jesus Christ to perform this miracle was an entire submission to his orders. This is likewise the most appropriate means we can use to obtain for ourselves an abundance of grace and to produce marvels, even miracles, in ourselves by helping us overcome ourselves. This led the Wise Man to say that it is the truly obedient who will sing of victories.[2]

For obedience to have this result, it must, first of all, be exact with regard to the thing commanded, so that the one who obeys is prepared to do everything prescribed and shows no greater preference for one thing than for another. This requires a strenuous effort to die to ourselves, for it is difficult not to appear more willing to do one thing rather than another.

You must overcome yourselves, then, to conquer all your dislikes so fully that anyone commanding you will not be able to judge or to discern, if possible, what pleases or displeases you when you are called to obey. Can it be said that you possess interiorly and exteriorly an entire indifference for whatever you are commanded or might be commanded to do? Are you faithful and exact to carry out in detail the orders of your superiors? The surest sign that you can give them of this is not to ask or to refuse them anything.

## 8.2 Second Point

The Gospel next observes that Jesus Christ told the waiters to fill the waterpots that were there for the Jewish purification rites. The waiters immediately filled them up to the brim.[3] This expression *up to the brim* gives us to understand that a truly obedient man not only does what he is told, but his exactitude in obeying also extends to the point of doing it in the manner indicated. These servants might have judged that they were obeying our Lord if they filled the waterpots more or less full, but this was not enough; they wanted to do exactly what was commanded of them, with regard to not only what was prescribed but also the manner of carrying it out. This is why they filled the water pots up to the brim. Eager to obey exactly, they took the word *fill* in the fullest sense possible.

This is how you ought to act when your superiors bid you to do something. You must do what is commanded and in the manner ordered. For instance, if you are told to do something using such or such an instrument, and you do it with another, thinking that this would be more convenient—or if you are supposed to use the signal when teaching, and you use words, thinking that this will be easier for you—then you are indeed obeying as to the thing commanded, but not as to the manner of doing it. This is not the way a perfectly obedient religious acts. In the future, if you wish to practice exact obedience, take care to be vigilant not to do anything in a manner other than what is prescribed.

## 8.3 Third Point

Another point that must be mentioned about obeying is the matter of time, for to obey properly, it is necessary that things be done at the prescribed moment, neither earlier nor later. Exactness in timing is as necessary to make obedience perfect as exactness in regard to the thing commanded and the manner of doing it. This is how Jesus Christ acted, as the servants also did at the marriage feast. The fact is that Jesus Christ shows us in this Gospel passage that he did not wish to perform this miracle until the moment his Father prescribed, as when he said to the most Blessed Virgin, his mother, *that his hour,* the hour for performing this miracle, had not yet arrived.[4]

The waiters serving at table *filled the waterpots with water* as soon as Jesus Christ told them to do so; similarly, as soon as our Savior told them, they drew off some of this water changed into wine and brought it to the head waiter of the feast to taste.[5]

Show a like exactness when you are instructed to do something, because God wants what is commanded done at that precise time, not at some other you might choose. For instance, you ring the bell late for an exercise, or you go to that exercise after it has begun, or you get up earlier than the Rule prescribes. In all these cases, you are not practicing exact obedience, because you are not doing all these things at the precise time appointed; therefore, you cannot be considered as having obeyed as you should have, because the circumstance of time is an element in exact and punctual obedience.

---

1. Jn 2:2–5
2. Prv 21:28
3. Jn 2:6–7
4. Jn 2:4
5. Jn 2:8

# Third Sunday After the Feast of the Kings

## GOSPEL: SAINT MATTHEW 8:1-13

*The faith that must be shown in obedience*

### 9.1 First Point

A centurion whose servant lay sick at his house, as today's Gospel tells us, begged Jesus Christ to come and cure him.[1] But then, having reflected that there was no need for Jesus to go to all this trouble, because it was sufficient for him to give a command to the servant to get well for him to be immediately cured, the centurion went to meet the Savior to tell him that a single word of his would suffice to heal the sick man. Jesus, admiring the faith of the centurion, said that he had not found such great faith in all Israel.[2]

This centurion makes known to us how excellent obedience is when it is inspired and sustained by faith. Those who obey their superiors with the conviction that they are obeying God elevate their obedience by this view of faith, so that it becomes one of the most eminent acts of the virtue of religion that we can elicit in this world, because it is addressed directly to God hidden under the veil of a person frail and mortal but endowed with divine authority. This is how the centurion acted when seeing in Jesus Christ only the external appearance of an ordinary man; nevertheless, he was profoundly convinced that to perform a miracle such as the cure of the sick servant, he possessed the authority of God and was consequently truly God.

Do you obey with like dispositions and with this pure and simple view of faith? Do you obey God hidden beneath the appearance of a man, a man who cannot command you except by reason of God's power residing in him? Is this view of faith the only motive that leads you to submit promptly and blindly? It is the only motive that will free your obedience from all human considerations.

### 9.2 Second Point

The centurion told Jesus that a single word of his would suffice to cure his servant. He confirmed this by his own behavior with regard to the soldiers in his command, to whom he needed to say only a word to be obeyed instantly.[3] The conclusion to be drawn from this is that if some, out of purely human considerations, show themselves so submissive to another whom they regard as their leader, with how much greater reason must those who have consecrated themselves to God and who ought to act only according to his Spirit be obliged to fulfill on the spot whatever is enjoined on them by their superior? They ought to have nothing but God in view when so acting, because they ought to be convinced that it is God who commands them in the superior's person.

Does it take only a word or a sign from your superior to make you set everything aside or to undertake anything right away for the sole motive that this word is a word coming from God and that this sign is made by God? This simple view of faith leads obedient people to transcend themselves and to see only God where he often is not apparent and to leave aside all the sentiments that human nature might suggest. Renew from time to time this view of faith regarding obedience. To be convinced more fully, often adore God in those who command you.

### 9.3 Third Point

The centurion was entirely right. As soon as he believed that Jesus could heal his servant with a single word, his servant was in fact cured.[4] This grace was granted, thanks to the excellence and vigor of his faith. In the same way, it takes only a word from a superior to a religious truly obedient and filled with lively faith to accomplish in that person great miracles and to bring about the most surprising effects of grace.

Obedience practiced this way leads the one who obeys to make no reply to the one who commands and to find no difficulty in executing the order. Even if a command is difficult to carry out, the love with which he obeys makes it agreeable, and everything is done with joy. In this way the person obeying has the simplicity of a child, who does not know how to choose or to argue, because the simplicity with which he obeys enlightens the mind with a view fixed on God and suppresses all other human reasoning and considerations.

Is this how you obey? Do you not advance reasons to be excused from doing what you have been commanded? If you do not do this openly and verbally, does not your mind, nevertheless, often take satisfaction in dwelling on the alternatives it considers good and even better and more appropriate than what the superior has ordered?

Pay attention to the fact that we must not obey by reason but by grace and through a simple view of faith. Whoever listens to reason acts only in a human manner, not as a disciple faithful to the voice of Jesus Christ, which must always guide us by the spirit of faith.

---

1. Lk 7:2–3       3. Mt 8:8–9       4. Mt 8:13
2. Mt 8:8–10

# Fourth Sunday After the Feast of the Kings

## GOSPEL: SAINT MATTHEW 8:23-27

*The fidelity in obedience we ought to have, in spite of the most violent temptations*

### 10.1 First Point

When Jesus was in a boat, there arose on the sea so great a storm that the vessel was covered by the waves. After the disciples appealed to him, he got up and commanded the winds and seas to be quiet, and there ensued a deep calm, which so astonished those present that they said, Who is this man whom winds and seas obey?[1]

To live in a community that is faithful to the Rule is to live in the boat with Jesus and his disciples, because those who live there have left the world to follow Jesus, have put themselves under his guidance, and have become his disciples. There they are protected from the waves of the stormy sea of this world, that is, from a great many occasions that are found there for offending God. Still, they are not entirely safe from all difficulties and temptations. Of these the most dangerous and most hurtful are those which lead us to fail in obedience or to obey in a faulty manner. Because we have entered the community only to obey, as soon as we separate ourselves from obedience, we forfeit the graces we need to persevere in this state of life. This is why it is so important that people living in community have at their disposal the means needed to protect themselves against temptations of this sort.

It is, therefore, very appropriate for you, who are exposed to such temptations every day, to have remedies to keep you from their evil consequences. Take great care about this, and give it your whole effort, because your faithfulness to your vocation ordinarily depends on this. What you ought, therefore, to beg most often of God is that he teach you how to obey and to obey well, in spite of the obstacles and difficulties that the demon will stir up in you to give you a dislike for obedience.

### 10.2 Second Point

The most considerable and most frequent temptations and difficulties concerning obedience arise either over those who command or over what is commanded. Those referring to the people who command stem from the fact that we look upon them as merely human, even though for us they hold the place of God and, consequently, must be considered only from this point of view. There is no power, says Saint Paul, that does not come from God,[2] particularly when it is a question of ordering, commanding, or forbidding anything referring to our salvation.

It is, no doubt, to make us realize and remember this truth that after most of the passages in the Old Testament where God gives injunctions, he adds: I am the Lord, or I am the Lord, your God.[3] For we cannot emancipate ourselves from the obligation of obeying God, nor, consequently, can anyone in a community fail in obedience to the superiors without becoming guilty of disobedience toward God. This is why, no matter what lack of sympathy we might experience with regard to a superior, this must refer only to the individual, never to the role, because in obeying we do not submit to a person but to God.

Never use your personal grievances as a pretext to dispense you from obeying your superiors, for this would direct your ill feeling against God.

### 10.3 Third Point

The second sort of temptation against the obedience due to superiors, and the most ordinary one, is to think that we cannot fulfill what they prescribe, because it is too difficult or because we experience too great a repugnance for it. Neither of these two pretexts can exempt us from obeying, if we consider that what is commanded and what we perform in obeying are God's will.

God knows what you are capable of, and he is not going to command you things above your strength.[4] If, indeed, they are difficult in themselves, it is up to him to impart to you the ability you need to carry them out. For, as Saint Paul says, God gives us not only the will to do what is right but also the grace to accomplish it.[5] A will fore-armed and sustained by God's grace to achieve something good finds nothing difficult, because God smoothes out all the obstacles encountered in the action.

This happened in the case of those inferiors who threw themselves into the fire and emerged unscathed or who did other equally difficult things at the first order given to them by their superiors. Did not Jesus Christ through obedience perform something extremely difficult when he died on a cross for the sins of all of us?

We must, therefore, overcome our repugnance and the other hindrances we find in what is commanded, for if we are determined to obey only in those things for which we feel a natural inclination, we intend to do our own will, not God's. We ought to be convinced that in obeying we are carrying out the will of God, as we learn from Saint Paul, who, speaking to those who are obliged to obey, urges them to do whatever they have to do with a willing heart, not as if obeying man but God.[6] Cassian also affirms that we must do what superiors enjoin as though they were commandments given to us by God from high heaven. No doubt, if we considered them in this light, we would not fail to be faithful.

---

1. Mt 8:23–27
2. Rom 13:1
3. Lv 11:44
4. 1 Cor 10:13
5. Phil 2:13
6. Eph 6:7

# Fifth Sunday After the Feast of the Kings

## GOSPEL: SAINT MATTHEW 13:24–30

*The excellence and merit of obedience*

### 11.1 First Point

Because obedience is a source of grace for a religious, it can be compared to the good seed sown in a field,[1] which produces a rich harvest for its owner. This, indeed, is the virtue that in people consecrated to God constitutes the entire merit of their actions, so that no matter how good these may be in themselves, they are valuable only insofar as obedience accompanies them. It may be said that what confers the crowning glory on their actions is obedience; however holy these works may be in themselves, unless obedience bestows on them their full luster, the beauty they possess is only apparent. This, it is true, suffices to dazzle those who do not look upon things with the eyes of faith, but truly enlightened people can discern all their falsity and vanity.

Those who live under obedience must take care that it not be said of them what was stated of the scribes and Pharisees, whom the Oracle of Truth called whitened sepulchers, attractive enough externally and beautiful to behold, as long as viewed from the outside, but filled with dead men's bones and corruption within.[2]

The same thing can be said about religious whose actions are not all performed under the control of obedience. These people seem to be virtuous in appearance, but in fact they are fundamentally bad and entirely displeasing to God, because they are not inspired by the virtue that alone must sustain them, the virtue of obedience. Without obedience their work, which seems good in the eyes of people, is only a body without a soul and cannot be considered as the work of a true religious.

### 11.2 Second Point

It sometimes happens that an activity ostensibly performed out of obedience is not totally guided and governed by this virtue, because the person has failed in something prescribed by the superior regarding either the time or the manner of complying. Such an action degenerates from what it was; because of this flaw, it becomes a deed inspired by self-will. This defect is the cockle that the demon sows amid the good seed.[3] It is certainly very unfortunate that a deed, good in itself, becomes bad for the want of such a circumstance and that this single deficiency makes it displeasing to God. This shows what great vigilance religious must exercise over all their conduct, so that their actions may what they ought to be to please God.

Take care, therefore, that all you do is guided by obedience and that in all your work there is not the slightest circumstance not subject to this virtue. For God has no regard for an action, even if performed through obedience, unless there is care to accomplish it without neglecting any detail in what is prescribed by the one who commands. According to a maxim of philosophers, to make an action good, everything connected with it must be good, whereas even the slightest defect makes it imperfect. It is no small flaw not to obey as we ought to obey, for this is to lack respect for God and not to show the esteem for him that we must have.

### 11.3 Third Point

The best way to do exactly what has been commanded by the superior is to place a higher value on obedience (which is what gives value to the action) than on the deed. Any act, however remarkable it might be in itself, if separated from obedience is not esteemed by God at all, because it lacks what precisely constitutes all its merit, whereas something that might seem of slight importance takes on considerable value in God's eyes, thanks to the care we take to do it in a spirit of obedience.

What constitutes the merit of a person living in a religious community is not the kind of actions done there but the perfection of the obedience with which they are done. This is what ought to distinguish a religious from a secular person. The deeds of the former are sanctified, because they are carried out through obedience, whereas for the latter, deeds are sanctified only by their intrinsic merit.

Let us examine whether obedience motivates and rules our conduct. We ought to give this question our most serious attention.

Another consideration that provides us with further and very notable proof of the excellence of the virtue we have been considering is that it rectifies everything; something bad becomes pleasing to God, thanks to obedience, when we are invincibly ignorant of the evil and we proceed in good faith and in all simplicity, having in mind no other intention except that of obeying God.

---

1. Mt 13:27          2. Mt 23:27          3. Mt 13:25

# Sixth Sunday After the Feast of the Kings

## GOSPEL: SAINT MATTHEW 13:31-35

*The great benefit produced by what is done through obedience, however insignificant it seems*

### 12.1 First Point

In today's Gospel Jesus Christ declares that the kingdom of heaven is like a grain of mustard seed, which is the smallest of all seeds but which, however, when it has grown, becomes a tree such that the birds of the sky come to rest in its branches.[1]

The same can be said of something done out of obedience, even though it may be quite insignificant in appearance; it is, nevertheless, quite considerable, because it is done out of obedience. Eating, for instance, gathering up the crumbs remaining on the table, or sweeping a room, washing dishes, attaching a pin: all such tasks seem to be trifles in themselves, but when performed through obedience, they become highly significant actions, because their object is God, whom we obey in performing them.

As a result, this virtue, more than any other, can be associated with the theological virtues, for faith is its principle and guide. It is always accompanied by hope and confidence in God, and it is a result of charity and the pure love of God.

Even the birds of the sky, that is, the virtues, which belong to the saints in heaven, rest[2] on those who obey, for they experience a joy, consolation, and interior peace which cannot be adequately expressed and which are not found in such perfection in anyone on earth, except in those who obey solely in view of God.

Experience how good the Lord is[3] and how true all this is, because throughout your entire life you must place all your affection in obeying.

### 12.2 Second Point

We can attribute to obedience what Solomon says of Wisdom, that all good things come to us along with it.[4] Indeed, whoever obeys in a spirit of religion possesses all the virtues: he is humble, because he must be humble to submit to another; he is gentle, because no matter how irksome the thing commanded may be, he does not complain; he is silent, because the truly obedient man has lost the use of his tongue and knows only how to do what is ordered without making any reply; he is patient, because he endures everything[5] and bears all the burdens imposed on him; he is charitable beyond measure, because obedience makes him undertake all things for the good of his neighbor.

This is why Saint Bonaventure says that obedience must enter into everything done in a community; without it all the most perfect actions cease to be good. Fasting, which is so meritorious before God, is rejected when inspired by self-will; in this case a person assumes the proprietorship of an action over which God alone possesses sovereign dominion and for which that person has the right only to do what God requires of him.

We ought to consider ourselves happy to be in a state that requires obedience of us; we ought to regard this virtue as the mother and the support of all the other virtues. But if you wish this to be true in your case, you must practice it with all possible perfection, for God gives this grace only to those who have renounced self-will and who regard his will as the rule and the principle of everything they do.

### 12.3 Third Point

The main benefit that obedience produces in a religious person is to procure for us the perfection proper to our state, to fortify us in it, and to assure perseverance. As Saint Dorotheus says, nothing helps us to fulfill our religious duties better than to renounce our self-will. This is the most appropriate means we can use to acquire all sorts of virtues. By often sacrificing our self-will, we acquire great control over our passions and inclinations and possess our souls undisturbed in every sort of circumstance. This is the highest perfection.

This is why Cassian says that a person achieves purity of heart and fervor in religion in proportion to the progress achieved in obedience. Saint Ignatius, in the third part of his Constitutions (chapter 1, paragraphs 21, 22, and 23), affirms that it is not only expedient but also most necessary in his community for all to practice obedience perfectly if they wish to advance in virtue and in the perfection of their state.

Nor is there anything that renders a religious more firm and unshakable, thanks to the respect and the love that it inspires for all the observances of the religious life. They are the safe and sure paths to acquire fully the spirit of your state and to persevere in it. For why do some fail to persevere? Is it not because they lose their love for the Rule and the practices of the community, eventually grow disgusted with them, and carry them out only grudgingly?

From this you can conclude how important it is that, above all else, you love the practice of obedience and give it your best effort. According to Sulpicius Severus, it is the first and most important of all the virtues that enhance a community. Rest assured that you will not love your state and will not have its spirit except insofar as you are faithful to obedience.

---

1. Mt 13:31–32
2. Mt 13:32
3. Ps 43:9
4. Wis 7:11
5. See 1 Cor 13:4–7

# Septuagesima Sunday

## GOSPEL: SAINT MATTHEW 20:1–16

*The need for people consecrated to God to be exercised in the practice of obedience*

### 13.1  First Point

There are many people in religious communities who could be asked with more surprise and more justice than those in the Gospel who were standing idle in the market place: Why have you stayed here all the day doing nothing?[1] These people have consecrated themselves to God and profess to be striving toward the perfection proper to their state, yet they remain in it without making any progress in virtue, especially the virtue of obedience. Although they are pledged in a special manner to practice it, they are not observed doing so to any great extent.

Often enough their superior must accommodate himself to their disposition or their inclinations. As a result, they do not practice obedience, or if they do, it is only a conditional sort of obedience, or else it varies from day to day or remains on a purely human level. We can truly say that they never do practice genuine obedience at all. Oh, how deeply are they to be pitied: they are not exercised in the practice of obedience, and they always remain newcomers in the practice of this virtue!

### 13.2  Second Point

It would seem that this disorder arises from two sources. The first lies in those who have undertaken the practice of obedience but do not offer themselves spontaneously to practice the virtue. They say that it is enough for them to follow the ordinary community activities and to carry out exteriorly, and all too often very negligently, their usual duties.

So, when it happens that they are given an order they did not expect, they cannot accept it; they say that this is too much for them and that they are not able to put up with such a trial. In this way they find everything enjoined on them to be above their strength and beyond their virtue; they are not readily disposed to be called upon to obey.

This defective conduct is also found in inferiors who wish to sell their submission too dearly. They are prepared to carry out orders only on certain conditions, which they claim the right to require of their superiors, or only when they are in a good humor.

Oh, how unhappy we are when we are obliged to obey and are not willingly disposed toward obedience! That is when the practice of obedience becomes difficult.

### 13.3 Third Point

The second source of this disorder comes from the superiors who leave their inferiors in a kind of laziness; they do not give them opportunities to practice obedience. The idle laborers say, No one has put us to work.[2] That is why some religious never acquire this virtue, for like all the others, it becomes easy only with practice. It even requires more effort than others, because to obey properly, we must overcome ourselves and renounce our own views and natural inclinations.

When such inferiors are told to do something, some of them do it only in part or only in an external manner; others answer back or plead reasons for excusing themselves from obeying; others even refuse outright to obey.

Oh, how unfortunate are those religious whose superiors give them no opportunity or scarcely any opportunity to practice obedience! For it is extremely important that those who profess to practice this virtue be given a chance to do so every day.

---

1. Mt 20:6          2. Mt 20:7

# Sexagesima Sunday

## GOSPEL: SAINT LUKE 8:4-15

*Three kinds of disobedient religious*

### 14.1 First Point

In a community the superior's word is like the seed in today's Gospel. It is heard by three kinds of poorly disposed people. The seed that fell on the road[1] is the word of a superior that is received by those who have only a weak desire to obey. They seem to have some liking for obedience; they speak well of it on occasion and even urge others to practice it. But all we discover in them is a kind of goodwill that has no consequence, because they find everything they are asked to do very difficult. They cannot bring themselves to practice obedience, and, in fact, they do not. This is because their heart has not been prepared ahead of time. To secure their compliance, the superior, before commanding them anything, first has to prepare them, so that they will like what he is asking them to do.

Are you not of this number? Are you always ready to obey? Be prepared in your heart to obey, so that your superior is able to call on you at any time with full confidence, knowing that he will find you always ready to do what you are asked.

### 14.2 Second Point

The seed that fell on stony ground[2] is like the word of a superior received by those who do what they are told only when they experience no disturbance or trouble in obeying. At the slightest temptation, the merest difficulty of spirit, or the least annoyance felt toward their superior, they become upset and cannot make up their mind to do what he has ordered, because they are not solidly grounded in virtue and have not been sufficiently exercised in the practice of obedience. Oh, how important it is that such people, weak and subject to temptation, be thoroughly exercised in obedience and that people of this character be contradicted and tested!

Often ask your superior not to allow such weaknesses in you, and ask God to give you an always docile heart.

### 14.3 Third Point

The seed that fell among thorns[3] is like the superior's word received by those who obey in everything they like and in which they find nothing difficult. But if they feel any repugnance toward what they are told, they cannot bring themselves to do it, because they are unable to overcome themselves and to do the violence to themselves that the occasion requires. To bring them to obey, the superior has to ask them to do only what they find agreeable; before venturing to give them an order, he needs to study their temperament and their inclinations.

This sort of obedience is entirely natural and human; in consequence, there is nothing religious about it, nothing meritorious before God. It obliges the superior to ask his inferior what he wishes to do, whereas it is the inferior who ought to say to his superior, What do you want me to do?[4] This is how you must always act if you wish to be truly obedient.

---

1. Lk 8:12        3. Lk 8:14        4. Acts 9:6
2. Lk 8:13

# Quinquagesima Sunday

## GOSPEL: SAINT LUKE 18:31-43

*Three sorts of people who obey without gaining the merit of blind obedience*

### 15.1 First Point

The blind man whom Jesus Christ cures in today's Gospel and whom he had previously asked: What do you wish me to do for you?,[1] is a figure of those people whose superiors are forced to ask them what is agreeable to them and who want to examine what they are going to be asked to do before showing that they are disposed to do it. There are three kinds of such self-willed religious. Some examine the order given; before obeying they must know what the superior intends to command them, so that they can consider whether it is acceptable to them, whether it will be too much trouble for them, or whether they have some condition to propose to make the execution easier and more convenient for them. They also have a number of other reflections to make, all completely natural.

Truly obedient people examine nothing and pay attention to nothing except that they must obey. Faith has full charge of their minds and forbids all these considerations.

### 15.2 Second Point

The second type of religious, those who want to see before believing and obeying, are those who give reasons to their superior, whether to dispense themselves from carrying out what is asked, to do the thing in some way other than asked, or to make the superior see that something else would be better than what he desires.

True obedience does not admit of any such reasoning, because it is based on faith, which is infinitely superior to reason. Hence, to obey properly, we ought not to use any reasons. If before we submit, we need to be convinced or at least persuaded by reason, it is no longer because God commands that we obey but because the order appears reasonable to us. We are, then, no longer acting like truly obedient people but like a philosopher, who prefers reason to faith.

Which of these two ways of acting guide you with regard to your superiors? Do you reason with them and try to bring them to command what you like? Is this not, in a certain way, to place you above them and to lay down the law to them?

### 15.3 Third Point

The third type of religious, those who cannot obey blindly, are those who by a shameful profanation of what is most sacred in religion, that is, the fulfilling of God's will, presume on their own lights to such a degree that they try to prove to their superiors that they are wrong to command such a thing, that what they have been told to do is contrary to good sense. Such was the behavior of the novice who deserved to be dismissed by Saint Francis for wanting to maintain his way of judging against that of the saint.

Look upon such conduct with intense horror, for it destroys obedience; regard it in a community as the abomination of desolation in the holy place.[2] Obedience, to be perfect, must be blind, and as such it cannot admit of any contradicting, reasoning, examining, or even the slightest reply.

---

1. Lk 18:41          2. Mt 24:15

# Ash Wednesday

*The spirit of penance we must have when receiving the ashes and in which we must live all during Lent*

### 16.1 First Point

The purpose of the Church in putting ashes on your head today is to make you realize that today you ought to be filled with the true spirit of penance. This sacred ceremony is a remnant of the Church's ancient discipline, which obliged public penitents at the start of their penance to receive ashes on their heads at the hands of the ministers of the holy altar, in full view of the faithful.

You ought to resolve to unite with this institution of the Church, to participate in it, and to begin on this holy day to prepare by a suitable disposition of heart for this holy practice, the soul of which is sincere compunction. This is how we ought to begin and to end this holy season of forty days.

### 16.2 Second Point

In receiving the ashes, ask God that this spirit of penance may inspire you, accompany your fasting, and sanctify it. External fasting is of little value; it must also humble your spirit while mortifying your flesh.

The effect that the reception of the ashes ought to produce in you is to make penance a part of all your behavior and to make you fast with your eyes, your tongue, and your heart: your eyes, by great recollection and a turning aside from whatever might distract you; your tongue, by exact silence, which will cut you off from creatures in order to be attached only to God during this holy season; your heart, by renouncing entirely all thoughts that might distract you, draw you away, and interrupt your communication with God.

The results of Christian fasting are mortification of the senses and of selfish inclinations and detachment from creatures.

### 16.3 Third Point

To encourage us to the spirit of fasting while depriving ourselves of sense pleasures and detaching us from all the satisfactions we might find in the use of creatures, the Church, by the voice of the priest who imposes the ashes on us, tells us to remember that being human, we are only ashes and will return to ashes.[1]

Nothing more strongly incites us to detachment from created things and to sincere penance than the thought of death. This is why the Church wants us to think about this truth during all the time we spend in the penitential exercises of Lent. She hopes that through this holy thought, we may be encouraged to practice penance with more affection and fervor.

We will die, and we will die only once. We will die well and with God only insofar as we have lived in the practice of penance and have deprived ourselves of the pleasures that the sensual seek in the use of creatures. Do we wish to die a holy death? Let us live as true penitents.

---

1. Gn 3:19

# First Sunday of Lent

## GOSPEL: SAINT MATTHEW 4:1-11

*Temptation*

### 17.1 First Point

Today's Gospel, which informs us that Jesus Christ went off into the desert,[1] does not say that he did this to withdraw from human company or to pray but to be tempted. This helps us understand that the first step we must take when we wish to give ourselves to God is to leave the world to prepare ourselves to fight this world and all the enemies of our salvation.

In seclusion from the world, says Saint Ambrose, we ought to expect to be tempted and tried in many ways. The Wise Man likewise forewarns us of this when he says that those who enter the service of God must prepare themselves for temptation.[2] It is very advantageous for them, because it is one of the best ways to free themselves entirely from sin and from affection for sin.

Have you always thought that to be devoted entirely to God, you must be prepared to be tempted? Are you not upset when some temptation comes to you? In the future be ready to meet temptation at any time and thus to draw from it all the benefit that God wishes it to accomplish in you.

### 17.2 Second Point

What ought to induce a soul truly given to God to be always ready to meet temptation is what Job says: human life is a temptation or, according to the Vulgate, a constant warfare.[3] From this we may conclude that if God wishes a soul to be tempted in this world, it is because there is a need to struggle constantly against the demon and our own passions and inclinations, which will continue to wage war as long as the soul will be in this life. This led Saint Jerome to say that it is impossible for our soul to escape temptation in this life, that if Jesus Christ, our Savior, was tempted, no one can hope to cross the stormy sea of this life without being exercised by temptation.

Have you been expecting to battle constantly with the demon and against you? Since you left the world, have you been as constantly on your guard against you as you must be? Do you have what you need to resist the demon and not to surrender to the pleasures of the senses? Be convinced that it is a great misfortune not to experience any temptation, because this is a sign that we are not victorious in any way and that we are allowing ourselves to be easily conquered by our passions.

### 17.3 Third Point

The angel who accompanied young Tobias said to his father, Because you were pleasing to God, it was necessary for you to be tested by temptation.[4] This ought to convince you fully of the necessity of trials of this sort, for it is temptation that will procure for you an abundance of grace. So, do not believe, as Saint Chrysostom remarks, that God has abandoned you when you are tempted. On the contrary, this is one of the greatest signs you can have that God is particularly concerned about your salvation, because he gives you the opportunity to fight and to practice virtue energetically and in this way to gain strength by it. Little by little, we acquire sublime virtue when we remain constant, unshaken, and inflexible in its practice in spite of the violent temptations that attack us.

So, consider it a great misfortune when you are not tempted. This is a sign of reprobation and of God's abandonment, for God exercises those he loves[5] and is pleased when he sees them tempted, as was the case with Job and Tobias, two of his most faithful servants.

---

1. Mt 4:1          3. Jb 7:1          5. Rv 3:19
2. Sir 2:1         4. Tb 12:13

# Second Sunday of Lent

## GOSPEL: SAINT MATTHEW 17:1-9

*Spiritual consolation*

### 18.1 First Point

When temptations and interior trials have been endured patiently, God ordinarily encourages a pure soul with spiritual consolation. The way God gives us this and the way we must respond when we experience it are brought home to us in today's Gospel, which tells about our Lord's transfiguration. This is a symbol of the spiritual consolation that God sometimes gives to souls who are leading a truly interior life.

The Gospel tells us that our Lord was transfigured while praying on a very high, lonely mountain.[1] This teaches us that God pours out his consolation on souls who devote themselves a great deal to prayer and who love this holy exercise.

Those souls who are half-hearted and lazy, who have little love for prayer, ought not to be surprised if they are not among those whom God favors in a special way and with whom he communicates familiarly. They do not enjoy an intimate union with him, because they do not give themselves to the exercise that unites us with God and in which we learn to enjoy God and to have, even on this earth, a foretaste of the joy of heaven.

· Be faithful to this holy exercise, so that all your actions may be done in the spirit of prayer.

## 18.2 Second Point

God is pleased to unite intimately with pure souls, who have no attachment to sin. Still, he does not wish them to become too strongly attached to his gifts, for this attachment in a soul is a defect that displeases him, because it shows that the soul is not seeking God but the gift of God and its own satisfaction.

This is why, when God makes use of consolation to strengthen souls and to give them a chance to rest a little after undergoing trials and tribulations, they must accept this little refreshment with a simple view of God's good pleasure, without being complacent about the personal enjoyment they find there.

The three Apostles who accompanied Jesus Christ on Mount Tabor lacked this balance. Unfamiliar with God's ways, they were more eager to prolong the delight they were enjoying in this mystery than to contemplate God's greatness and goodness, which on this occasion ought to have filled their minds and absorbed all their attention. As a result, the exterior glory of Jesus Christ vanished in a moment and disappeared from their sight.[2]

That is God's way. He deprives us of the sensible pleasure found in consolation when we are too attached to it and enjoy it with too much self-satisfaction.

## 18.3 Third Point

Jesus' transfiguration lasted only a short time. This shows us that the consolations that God sometimes allows in this life are only a respite he sends to holy souls in the midst of their interior desolation to help them endure these trials with more courage and to augment their affection, which sometimes slackens off because of the weakness of nature.

Hardly had Jesus Christ enjoyed a moment of consolation in his transfiguration when he found himself once more alone,[3] deprived of everything and with no thought of anything other than of the torments he would have to undergo in Jerusalem,[4] *of which he had conversed with Moses and Elias* and which had been the subject of his conversation with his disciples as they came down from the mountain.[5]

We can understand from this that the passing consolations ought to help us to stir up our courage and to confirm us in the love of suffering and the love of interior and exterior trials, from which we must not expect to be exempt in this life.

---

1. Mt 17:1–2      3. Lk 9:36      5. Mt 17:9–12
2. Mt 17:4–8      4. Lk 9:31

# Third Sunday of Lent

## GOSPEL: SAINT LUKE 11:14-28

*Simplicity and openness of heart*[1]

### 19.1  First Point

Today's Gospel relates that Jesus Christ delivered a man possessed by a dumb demon,[2] that is, one who prevented the victim from speaking. This is a figure of those who remain mute in their relationship with their superiors, who do not open to them the depths of their hearts. This is very harmful, often the most harmful thing an inferior can do.

When you are sick, you can scarcely be cured if you cannot explain what is wrong; so too if you do not expose the wound in your soul to your spiritual physician, you run the risk of remaining ill for a long time. What was at first only a slight spiritual difficulty becomes a strong temptation, because the sufferer did not have the courage to discuss it openly with his Director. A fault thus concealed is followed by another still more serious, and in the end the problem becomes incurable because it was not brought to light at the beginning, when nothing would have been easier to remedy.

### 19.2  Second Point

It is pride or human respect that ordinarily prevents us from revealing our interior difficulties to our superior. It is pride, because we are ashamed to expose the depths of our soul and because our self-love suffers keenly when we have to admit certain weaknesses. So it seals our lips, persuading us that we would dishonor ourselves if we spoke sincerely to a superior, who then would get a bad impression of our behavior. This is what the demon does not fail to suggest to us on such occasions, taking pains to magnify things in our eyes, preventing us from surmounting the momentary confusion we experience in acknowledging these faults.

The remedy for this pernicious notion is to love the humiliation we experience in such an openness of heart, to carry out this duty as a powerful way to humble ourselves, and at the beginning simply to tell our superior everything that is most humiliating in the account we are giving of our conscience.

### 19.3 Third Point

The second reason why we ordinarily find it difficult to open ourselves fully to our superior is human respect. When we reflect that the fault in question concerns the very person to whom we must make it known, we do not know exactly how to go about it. We fear to cause pain, and so we sometimes resolve to say nothing. What a frivolous reason! What an ill-founded fear! For in such cases what happens is just the opposite of what we had imagined.

A superior to whom an inferior reveals everything going on interiorly, whether this has to do with the superior or with others, ought to feel, and usually does feel, a very special affection and esteem for the person who shows this kind of confidence. Such a superior is as unaffected as a stone by anything personal and does not become concerned about any revelations, except to apply the most appropriate remedy.

In the future consider all the thoughts that might prevent you from revealing yourself in all simplicity to those who are appointed to guide you as temptations from the demon, most dangerous and harmful to the good of your soul.

---

1. This meditation concerns the manifestation of conscience by the Brothers to their Directors and the Superior. Owing to the Holy See's Decree *Quemadmodum* of December 15, 1890, this meditation was modified in subsequent editions, substituting *confessor* for *superior*. The present translation follows the first edition.
2. Lk 11:14

# Fourth Sunday of Lent

## GOSPEL: SAINT JOHN 6:1-15

*Abandonment to God during trials and dryness*

### 20.1 First Point

It seems in today's Gospel that Jesus Christ wants to suggest that there are times of trial and dryness when souls cannot find much help from other people, either because these people are not sufficiently enlightened by talent or experience or because God does not give them a sufficiently great abundance of graces to relieve those who are in difficulty.

Souls in this circumstance, nevertheless, must not hesitate to speak with their spiritual directors, because this is the means established by God and because these directors can always help to some extent.

On this occasion in today's Gospel, *Jesus Christ did not hesitate to speak to his disciples to tell them to provide for the needs of the people*, even though they were not able to do so. At the same time, he made use of them to distribute the bread that he had multiplied to feed everyone.[1]

This is how God wants you always to turn to those who guide you, represented in this Gospel by the Apostles, even though at times and in certain difficulties, doing this may seem to you quite useless. God wishes you always to use, insofar as you are able, the ordinary means that he provides for your guidance, even if this is without any success.

### 20.2 Second Point

In your times of trouble, when you have had recourse to those who are appointed to guide you and they have been unable to provide a suitable remedy for your difficulty, God wants you, then, to remain completely abandoned to his guidance, awaiting from him alone and from his goodness all the help you need. Follow the example of this crowd of people who had come following Jesus Christ and who waited patiently for him to provide for their nourishment without even taking the trouble to lay their needs before him.

You ought to be convinced that God will not allow you to be tempted and burdened beyond your strength.[2] When people can do nothing to help you, then it is that God does everything for you, wonderfully showing at one and the same time his power and his goodness. This is why you must abandon yourself to God, as the people who followed our Lord did, to suffer as much as it pleases him (as being an advantage for you) or to be delivered from your trials by the means that God judges most profitable for you, without worrying about trying to achieve peace by your own efforts, which will often be useless.

### 20.3 Third Point

After we have abandoned ourselves to God like this, it usually happens that God makes us experience very extraordinary effects of his goodness and protection, as he shows us in the Gospel today: after he multiplied the five loaves and the two fishes offered to him and five thousand people—not counting the little children—had eaten their fill, there still remained a large quantity.[3]

Be assured, then, that once you have placed yourself in God's hands, willing to suffer whatever and as much as he may desire, although he still leaves you in sorrow, he will help you by his grace to endure this trial, perhaps in a way that is not obvious, or else he will deliver you from it by surprising means and at a time when you least expect it. This is what David assures us he experienced in his own difficulties, when he says: I waited on the Lord with great patience, and finally he heard me; he granted my prayers and withdrew me from the depths of misery and from the deep pit. He set my foot upon a rock and guided my steps. Many people, on seeing this marvel, have learned to revere God and to place all their confidence in him.[4]

---

1. Mt 14:16, 19      3. Jn 6:9–13      4. Ps 40:2–4
2. 1 Cor 10:13

# Passion Sunday

## GOSPEL: JOHN 8:45–59

*In what spirit we must hear and receive the words of our superiors*

### 21.1 First Point

With good reason Jesus Christ complains in today's Gospel that the Jews did not believe his words,[1] in spite of the fact that he told them nothing but the truth and spoke to them as his Father enjoined him to do,[2] for this was a sign that they did not recognize him as the Son of God.

The same complaint can often be made about many religious people who lack confidence in their superiors because they do not consider them as holding God's place. As a result, they do not profit by the advice given them and do not carry out faithfully what they have been commanded.

To remedy this defect, which can have very serious consequences, all those who live under the direction of a superior must believe that his words are the words of God. Jesus Christ requires this in the holy Gospel when he says, in the person of the Apostles to all those who guide others, whoever hears you, hears me.[3] We ought to be firmly convinced that superiors are the ministers of Jesus Christ, that God is in them and causes them to speak, and that the words of our superiors are the truth that they have learned from God. Is it not true that if you had always had such dispositions, you would have believed with simplicity all that your superiors said to you and would never have hesitated a single moment over following their advice and obeying their commands? Admit that if you committed any faults in their regard, it was only because you did not consider God in them and did not hear their words as those of God.

### 21.2 Second Point

Not only ought religious people to believe the words of their superiors, they ought likewise to listen to them with respect and humility in the same dispositions with which wellborn children listen to their parents' voice. Then Jesus Christ would not have to make to them the same reproach that he addresses to the Jews in today's Gospel, namely, that they do not listen to his words because they are not born of God. He who is born of God, says our Lord, hears the words of God.[4]

If religious possess the Spirit of God within them, they will gladly listen to the words of their superiors, because they will recognize the language as that of God. They will be convinced that God's truth is in their superiors and that they do not speak by their own initiative but by the impulse of the Spirit of God,[5] to whom in them they ought to listen, as Jesus Christ, our Lord, says.

Is this how you listen to your superiors? Do you not at times examine critically what they tell you? Do you not entertain thoughts contrary to what they advise or command you? If so, you are insulting God in their person.

### 21.3 Third Point

You are also obliged to practice with docility the advice and the orders of your superiors, for, as Saint John says, we show that we truly know God if we keep his commandments.[6] At the same time, the chief witness you can give that you recognize as your superior the one who commands you is that you carry out promptly and exactly not only everything you are ordered but everything you are told, even simple counsels.

Just as the one who pretends to know God but does not observe his commandments is a liar and the truth is not in him,[7] as Saint John adds, so too the one who does not do everything his superior tells him and shows by his conduct that although he may say that the one who speaks to him is, in fact, his superior, he does not recognize him as such, for what makes known that he is truly united with him in that role and dependent on him is whether he does what his superior tells him. So too, according to this holy Apostle, what proves that we are in God is whether we keep his words.[8]

Judge from this how you ought to act with regard to what your superior tells you to do.

---

1. Jn 8:46
2. Jn 7:16
3. Lk 10:16

4. Jn 8:47
5. Lk 10:16;
    see 2 Pt 1:21

6. 1 Jn 2:3
7. 1 Jn 2:4
8. 1 Jn 2:5

# Palm Sunday

## GOSPEL: SAINT MATTHEW 21:1–9

*The Kingship of Jesus Christ*

### 22.1 First Point

Jesus Christ came to this earth to reign here, but not, says Saint Augustine, as other kings do, to raise tribute, enroll armies, and visibly do battle against his enemies, for Jesus Christ assures us that his kingdom is not of this world[1] but is to establish his reign within our souls, according to what he says in the holy Gospel, that his kingdom is within us.[2]

So that Jesus Christ may reign over your souls, you must pay him the tribute of your actions. All of them must be consecrated to him; in them there must be nothing that is not pleasing to him. They ought to have no other intention than to accomplish his holy will, which ought to direct all of them, so that there may be nothing human in them.

Because the reign of Jesus Christ is divine, all that has any connection with it must be either divine or divinized by the relationship that it has with Jesus Christ. The main purpose he had in this world was to accomplish his Father's will,[3] as he declares in several passages in the Gospel.

He also wishes that you, who are his members and his servants, be united with him and have this same purpose in your actions. Examine whether this is what you intend to do.

### 22.2 Second Point

So that Jesus Christ may reign in your soul, you must wage war under his leadership against the enemies of your salvation, who are also his enemies. Because he wishes to establish his peace within you, a peace which, according to Saint Paul, ought to reign in your hearts,[4] he must overcome—and you must overcome with him and by his help—anything that is able to be an obstacle, such as your passions and evil inclinations. You must eliminate within you the man of sin who in the past has reigned over you. Then you will deliver yourself from the shameful slavery to which sin has reduced you.[5]

Be disposed today, then, to receive Jesus Christ fully by abandoning yourself entirely to his guidance and by letting him reign over your whole interior life, so absolutely on his part and so dependently on yours that you may in truth say that it is no longer you who live but Jesus Christ who lives in you.[6]

### 22.3 Third Point

If you wish Jesus Christ to fight within you the enemies who want to keep him from reigning there, he must be able to raise an army of virtues that will equip your soul and enable him to be the complete master of your heart. You also need to fight valiantly under his standard, making use of the weapons he places in your hands.

*You must*, says Saint Paul, *be girded with the belt of truth and put on the breastplate of justice*, that is, a love for the duties of your state. You must take up the shield of faith, with which you will be able to extinguish all the fiery darts of the devil. Hope of salvation must serve as your helmet and the word of God as your sword.[7] By such weapons, declares the same Saint Paul, the peace of Jesus Christ will truly reign in your hearts.[8]

---

1. Jn 18:36
2. Lk 17:21
3. Jn 6:38

4. Col 3:15
5. Rom 6:6
6. Gal 2:20

7. Eph 6:14–17
8. Col 3:15

# Monday in Holy Week

*The plot of the Jews to put Jesus Christ to death*

### 23.1 First Point

The Jews, indignant because Jesus Christ performed a great number of miracles and, therefore, everyone flocked to him and considered him as a Prophet, plotted to bring about his death and called a council among themselves[1] to determine how they would go about arresting him. Because they feared the people,[2] who esteemed him highly, they had to act cautiously. Out of hatred for him, they spread the word that he was a preacher of new doctrines, and they used this pretext as a way to do away with him.

Consider with amazement the hatred that the Jews felt for Jesus Christ and the opposition that he endured from them, especially from the Pharisees, who brought about his death. Reflect on the excesses into which the envy and rage of these wicked men led them, for they did not hesitate to cause the death of an innocent man, a saint, a Prophet, one who possessed all the exterior signs of divinity.

### 23.2 Second Point

Despite the hatred that the Jews had for him and the wicked plot they had against him, Jesus Christ did not stop speaking to them about himself with all imaginable kindness. On one occasion, he reminded them of the many good works he had performed among them and asked them for which of these they wanted to put him to death.[3] In their assembly they openly admitted their motive. If we let him continue to live, they said, the whole world will believe in him.[4]

What evil has he done? Pilate said to them. I find no crime in him that deserves death.[5] But it sufficed that Jesus Christ was hated by the Jews, because he reproached them for their vices, and this was reason enough for their tribunal to find him guilty and worthy of death. Let us condemn him to a shameful death,[6] they said, borrowing the words of the Wise Man.

Adore Jesus' interior disposition in all these plans of the Pharisees' intrigue. He courageously endured the accomplishment of their designs, because this was in accord with the plan of his Eternal Father. You would have no power over me, he told Pilate, unless it were given to you from above.[7]

### 23.3 Third Point

Another reason the Jews gave in their assembly as a reason for wanting to put Jesus to death was that *a great number of people were believing in him, following him, and honoring him as their king.* They feared that because of this, the Romans would come and destroy their city and nation.[8] In this, says Saint Augustine, they were strangely blinded, because it was as a result of the cruelty they showed to the Anointed One of the Lord that their city was besieged, taken by the Romans, and so completely destroyed, as Jesus Christ had foretold, that not a stone remained upon a stone.[9] All this took place, according to the testimony of Josephus, a writer who lived in those times and who belonged to the party of the Pharisees, only because they had put Jesus Christ to death.

God, as a rule, overturns the plans of men and causes the opposite of what they proposed to happen, so that they may learn to have confidence in him and abandon themselves entirely to his Providence, not undertaking anything on their own, because they ought to desire only what God wants.

---

| | | |
|---|---|---|
| 1. Jn 11:47,53 | 4. Jn 11:48 | 7. Jn 19:11 |
| 2. Lk 22:2 | 5. Lk 23:22 | 8. Jn 11:48 |
| 3. Jn 10:32 | 6. Wis 2:20 | 9. Mt 24:2 |

# Tuesday in Holy Week

*Jesus Christ's acceptance of suffering and death*

### 24.1 First Point

It is admirable that at one time Jesus Christ hid from the eyes of his enemies, escaped from their hands, kept away from them, and did not want to appear in public, because he knew that they were planning to put him to death,[1] while at another time he went to the place where he knew that those who wanted to kill him would come looking for him. When they came for him, he stepped forward, presented himself before them, and allowed himself to be arrested, bound, and led away, knowing, as the Gospel says, everything that would happen to him[2] and that he would be delivered into the hands of sinners.[3]

Adore these different dispositions of Jesus Christ, which were conformable to the plans God had for him. As he said, the will of his Father was his nourishment,[4] that is, the rule and, as it were, the soul of his conduct.

Strive after the example of your divine master, Jesus Christ, to want only what God wants, when he wants it, and in the way he wants it.

### 24.2 Second Point

The Gospel tells us that the reason for these different dispositions of Jesus Christ is that on the prior occasions his hour had not yet come[5] and that later on he knew that the time and the hour for leaving this world and going back to the Father had indeed arrived.[6] This is why, when Judas went out to do what he had agreed upon with the enemies of Jesus, Jesus told him: Be quick about what you are going to do.[7]

This was to give us to understand that he had waited to allow himself to be arrested and to deliver himself up to death until the hour that had been determined by his Eternal Father. This shows us that Jesus Christ followed in detail his orders from heaven and wanted everything he had to do and to suffer to be prescribed for him by his Father.

Imitate this admirable example given to you by Jesus Christ. Do nothing on your own initiative, but let everything you have to do, down to the slightest detail, be ruled and prescribed by your superiors.

### 24.3 Third Point[8]

This is how Jesus Christ abandoned himself entirely to the will of his Father to suffer and die when and in the way God willed. He did this when he was preparing for his Passion and death while he waited and prayed in the garden of olives. He declared to his Father that despite the repugnance he felt for the death that he knew was imminent, he desired nonetheless that no account be taken of his own will but that of his Father,[9] to which he gave himself entirely, just as he had always been abandoned to his Father's will during his life, not coming into the world, as he says in several places in the Gospel, to do his own will but the will of the One who sent him.[10]

O lovable abandonmeent of Jesus' human will, submitting to the divine will in all things and having no preference for either life or death, for the time or the way he was to suffer, other than what was chosen for him by his Eternal Father! Become disciples of Jesus in this way in order to have no other will than God's.

---

1. Jn 8:59; Jn 11:53–54
2. Jn 18:4; Jn 18:12–13
3. Mt 26:45
4. Jn 4:34
5. Jn 7:30
6. Jn 13:1
7. Jn 13:27
8. The first edition does not separate a third point at this juncture.
9. Lk 22:42
10. Jn 6:38

# Wednesday in Holy Week

*The desire that Jesus Christ had to suffer and die*

### 25.1 First Point

Jesus Christ came down from heaven only to procure the salvation of all people. He knew that this purpose would not be accomplished unless he suffered much and died on the cross. Therefore, at the moment of his incarnation, he offered himself to the Eternal Father to suffer whatever would be in accord with his will to satisfy for our sins.

For *it was impossible,* says Saint Paul, *that sins be blotted out by the blood of goats and bulls. For this reason,* continues the same saint, *Christ said to God: Holocausts and sin offerings have not pleased you; then said I, behold, I come to fulfill your will. This same will,* affirms the same Apostle, has sanctified us by the offering that Jesus Christ made, once for all, of his body.[1]

Adore the holy disposition that Jesus Christ had on coming into the world, which he always continued to maintain: to suffer and to die for our sins and for those of all people. Thank him for such goodness, and become worthy to receive the benefits of salvation by your own sharing in his sufferings.

### 25.2 Second Point

The tender love that Jesus Christ has for sinners not only inspired him with this willingness to suffer and to die for us but also made him conceive a great desire to do so. This made him say, longing for the destruction of sin, I have come to bring fire upon the earth, and what do I desire except that it be kindled?[2]

But as he saw that this fire of God's love could not exist in us except through the destruction of sin and because sin could only be destroyed by his suffering and death, he added, speaking of his death, I have a baptism with which I am to be baptized; Oh, how I long that it be accomplished![3] By these words he indicated how great was the anguish he experienced because this plan for his death, which was to be so very advantageous to all people, was taking so long to be accomplished, for this delay also delayed their salvation.

Are you not ashamed that Jesus Christ had such a great desire for your salvation and still desires it so strongly today, while you correspond so little to his ardent desire?

### 25.3 Third Point

Jesus Christ was not content to have had this yearning to die for us all during his life. When he saw the time of his death approaching, he testified to his joy. This is what made him say to his Apostles, when he celebrated the Last Passover with them, that he had for a long time desired to eat this meal with them and that he had a very strong desire to celebrate this Passover with them.[4] He knew that this was to be the final act of his mortal life and the last meal he would eat with his Apostles before suffering and dying for us, which was what he had most at heart.

This is also what made him cry out, shortly before dying, that he was thirsty.[5] The holy Fathers understand this thirst as the longing for our salvation which impelled him. This was also what made him say these words as he was dying: All is consummated,[6] because what he had so longed for—to suffer for our salvation—had finally been accomplished.

All that remains on your part, Saint Paul says, is to complete what is lacking in the Passion of Christ,[7] that is, the application that you ought to make of the Passion through your sharing in his sufferings. Become worthy, then, of such a grace.

---

1. Heb 10:4–7, 10
2. Lk 12:49
3. Lk 12:50
4. Lk 22:15
5. Jn 19:28
6. Jn 19:30
7. Col 1:24

# Holy Thursday

*Institution of the sacrament of the Eucharist*

### 26.1 First Point

This sacred day is a happy one for all the faithful. It is the day on which Jesus Christ instituted the sacrament of his body and blood. He multiplies himself in it in order to be always with the faithful, to make them sharers in his divinity,[1] and to change their hearts and bodies into living tabernacles.[2] There he can remain as in a place pleasing to him and honorable for those who receive him and in a way that is most advantageous for them.

For the sake of his disciples and for those who share their spirit, Jesus Christ instituted this sacrament. To let them share in his Spirit, he gives them his body in this august sacrament.

Adore Jesus Christ in this action. Unite with his intention, and take your full and proper part in this holy institution.

### 26.2  Second Point

In instituting this divine sacrament, Jesus Christ changed bread into his flesh and wine into his blood. On this very day he became the living Bread come down from heaven[3] to unite himself with us, to incorporate himself in us, and to communicate himself to the lowliness of a vile creature.

This heavenly Bread unites him to our soul to nourish it with God and to make it grow strong, to use Tertullian's expression, with the flesh of Jesus Christ.

He puts aside all the splendor of his divinity to take on the appearance of ordinary bread, an appearance that has no proportion to what it contains. What takes the place of the bread is his own true substance, which is the object of veneration for angels and for all his people.

Admire this holy institution; become worthy to profit from it by a holy life, and today pray to Jesus Christ, who comes to you to destroy entirely your own inclinations and spirit, so that you may have no other inclinations except his and may no longer be guided except by his Spirit.[4]

### 26.3  Third Point

The love of Jesus Christ for us led him to institute this divine sacrament in order to give himself entirely to us and to remain always with us. He knew that immediately afterward he would suffer and die for us, that this offering he would make of himself on the cross would occur only once,[5] and that after his Ascension into heaven, he would no longer appear among us. This is why, to give us a sign of his tender love and goodness before dying, he left to his Apostles and to the whole Church in their person, his body and blood to be for us in the ages to come a precious proof of the tender love he feels for us.

Today, receive this gift with respect and thanksgiving. Give Jesus love in return for his love, considering what a great benefit you receive. May this love you have for him and the desire you have to be united with him lead you to have a great love for frequent Communion.

---

1. 2 Pt 1:4          3. Jn 6:51          5. Heb 10:10
2. 1 Cor 6:19        4. Rom 8:13

# Good Friday

*The Passion of our Lord Jesus Christ*

### 27.1 First Point

No one can understand how great the sufferings of Jesus Christ were in his Passion. He suffered in all parts of his body; his soul was oppressed with such painful and extreme sorrow that he could not express it, but he said that there could not be any greater sorrow without dying.[1] This sorrow affected him so much that it caused him to sweat blood,[2] and he fell into such great weakness that the Eternal Father was obliged to send him an angel to strengthen him,[3] encourage him, and make it possible for him to suffer all the torments of his Passion to the end. In addition to this, he was overwhelmed with shame and confusion; he was loaded with insults, curses, and calumnies; a revolutionary, a murderer, a criminal, was preferred to him.

Such was the state to which our sins reduced that Person who deserves every kind of esteem, honor, and respect.

### 27.2 Second Point

Jesus Christ suffered no less in his body than in his soul. He was bound and shackled disgracefully by the soldiers.[4] His head was crowned with thorns,[5] which were beaten in by heavy blows from a rod. Several soldiers spat in his face; others slapped him.[6] He was so cruelly whipped[7] that the blood flowed from every part of his body. They hoisted a heavy cross onto his shoulders;[8] they gave him gall and vinegar to drink,[9] and finally they crucified him between two thieves,[10] piercing his hands and feet with large nails and his side with a lance.[11]

What crime had Jesus Christ committed to be treated this way? Yet the rage of the Jews was not satisfied, says Saint Bernard, not even after making him undergo such great torment unjustly. How is it possible to treat like this that Person who had only tried to do good to everyone?

### 27.3 Third Point

Jesus Christ suffered from all sorts of people. One of his Apostles betrayed him;[12] another denied him;[13] all the rest ran off and abandoned him[14] to the hands of his enemies. The high priests sent soldiers to seize him;[15] the soldiers treated him outrageously;[16] the people mocked him;[17] a king insulted him and dismissed him with scorn, considering him as a lunatic.[18] The governor of Judea condemned him to death.[19] All the Jews regarded him as a malefactor;[20] all the passersby blasphemed him.[21]

Can we contemplate the man-God in such a pitiful state without feeling horror for sin and a great sorrow for those we have committed? We cannot be ignorant that our sins were the cause of his death and of all his agony. If we will not stop sinning, it means we want him to continue suffering. Do we not know that every sin we commit causes him new torments? We crucify him again,[22] says Saint Paul, and we make him die another death even more painful and cruel than the first one.

---

1. Mt 26:38
2. Lk 22:44
3. Lk 22:43
4. Jn 18:12
5. Mk 15:17; Mt 27:29
6. Mk 15:19; Mt 27:30; Jn 19:3
7. Mt 27:26; Jn 19:1
8. Jn 19:17
9. Mt 27:34, 48
10. Mt 27:38
11. Jn 19:34

12. Mt 26:14–16, 48–50
13. Mt 26:69–75
14. Mt 26:56
15. Mt 26:47
16. Mt 26:50
17. Mt 27:39–40
18. Lk 23:11
19. Lk 23:24–25
20. Lk 23:18–23
21. Mt 27:39–43
22. Heb 6:6

# Holy Saturday

*The five wounds of Jesus Christ*

### 28.1 First Point

Adore the five wounds of Jesus Christ, our Lord, and consider that he has kept them in his sacred body as glorious trophies of the victory he gained over hell and sin, from which he rescued us by his sufferings and his death. Know, says Saint Peter, that you have been redeemed from a life of vanity, which you learned from your forefathers, not by silver or gold but by the precious blood of Jesus Christ, the Lamb without blemish.[1] These sacred wounds from which this precious blood poured remind us of such an extraordinary favor.

Often let your eyes rest on this sacred object. Regard the wounds in your Savior's body as so many mouths that reproach you for your sins; keep in mind all that he suffered to efface them.

## 28.2 Second Point

These sacred wounds not only honor the body of Jesus Christ but also, as Saint Peter declares, help us recognize that Jesus Christ suffered to give us an example, so that we might follow him and walk in his footsteps. He bore our sins in his own body on the tree of the cross, so that we might die to sin and live for justice, having been healed by his bruises[2] and by these lovable wounds.

According to the same Apostle, because Jesus Christ suffered death in his flesh,[3] realize, when you contemplate the wounds of your Savior, that they ought to induce you to die to self, that whoever is dead to the flesh sins no more, and that for as long as we remain in this mortal body, we ought to live no longer according to passions but according to God's will.[4] Such is the conclusion we ought to draw from these words of the Prince of the Apostles. The benefit we can derive from the contemplation of our Lord's wounds is to renounce sin entirely, to mortify our passions, and to oppose our too human and too natural inclinations.

## 28.3 Third Point

These sacred wounds can procure for us another benefit: to inspire us to a love for suffering, for his wounds show us how powerfully Jesus Christ was impelled to suffer. In his glorious body he has preserved the scars of his wounds as so many ornaments and marks of honor.

As members of Jesus Christ, you ought likewise to consider it an honor to suffer like him and for him. After the example of Saint Paul, you glory only in the cross of your Savior.[5] Often kneel before these divine wounds; lregard them as the source of your salvation. With Saint Thomas, put your hand into the wound of the side,[6] not so much to strengthen your faith as to penetrate, if possible, even to the heart of Jesus and to draw from there into your own heart sentiments of truly Christian patience, entire resignation, perfect conformity to God's will, and courage that will lead you to seek opportunities to suffer.

---

1. 1 Pt 1:18–19
2. 1 Pt 2:21–24
3. 1 Pt 4:1
4. 1 Pt 4:1–2
5. Gal 6:14
6. Jn 20:27

# Easter Sunday

*The Resurrection of Jesus Christ*

### 29.1 First Point

This feast is a day of joy for the entire Church; that is why we so frequently and so solemnly sing these words of the Royal Prophet: This is the day the Lord has made; let us rejoice and be glad in it.[1] Indeed, the Resurrection of Jesus Christ is at once very glorious for him and highly advantageous for all the faithful.

It is glorious for Jesus Christ, because by it he overcame death. This led Saint Paul to affirm that Jesus Christ was raised up for the glory of his Father and that once risen, he dies no more, because death will no longer have power over him.[2]

It is advantageous for us, because it is an assurance of our own resurrection. Certain it is, adds the Apostle, that just as all died in Adam, so too all will rise again in Jesus Christ.[3] According to this same Apostle, it was on this happy day that death was destroyed[4] once and for all. Rejoice with the whole Church over so great a favor, and thank Jesus Christ, our Lord, very humbly for it.

### 29.2 Second Point

The Resurrection of Jesus Christ was glorious for him and advantageous for us in another sense, because, according to Saint Paul, he destroyed sin and rose again only that we might live with a new life. For it is certain that if we are united with him through likeness to his death, we will also be united with him through likeness to his Resurrection, and if we die to sin with Jesus Christ, we will also live with him.[5]

Because by rising Jesus Christ destroyed sin, you must take care, following Saint Paul's advice, that sin may no longer reign in your mortal body.[6] Attach that body with all your disorderly affections to the cross of Jesus Christ;[7] this will make your body share in anticipation the incorruptibility proper to his body by preserving you from sin, the source of all corruption.

### 29.3 Third Point

The Resurrection of Jesus Christ also ought to procure for you the benefit of making you rise spiritually by causing you to live according to grace. This means that it will cause you to enter an entirely new and heavenly life.

To enter into these practices and to show, according to Saint Paul, that you are risen with Christ, seek the things that are above; love the things of heaven, not those that are on earth.[8] Be separated from human association so thoroughly that your life may be hidden and be totally in God with Jesus Christ.[9]

Mortify your earthly body, continues the same Apostle, and put off the old man, in order to be clothed in the new.[10] Show by your conduct that the Resurrection of Jesus Christ has produced these happy effects in you.

---

| | | |
|---|---|---|
| 1. Ps 118:24 | 5. Rom 6:4–5, 8 | 9. Col 3:3 |
| 2. Rom 6:4,9 | 6. Rom 6:12 | 10. Col 3:5, 9–10 |
| 3. 1 Cor 15:22 | 7. Gal 5:24 | |
| 4. 1 Cor 15:55 | 8. Col 3:1–2 | |

# Easter Monday

*How we ought to regulate our conversation*

### 30.1 First Point

One of the first things to be done by those who have risen with Christ and who wish to lead a new life[1] is to regulate their conversation properly, making it holy and pleasing to God.

Ordinarily, especially in communities, it is in our talk that we commit most of our faults and the most serious ones. It follows that conversation is one of the things that we need to watch over the most so that it does not become harmful.

For this we cannot do better than model our conversation on the one that Jesus Christ had with his two disciples who were on their way to Emmaus and also the one that the two disciples had with each other before Jesus Christ joined them and after he left them.[2]

In your conversations and recreations, are you careful to take Jesus Christ for your model? Is it with the purpose of edifying one another that you participate in them? On leaving them are you all on fire with divine love, as were the two disciples who were traveling to Emmaus? Like them, are you better instructed regarding your duties? Are you more encouraged to perform these duties well? Are their topics of conversation the same as yours? Are their maxims and ways of acting sometimes the subject of your discussions? That is how you will benefit from the moments of recreation that obedience grants you to relax from your work and to restore your energy.

## 30.2 Second Point

To model your conversation on that of the two disciples and Jesus Christ with them, it is good for you to know, first of all, what these two disciples were talking about. *They spoke* only of good things, of what had happened in Jerusalem at the death of Jesus Christ, about his holy deeds and miracles, and about the admirable life that caused him to be so greatly honored by the entire people that they regarded him as a great Prophet and even as the Messiah who was to deliver Israel. They also spoke about the rumors that were spreading about his Resurrection.[3]

Topics of this kind ought to make up the ordinary matter of conversation among religious and those who live together in community. Since they have left the world and live apart from it, their conversations must also be entirely different from those of worldly people. It would be of slight advantage for them to be separated from the world in body if they were not taking on a spirit quite opposed to that of worldlings; this they ought to show particularly in their conversations.

## 30.3 Third Point

The good effects that the conversation of the two disciples produced in them were, first of all, that Jesus Christ joined them.[4] This is also a benefit we derive from good conversations, to have Jesus present with us by faith.

Secondly, their hearts were filled with ardor[5] for doing good and on fire with the love of God. This too is an advantage that good conversations procure for us; when we have been speaking this way in recreation, we leave it filled with enthusiasm and eager to do good.

Thirdly, Jesus Christ was so pleased by the disciples' conversation that he went with them to the place where they stopped and remained there with them.[6] Similarly, Jesus will be glad to be with you when you take pleasure in speaking of him and of what can lead you to him.

Fourthly, Jesus gave them his sacred body, and they recognized him.[7] A similar happiness will be yours when you willingly converse on holy topics. Jesus Christ, who is in your midst, will give himself to you, and he will communicate his Spirit to you. To the degree that you talk about him and about what pertains to him, to that degree you will learn to know him and to appreciate what is good and his holy maxims.

---

1. Col 3:1
2. Lk 24:13–32
3. Lk 24:19–24

4. Lk 24:15
5. Lk 24:32
6. Lk 24:29

7. Lk 24:30–31

# Easter Tuesday

*Interior peace and the means to preserve it*

### 31.1 First Point

On the day of his Resurrection, Jesus Christ appeared to his disciples and said to them, Peace be with you![1] to teach us that one of the principal signs that a person is leading a new life, that is, an interior and spiritual life, and is risen with Jesus Christ is when the person enjoys interior peace.

There are many people who seem to be spiritual and to possess interior peace but who lack it. We might say of them what Jeremiah says, that they desire peace, yet peace does not exist in them.[2] Such people appear to be the most pious and devout people in the world; they speak very eloquently and most willingly about interior things. They often experience the presence of God in prayer. But just say a sharp word to them or do something to irritate them, and immediately they are quite upset. They lose their peace because they are not solidly grounded in virtue and have not worked hard enough to get rid of their natural impulses.

Are you not counted among these people? You must give yourselves more resolutely and more truly to God.

### 31.2 Second Point

Because true interior peace proceeds from charity, nothing is more able to destroy it than whatever makes us lose the charity and the love of God. *What will separate us*, asks Saint Paul, *from the love of Jesus Christ?*

*Will it be tribulation*, that is, either interior or exterior trials?

*Will it be desolation*, that is, whatever can cause you some vexation, like separation or privation of something to which you are attached?

*Will it be hunger*, because you live in a poor community, where you are poorly nourished?

*Will it be nakedness*, because you are given worn and patched clothes that cause you embarrassment in public?

*Will it be some danger* in which you might lose your health or even your life?

*Will it be some persecution* that will come against your community or against you in particular, such as insults and vicious treatment directed against you?

Will it be the sword,[3] a calumny someone has spread against you or some severe reprimand you will get for a fault someone blamed on you?

None of these things can make you lose your interior peace if it is a true peace, because none of them can cause you to lose charity.

Are you in this disposition? If you are not, try to acquire it by frequently doing violence to yourself.

### 31.3 Third Point

The reason given by Saint Paul to explain why none of the misfortunes he mentions or anything else can make you lose charity and interior peace is that you must be prepared to mortify yourselves interiorly and exteriorly and to be mortified by others all day long for the love of God.

Another reason is that you ought to be content to be considered and to consider yourselves like sheep destined for the slaughter;[4] they allow their throat to be cut by the knife without complaining or resisting in any way.

This is why, adds the same Apostle, among all the misfortunes that may overtake you, you must always remain victorious because of the One who has loved you, Jesus Christ. For neither death nor life nor any creature can ever separate you from the charity of God, which unites you to Jesus Christ, our Lord.[5]

---

1. Lk 24:36
2. Jer 6:14
3. Rom 8:35
4. Rom 8:36
5. Rom 8:37–39

# Quasimodo or Low Sunday

## GOSPEL: SAINT JOHN 20:19–31

*The faith that ought to permeate a soul who has risen according to grace*

### 32.1 First Point

On this day, Jesus Christ entered the upper room where the Apostles have gathered after his Resurrection. The doors were all shut,[1] which symbolizes that every approach to a soul who does not live a renewed life, a life of grace, is closed to all interior action of the Spirit of God and has only human and natural impulses to act. This is the result of the blindness of spirit and the hardness of heart that sin brings about in us. It makes people who are quite enlightened about the things of this world lose all understanding of and all openness to what concerns God and his service.

This is what Jesus Christ teaches us when he says that the children of this world are often wiser and more prudent with regard to temporal matters than most of the children of light[2] with regard to their spiritual welfare and the salvation of their souls. Are you not of their number?

### 32.2 Second Point

On entering the upper room, our Lord radiated such an aura of his divinity that Saint Thomas, unbelieving until then, catching sight of Jesus Christ and of his wounds, was deeply moved,[3] for at that moment Jesus Christ filled him with faith and made him understand in one instant by a vision and a deepening of his faith what previously had been hidden from him.

In this way Jesus Christ, entering a soul, raises it so far above all human sentiments, through the faith that enlivens it, that it sees nothing except by the light of faith. No matter what anyone does to such a soul, nothing can disturb its constancy, make it abandon God's service, or even diminish in the least degree the ardor it feels for God, because the darkness that previously blinded its spirit is changed into an admirable light.[4] As a result, the soul no longer sees anything except by the eyes of faith.

Do you feel that you have this disposition? Pray to the risen Christ to give it to you.

### 32.3 Third Point

At the sight of Jesus Christ, Saint Thomas, filled with this light and this conviction inspired by faith, cannot keep from crying out: My Lord and my God![5] because up to then he saw Jesus Christ only with eyes weakened and blinded by the darkness of incredulity. He was not able to perceive the divinity veiled beneath the shadows of human nature. But now, thanks to this light of faith, which the presence of the Risen Savior strongly imparted to him, he sees all that is divine in our Lord. His faith, strengthened this way, gives him the courage to confess that he who had died on the cross and had been buried in the tomb is his Lord and his God.

In this way a soul is filled with views of faith and is so raised up into the life of God that it no longer understands things apart from God; it values everything in terms of God and finds no joy except in God. As a result, it can no longer be preoccupied by anything but God, because, enlightened by this supernatural radiance, it no longer feels any interest in worldly things and looks upon them only with disdain. This was how Saint Francis felt when, enlightened by faith and filled with love for God, he kept saying all his life, "My God and my all!" Today, try to have a similar disposition.

---

1. Jn 20:19     3. Jn 20:24–29     5. Jn 20:28
2. Lk 16:8      4. 1 Pt 2:9

# Second Sunday After Easter

## GOSPEL: JOHN 10:11-16

*How teachers ought to act toward their students*

### 33.1  First Point

In today's Gospel Jesus Christ compares those who have charge of souls to a good shepherd who has great care for the sheep.[1] One quality he must possess, according to our Savior, is to know each one of them[2] individually. This ought also to be one of the main concerns of those who instruct others: to be able to understand their students and to discern the right way to guide them.

They must show more mildness toward some, more firmness toward others. There are those who call for much patience, those who need to be stimulated and spurred on, some who need to be reproved and punished to correct them of their faults, others who must be constantly watched over to prevent them from being lost or going astray.

This guidance requires understanding and discernment of spirits, qualities you must frequently and earnestly ask of God, because they are most necessary for you in guiding those placed in your care.

### 33.2  Second Point

It is also necessary, says Jesus Christ, that the sheep know their shepherd[3] in order to be able to follow him. Two qualities are needed by those who lead others and must be particularly evident in them.

The first is a high level of virtue, in order to be models for others, who would not fail to go astray following their guides if the guides themselves did not walk in the right way.

The second is the great tenderness they must show for those entrusted to their care. They must be very alert to whatever can harm or wound their sheep. This is what leads the sheep to love their shepherds and to delight in their company, for there they find their rest and comfort.

Do you want your disciples to do what is right? Then you do so too. You will persuade them much more readily through your example of wise and prudent behavior than through all the words you could speak to them. Do you want them to keep silence? Then be silent too. You will make them prudent and self-controlled only insofar as you act that way.

### 33.3 Third Point

The members of the flock of Jesus Christ are also obliged to hear their shepherd's voice.[4] It is, then, your duty to teach the children entrusted to you; this is your duty every day. Because they must understand what you say, you must give them instructions that are adapted to their capacity; otherwise, what you say will be of little use. For this purpose, you must prepare and train, so that your questions and answers during the catechism lessons are understood well and so that you can explain the text clearly and use words that will be easily understood.

In your exhortations to your students, explain their faults simply, and show them how to correct them. Make known to them the virtues they ought to practice, and help them see how easy this is. You must inspire them to have a very great horror for sin and to avoid bad companions. In a word, speak to them of everything that can lead them to piety. This is how your disciples ought to hear the voice of their teacher.

---

1. Jn 10:11      3. Jn 10:14      4. Jn 10:16
2. Jn 10:14

# Third Sunday After Easter

## GOSPEL: JOHN 16:16–22

*The false joys of the world and the true joys possessed by the servants of Jesus Christ*

### 34.1 First Point

In today's Gospel Jesus Christ says that the world will rejoice, whereas for a time the servants of God will be made sorrowful, but that their sorrow will be turned into joy.[1] This ought to lead you to consider the difference between the joy of worldly people and that of God's servants.

The world's joy will be brief; that of God's servants will have no end. This much is clear from the words of the Gospel. Worldlings, says Jesus Christ, will rejoice, but for how long? At most, for as long as they remain in this world, but as soon as they leave this earth, that is, after this present life, their joy will end, and the sadness that will follow will be eternal.

As for the joy of God's servants, it will be such, says our Lord, that no one will be able to take it away from them.[2] If now they experience trials and sorrows, these will last only for a short time;[3] the joy that will follow their pains will have no end.

Woe to those who think only of satisfying themselves in this world, for this satisfaction will not last!

### 34.2 Second Point

A second difference between worldlings' joy and the joy of God's servants is that the former is only superficial, whereas the latter is very deep. This difference is seen in our Lord's words. The world will rejoice,[4] he tells us, whereas for the servants of God, he says, Your hearts will rejoice.[5] This shows us that the joy of the former is only apparent. The world knows only the pomp and the outward show of joy, but when God's servants have joy, it is their hearts that rejoice.

The heart is the source of life in a person because it is the last thing in the person to die. The joy of the just, according to our Lord, will be unshakable and not easily subject to change because it is founded on what sustains the life of grace in them, namely, the love of God and union with God by prayer and the reception of the sacraments. In this way God maintains and nourishes their joy; it is solidly based because it is based on God.

Your joy is genuine if you rejoice in the midst of suffering and all the most painful trials. But if you make your joy consist in sensual pleasures, ah, how true it is that your joy is completely superficial, for it has the same nature as its object, in this case, a fragile and perishable good!

### 34.3 Third Point

There is still a major difference between the joys of worldlings and those of God's servants. The former are entirely external; the latter are interior, for they are in the heart. Hence, in the case of worldlings, the least trouble disturbs their joy and throws them into dejection, whereas the joy of God's servants, being within them, is immune to anything external that might detract from it. Nothing external can penetrate the depths of their hearts, for God's servants are not affected by outward things, except when they allow themselves to be deceived by the senses.

Because the joy of the just is caused by God's love deep in their hearts and because this love is directed to a good that is inalterable, immutable, and eternal, it follows that the just cannot be disturbed in the possession of that delightful satisfaction as long as charity unites their souls to God.

Does your joy come from within? Or are you not sometimes self-absorbed by vain and entirely exterior joys?

---

| | | |
|---|---|---|
| 1. Jn 16:20 | 3. Jn 16:16 | 5. Jn 16:22 |
| 2. Jn 16:22 | 4. Jn 16:20 | |

# Fourth Sunday After Easter

## GOSPEL: SAINT JOHN 16:5-14

*The advantages of trials, whether interior or exterior*

### 35.1 First Point

When Jesus Christ told his Apostles that he was going back to the One who had sent him, their hearts were at once filled with sadness.[1] Because the presence of their Master was their entire consolation and support, they felt great sorrow on learning that they would soon be parted from him, because they were sure that when Jesus Christ no longer walked visibly among them, they would be deprived of a help without which, they believed, they could not survive. Because they had not yet received the Holy Spirit, they were attached to what impressed their senses without rising any higher.

When we turn our backs on the world and when by this separation we renounce the pleasures of the senses, it sometimes happens that we only make this renunciation out of a mere feeling and sensible attraction for God and the things of God, which gives us a satisfaction incomparably superior to those of the senses. To enjoy this greater satisfaction, we deprive ourselves willingly of another satisfaction that is far less; this shows that we have not yet attained complete detachment.

Earnestly beg God for this total detachment, so that you may give yourself to him alone in whom is all happiness in this life and in the next.

### 35.2 Second Point

Seeing that his Apostles had been saddened when he announced that he would soon depart from them, Jesus Christ told them that it was better for them that he was leaving.[2]

Those who have given themselves to God often believe that God's sensible presence is the only thing that can confirm them in piety. They think that when they experience interior difficulty and dryness, they have completely lost the degree of holiness to which God has raised them. Having lost a certain relish for prayer and a facility for praying, they imagine that they have lost everything and that God has completely rejected them. Their inner life is desolate, and they suppose that all paths leading to God are blocked before them.

Such people ought to be told what Jesus Christ said to his Apostles: that it is better for them that God withdraws from them on a feeling level and that what they consider a loss is for them a great gain if they willingly endure this trial.

### 35.3 Third Point

The main reason why Jesus Christ said to his Apostles that his leaving was better for them was that if he did not go, the Consoler Spirit would not come to them at all, but if he did go, he would send this Spirit to them.[3]

By this let us understand that it is sometimes more advantageous to be deprived of spiritual consolations than to have them. The more detached we are from what pleases the senses, the easier it is for us to seek God purely and in a spirit of entire detachment from all creatures. Then it is that the Spirit of God comes to us and fills us with his grace.

Do not complain any more, then, when you suffer trials, whether interior or exterior; be convinced that the more you are tried, the more opportunities you will have to belong entirely to God.

---

1. Jn 16:6         2. Jn 16:7         3. Jn 16:7

# Fifth Sunday After Easter

## GOSPEL: JOHN 16:23-30

*The necessity of prayer*

### 36.1 First Point

Ask, and you will receive.[1] By these words in today's Gospel, Jesus Christ wishes to make known to us that because we need to receive his graces, we must ask him for them; also, that because God wants to give us his graces, he has provided us with a sure means to obtain them, namely, prayer.

This is all the easier for us, because God is always present to us, and whenever we wish to do so, we can turn to God. This led Saint Augustine, to make clear to us how easy it is for us to do good, to say, If you are powerless to act, whether because of your weakness, the violence of temptation, or any other reason, you must turn to prayer, which will infallibly give you the power to accomplish what is beyond your natural strength.

When you find the practice of virtue difficult, strive to make it become easier by your application to prayer. Have recourse to prayer promptly, calling to mind the words of Jesus Christ, *Ask, and you will receive.*

### 36.2 Second Point

What ought especially to lead you to pray is the weakness to which sin has reduced you, a weakness that makes you incapable of accomplishing any supernatural good. Because we become weaker every day by falling into new sins daily, we also have a much greater need for God's help every day.

Prayer, says Saint John Chrysostom, is a divine medicine that drives out of our hearts all the malice it finds there and fills them with all justice. This is why, if we wish to deliver ourselves from sin completely, we cannot do anything better than to devote ourselves to prayer.

No matter how many sins a person who loves prayer commits, he still has, even in the midst of a greatly disordered life, a quick and easy recourse, which is prayer, to obtain the grace of repentance and pardon.

Ask God, then, to give you a pure heart that has an aversion and a horror not only for the most grievous sins but also for whatever can stain your conscience and make you displeasing to God.

### 36.3 Third Point

We are so subject to temptation that, as Job says, our life is a constant temptation.[2] This made Saint Peter say that our enemy, the demon, like a roaring lion, is always roaming around us seeking endlessly some way to devour us.[3] Prayer puts us in a position to resist him.

Jesus Christ even says of the demon of impurity that he cannot be put to flight except by prayer and fasting.[4] He puts prayer before fasting to teach us that although mortification is most necessary to vanquish the unclean spirit, it is even more important that we arm ourselves with prayer when we are assailed.

When you feel attacked by the tempting spirit, do not stop praying until you have driven it completely away.

---

1. Jn 16:24
2. Jb 7:1
3. 1 Pt 5:8
4. Mt 17:21; Mk 9:29

# Rogation Monday

*Our obligation to pray for those whom we are appointed to teach*

### 37.1 First Point

In today's Gospel Jesus Christ presents a parable that lets you know your duty to be concerned about the needs of those whom you instruct. It is as if one of you, he says, goes at midnight to find one of your friends and tells him, "Lend me three loaves of bread, because a friend of mine on a journey has just arrived at my house, and I have nothing to give him."[1]

In his explanation of this parable, Saint Augustine says that this traveling friend is someone who has walked the way of sin, seeking to satisfy his passions in the world and finding there nothing but vice and vanity, misery and disappointment, and who turns to you in distress, looking for help, persuaded that you have received the grace to support the weak, to teach the ignorant, and to correct the wayward.[2] Your friend comes to you like the weary and exhausted traveler, and he begs you to help him in his destitution.

Such is the plight of those whom Providence calls upon you to teach and whom you must train in piety. God has led them to you; God makes you responsible for their salvation;[3] God gives you the responsibility to provide for all their spiritual needs. To do this ought to be your constant effort.

### 37.2  Second Point

The children who come to you either have not had any instruction and have been taught the wrong things or, if they have received some good lessons, bad companions or their own bad habits have prevented them from benefiting. God sends them to you, so that you can give them the Christian spirit and educate them according to the maxims of the Gospel.

You are obliged, says Saint Augustine, to learn these things. You have a reason to be ashamed if you have to teach these children what you do not know or to exhort them to practice what you do not do. Ask God, then, for what you lack and to give you what you need in full measure, namely, the Christian spirit and deep religious convictions.

Those who come to you do so in the middle of the night,[4] which, says Saint Augustine, symbolizes their great ignorance. Their need is pressing, and you have nothing to satisfy their need. Your simple faith in the mysteries might be enough for you but not sufficient for you to be able to give them what they need. Will you, then, abandon them and leave them without any instruction? Have recourse to God; knock on the door; pray and beg him insistently, even importunately.[5]

The three loaves that you ought to ask for, continues the same Father, represent knowledge of the three Divine Persons. If you obtain this from God, you will have what will satisfy those who come to you in their need for instruction.

### 37.3  Third Point

You ought to look upon the children whom you are appointed to teach as poor, abandoned orphans. Although the majority of them do have a father here on earth, they are still as if they had none and are abandoned to themselves for the salvation of their souls. This is the reason God places them as if under your guardianship.

God looks on them with compassion and takes care of them as being their protector, their support, and their father,[6] and it is to you that God entrusts this care. This God of goodness places them in your hands and undertakes to give them everything you ask of him for them: piety, self-control, reserve, purity, and the avoidance of companions who could be dangerous to them.

Because God knows that of yourself you have neither enough virtue nor enough ability to give all these things to the children he has entrusted to you, God wants you to ask him for these blessings for them frequently, fervently, and insistently. In this way and thanks to your care, nothing that they need for their salvation will be lacking to them.

---

1. Lk 11:5–6
2. 1 Thes 5:14
3. Heb 13–17
4. Lk 11:5
5. Lk 11:9
6. Ps 68:6

# Rogation Tuesday

*Love for prayer*

### 38.1  First Point

To induce us powerfully to pray, Jesus Christ assures us explicitly that we will receive everything that we ask for. Whoever asks, he says, will receive.[1] Prayer has this efficacy in itself; this is precisely what God promises us. The more we ask of God, the more he gives, because he takes great delight in granting our prayers. God would not urge us so strongly to make requests of him, says Saint Augustine, if he were not disposed to give us what we ask and if he did not will this effectively.

Be ashamed, then, to be so slothful and negligent in praying to God, who has a greater desire to give than you desire to ask. He has more compassion on your wretchedness than you have the desire to be delivered.

Have the courage, therefore, to believe the One who so strongly addresses you. Be worthy of his promises, and take pleasure in having recourse to him. Is there anyone,"asks Saint Augustine, who has been confident of obtaining something from God and has been disappointed?

### 38.2  Second Point

In the Gospel Jesus Christ gives two reasons for the efficacy of prayer. The first is the faith and confidence we have in praying. Whatsoever you ask in prayer with faith, says Jesus Christ, you will receive.[2] He says all whatsoever, and he makes no exceptions. Would anyone believe that faith would have such an effect that we would obtain infallibly whatever we ask of God, if the Son of God, who is Truth,[3] had not assured us of this?

He not only made this known to you by his words but also gave you a great example of it in the Canaanite woman.[4] She had insistently prayed and entreated with Jesus Christ to deliver her daughter, who was possessed by a demon. Because of her faith, she merited that Jesus Christ give her what she requested. O woman! exclaimed Jesus, how great is your faith! Let it be done as you desire.[5]

Be convinced, then, that God is ready to refuse you nothing that you ask of him with faith and confidence in his goodness.

### 38.3  Third Point

The second reason why God grants everything to those who pray is the humility with which they ask him for what they need. As the Wise Man so rightly says, God resists the proud and gives his grace to the humble.[6] In other words, he grants nothing to the proud and refuses nothing to the humble.

This is what Jesus Christ made abundantly clear in the parable of the Pharisee and the publican, who were both praying in the Temple. *The publican went home justified,* says our Lord, *but not the Pharisee.* The reason for this, as he immediately adds, is that whoever exalts himself will be humbled, while whoever humbles himself will be exalted.[7] This was like saying that the Pharisee's prayer was not heard, because it was accompanied by sentiments of pride, whereas the publican, in spite of the serious sins he had committed, received a full pardon for them on account of the contrition and the humility he showed in the presence of God, and he went home justified.

When you pray to God, then, let it be with such deep humility that God will not be able to refuse you anything you ask.

---

| | | |
|---|---|---|
| 1. Lk 11:10 | 4. Mt 15:21–28 | 7. Lk 18:14 |
| 2. Mt 21:22 | 5. Mt 15:28 | |
| 3. Jn 14:6 | 6. Prv 3:34 | |

# Eve of the Ascension of Our Lord Jesus Christ

*What we ought to ask of God in prayer*

### 39.1  First Point

In today's Gospel and in the rest of the same chapter, which gives us the prayer he addressed to his Father for his holy Apostles, Jesus

Christ teaches us what we ought to ask of God in our prayers. He does not ask for human and temporal favors for them, because he had not come into this world to procure such benefits for us. He knew that it was the Eternal Father who had given him his disciples, that they belonged to him,[1] and that the Father had destined them to preach his Gospel[2] and to work for the salvation of souls. He realized, therefore, that he must pray to his Father to give them only those things that might contribute to the end for which he had called them.

This is why in this prayer Jesus Christ asked his Eternal Father for three things in particular: first, to keep them from sin, by the words, keep them from evil.[3] This is what you must first of all ask of God until you have obtained it. You ought to have such a horror for anything that even comes close to being sinful that, as Saint Paul urges, you will keep away from anything having the shadow or the appearance of sin.[4] Because you cannot procure this benefit, it is essential that you constantly ask God's help to obtain it.

Beg him, therefore, most earnestly that nothing may make you displeasing in his sight, because you are obliged to inspire his love in the hearts of those whom you instruct. Is this how you relate to them? Is this what you ask of God in the prayers you offer to him?

### 39.2  Second Point

The second thing in this prayer that Jesus Christ asks of his Eternal Father for his holy Apostles is that he sanctify them in truth;[5] in other words, he does not want them to be holy with a merely external justice, like that required under the Old Law. He wants their hearts to be purified and sanctified by grace and by a sharing in the divine holiness which is in Jesus Christ. They need to participate in this holiness if they are to contribute to the sanctification of others. He adds that this is why he is offering himself to the Father and that he wishes to be made holy[6] by the death he is about to undergo on the cross.

Because in your state of life you are called to procure the sanctification of your students, you ought to be holy in no ordinary degree, for you must communicate this holiness to them, both by your good example and by the words of salvation that you must address to them every day. Interior application to prayer, love for your exercises, fidelity in performing them well and in carrying out all the other community practices will especially help you to acquire this holiness and the perfection that God wishes you to have. Beg God for it daily with great earnestness. Have this so much at heart that you never cease praying for it until you have obtained it.

### 39.3 Third Point

The third favor that Jesus Christ asks of his Eternal Father for his holy Apostles in the prayer we read in today's Gospel *is great union among themselves.* He desires that this union be so close and stable that it resembles the union among the three Divine Persons.[7] It will not be exactly the same, because the three Divine Persons have only one essence, but the union among the Apostles would participate in the union of the Trinity in such a way that their union of mind and heart, desired by Jesus Christ for them, would have the same effect as the essential union of the Father, Son, and Holy Spirit. They would all have one and the same convictions, the same will, the same affections, the same maxims and practices.[8] This is what Saint Paul recommended to the faithful when writing to them. This is also what was so noticeable among the holy Apostles and among the early disciples of Jesus Christ. As Saint Luke tells us in the Acts of the Apostles, they had but one heart and one mind.[9]

Because God has given you the grace of calling you to live in community, there is nothing that you must more earnestly ask of him than this union of mind and heart with your Brothers. Only by means of this union will you acquire the peace that ought to be all the joy of your life. Entreat the God of hearts to keep your heart and those of your Brothers one in the heart of Jesus.

---

| | | |
|---|---|---|
| 1. Jn 17:6, 9 | 4. 1 Thess 5:22 | 7. Jn 17:22–23 |
| 2. Jn 17:18; Mt 28:19 | 5. Jn 17:17 | 8. Phil 2:2; 1 Cor 1:10 |
| 3. Jn 17:15 | 6. Jn 17:19 | 9. Acts 4:32 |

# Ascension of Our Lord Jesus Christ

### 40.1 First Point

Jesus Christ, having come to this earth only to give us a new law and to accomplish the mysteries of our redemption and having entirely fulfilled everything relating to the duties of his ministry as Legislator and Redeemer, had nothing left to keep him in this world. He seemed to be in a sort of constrained condition, for the center of his glorious body was in heaven, and his proper place was at the right hand of his Father.[1] But the dealings he was still obliged to have on earth made it necessary for him to veil the radiance of his glory in his apparitions to his disciples.

You, who have left the world, ought to be entirely freed from all human inclinations that tend only earthward. You ought to aspire only toward heaven and to lift your mind and heart heavenward,[2] because you are destined only for heaven and to work only for heaven and because you will not find perfect rest until you are in heaven.

### 40.2 Second Point

On this day Jesus Christ left the earth and ascended into heaven, where he has fixed his dwelling forever. On this day his sacred humanity received the adoration of all the angels and all the just who entered heaven with him to take possession of their eternal happiness.

With all the saints, adore this sacred humanity, to whom all power has been given in heaven and on earth.[3] Unite with all the saints to acknowledge and to honor this humanity as it deserves.

Look upon the humanity of Jesus as being the One in whom, as Saint Paul says, are all the treasures of God's wisdom and knowledge.[4] From his humanity our Savior draws, as from their source, all the graces that he pours out on those who by their good works and by their prayers make themselves worthy to share in them.

When will you be able to say, with Saint Stephen, that you see the heavens open and Jesus Christ, who is there[5] and is ready to share his graces with you? Beg of him especially for the grace to be no longer preoccupied with anything except the things of heaven.

### 40.3 Third Point

Acknowledge that it is, indeed, a great advantage for you that Jesus Christ ascended into heaven; from there come all the gifts that ought to enrich and adorn your soul. By virtue of the power over all creatures, both in heaven and on earth, that Jesus Christ received this day, he is generous toward his people.

As their head, he makes them share in the life of grace, the fullness of which dwells in him, and as your mediator, he presents your prayers and good works to God, his Father.[6]

He prays for you[7] to draw down God's mercy on you and to prevent God from turning his anger against you when you offend him. Say with Saint Augustine, then, that the Ascension of Jesus Christ is your glory, the motive of your hope, and the promise of your happiness. Become worthy to have Jesus Christ as your Sovereign, your Head, and your Mediator in heaven.

---

1. Mk 16:19  4. Col 2:3  7. Heb 7:25
2. Col 3:1–2  5. Acts 7:56
3. Mt 28:18  6. Col 1:18–20; Jn 1:16

# Sunday in the Octave of the Ascension

## GOSPEL: SAINT JOHN 15:16-17 AND 16:1-4

### 41.1 First Point

In today's Gospel Jesus Christ predicts to his Apostles the persecutions they will have to suffer from the Jews, who will drive them out of their synagogues and assemblies and consider them as excommunicated,[1] unworthy to associate with them. This is how worldly people regard those who belong to God, especially those who have withdrawn from the world. They harass and insult them, outrage them, and maltreat them as though they were evildoers, all because they do not belong to the world,[2] as our Lord says.

This is how you must expect to be treated as long as you live according to the spirit of your Institute and work usefully for your neighbor, because the demon will hate you, and the world, his close ally, will not be able to endure you. You must put yourself in the same place as far as the world goes; this will be one of the best ways to preserve your piety, your seclusion, and your separation from the world.

### 41.2 Second Point

Jesus Christ foretold to his Apostles not only that they would be driven away and insulted by the Jews but also that those who would put them to death would think they were doing a great service to God.[3] Although today those who belong to God and who work for his glory are not put to death, people do almost anything to rob them of their honor by the most atrocious calumnies, treating them as though they were unworthy to live.

You ought to be glad to be treated this way, for you must be dead to the world and have no dealings with it. If you truly belong to God, you are the world's enemy, and the world is your enemy, because it is God's enemy.[4] Therefore, behave toward it as such, and hold in horror all dealings with the world. Do not allow it to have the least opening to you, for fear that by dealing with it, you will share its spirit.

### 41.3 Third Point

The reason why the world maltreats and insults the disciples of Jesus Christ is, as our Lord declares, because this world has not known him or his Father who sent him.[5] Indeed, the people of the world, as a rule, have no love except for people like themselves, that is, for those who enjoy nothing but what caters to their senses. Because they have only a very imperfect knowledge of God, they do not think about God, never speak about God, do not willingly hear about God, and scarcely ever pray to God. It follows that they have only disdain for God's faithful servants and friends and often make this manifest.

At times you may have to teach children who do not know God, because they have been brought up by parents who do not know God. Strive to know God so well through reading and prayer that you may be able to make him known to others and make him loved by all those to whom you have made him known.

---

1. Jn 16:1
2. Jn 15:19
3. Jn 16:2
4. Jn 15:18–19
5. Jn 16:3

# Eve of Pentecost

*Dispositions for receiving the Holy Spirit*

### 42.1  First Point

In today's Gospel Jesus Christ points out to us three dispositions we need to receive the Holy Spirit, which he expresses in these words: If you love me, keep my commandments, and I will ask my Father, and he will give you another Consoler to be with you always.[1]

The first disposition is to love God and to give yourself entirely to him. For this you must be detached from all creatures and love God alone. Whoever is attached to the world and to its goods is incapable of receiving the Spirit of God, who communicates himself only to those he finds empty of all that is not God. This is why, as Jesus Christ observes, the world cannot receive this divine Spirit,[2] because it loves only the concupiscence of the flesh, the concupiscence of the eyes, and the pride of life.[3]

Be detached from all things, then, and be attached to God alone, if you wish to be in a state to receive the Spirit of God.

### 42.2  Second Point

The second disposition required to receive the Holy Spirit is to keep God's commandments faithfully and to strive to do his holy will in all things. Jesus Christ says that this divine Spirit will always be in and with those who receive him[4] and that he cannot be pleased except with those who try always to do what God desires of them and to be in harmony with his holy will. We must, then, not expect to receive the Holy Spirit if we do not try to accomplish the holy will of God in all things.

You have left the world, no doubt, to give yourself entirely to God and to possess abundantly his divine Spirit. Do not expect to achieve this, however, unless you punctually fulfill what you know is God's will for you. Be very careful to observe your Rule exactly.

### 42.3 Third Point

Nothing disposes us better to receive the Holy Spirit than prayer. This is why Jesus Christ assures us that our heavenly Father will give his Spirit, full of love and goodness for us, to all those who ask him.[5] Yet, because he knows that the fullness of this divine Spirit is difficult to obtain and because he desires to give the Spirit to his Apostles, he promises them that he will pray to the Father for them,[6] so that they will receive his Spirit in profusion.

If you wish to be disposed as perfectly as God asks of you in order to be filled with the Spirit of God on Pentecost, apply yourself with attention and fervor to interior prayer in order to be filled with God's grace. For this is the day on which he generously pours out his graces; on this day he gave himself to the holy Apostles and to all those who then made up the Church. Do not fail to pray to him during all these holy days, and often repeat with the Church these holy words: Send forth your Spirit to give us a new life, and you will renew the face of the earth.[7]

---

| | | |
|---|---|---|
| 1. Jn 14:15–16 | 4. Jn 14:16–17 | 7. Ps 104:30 |
| 2. Jn 14:17 | 5. Lk 11:13 | |
| 3. 1 Jn 2:16 | 6. Jn 14:16 | |

# Pentecost Sunday

## GOSPEL: SAINT JOHN 14:23–31

### 43.1 First Point

The holy Apostles remained in seclusion and applied themselves to prayer[1] from the Ascension of Jesus Christ until the day of Pentecost. This was a feast that the Jews celebrated in memory of the giving of the Old Law to Moses on Mount Sinai.

On this day the Holy Spirit descended on the Apostles and on all those who were gathered together with them[2] in the large upper room. He came to bring them a new law, the law of grace and love, and he poured himself out upon them like a strong, driving wind.[3]

This was to show that just as God in creating man had,[4] as Holy Scripture expresses it, breathed into him the breath of life,[5] so too in communicating a new life to his disciples to live only by grace, he breathed into them his divine Spirit to give them some share in his own divine life.

The Spirit of God also ought to come and to rest upon you on this sacred day, to make it possible for you to live and to act only by the Spirit's action in you. Draw him within you by offering him a well-disposed heart.

### 43.2 Second Point

The Acts of the Apostles tells us that *this wind*, the symbol of the Spirit of God, who poured himself out upon the disciples of Jesus Christ, *filled the entire house*. This illustrates what is said immediately afterward, that those who were gathered there were all filled with the Holy Spirit.[6] At that moment the holy Apostles received such an abundance of grace that all Jerusalem was filled with the sound of their voices.[7] They spoke about nothing except the risen Jesus Christ. They had the words of Holy Scripture constantly on their lips, and these words served to guide them in all they did.

They had all fled after seeing Christ die on the cross; they had gone into hiding, afraid of death. But after receiving the Holy Spirit, they came together again and gathered in the same place; there *they encouraged one another* and urged one another *to suffer for the name of Jesus Christ*. In such suffering they considered themselves blessed, and they rejoiced.[8]

You need the fullness of the Spirit of God in your state, for you ought to live and be guided entirely by the spirit and the light of faith; only the Spirit of God can give you this disposition.

### 43.3 Third Point

The Acts of the Apostles adds that when the disciples were all gathered together, there appeared to them separate tongues of fire, which came to rest on each of them. Immediately they began to speak in various languages, according to the grace given to them by the Holy Spirit.[9]

It is amazing that these men, up to then so earthly minded that they could not grasp the sacred truths that Jesus Christ taught them, were all at once so enlightened that they could now explain clearly and with all imaginable accuracy the words of Holy Scripture! As a result, those present were completely surprised and filled with amazement.[10] In a little time they converted a very great number of them,[11] because, as Saint Peter told them, the Spirit of God had been poured out upon them.[12]

You carry out a work that requires you to touch hearts, but this you cannot do except by the Spirit of God. Pray to him to give you today the same grace that he gave the holy Apostles. Ask him that after filling you with his Holy Spirit to sanctify you, he will also communicate himself to you to procure the salvation of others.

| | | |
|---|---|---|
| 1. Acts 1:13–14 | 5. Gn 2:7 | 9. Acts 2:3–4 |
| 2. Acts 2:1–4 | 6. Acts 2:2–4 | 10. Acts 2:12 |
| 3. Jer 31:33–34; Rom 8:2 | 7. Acts 2:5–6 | 11. Acts 2:41 |
| 4. Acts 2:2 | 8. Acts 5:41 | 12. Acts 2:33 |

# Monday in the Octave of Pentecost

*The first effect produced by the Holy Spirit in a soul is to make it consider things with the eyes of faith.*

### 44.1 First Point

In today's Gospel Jesus Christ says that the light had come into the world, but the world preferred darkness to the light.[1] By the descent of the Holy Spirit, the true light came into the world. The first effect that this light produces in a soul fortunate enough to receive it is to cause it to see spiritual things altogether differently from those who live according to the spirit of the times. This is why Jesus Christ, in another place in the Gospel, told his Apostles that when this Holy Spirit, whom he calls the Spirit of Truth, would come, he would teach them all truth.[2] He would make all things known to them by showing things not only as they appear outwardly but as they are in themselves and as we can know them when we understand them truly with the eyes of faith.

Do you make use of this light to judge all visible things and to learn what is true and false about them, what is only apparent and what is substantial? If you act as a disciple of Jesus Christ enlightened by God's Spirit, this is the only light that ought to guide you.

## 44.2 Second Point

The truths that the Holy Spirit teaches to those who receive him are the maxims found in the holy Gospel. He helps them to understand these maxims and to take them to heart, and he leads them to live and to act in accordance with them.

Only the Spirit of God can give us a correct understanding of these maxims of the Gospel and inspire us to put them into practice, because they are above the level of the human spirit. How, indeed, can we ever realize that blessed are the poor,[3] that we must love those who hate us[4] and rejoice when we are calumniated and when people say all sorts of evil against us,[5] that we must return good for evil,[6] and so many other truths entirely contrary to what nature suggests, unless the Spirit of God teaches them to us?

You are obliged to teach these holy maxims to the children you are appointed to instruct. You must be thoroughly convinced of them, so that you can impress them deeply on the hearts of your students. Be docile, therefore, to the Holy Spirit, who can in a short time procure for you a perfect understanding of these truths.

## 44.3 Third Point

Although these great truths are so admirable and exalted and the Spirit of God, the true Light, enlightens souls concerning them, the majority of people understand nothing of these truths, because, as the Gospel says, they prefer darkness to the light and know neither the Spirit of God[7] nor what the Spirit is capable of inspiring and producing in souls.

The reasons for this, according to Jesus Christ, are that their works are evil and that everyone who does evil hates the light.[8] Because the world is blinded by sin, it follows maxims entirely contrary to those that the Holy Spirit teaches to holy souls. The world is guided by these false precepts, which are the source of its sins and of the corruption of hearts.

There is nothing you ought to omit in order to eradicate from the spirit of your disciples the maxims and the practices of the world and to inspire them with a horror for them. The more aversion you feel for the world, the more you will hate its behavior and its maxims in you and in others.

---

1. Jn 3:19
2. Jn 16:13
3. Mt 5:3
4. Mt 5:44
5. Mt 5:11
6. Lk 6:27
7. Jn 3:19
8. Jn 3:19–20

# Tuesday After Pentecost

*The second effect produced by the Holy Spirit in a soul is to make it live and act through grace.*

### 45.1  First Point

In today's Gospel Jesus Christ declares that he has come so that those who belong to him may have life and have it more abundantly.[1] This is also something we ought to attribute to the action of the Holy Spirit, who comes in a soul only to give it the life of grace and to cause it to act with grace.

Because we must be alive in order to act, the first impulse the Spirit of God must give to a heart when he takes possession of it is to produce the life of grace within it. For this reason Saint Paul calls him the Spirit of Life, and he adds that it was by this Spirit that he had been delivered from the law of sin.[2]

You ought to have been freed from this shameful law when you left the world and became free with the liberty of God's children,[3] a title with which Jesus Christ honors you.

Take care, then, to preserve this grace of freedom that is given to you, which Jesus Christ won for you with so much suffering. Do not subject yourself again to the yoke of the slavery[4] of sin; this would be to wrong Jesus, who merited the grace of freedom for you by all his agony. It would also sadden the Holy Spirit,[5] who has given this grace to you with such goodness.

### 45.2  Second Point

It is not enough for a person who has withdrawn from the world to live a life of grace; he must also oppose whatever might cause him to lose it. This is another effect brought about in him by the Holy Spirit. The flesh, says Saint Paul, fights with its desires against the spirit, and the spirit against the flesh, and they are opposed to each other.[6] For this reason, declares the same Apostle, if by the Spirit you put to death the deeds of the flesh (that is, by the Spirit of God, who dwells in you), you will live.[7]

This tells you that you cannot preserve the life of grace except by mortifying in you the inclinations of corrupt nature, what Saint Paul calls the flesh. The more you resist these inclinations, the more you will strengthen the life of grace in you.

Only in this way will you belong entirely to Jesus Christ, because those who belong to Jesus Christ, as the same Apostle says, have crucified their flesh with their vices and their passions.[8]

Mortify your members, then,[9] he continues, and you will avoid yielding to the desires of the flesh, and you will strengthen the life of grace within you.

### 45.3 Third Point

Although it is a very special effect of God's goodness to preserve you in his holy grace, this is not sufficient for you in your profession. To live according to the spirit of your state, you must act under the influence of grace and make it plain that you are guided by the inspiration of the Spirit of God. This, says Saint Paul, is an indication that you are in God's grace. If you live by the Spirit, he says, then act by the Spirit.[10]

You must, then, act in such a way and be so watchful over self that nature will have no part in what you do and that there will be nothing in your conduct that is not produced by grace. Do you not do a great many things for purely human and natural motives, just because you feel like doing them? Do you do everything as being done in God's presence, as being done for God, and do you act as having nothing else to do but to please God?[11]

---

1. Jn 10:10
2. Rom 8:2
3. Rom 8:21
4. Gal 5:1
5. Eph 4:30
6. Gal 5:17
7. Rom 8:11–13
8. Gal 5:24
9. Col 3:5
10. Gal 5:25
11. 1 Cor 7:32

# Trinity Sunday

## GOSPEL: SAINT MATTHEW 28:18-20

### 46.1 First Point

Adore this sacred mystery, which is entirely above our senses and even above our reason. The angels and the saints pay it their homage without ever being able to understand it fully. Be content to honor it with them, acknowledging in mind and heart your nothingness before this mystery. Declare that all you can say of it, all you can conceive of it, is that it is the mystery of one God in three Persons, the Father, the Son, and the Holy Spirit.

This is the object of the Church's most profound veneration in heaven as well as on earth. In the presence of this ineffable mystery, every knee must bend in heaven, on earth, and in hell.[1] You too must declare with all the heavenly spirits that Holy, Holy, Holy is the Lord God almighty and that the whole world is filled with his glory and majesty.[2]

For it is he who deserves all glory; to him alone it belongs, because he is the only One who exists of and by himself.

Today, pay your homage to this divine mystery, and acknowledge that this is the mystery above all mysteries, for it is the source of all the others.

### 46.2 Second Point

With good reason we can call the Holy Trinity the mystery of faith, because nothing but faith can throw light on this mystery.

Faith alone can enable us to know it, although only in a superficial manner; nevertheless, we do know it as far as it can be grasped in this life.

Faith alone keeps our mind fixed on the consideration of this supreme mystery, which is infinitely beyond the range of the human mind.

Faith alone, drawing the mind from the darkness[3] of infidelity, leads it deep into this sacred obscurity in which faith holds us captive.[4]

Blessed darkness, which veils our understanding and humbles our reason! Other mysteries are accompanied by something tangible that gives our senses and our reason some help, but in this one neither senses nor reason find any assistance.

Ask God, therefore, for a deep faith to believe this sacred mystery, and while firmly professing that God is One in Three Persons, proclaim that blessed are those who have not seen but yet believe.[5]

### 46.3 Third Point

If it is true that this mystery, which has no equal in dignity and in holiness, is the first object of all the veneration of the faithful, it ought to be all the more important for you, because you are obliged to teach it and to make it known to children, who are living plants in the field of the Church.[6]

They too were consecrated to the Most Holy Trinity in Baptism, just as you were; they bear in their souls[7] the indelible character of their belonging to God. They are indebted to this adorable mystery for the anointing with grace that has been poured into their hearts.[8]

It is only right that you, who are responsible for explaining this mystery to them as far as faith allows, must recognize it as the source of all enlightenment, the foundation of faith, and the basis of our religion.

With this in view, today pay very special honor and be dedicated entirely to the Most Holy Trinity to contribute as far as you will be able to extend its glory over all the earth.[9] For this purpose, enter into the spirit of your Institute, and stir up in you the zeal that God wishes you to have in its fullness, so that you can give your students some understanding of this sacred mystery.

| | | |
|---|---|---|
| 1. Phil 2:10 | 4. 2 Cor 10:5 | 7. Eph 4:30 |
| 2. Is 6:3 | 5. Jn 20:29 | 8. 1 Jn 2:20, 27 |
| 3. Col 1:13 | 6. Ps 128:3; 1 Cor 1:3–9 | 9. Is 6:3 |

# Feast of the Most Blessed Sacrament

### 47.1  First Point

It is no doubt a great honor for us that God desires so much to dwell with us continually and to make himself in some way tangible to us in the Most Blessed Sacrament of the Eucharist, in order to procure for us a great number of graces, both interior and exterior. The angels offer their adoration to him there; they acknowledge their nothingness before this sacred treasure, the consolation of everyone on earth.

Today the whole Church celebrates; all the faithful join in mind and in heart to show themselves grateful for such a great benefit.

Strive to share these sentiments and to offer Jesus Christ in this mystery your very humble thanks for the goodness he has shown by communicating himself to you in this sacrament and by being always ready to impart to you an abundance of his graces.

### 47.2  Second Point

The love that Jesus Christ shows for you in this great sacrament certainly deserves that today you show an altogether special return of love for him by a very deep respect, both interior and exterior, for this adorable mystery. On this day in the Church, we try to pay the greatest possible external respect to this hidden God.[1] This is why the Blessed Sacrament is exposed on the altar during the entire octave and is solemnly carried in procession, so that Christians may encourage one another to honor it during these holy days and to pay frequent visits to the churches.

Have a deep reverence for this sacred mystery; take care that your disciples pay it homage and visit the Most Blessed Sacrament with more than ordinary piety during these holy days.

### 47.3 Third Point

This external veneration would mean little to God and to Jesus Christ if it were not accompanied by the interior acknowledgment of our utter nothingness, which is the only thing that can make our exterior homage, no matter how great it may be, truly worthy of God.

There are those who are content to receive external honors without concerning themselves whether there are corresponding sentiments in the heart. God, however, wants the honor given to him and the respect shown to him to be more interior than external.

This is also what Jesus Christ expects of you in the Holy Eucharist. He wants your soul to forget itself completely in his presence at the thought of this God of love. He wants you to make known to him that you honor him interiorly, as he requires of you, through the continual attention you pay to the goodness he has shown you by giving himself entirely to you in this great sacrament. Be faithful to this.

---

1. Is 45:15

# Friday in the Octave
# of the Blessed Sacrament

*Jesus Christ in the Holy Eucharist, bread that nourishes our souls*

### 48.1 First Point

The Jews gloried in the fact that Moses had given their forefathers a bread from heaven, but Jesus Christ told them that they were mistaken, that it was his Eternal Father who gives the true bread from heaven and that he is this living Bread come down from heaven.[1]

Indeed, he is living in those who receive him, for when they receive the sacrament of the holy Eucharist with holy dispositions, he gives himself generously to all the faculties of their souls and carries out there the actions of life. He guides and directs them by his divine Spirit, by whom he lives and acts in them.

When Jesus Christ is in you, is he there as a living bread? Do you allow him complete freedom to communicate his divine Spirit to your soul? Is he living in you to the extent that you can say that it is no longer you who live but that it is Jesus Christ who lives in you?[2]

## 48.2 Second Point

Jesus Christ told the Jews that he was the true bread come down from heaven. He added that this bread gives life to the world. He says even more that whoever eats this bread will never be hungry.[3] How fortunate we are to be able to satisfy our hunger with such bread as often as we wish! ·

This is the bread that nourishes you so well that you find in it all the spiritual sustenance and vigor you need. This is why the Fathers of the Church say that this is the supersubstantial bread[4] spoken of in the Lord's prayer according to Saint Matthew. For nothing is better able to sustain our soul and to give it such surpassing strength to walk vigorously in the path of virtue.

The bread that Elias ate before reaching the summit of Mount Horeb, which alone sufficed to strengthen him for his journey of forty days,[5] is also regarded as a figure of the sacred bread of the Eucharist.

Eat this divine bread, then, gladly, with love, and as often as you can. If you learn how to find in it all the encouragement it contains, it will give your soul a truly heavenly life here on earth.

## 48.3 Third Point

Seeing that the Jews found it difficult to believe what he was telling them, Jesus Christ added that he was himself the bread of life, that their forefathers who had eaten the manna had all died, but that those who eat of this bread come down from heaven will never die; that if anyone eats of this bread, he will live forever; that this bread which he will give is his own flesh.[6]

When we receive the body of Jesus Christ, we have the advantage of sharing in our Savior's life, of having in us an assurance of eternal life. We are even guaranteed to live forever if we preserve in ourselves the Spirit of Jesus Christ, which is what he leaves in us.

Is it possible that Jesus Christ promises that you will live with an eternal life by eating this bread, which is God, and that you want either not to eat it or to eat it only rarely? Taste and see[7] how good this bread is for you, how pleasing it is to your taste, and how beneficial for your soul.

---

1. Jn 6:31–32, 51
2. Gal 2:20
3. Jn 6:51, 33, 35
4. Mt 6:11
5. 1 Kgs 19:7–8
6. Jn 6:48–51
7. Ps 34:9

# Saturday in the Octave
# of the Blessed Sacrament

*Jesus Christ in the Eucharist, food that sustains the life of our souls*

### 49.1 First Point

In the Gospel Jesus Christ calls the Holy Eucharist not only bread but also meat. My flesh, he says, is food.[1] As such, it gives the soul a vigor that makes it easy to overcome all the difficulties found in the practice of virtue.

Nothing, in effect, can disturb the soul, because Jesus Christ communicates to it in some manner the energy that can withstand whatever opposes its good. He also gives the soul courage to reassure it against whatever it might fear in the attacks of its enemies.

We even grow stronger, says Tertullian, by this flesh, which is why it is more necessary for us to feed upon it to procure for our soul an abundance of grace than to nourish our body with ordinary meat to preserve life.

The more virtue and perfection your state demands of you, the more strength and generosity you need to achieve this and not allow yourself to be laid low by fear of the sufferings you will encounter on your way. Nourish yourself with this Eucharistic meat to be strengthened interiorly and to overcome all the obstacles to your salvation.

### 49.2 Second Point

This divine meat of the Eucharist produces another effect in us; those who eat it live in Jesus Christ, and Jesus Christ lives in them.[2] He assures us of this in the holy Gospel. This shows that between Jesus Christ and the person who eats his flesh, such a close and intimate union is brought about that only with difficulty can one be separated from the other. This sacred food is incorporated in the soul that receives it with fervor, so that this soul shares in the virtues of Jesus Christ, and what was said of the spouse in the Canticle takes place: My lover belongs to me, and I belong to my lover.[3]

Are you thus so closely united to Jesus Christ when you receive him that nothing is able to separate you from him? After receiving Communion, can you say with Saint Paul, Who will separate me from Jesus Christ? Will it be tribulation, poverty, persecution, hunger, nakedness, or danger?[4] Can you add, with all the confidence of the Apostle, that no creature can ever separate you from your Savior?[5] See to it that your holy Communion produces between you and Jesus Christ a union so strong that you will never be separated from him.

### 49.3 Third Point

Another admirable effect produced in a soul by the divine meat of the Eucharist is that it makes the soul live an altogether supernatural and divine life. This is made clear when Jesus Christ says: As my Father who sent me lives and as I live by my Father, so too the one who eats me will live by me.[6]

A soul who eats, then, this flesh of Jesus Christ and is nourished by this meat no longer lives a natural life, no longer seeks to satisfy its senses, no longer acts by its own spirit but by the Spirit of its God, who has become its nourishment.

Are these the effects produced in you by union with Jesus Christ in the Eucharist?

---

| | | |
|---|---|---|
| 1. Jn 6:55 | 3. Song 6:3 | 5. Rom 8:39 |
| 2. Jn 6:56 | 4. Rom 8:35 | 6. Jn 6:57 |

# Second Sunday After Pentecost
# in the Octave of the Blessed Sacrament

## GOSPEL: SAINT LUKE 14:16–24

*God's honor to us by inviting us to receive Jesus Christ in the Holy Eucharist*

### 50.1 First Point

You are the ones whom the Eternal Father today invites to his banquet in order to receive his Son, Jesus Christ, in the Eucharist. Worldly people excuse themselves from attending. One says that he has bought a farm and must therefore go out and inspect it; another wishes to test five yoke of oxen that he has acquired; a third says that he is married.[1] Some excuse themselves because of their business; others, because of the pleasures they want to enjoy. Both prefer their affairs and their personal satisfaction to the practices of piety and of religion, and especially to the greatest honor they can ever enjoy on earth—and which ought to be supremely agreeable to them in this world—namely, to receive Jesus Christ in the Eucharist.

Deplore the blindness of those who live in the world and who follow worldly maxims. They prefer temporal advantages to sharing in this most delightful food, which is Jesus Christ, who by coming to them, makes them participants in the divinity.[2]

## 50.2 Second Point

It is hard to imagine that people who are born for heaven, who in Baptism have undertaken to live a holy life, would neglect the means given to them by God to sanctify themselves, especially the greatest of these means, namely, Communion with the body of Jesus Christ. By uniting himself with them, he gives them in abundance the graces they are able to receive and that he has prepared for them.

If, as our Lord says, the body is more important than the clothing,[3] what is the body compared with the soul? Is it not more reasonable to disregard the body and everything temporal in order to think first of all of the soul and to provide what it needs?

If a king wanted to honor his people, who were taken up with worldly concerns, and proposed to visit them in their homes, would they offer him such frivolous excuses for not welcoming him? We can, therefore, with much reason apply to those who generally refuse to receive Communion because of their temporal affairs what Jesus Christ says in the Gospel: When the Son of Man comes, that is, when he offers himself to be the spiritual nourishment of his people, do you think he will find faith on earth?[4] A lack of faith, indeed, makes people stay away from Communion.

## 50.3 Third Point

You have had the good fortune to withdraw from the world. To become worthy of your ministry, you must lead a life resembling that of the angels; therefore, you ought to consider yourself fortunate to receive so frequently this bread of angels that Jesus Christ presents to you in person and with which he desires to satisfy you completely.

Could you, then, very well excuse yourself from such a delightful banquet at which a heart that loves God finds full satisfaction?

Jesus Christ tells us that what one person does not have will be taken away and given to another who already has.[5] From this we may conclude, with regard to this holy sacrament, that the graces which would have been received by those who stay away are given to those who have the happiness to come.

To profit by such a great blessing, make an effort to receive Communion, and come to it with faith. You commit a great wrong if you excuse yourself from Communion, because you have so many opportunities to receive it with such great ease. Be convinced that no matter what excuse you give to Jesus Christ to dispense yourself from receiving him, he is not disposed to accept it.

---

1. Lk 14:18–20      3. Lk 12:23      5. Lk 19:26
2. 2 Pt 1:4         4. Lk 18:8

# Monday in the Octave
# of the Blessed Sacrament

*To omit Communion is often poor advice, for Communion is the remedy for all the weaknesses of our soul.*

### 51.1 First Point

One of the most frequent excuses offered by those who are negligent in the service of God to dispense themselves from receiving Communion is that they are not prepared. This excuse would seem to be ill-founded, for it means either that they are not prepared because they do not wish to be prepared or that they cannot be prepared. If they do not wish to be prepared, this is a sign that they have very little love for God, who feels such great tenderness for us that he gives us his own Son[1] to nourish our souls and at the same time to remedy all our spiritual maladies.

Do you want to let your soul faint away for lack of nourishment? Do you want to abandon it to the disorder either of sin or of your passions, which will infallibly lead to sin, because you do not use the remedy that could in a short time deliver your soul from all corruption?

### 51.2 Second Point

If people say that they are not prepared to receive Communion because they are unable to prepare, let them carefully examine themselves to see whether it is true that they cannot prepare themselves. They must, indeed, prove themselves before receiving Communion,[2] as Saint Paul enjoins, in order not to make an unworthy Communion. Without doubt, only mortal sin can make it impossible for them to receive Communion, no matter how much they desire to receive, no matter how much they are urged to receive, for it would be a sacrilege to receive Communion in that state.

But is it possible that you would want to stain your soul with such a sin, you to whom God has given so many graces and to whom he still gives such special and notable graces every day?

Could your heart, which Jesus Christ has chosen for his dwelling place and which ought always to be guided by his action, offer him such an affront as to attach itself in criminal fashion to creatures?

Do you want to render useless the benefit of his Passion and become an enemy of God and the slave of the devil after Jesus Christ, with so much suffering and anguish, has destroyed the power Satan had over us?

### 51.3 Third Point

But, you say, you are not prepared to receive Communion, because your spirit is in turmoil or because you are experiencing severe temptations. Do you not know that turmoil and temptations, far from making you unfit to receive Communion, do nothing of the sort? On the contrary, the more anxiety and temptation you experience, the more you must have recourse to Communion, which is a sure remedy to ease your anxiety and to weaken your temptations.

Perhaps at other times you say that the reason you do not receive Communion is that you cannot concentrate on God. You feel completely dry; your mind is filled with evil or useless thoughts. Because of this, you are not able either to prepare to receive Communion or to make a worthy thanksgiving after it.

Beg Jesus Christ, living in you, to make up for your powerlessness, to prepare you, and to make thanksgiving in you and for you. In this way what you lack will be fully supplied, and God will be most satisfied with you and with your Communion. Do not, then, listen any further to what your spirit may suggest to dispense you from receiving Communion.

---

1. Jn 3:16       2. 1 Cor 11:28

# Tuesday in the Octave of the Blessed Sacrament

*Causes and remedies of a bad Communion*

### 52.1 First Point

A bad Communion is a very serious crime; nevertheless, it can happen in the life of people who appear to have and who might, in fact, have a certain piety. This evil can occur even in the holiest communities. Judas was in the company of Jesus Christ, and he committed this crime and many more, because, as Jesus Christ testified, he was a devil.[1]

A devil in the company of Jesus Christ! Who could imagine such a thing? He received, day after day, the instructions of such a good teacher, and yet to what an extent he abused them! What perfidious conduct! What ingratitude! To be warned about his crime even before he fell into it, yet to be brazen enough to commit it!

Oh, how hardened must a person's heart be not to hold a sin like this in horror! Yet what happened to this Apostle can happen to anyone else. Tremble at the thought, and be on your guard in fear of such a shameful disorder.

## 52.2 Second Point

As a rule, what leads a person to a bad Communion is either hypocrisy or embarrassment over confessing sins. These were the reasons why Judas sinned. Outwardly, he seemed to act like the other Apostles. He stayed with them for three years without anyone's having noticed anything out of place in his conduct. Although Jesus Christ was able to speak to Judas before he committed his crime, to inspire him with horror for it, nothing was able to touch him, and he never declared either to Jesus Christ or to anyone else the least word that might have revealed the evil state of his conscience.

This is also what causes this horrible sin in those who commit it. They want to appear as pious and as faithful to the Rule as everyone else, while going about with a soul sullied with crimes. They do not dare to reveal themselves to those who are in charge of their souls, and they criminally abuse the goodness of Jesus Christ, who does them the favor of giving himself to them.

## 52.3 Third Point

The way to avoid falling into such a lamentable situation and to remedy it is, first of all, to be very humble and to be accustomed to accuse yourself simply and humbly of all your faults, without concealing or disguising a single one. Otherwise, the devil will surprise you when you least expect it, and he will make you fall into his snares. Secondly, let there be nothing in you hidden from those who guide you. By these two means you will surely avoid making an unworthy Communion.

A person does not fall all of a sudden into such a detestable crime, but if he does commit one, it is only after he has, little by little, closed his heart firmly against grace by keeping it shut to those whom God has commissioned to lead him to heaven. Such a heart is blinded and does not know the path that leads to God, unless someone shows the way. Woe, then, to those who guide themselves, because they are not capable of sustaining themselves! If they fall, they will have no one to help them rise.[2]

---

1. Jn 6:70–71     2. Eccl 4:10

# Wednesday in the Octave
# of the Most Blessed Sacrament

*Causes and remedies of a Communion that is of little benefit*

### 53.1 First Point

It is true that to receive the grace of the sacrament of the Holy Eucharist, which is to nourish our souls and to prevent them from falling into sin, it is sufficient to be without mortal sin. However, if we wish to profit by Communion as we ought when we receive Communion often, we need to confess our venial sins and to give up any attachment to them. We must be resolved to correct ourselves; otherwise, our Communion will be of slight benefit. We go to Communion to become holy; to achieve this, we must strive to have this disposition as far as we are able, so that in receiving Communion, we are strengthened in the life of grace, obtain new graces, and practice virtue more readily.

Have you observed whether your Communions produce these effects in you? Do they make you more recollected, more reserved, more charitable toward your Brothers, more patient, and more self-controlled? Do you use more violence to overcome yourself? Do you experience more rarely the revolt of your passions? Do you watch more carefully in order not to succumb to them? See to it that your Communions produce these good results.

### 53.2 Second Point

Quite often, what causes our Communions to fail to have the good results we ought to draw from them is the fact that we receive Communion with considerable, although venial, sins that we have not confessed.

To receive Communion without Confession, for example, after having lied, murmured against our superior or our Brothers, scandalized them because we did not do a penance or else refused to accept some penance, allowed ourselves to yield deliberately to curiosity, or committed similar faults shows that we do not have much horror for sin.

By doing this we take little trouble to purify our heart when we wish to go to Communion, and we take very lightly the sins of this sort, which are, nonetheless, serious in a person who makes profession of piety.

To draw all the good you possibly can from your Communions, take care to purify your conscience thoroughly before receiving Communion; otherwise, you show little love for God and little respect for Jesus Christ, whom you are going to receive.

### 53.3 Third Point

Another reason why Communions sometimes produce meager results is that people make little effort to correct themselves of venial faults, even though they do confess them. Such base behavior and negligence are signs of spiritual indifference, which is why God, in turn, neglects a soul, looking upon it as unworthy of his graces, because it cares so little about him and makes so few efforts to make itself entirely pleasing to him. A soul that behaves so negligently often makes little effort both to prepare for Holy Communion and to make thanksgiving afterward.

These defects arise from a heart that is little disposed to give itself totally to God and not from Communion or its frequent reception, for the effect proper to Communion is to nourish our souls and to increase grace in them.

Act, then, in such a way as to make sure that each time you receive this sacrament, it will produce all the good that God intends it to have, and you will place no obstacle in the way.

# Octave of the Most Blessed Sacrament

*Frequent Communion*

### 54.1 First Point

The first disciples had the habit of receiving Communion daily,[1] a practice followed for a long time in the Church. People who attended Mass did not fail to communicate. Several Fathers of the Church demonstrate that this custom was conformable to the purpose Jesus Christ had in instituting the Eucharist when they apply the words of the Lord's Prayer, our daily bread,[2] to the body of Jesus Christ, which we receive in Communion. They consider it as the bread with which we ought to nourish our soul daily, for it needs to be nourished and strengthened as much as our body; otherwise, it is not possible to maintain it in piety.

What happiness you enjoy to be able to communicate often so as to preserve you in grace, which would soon abandon you if you were to abandon Communion. In it you find relief in your difficulties, strength in your temptations not to succumb to them, and an easy way to acquire virtue. Do not neglect so holy a practice.

### 54.2 Second Point

The effects of Holy Communion are so admirable and procure such great good for our souls that we ought to be especially committed to approach it often. This divine sacrament, says Saint Bernard, produces two considerable effects in us: it diminishes our susceptibility to the approach of slight sins, and it prevents us from consenting when we are tempted to serious sins. If anyone, adds this Father, is not at present assailed by movements of anger, envy, impurity, and the like, you ought to give thanks to the body and blood of Jesus Christ, because this is the effect of the power of the sacrament of the Eucharist operating in you.

Because you cannot find a more prompt and efficacious remedy for your temptations and falls than the reception of the body of Jesus Christ, receive it often, so that by this means your soul may fall less easily into any sin.

### 54.3 Third Point

Saint John Chrysostom attributes another effect to Holy Communion that is greater than anything we can imagine and raises us to great heights indeed. It unites us so intimately with Jesus Christ that we become one body with him, the body of Jesus Christ. Many grains of wheat, says the saint, become one bread, and they cannot be distinguished from one another any longer, because they have become the same thing. This is also the effect of food, which produces a union so intimate that it is united substantially with the entire body of the person who consumes it.

Similarly, Jesus Christ unites with you in Holy Communion to transform you into him and to make you be one and the same heart and one and the same mind with him. The interior dispositions in him pass over into you and become your own.

How happy you ought to think you are to be in a state where Communion is received very often, where you can always be one, and only one, with Jesus Christ, possess his Spirit, and act only by him.

---

1. Acts 2:42          2. Lk 11:3

# Friday After the Octave
# of the Most Blessed Sacrament

*Reasons used by some people as pretexts for not receiving Communion often*

### 55.1 First Point

The great benefits that come from receiving Communion often are the reason why the devil does all he can with various false pretexts that he puts into their minds to persuade many people to receive Communion only rarely.

Some fear, they say, to commit a sacrilege. They do well to fear this, but to commit a sacrilege, we must receive Communion in a state of mortal sin. Is it possible that you could be in such a state?

Others claim that they are not worthy to receive Communion so frequently. They must not wait for what will never be; all people who receive Communion, whoever they are, acknowledge their unworthiness before coming to receive.

But, say others, I am so full of defects; how can I dare go to Communion so often in this state? If you wait until you are without defects before receiving Communion, you will not receive Communion in your lifetime.

The fact that you do not fall into more serious faults than those you ordinarily commit is something that you ought to see as a result of frequent Communion. This will encourage you to continue in this practice.

### 55.2 Second Point

Some fear to receive Communion because they are falsely convinced that they derive no benefit from it and that it is an abuse of so great a mystery to take part in it so often with no profit for the good of their soul. Do they count for nothing the fact that Communion preserves them from mortal sin? This is without doubt a priceless favor that ought to make them desire to receive Communion daily.

But, you may say, as others do, that this sacrament contains the essence of holiness and demands great holiness in those who receive it so often. To reason this way is to regard as the preparation for this sacrament what are its effect and its purpose. We go to Communion to become holy, not because we are holy. If you said in like manner that you must be a saint to live in community, you would be told that people come to religious life to become saints, not because they are saints.

Is not the union with Jesus Christ that you obtain by receiving him capable of making you share in his holiness? This is precisely the reason why you ought to receive Communion often.

### 55.3 Third Point

Because the Eucharist is a sacrament of love, in receiving it, we must have a tender love for Jesus Christ. This is why devotion is one of the main dispositions that we ought to bring to this action.

How, then, some say, can I communicate so often, when I do not have any devotion? To receive Communion, it is not necessary to have a sensible fervor. You can be certain that the true and least suspect devotion consists in a great horror for sin.

But when we go to Communion so often, must we not fear to receive Communion out of mere custom? Do you think such a custom is a bad one or that we ought also to forego attending daily Mass for fear of doing so out of custom?

Take great care not to be misled by any of these reasons for excusing yourself from Communion, as long as you do not have any fundamental impediment.

Because you have withdrawn from the world, your first care must be to unite with God. Draw near to him often, then, through Holy Communion; it is the easiest and most sure means that God has left you to unite with him. Even if you feel hesitant about communicating because of your faults, provided that none of them is mortal, be sure that if you go to Communion out of obedience and ask God to eliminate the faults that are in you, your Communion, thanks to your obedience, will be pleasing to God and will draw down upon you many graces.

# Third Sunday After Pentecost

*That the first concern of those who teach children ought to be to help them avoid sin*

### 56.1 First Point

Because you are God's ministers in the work that you have to do, you ought to cooperate with him[1] and enter into his plan to procure the salvation of the children entrusted to you, especially the ones most inclined to lead a wayward life. Today's Gospel tells you that you must watch over these more closely than over those who spontaneously embrace what is right and practice piety. This our Lord teaches when he tells us the parable of the Good Shepherd, who, when one of his one hundred sheep went astray, left the ninety-nine others alone to go searching for the one that was lost.[2]

You must do all you can to help those come back to God who might be subject to some vice, because, as Jesus Christ says, it is not the will of your Father, who is in heaven, that even a single one of these little ones would perish.[3] Because he is the one who employs you to guide them in the way of salvation, see to it that none of them goes astray, or if some do, that they come back without any delay. Your duty is to make them follow the right path.

### 56.2 Second Point

One of the main things that most contributes to the corruption of young people is keeping bad company. Few go astray from malice of heart. The majority are corrupted by bad example and by the circumstances they encounter. This is why there is nothing that those who guide children ought to pay more attention to than to prevent them from being led astray by either of these two causes.

If human weakness is great, because of our inclination to sin, that of children is much greater, because they have little use of their reason and because nature is, consequently, more lively in them and strongly inclined to enjoy the pleasures of the senses. As a result, they can easily be led into sin.

Act, therefore, with all possible care to keep your disciples away from bad companions. See to it that they associate only with good ones, so that in this way, having only good example, they will practice what is good with great ease.

### 56.3 Third Point

God has given us two sure means to keep from sin and to preserve grace, namely, prayer and the sacraments. There is, consequently, nothing that we must more strongly inspire in children to give them a horror for vice than the love of prayer and the frequent use of the sacraments. You must get them to pray to God often and to pray with attention. You must teach them the holy dispositions that they ought to bring to receive the sacraments well and urge them to do so frequently to keep their conscience free from all sin. These are the two main things that you must have in mind in the instructions you give your students to keep them away from sin.

You ought also to pray much to God for those you see less inclined to piety, so that God will put in their hearts a desire for salvation. You are mediators for them, and God uses you to teach them the way they are to be saved.[4] Fulfill, then, the position that God has entrusted to you; otherwise, God will make you accountable for their loss if they fall into disorder for lack of having been kept from sin and encouraged to do good.

---

1. 1 Cor 4:1; 3:9
2. Lk 15:4
3. Mt 18:14
4. 1 Cor 3:5

# Fourth Sunday After Pentecost

## GOSPEL: SAINT LUKE 5:1–11

*That we always succeed in what we do through obedience*

### 57.1 First Point

It frequently happens that what we attempt does not succeed as expected because we undertook it on our own initiative and because we follow no other rule and no other guide than what our own mind is able to propose. This is what today's Gospel gives us to understand in the person of Saint Peter. He told Jesus Christ that he had labored all night without catching a single fish;[1] the reason is that he had acted entirely on his own.

So too it can sometimes happen that you believe you are doing good, and yet you do none at all for you or for others, because in what you undertake, you have no other guide, no other leader, than your own mind. When we act this way, we are laboring in the darkness of night, because often enough our mind merely leads us astray, for the light that is in it is, most of the time, only darkness.[2] Follow a more reliable guide, then, if you do want neither to go astray nor to render all your work useless.

### 57.2 Second Point

Saint Peter had not succeeded in his work when he acted on his own, but as soon as Jesus Christ commanded him to throw the net and pointed out the place he ought to throw it, Peter showed such great submission to what the Savior had just told him that he and his companions caught such a great quantity of fish that the net was about to tear.[3]

There you see the result of obedience. It draws down God's blessing so well on what we do that by this means we obtain whatever we desire; we acquire great facility for doing good and touching hearts when we have the happiness of working for the salvation of souls and do so through simple obedience.

If you fall into many defects, if you do not achieve as much good as you could in your work, blame this on the fact that often you are not sufficiently faithful to the Rule and are not guided enough by obedience. Compare what you do under the motive of obedience with what you do of your own accord, and consider the former as God's work and the latter as human work.

### 57.3  Third Point

People who live in community have this advantage over seculars, that they can say to Jesus Christ every day, with Saint Peter, Lord, it is at your word I am going to let down the net.[4] At your word I am going to do this action, and this is what makes me feel confident that you will bless it and will be pleased with it.

Indeed, it is enough for an action to be performed through obedience for it to please God when it is accomplished with such simplicity that you have in view only to obey. From this it sometimes happens, through a special guidance of God, that an act that was bad in itself becomes good when done through simple obedience.

Because obedience procures such a great advantage, let it be inseparable from all your actions, what makes them worthy of God, and what puts you in a position to do good for the souls you must lead to God and educate as Christians.

---

1. Lk 5:5          3. Lk 5:6          4. Lk 5:5
2. Mt 6:23

# Fifth Sunday After Pentecost

## GOSPEL:  SAINT MATTHEW 5:20-24

*That religious ought to be far more virtuous than secular people*

### 58.1  First Point

In today's Gospel Jesus Christ tells his holy Apostles that unless their virtue surpasses that of the Pharisees, they will not enter the kingdom of heaven.[1] Apply these words to you. Be convinced that Jesus Christ is addressing them to you, that if you do not have more virtue than people in the world, you will be more liable to condemnation than they will be on the day of judgment.

People of the world, like the Pharisees, are satisfied with observing the external and outward practices of religion. They go to Mass, listen to sermons, and sometimes follow the Divine Office, but they do all these things and a number of others without any interior spirit.

You, who gave yourself to God and, consequently, ought to consecrate to God every moment of your life, must do everything in a spirit of religion without being content to do only what is exterior in the duties of your state. Even if people are satisfied with what is external in actions, God, who looks into the heart,[2] will not put any value on them.

### 58.2  Second Point

Some people in the world, who have a certain amount of piety, believe that they have fulfilled their obligations when they do not show any outstanding vices and when their exterior conduct is not wholly reprehensible, but Jesus Christ condemns this attitude in those who claim to be serving him faithfully.

He does not want us to approach him in prayer or to participate in the Eucharist if we entertain the least coldness toward one of our Brothers.[3] He wants us, far from hating our enemies, to love them, to do good to them, and to pray for them.[4]

This is what God requires of you and how he desires that your justice be more than that of people of the world:[5] that you not only keep his commandments exactly but also are faithful to the practice of the counsels of the Gospel and, consequently, to the observance of your Rule. Have you nothing with which to reproach you concerning all these matters?

### 58.3  Third Point

People living in the world think very little about God and have little concern about their salvation. Their sole occupation is usually with their temporal affairs and the needs of the body. It would seem that most have nothing to hope for or to fear beyond this present life. If we speak to them about God, about what leads us to God, about the essential duties of a Christian, about the practice of what is right, and about avoiding occasions of sin and dangerous company, they then have ears and hear nothing,[6] because all they can grasp is what strikes their senses.

You have withdrawn from the world to lead a life above nature and human inclinations and to labor for the salvation of your neighbor; therefore, you must not be attached and devoted to anything but

God and the ministry with which he has honored you. All your concern ought to be concentrated on purely spiritual matters.

---

1. Mt 5:20    3. Mt 5:23    5. Mt 5:20
2. Rom 8:27   4. Lk 6:27–28  6. Ps 115:6

# Sixth Sunday After Pentecost

## GOSPEL: ST. MARK 8:1–9

*That those who have given themselves to God must love mortification and poverty*

### 59.1 First Point

Over four thousand people had followed Jesus Christ into the desert,[1] drawn by the example of his holy life and by the zeal he showed for the conversion of souls in his fervent preaching. These people did not grow weary in our Lord's company, even though they were in a deserted place, had nothing to eat, and could not procure any food. They accompanied him for three whole days[2] without being concerned about the nourishment of their bodies.

If they acted this way, it was because they were convinced, as followers of Jesus Christ, that they ought no longer to be concerned about their bodies but only their souls and that to perfect their souls, they needed to mortify their flesh and to bring it into subjection,[3] as Saint Paul says. The more the body is humbled and mortified and the soul is purified, the more pleasing to God the soul becomes and the more able to acquire the perfection proper to it.

You have left the world to follow Jesus Christ in seclusion. Let all your care be to give yourself entirely to him.

### 59.2 Second Point

Jesus Christ, seeing that these people took no care for their bodily nourishment, took care of it and undertook to provide for those who had consecrated themselves entirely to him.

It is right to let him act in such circumstances, because the more fully we abandon ourselves to the care of Providence, the more attentive God is not to let us want for anything.

A marvelous thing indeed! During three days these people did not say a single word to complain or to show their distress, because it was enough that Jesus Christ knew their needs.

Has he ever abandoned those whose only desire is to please him and who think only of following him?

Is this the way you look upon your relationship with him? Are you so firmly attached to Jesus Christ that you no longer think of yourself? Is it your one concern to nourish your soul on the maxims of the holy Gospel by studying how to put them into practice and by being devoted with so much affection to what promotes your spiritual advancement that you neglect the needs of your body?

### 59.3  Third Point

Admire the goodness of Jesus Christ regarding these people who had followed him. I have compassion on these people,[4] he said, and he performed a miracle to feed all of them. He multiplied the seven loaves to be able to feed such a great number of people. All could eat their fill, and a great deal remained left over.[5]

In like manner God fed the Jewish people in the desert during forty years. In all that time, no one had to make any effort during so many years to provide for his own needs.[6]

Similarly, God will furnish you with all that you need, if your only thought is to be sanctified and to fulfill well the duties of your state. This is why God told Saint Catherine of Siena that she ought to think of him and that he would think of her.

God, who created all people, desires them to receive what they need, and when other means fail, God provides for them. In your state you are doing God's work.[7] Rest assured that he will take care of you, provided that you serve him faithfully and omit nothing that he asks of you.

---

1. Mk 8:9
2. Mk 8:2
3. 1 Cor 9:27

4. Mk 8:2
5. Mk 8:8
6. See Neh 9:21

7. 1 Cor 3:9

# Seventh Sunday After Pentecost

## GOSPEL: SAINT MATTHEW 7:15-21

*That holiness does not consist in the habit worn but in actions*

### 60.1 First Point

In today's Gospel Jesus Christ says that many have the coat of sheep, but beneath this coat ravening wolves are hiding.[1] This happens sometimes in the holiest communities, which is why the Council of Trent says that the habit does not make the religious.

This habit, simple and plain, gives a pious and reserved appearance that edifies the world and imposes a certain external restraint on those who wear it.

It is a holy habit because it is an exterior sign of the commitment made by those who wear it to live a holy life.

If it is true that this habit ought to remind them constantly of this, it is also true that it is not this habit that makes them holy; it happens only too often that it serves to cover great faults.

Consider seriously whether you *laid aside all* the false maxims of the world when you *gave up its clothing* and whether when you put on a new habit, you also renewed yourself in spirit.[2] If you have entirely *renounced the practices of people of the world,* your life, as well as your habit, ought to be entirely different from theirs.[3]

### 60.2 Second Point

The Gospel adds that we must be concerned not about the clothing we wear but about the harvest we produce. You will know, it says, by the results.[4]

You must produce two kinds of fruit. The harvest of grace in your own regard consists in the holiness of your actions. Because you wear a habit entirely different from that in the world, you ought to be a new man, created in justice and holiness,[5] as Saint Paul says.

Everything about you, within and without, ought to reveal the holiness to which your profession obliges you. Your exterior must be holy because it must be edifying. You must be so recollected, self-controlled, and reserved that it is clear that God dwells in you and that you have only God in view in all your conduct.

Your actions ought to be holy, done through a holy motive, with attention to God and according to the Rule prescribed for you, which is the proper means to sanctify you. Such is the harvest that you must produce in the state where God has placed you.

### 60.3  Third Point

There are other benefits that you ought to realize regarding the children whom you are required to instruct. Your duty obliges you to teach them their religion. If they do not know it because you do not know it well or because you are careless in teaching it to them, you are a false prophet. You are responsible for making God known to them, but you allow them to be in an ignorance liable to damn them because of your negligence.

You must inspire them with horror for vice and for all that can lead them astray. Perhaps you take little care whether they associate with bad companions, abandon themselves to gambling, or spend a great part of the day in thoughtless behavior and disorderly conduct. In that case you are for them a false prophet who produces only bad results.[6]

You ought to try to procure for them a spirit of piety and help them love prayer and be attentive in church and in devout practices. Thus, if they show themselves to be distracted in church, lacking self-control, not praying to God, or praying without devotion, people will be able to see by their exterior conduct that you lack piety and that because you produce no good,[7] you are unable to help others produce any good.

---

| | | |
|---|---|---|
| 1. Mt 7:15 | 4. Mt 7:16 | 7. Mt 7:19 |
| 2. Eph 4:22–23 | 5. Eph 4:24 | |
| 3. Eph 4:17 | 6. Mt 7:15–17 | |

# Eighth Sunday After Pentecost

## GOSPEL:  SAINT LUKE 16:1–9

*The account you must give on the manner in which you have done your work*

### 61.1  First Point

A manager was accused of wasting the property of his employer, who called him and said: What is this that I hear about you? Give me an account of your management.[1]

You are in a holy work where God has placed you. You must be convinced that these words are addressed to you. At the close of each day and at the end of each performance of your work, you ought to reflect that God calls you to give him an account of the way you have behaved. For this reason you must reflect on and examine this account, so that you will always be ready to give it. You must act in such a way that God, to whom you have to make this report, will find no fault with it.

If you wait to prepare your account until God comes to ask it of you, you must greatly fear that he will find you wanting.

### 61.2  Second Point

You have two accounts to give to God regarding the spiritual good you ought to achieve in your work. The first has to do with your duty to teach catechism and the Gospel maxims to the children. Not one of your students must go without being instructed in his religion; it is, above all, for this purpose that the Church entrusts them to you.

This is why you must regard yourselves as people to whom the deposit of the faith has been confided,[2] so that you can pass it on to them. This is the good that God has placed in your hands and of which he has made you the manager.

In the account God will require of you, will he not find many of the children ignorant of the principal mysteries of religion? If he does, you will be more to blame than they are, because by your negligence you have caused this ignorance in these children. Faith, according to Saint Paul, is communicated only through hearing, and what is heard is nothing less than the word of Jesus Christ.[3]

### 61.3  Third Point

The second account you must give will have to do with piety, whether you take care to impart it to your disciples: whether they are self-controlled and reserved in church, whether they pray to God all the time they are there, whether they do not talk there, whether they do not sometimes play there, whether they pray to God every morning and evening, whether when they pray in school they pray with attention, whether they have a horror for taking oaths and improper language, whether they respect their parents and obey them faithfully, whether they avoid bad companions, whether you encourage them in all these practices, whether you watch diligently over their behavior as far as necessary to help them carry out these practices, whether you take care that they go to Confession from time to time, and whether you obtain good confessors for them.

Because you are responsible for the good of their souls, God will ask you for an account of all these things.[4] Are you ready to give it? Is there nothing about which your conscience feels uneasy? For in these matters you are taking the place of the pastors of the Church and their fathers and mothers.

---

1. Lk 16:1–2        3. Rom 10:17        4. Heb 13:17
2. 1 Tim 6:20

# Ninth Sunday After Pentecost

## GOSPEL: SAINT LUKE 19:41–47

### 62.1 First Point

Entering the Temple of Jerusalem, Jesus Christ found people there who were selling and buying, thus profaning the Temple of the living God. He drove them out, telling them that his house is a house of prayer and that they are making it a den of thieves.[1]

You are here in a house of prayer, and prayer ought to be your principal occupation. God's Spirit will not reside here, and God will not pour out his blessings here, except insofar as it will be a house of prayer. When you lose the spirit and the love of prayer, God will look upon you with displeasure as someone who is both unworthy of a work that is his own work[2] and like those who make his house a den of thieves.

Is it not to be a thief to attribute to ourselves a work such as preserving souls in innocence or converting them? Such work can belong to God alone and to those whom he employs for it, who belong entirely to him and have recourse to him continually to procure so great a good.

If, then, you do not belong to God, if you do not frequently turn to God in prayer, if you teach only external matters to children, and if you do not put all your care to give them the spirit of religion, must you not be considered by God as a thief who has broken into his house, who remains there without his consent, and who, instead of inspiring students with the Christian spirit as you ought to do, only teaches them things that will be of use to them in this world?

### 62.2 Second Point

Not only do you live in a house of prayer but also your body is a house of prayer. *Do you not know,* as Saint Paul says, *that your body is the temple of the Holy Spirit, who dwells in you, who has been given to you by God, and that you are no longer your own since you have been bought at a great price?* From this Saint Paul concludes, Glorify God, therefore, and bear him in your body.[3] This is true if your body is a house of prayer. In this same spirit and in this sentiment, Saint Paul in another passage implores you, by the mercy of God, to offer God your body as a living sacrifice, holy and acceptable in his eyes.[4]

Do you sometimes reflect on what a blessing it is for you that the Holy Spirit dwells in your body as in his temple and that he prays in you and for you?[5] Do you surrender entirely to this divine Spirit, so that he may ask of God all you need to have for the good of your own soul and for those in your care and so that you may act only by him?

### 62.3 Third Point

The Holy Spirit, who dwells in you, must penetrate the depths of your soul, where this Holy Spirit ought especially to pray.

In the interior of the soul, this Spirit communicates and unites with the soul and makes known what God asks in order to belong entirely to him.[6]

There he shares with the soul his divine love, by which he honors holy souls, those who are no longer attached to earth.

When they are disengaged from all affection for creatures, he makes them his sanctuary, helping them to be constantly attentive to God, living only in God and for God.

Because Jesus Christ is your Mediator[7] and because you can go to God only through him,[8] beg him that he will always be in your soul to pray in it and to guide it to him. Ask him to make his dwelling in your soul as in his temple throughout time, so that your soul may then make its home in him throughout all eternity.

---

1. Mt 21:12–13
2. 1 Cor 3:9
3. 1 Cor 6:19–20
4. Rom 12:1
5. Rom 8:26
6. Rom 8:27
7. 1 Tim 2:5; Heb 8:6
8. Jn 14:6

# Tenth Sunday After Pentecost

## GOSPEL: SAINT LUKE 18:9–14

*Self-contempt*

### 63.1 First Point

One thing that contributes the most to the acquisition of virtue is self-contempt, for the source of all sin, says the Wise Man, is pride[1] and the good opinion of yourself. There is no one, however holy, however richly endowed with grace, who ought not to feel contempt for himself and for everything about himself.

What contempt does he not deserve whose very being is not his own but belongs to God, who gave it to him and who can take it back and annihilate him whenever it may please him!

What esteem can we feel for man, whose life is only sin, and who of himself can never free himself from it!

Such is your condition; yet it seems, to hear you speak, that you are something! Do not imitate the Pharisee, who instead of praying to God, thought only of praising and congratulating himself.[2]

### 63.2 Second Point

Seeing that most people are so filled with themselves that generally if they speak, it is of themselves and in their favor, Jesus Christ proposes to us today in his Gospel the parable of a publican and a Pharisee. *The latter pretended to pray, but his mind was full of nothing but his good qualities, and the former, considering himself a miserable sinner, humbly begged God for mercy and was justified* because of the simple and humble manner in which he prayed. The other man, on the contrary, reaped only confusion,[3] because he had insulted God instead of praying to God.

This is the model that Jesus Christ gives you, which must frequently be before your eyes to induce you never to speak or to think about you and, when thinking of yourself in God's presence, to do so only to be humbled and to seek the means to correct your defects. When you pray, often say with David, my sin is always before me.[4]

### 63.3 Third Point

It is impossible to carry self-contempt too far. Saint Francis, great saint that he was, called himself the world's greatest sinner. Others have done things unbecoming a human being in order to draw down contempt upon themselves.

You who have crucified Jesus Christ by your sins,[5] imitate him by thoughts of humility;[6] look at yourself with the eyes of faith, and pay attention only to what can inspire in you lowly thoughts about you in relation to God and to others.

Because God gives his grace to the humble,[7] contempt for you, coming from outside or from within, must be your lot, and you must find your satisfaction in it.

You have many opportunities for this in your state and in your work. To encourage you to profit fully by them, regard them as among the best means to be sanctified; consider that you are the weakest of all people and the least capable of doing any good. Thank God for the grace he gives you to be despised, to be covered with opprobrium and calumnies, and never show any esteem for what you do, for it is God, by his goodness and his grace, who is the author of all the good there is in you.[8]

---

1. Sir 10:13
2. Lk 18:11
3. Lk 18:11–14

4. Ps 51:5
5. Heb 6:6
6. Phil 2:5–6

7. 1 Pt 5:5
8. Phil 2:13

# Eleventh Sunday After Pentecost

## GOSPEL: SAINT MARK 7:31–37

*Spiritual deafness*

### 64.1 First Point

In today's Gospel Jesus Christ cures a deaf-mute.[1] This man represents three kinds of deaf people who can be found occasionally in communities. The first group includes those who are deaf to God's inspirations, either the inspirations that lead them to observe their Rule faithfully (the only thing that can maintain in them the grace of their state) or those that lead them to practice something special that God is asking of them.

The second kind of deafness is found in those who are deaf to the voice of their superiors. Because obedience is what draws down on a community the greatest abundance of graces, both communal and individual, and because it is the best way to preserve the grace of God there, this kind of deafness, unless early efforts are made to remedy it, nearly always becomes incurable.

The third kind of deaf people are those who cannot hear God spoken of or who cannot appreciate his word in reading sacred books or books of piety. The consequence is that they never give themselves to God, because it is ordinarily the reading of holy and pious books that fills us with his Spirit.

What efforts our Savior has to make to cure these types of deafness! The reason for this is that he no longer finds the fervor of his grace in people so afflicted. *He needs to draw them aside*, because it is only in seclusion that they will dispose themselves to listen to God's voice. Jesus then raises his eyes to heaven, heaves a great sigh, puts his fingers into the deaf man's ears, and says, Be opened.[2] Oh, how difficult and rare it is to cure a soul when this deafness is firmly established!

### 64.2  Second Point

This man whom Jesus Christ cured was both mute and deaf. Just as there are three kinds of deaf people, there are also three kinds of mute people. The first are those who do not know how to speak to God. The reason for this is that there is no communication between God and them.

We learn to speak to God only by listening to him, for to know how to speak to God and to converse with him can only come from God, who has his own language, which is special to him and which he shares only with his friends and confidants, to whom he gives the happiness of frequently conversing with him.

The second kind of mute people are those who are unable to speak about God. There are many people like this; they rarely think of God and hardly know him, because they are full of the thoughts of the world and of worldly amusements. They cannot, as Saint Paul says, grasp the things of God[3] and are as little able to speak about him and of what concerns him as are newborn children.

The third kind of mute people are those whom God has not favored with the gift of tongues,[4] who cannot speak for God. The gift of tongues is the ability to speak in order to attract souls to God, to procure conversion,[5] and to tell everyone what he needs to hear. For God does not win over all souls by the same means; we need to know how to speak in the right way to each one of them[6] in order to engage them to give themselves entirely to God.

Because you are in charge of instructing children, you ought to become an expert in the art of speaking to God, speaking about God, and speaking for God. Be convinced that you will never speak well to your students and win them over to God except insofar as you have learned well how to speak to God and to speak about God.

### 64.3 Third Point

It is not enough to know about the different kinds of deaf and mute people; you must also know the remedies that can cure them. As a rule, it is deafness that leads to muteness; consequently, it is easier to cure a mute person than a deaf one, because as soon as the deaf man is able to hear, he right away is able to speak.

Also for this reason, the man mentioned in today's Gospel recovered the use of his tongue before that of his ears. To enable him to speak, Jesus Christ merely had to place some saliva on the tongue in his mouth; at once the tongue was unloosed, and he spoke very distinctly.[7]

To cure his deafness, Jesus Christ placed his fingers in the deaf man's ears,[8] which indicates that Jesus Christ must touch a soul interiorly to make that person hear, understand, and appreciate what he says.

He had to take the man aside, so that the noise of the world could not prevent him from hearing his words and appreciating them.

Then he raised his eyes to heaven and heaved a deep sigh[9] to show how much he suffers before God because of the blindness of this soul caused by its spiritual deafness.

He even had to make an effort and say in a loud voice in the deaf man's ears, Be opened.[10] This he did to open his ears wide enough to hear the words of Jesus Christ easily and to become docile to them.

He cured the mute by placing some saliva on his tongue to show him that it would be of little use to speak unless he spoke wisely.

Let your ears, then, be always open and attentive to God's word; learn to speak little and to speak only with wisdom.

---

1. Mk 7:32
2. Mk 7:33–34
3. 1 Cor 2:14
4. Acts 2:4
5. Acts 2:41
6. Acts 2:8
7. Mk 7:33
8. Mk 7:33
9. Mk 7:34
10. Mk 7:34

# Twelfth Sunday After Pentecost

## GOSPEL: SAINT LUKE 10:23-37

*The union that ought to exist among Brothers*

### 65.1 First Point

In today's Gospel Jesus Christ proposes to us an example of charity. There was a Samaritan who came upon a man lying half dead on the roadside; he bound up his wounds and left him with an inn-keeper to be cared for until he recovered completely.[1] Our Savior, in detailing for us all that this charitable man did, gives us a clear picture of the kind of charity we ought to have for our Brothers and how closely we ought to be united with one another.

This is one of the things we must take most to heart because, as Saint Paul says, if you do not have charity, whatever good you may do will profit you nothing.[2]

Experience brings home to us the truth of this saying. A community without charity and union is a hell: one grumbles; another slanders his Brother because of the ill-will he feels toward him; another gets angry because someone has irritated him; another complains to his superior about what one of his Brothers has done to him. All we hear, in short, are accusations, murmuring, and backbiting, which of course cause much irritation and disquiet.

The only remedy for all these disorders is union and charity, because charity is patient, as Saint Paul says.[3] This holy Apostle even desires that patience, which is the result of charity, must go so far as to endure all things.[4] Whoever says "all" makes no exceptions.

If, then, we have charity and union with our Brothers and must endure all things from everyone, we can no longer say, I cannot put up with this from that person; I cannot stand such a defect in this other one; he has to give in to my whims or my weakness in something. To speak like this is not to endure all things from everyone. Think carefully over this maxim, and practice it exactly.

### 65.2 Second Point

Charity is kind;[5] this is the second characteristic given to charity by Saint Paul. It is not by scolding, murmuring, complaining aloud, or quarreling that we show our love and union. It is by speaking in a kind and affable way, in humbling ourself before our Brothers. A kind word, says the Wise Man, turns away wrath, while a harsh reply stirs up fury.[6]

For this reason, our Lord, in the Sermon on the Mount, said to his Apostles: Blessed are those who show kindness toward others, for they will possess the land.[7] This means the whole earth, because those who possess the hearts of others do possess the whole earth, which is what people whose temperament is kind and moderate easily achieve. They gain entry so well into the hearts of those with whom they speak and relate that they win them over, little by little, and obtain from them whatever they desire. That is how we gain possession of hearts and get them to do whatever we wish. In this way those who were born with this fortunate disposition or have acquired it with the help of grace make themselves, as it were, masters of others and turn them whichever way they like.

Oh, what a great advantage it is to learn well and to practice well this lesson given us by our Lord: Learn of me, for I am kind and humble of heart![8]

However, this is not the only benefit we can derive from kindness. The main one is that through it we can acquire the most exalted virtues. By it we restrain our passions and prevent them from breaking out of our control; by it we will in the end succeed in preserving union with our Brothers.

Never speak to anyone except with kindness, and if you fear to speak otherwise, keep silent.

### 65.3 Third Point

Charity is generous;[9] this is the third quality attributed to charity by Saint Paul. Also by this quality, the Samaritan of the Gospel showed the goodness of his heart. Finding this poor man, whom bandits had robbed, covered with wounds and left half dead, he was so moved that after pouring oil and wine on the victim's wounds and bandaging them, he put him on his own horse and brought him to an inn, where he took care of him for some time. When he had to leave, he made the innkeeper responsible to look after him with great care, gave him two silver coins, and assured him that on his return he would pay him for the entire expense.[10]

Admire the extreme charity of this good Samaritan. He was a foreigner among the Jews; people from his country were considered as schismatics by the Jews, and each hated the other. Still, this Samaritan did everything he could for the unfortunate traveler, whom a priest and a Levite, both Jews, had not even wanted to look at. He even showed a great disinterestedness in his charity, for after all he had done to help this poor man, he gave money to the innkeeper to care for him, and he promised him that when he came back, he would pay for all that he had spent on this man.[11]

This is also one of the conditions that Saint Paul requires for true and genuine charity. He wants it to be disinterested.[12] However, it often happens, even in communities, that we do a service for a Brother because he has done one for us or that we refuse a service, or at least do not do it willingly, because something about the Brother irritates us: he has given us trouble, or he has irked us in some way. Oh, how human is such charity, how little Christian; how little does it deserve to be called generous!

---

1. Lk 10:30–35
2. 1 Cor 13:3
3. 1 Cor 13:4
4. 1 Cor 13:7
5. 1 Cor 13:4
6. Prv 15:1
7. Mt 5:4
8. Mt 11:29
9. 1 Cor 13:4 The third quality of charity in Saint Paul's list (in the original Greek as well as in English translations) is "not jealous." Where did De La Salle find generous *(bienfaisante)* to be the third quality? It is not in the 1668 New Testament presumably used by him (CL 47, pp. 16ff) in writing these meditations. However, this word is in the 1708 edition by the same translator, which might indicate that he was using this later edition.
10. Lk 10:30ff
11. Lk 10:35
12. 1 Cor 13:5

# Thirteenth Sunday After Pentecost

## GOSPEL: SAINT LUKE 17:11–19

*Temptations to impurity and how to overcome them*

### 66.1 First Point

The ten lepers who presented themselves to Jesus Christ, as today's Gospel relates, are figures for us of temptations to impurity, because leprosy is a disease that makes the body unclean and corrupt.[1] The manner in which our Lord cured the lepers shows us the most sure remedies that we can use to be rid of this trouble. The Gospel reports that these lepers, seeing Jesus Christ from a distance, stopped and raised their voices, saying to him: Jesus, Master, have pity on us![2]

The lepers kept their distance.[3] This detail shows us how far removed impure people are from our Lord, who, being pure, does not want to have any association with those who even to the least degree manifest this vice, just as lepers were not allowed to have any association with other Jews.

They cried out in a loud voice to beg Jesus Christ to have compassion on them. This reminds us of what our Lord says in another place in the Gospel, that the first remedy for impurity and for the temptations that lead to it is to have recourse to prayer.[4] These clamorous, insistent voices are a figure of the fervor and the insistence with which we ought to pray to obtain the cure of this infirmity.

According to the Wise Man, we cannot be pure unless God gives us the grace for it;[5] therefore, we cannot ask this of him too often or with too much earnestness, because this malady is very dangerous and has very unfortunate consequences. If you sometimes feel tormented by impure thoughts, do not cease imploring God until you are completely delivered from them.

### 66.2 Second Point

The second remedy that the Gospel proposes and that *Jesus Christ orders the lepers to use* is to go show themselves to the priests.[6] The Old Law prescribed that when lepers were cleansed, they must let the priests see them, so that they could learn whether the leprosy was indeed healed. If it had been cured, these priests gave permission for them to associate with other Jews.[7]

But in the New Law, the prescriptions of Jesus Christ have quite a different power than those given by Moses. For when Jesus Christ ordered the ten lepers to go and show themselves to the priests, they were cured of their shameful illness; they were perfectly cured while on their way.[8]

In a community we must manifest our malady to our superiors and make ourselves known just as we are. This is an effective means for obtaining a prompt cure. This is what Saint Dorotheus, a skilled master in guiding souls, says that he experienced in his own case. He declares that the impure spirit fears nothing so much as to be exposed; when he has been discovered, he cannot harm us any more.

The saint adds that a soul finds security by the declaration it makes of all its inner dispositions. When the superior tells it to do this or not to do that, this is good or that is bad, the devil no longer finds an opening to penetrate the heart of the ailing soul. Its salvation lies in the care that it takes to be open with its superior and to act in all things according to the superior's advice. Be faithful, then, to this practice because it is so effective.

### 66.3 Third Point

In the Old Law, *when lepers were cured*, they were commanded to offer a sacrifice before associating with others, in order to purify themselves exteriorly of the legal impurity contracted by leprosy.[9] This sacrifice is a symbol of the mortification that Jesus Christ recommends as a remedy for the lepers we are speaking about, those who are afflicted by the leprosy of impurity or who are attacked by the impure devil. *Jesus Christ even says that we cannot be completely cured of this infirmity* or entirely delivered from these temptations except through fasting,[10] that is, mortification.

By this sacrifice *we offer God our body*, to use an expression of Saint Paul, as a living victim, holy and acceptable to God.[11] Mortification procures for us this advantage, to make the body share in the life of the spirit, which made Saint Paul also say: *If by the Spirit you mortify the flesh and all its actions, you will live. On the contrary*, as the same Apostle adds, *if you live according to the flesh* and if you give in to the flesh to satisfy its senses, you will die.[12] Impurity, in other words, by making you die to the life of grace, will pervert your spirit and make it in some way wholly material, and your soul will become like that of animals.

Let mortification, then, be for you the perpetual sacrifice that was prescribed in the Old Law.[13] Always carry about in your body, as Saint Paul says, the mortification of Jesus Christ, so that the life of Jesus Christ may also be revealed in your body.[14] This is the admirable effect that this excellent sacrifice will produce in you.

---

| | | |
|---|---|---|
| 1. Lv 13:45–46 | 6. Lk 17:14 | 11. Rom 12:1 |
| 2. Lk 17:12–13 | 7. See Lv 14:1–32 | 12. Rom 8:13 |
| 3. Lv 13:46 | 8. Lk 17:14 | 13. See Lv 6:1ff |
| 4. Mk 9:29 | 9. See Lv 14:10–20 | 14. 2 Cor 4:10 |
| 5. Wis 8:21 | 10. Mk 9:29 | |

# Fourteenth Sunday After Pentecost

## GOSPEL: SAINT MATTHEW 6:24-33

*Abandonment to Providence*

### 67.1 First Point

To you especially Jesus Christ addresses these words of today's Gospel: Seek first the kingdom of God.[1] You ought not to have come to this community except to seek here the reign of God: first, for you, and second, for those whose instruction God has entrusted to you. Here you ought to seek only to establish this reign of God within your soul, both in this life and in the next.

For this present life, you must not be concerned about anything except to make God reign in your heart by his grace and by the fullness of his love. It is for God that you ought to be living; it is the life of God that ought to be the life of your soul.

You nourish the life of your soul with God's life by being occupied with his holy presence as much as you are able. What characterizes the life of the saints is their continual attention to God; this ought also to be true of souls consecrated to God, who seek only to do his holy will, to love him, and to cause him to be loved by others.

This must be your entire preoccupation on earth; to accomplish this ought to be the goal of all your work. Hence, help those you teach to regard sin as a shameful sickness that infects their souls and makes them unworthy to draw near to God and to appear before him. Inspire them with love for virtue; impress upon them sentiments of piety, and see to it that God does not cease to reign in them. Then they will have nothing to do with sin, or at least they will avoid serious sins, which cause death to the soul.

Often recall to mind the purpose of your vocation, and let this inspire you to do your part to establish and to maintain the kingdom of God in the hearts of your students. Do you reflect that one of your best ways to procure such an advantage is, first of all, to make God reign in your students in such a way that they no longer act or have any inclination except by God?

### 67.2 Second Point

To focus your attention only on how to make God reign in you and in the souls of those whom you instruct, it is important not to be taken up with the needs of your body, because these two kinds of concerns do not go well together at all. Preoccupation with external things destroys in a soul the care for those things that refer to God and his service.

This is why Jesus Christ, when he entrusts the salvation of the world and the establishment of his kingdom on earth to his Apostles, recommends in the same Gospel that they not be anxious, saying, What will we eat? What will we drink? What are we to wear? Such concerns are proper only to pagans.[2] Insofar as they are so disturbed by such things, they show that they have no faith.

To give them a convincing proof of this, he says, Look at the birds in the sky. They do not sow or reap; they gather nothing into barns. Consider also the lilies of the field. They neither work nor spin; nevertheless, not even Solomon in all his glory was ever clothed like them.[3]

Have you, then, so little faith as to fear that if you accomplish your duty and are devoted entirely to bring about God's reign in your heart and in the hearts of others, God would allow you to lack something necessary for you to live and to be clothed?

### 67.3  Third Point

Jesus Christ assures you that God will take charge of providing your food and your support. Your heavenly Father, he says, knows that you need all these things.[4] He is the one who feeds the birds of the sky. Are you not far more valuable than they? Are you not far dearer to him than birds?[5]

If God, he adds, takes care to clothe the grass of the field, which is underfoot today and will be cut down tomorrow, with how much more care will he not clothe you, O man of little faith![6]

Be convinced, concludes Jesus Christ, that if you truly seek the kingdom of God and his justice, all these things will be given to you besides,[7] because God takes responsibility for the care to provide for you. As Saint Paul says, You shall not muzzle the ox that treads out the grain.[8]

If, then, you are devoted to work in the harvest of souls,[9] how can you fear that the One who employs you in this task as his coworker[10] will refuse you the food that you need to do his work? The more you are abandoned to God for what concerns your temporal needs, the more care he will take to provide for you.

If, on the contrary, you want to provide for yourself in these matters, God will leave you with the concern to do so, and it could often happen that you will be in need; God will want to punish you for your lack of faith and for your distrust.

Do, then, what David says: Turn your thoughts to God; place all your trust in him, and he will feed you.[11]

---

| | | |
|---|---|---|
| 1. Mt 6:33 | 5. Mt 6:26 | 9. Mt 9:37–38 |
| 2. Mt 6:31–32 | 6. Mt 6:30 | 10. 1 Cor 3:9 |
| 3. Mt 6:26, 28–29 | 7. Mt 6:33 | 11. Ps 55:23 |
| 4. Mt 6:32 | 8. 1 Cor 9:8 | |

# Fifteenth Sunday After Pentecost

## GOSPEL: SAINT LUKE 7:11–16

*That those who have given up the spirit of their state must take the means to regain it*

### 68.1 First Point

Today's Gospel relates that a young man from the town of Naim, whose mother was a widow, was being carried out to be buried.[1] This Gospel admirably portrays the plight of those who have lost the grace of their state.

The deceased was a young man who by his tender years represents for you those in whom piety has not yet struck deep roots[2] and whose hearts are not yet firmly set on what is good. This makes them think, without good reason, that they will easily save themselves elsewhere, that they have spent enough time away from the occasions of sin, and that when they are again exposed to them, they will be strong enough not to succumb.

A person dies quickly when, being ill, he does not believe that he is sick or when he imagines that he can cure himself by his own effort and with no medicine. This is what the devil ordinarily suggests to those who fall into this kind of temptation and who are not docile to the advice of their superiors. They sink into such an extremity that their malady becomes incurable, and they cannot help abandoning the holy state that they had embraced.

Have you not sometimes been or are you not now in this deplorable disposition? If so, grieve before God on account of it, and beg him earnestly to rescue you as quickly as possible, because the remedy for this illness needs to be applied promptly.

## 68.2  Second Point

They were carrying the young man out to be buried.[3] The end result and the final effect of this spiritual death is to bury the soul attacked by it.

These souls think of nothing but the earth, that is, of the world and the things of the world, because they no longer have any taste for God and for what leads to him. To hear God spoken of is for them a torture; to spend time in prayer is a martyrdom. Communion is insipid; they stay away from Confession because they do not want to make their sickness known.

They are guided only by their own light, and their light is false. Thus all the means that help to maintain the life of the Spirit are useless in their case because they reject them. This results from their having lost the spirit of the life that they once possessed, which is the spirit of their state.

The crowd of people who accompanied the dead man as he was being carried out to be buried[4] represents those who urge you to go back into the world. Bereft of grace, what good advice can they give you? Yet some people believe what these people of the world say and follow the action they propose all the more readily because what they are trying to advance is more agreeable to the inclination of corrupt nature. Oh, what a sorry state! What a sad situation! Beg God fervently not to abandon you to such an extent.

## 68.3  Third Point

Jesus Christ, drawing near to the dead man, touched the litter, and those who carried it stood still. Then he said to this young man, I bid you, get up. Immediately the dead man sat up, uncovered his face, and began to speak. Then Jesus gave him back to his mother.[5]

These words make known the means to recover the grace of our vocation. The first is to resort to prayer to bring Jesus Christ near to us. The second is to stop the flow of all the thoughts that have led us to the brink of the precipice. The third is to listen to the voice of Jesus Christ, who speaks to us through our superiors. The fourth is to raise ourselves up to God as soon as we hear his word.

In this way and little by little, we recover the spirit of our state and begin again to fulfill the duties expected of us. Then Jesus will give us back to our mother, which is our community to which we have committed ourselves. The community will again regard us as beloved children, and we will be for our Brothers a source of consolation and edification.

This is what ought to be done by those who have lost or have put themselves in danger of losing their vocation and, as a result, of losing God's grace and of falling into a disorderly life, the inevitable consequence of this loss.

---

1. Lk 7:12
2. Mt 13:21

3. Lk 7:12
4. Lk 7:12

5. Lk 7:14–15

# Sixteenth Sunday After Pentecost

## GOSPEL: SAINT LUKE 14:1-11

*The obligation of Brothers to edify their neighbor*

### 69.1 First Point

It is told in the Gospel of today that when Jesus went into the house of a leader of the Pharisees to take a meal with him, those who were there watched him maliciously.[1] You are in a work that allows everyone to observe you and, consequently, that obliges you to practice the advice Saint Paul gave to Titus, his disciple, the bishop of Crete. He told him to make himself in all things a model of good works in his teaching by his irreproachable morals, the good example of his behavior, and his seriousness.[2]

In the first place, your students observe you; this is why you are obliged to give them good example by your teaching, imitating our Lord in this, who, according to what Saint Luke tells us in the Acts of the Apostles, began to do before teaching.[3]

This is also something that will make you esteemed by your students; this is why, to accomplish your duties worthily in their regard, it is important that your actions teach them more than your words do. As the same Saint Paul adds to Titus, *Let your words be without reproach, not only as to sound doctrine but also as a sign and effect of your virtue.* Those whom you instruct, then, as Saint Paul adds, will not find anything to criticize in what you tell them,[4] seeing that it conforms with what you do.

Is this how you act? Do you teach your disciples anything you do not practice? When you tell them to be self-controlled, are you the very first to act that way? When you urge them to pray to God with piety, do you do so? Do you have the same charity for them that you want them to have for their companions? By conduct of this sort, you will be a model of good works in all things, especially in what concerns doctrine.

### 69.2 Second Point

Because you are living with your Brothers under the same Rule and the same uniform behavior, they observe you constantly, and so it is especially to them that you ought to be an example in all things. Because scandal is dangerous and extremely harmful in a community, watch carefully that you do not give any occasion for it in the ordinary actions you perform every day with your Brothers, lest you become responsible for the faults that they might commit because of your bad example.

There might be some weak people among you on whom your way of acting with little respect for the Rule and destructive of good order could make a bad impression and be an occasion for them to fall into disregard for the Rule. This is why Jesus Christ says in the Gospel that it would be better to have a millstone put around our neck and for us to be thrown into the sea rather than to scandalize the least of the children[5] confided to our care. What frightful words for a soul who fears to offend God or to have others offend him!

Often reflect that you must be a model of innocence and fervor for your Brothers. You must keep your Rule exactly, not only to take the means given to you by God for your own salvation but also to edify your Brothers.

### 69.3 Third Point

The profession you exercise places you under the obligation of being among people of the world every day, where even the least of your actions is observed. This ought to motivate you not to omit anything to be an example of all kinds of virtues in the eyes of the secular people among whom you must live.

You ought to seek to edify them particularly by your seriousness and self-control. If they notice in you any signs of levity or thoughtlessness, they will easily be scandalized, whereas if you go among them in a reserved manner, they will have a high regard for you.

To this might be added what the Wise Man says, that people judge others by their external appearance.[6] So people will readily come to the conclusion that there is little piety and recollection in you whenever they see you in thoughtless behavior. But if you show a simple and serious exterior, people will soon conclude that your inner life too is well-controlled and that there is reason to believe that you are fit to educate your disciples in the Christian spirit.

See, then, how important it is for you and for the honor of your work to show a self-controlled exterior when you are among people of the world, if you wish to edify them.

---

| | | |
|---|---|---|
| 1. Lk 14:1 | 3. Acts 1:1 | 5. Lk 17:2 |
| 2. Ti 2:7 | 4. Ti 2:1, 7–8 | 6. Sir 19:26 |

# Seventeenth Sunday After Pentecost

## GOSPEL: SAINT MATTHEW 22:34–46

*The manner in which we ought to love God*

### 70.1 First Point

When a doctor of the Law asked Jesus Christ what is the greatest commandment in the Law, Jesus answered him: You shall love the Lord your God with all your heart, with all your soul, with all your mind, and with all your strength.[1] This is indeed a great commandment, for its scope is very great, and the manner in which Jesus Christ says we must love God requires great courage of us. This will form the subject of our reflections today.

We must, then, first *love God with all our heart*, that is, with all our affection, without reserving even the smallest part of it for any creature. We must desire wholeheartedly to love only God, who alone is lovable, because God alone is essentially good.

To love anything other than God is to wrong him and to prefer something that is infinitely beneath him. If a creature has some goodness or lovableness in it, this is only an overflow from and a participation in the goodness that comes from God, a goodness that belongs uniquely to God and that God imparts to his creature.

Besides, because God is infinitely good and the inexhaustible source of all created goodness, we are not allowed to give ourselves and to yield our heart completely to anything but God, because everything has been created for God. If we love anything in creatures, it ought to be loved in God, in whom we will find all that is lovable in creatures as in their source.

### 70.2 Second Point

It is not possible for us to love God with all our heart without loving him also with all our soul.[2] This means that we are prepared to give up not only all external and sensible goods but also our life, signified by the word *soul,* rather than be for a single instant deprived of the love of God.

This is because we ought to prefer God to everything else that might be the object of our love. For God is, in fact, infinitely superior to all created things, such as our life, which does not deserve any consideration on our part if we compare it with the One who is its author.

Must you not, then, offer your life willingly to God and sacrifice it to him to preserve his holy love or to increase it in you? God has given you this life out of an entirely gratuitous goodness. It is quite right, then, that you show God how much you are indebted to him and how totally you belong to him by paying homage to God for your life as something that belongs to him and of which you are only the guardian.

It is truly to sacrifice your life for God and to spend it only for him. This is what you can do in your profession and your work, not being concerned whether you die in a few years, provided that you are saved and that you win souls for God.

They will help you rise to heaven because you have tried to help them procure admittance there, have taught them how to enter, and have helped them take all possible means of doing so. In this way you will show God that you love him with all your soul.[3]

### 70.3 Third Point

God has put us in this world only for himself, according to the Wise Man, who says that God made all things for himself.[4] God thinks constantly of us and has given us a mind that can think of him. Jesus Christ, then, has reason to say in this Gospel passage that we must love God with all our mind.[5]

By thinking about God at all times, we fulfill this commandment and also by referring to him all our thoughts about creatures in such a way that we do not think about anything that relates to them unless it leads us to love God or keeps us in his holy love.

Nothing shows better that we love another person than when we cannot help thinking about that person.

How happy you would be if all your thoughts tended only to God and were only for God! Then you would have found your paradise in this world, because you would be engaged in the same activity as the saints, and the happiness that they are enjoying would be yours. True, there would still be this difference, that the saints see God clearly in his own nature, whereas we enjoy God only by faith. But this view of faith gives so much pleasure and joy to a soul who loves God that even in this life it has a foretaste of the delights of heaven.

Does your soul enjoy this benefit? If you are not fortunate enough to possess it, try to be devoted to God in your prayer and by frequent short prayers to procure this benefit. It is the greatest good you can enjoy in this world.

---

1. Mt 22:35–37
2. Mt 22:37
3. Mt 22:37
4. Sir 43:37
5. Mt 22:37

# Eighteenth Sunday After Pentecost

## GOSPEL: SAINT MATTHEW 9:1-8

*The means for curing spiritual infirmities, whether voluntary or involuntary*

### 71.1  First Point

It sometimes happens that God's servants find themselves in a kind of inability to do good, whether because of temptations they can barely resist, because of interior trials, or because of the strength of their passions. This is illustrated for us by the paralytic spoken of in today's Gospel.

Such people do not find it easy to go to God, for lack either of light or of help from those who guide them. Sometimes this type of trial also lasts a long time. God leaves souls in this situation to make them experience the fact that they can do nothing without him. They cannot take the steps needed to approach him unless they are helped by his grace, but, on the contrary, they can do everything when God strengthens them.

They must, then, patiently wait until Jesus passes by, bringing a remedy for their ills. Because he has won for us the grace of redemption, he knows how to strengthen our soul and to give back the movement it has lost.

We must make sure only that we are faithful to be carried to Jesus Christ when he passes by, as did this paralytic lying on his stretcher,[1] being content to endure his infirmity until Jesus would cure him. In maladies of this sort, ordinarily, Jesus alone can bring a cure; all we can do is to watch over ourselves to avoid doing evil. Also we must pray much and be satisfied to implore God with David: My God, create a clean heart within me; renew your Spirit in me to lead me straight to you.[2]

### 71.2 Second Point

When we are in the presence of Jesus, that is, when some passing inspiration enlightens us, whether it comes on our part or from those who guide us, let us wait until Jesus speaks to us and restores our health and movement, as he did for the paralytic.[3] Let us rely on the firmness of our faith, even though we have no feeling of God and are without any movement toward God.

Let us be assured that this view of faith will be very pleasing to God and that after he has helped us and stirred up our confidence, he will say, as he did to the paralytic, Stand up,[4] that is, rise up to God.

All our strength will return to us; we will easily rise. We will find nothing to hold us back any longer, no obstacle to hinder our exterior movements and to prevent us from going to God. This is why, as soon as Jesus says to us, Go home,[5] we will find it so easy to go to God and to converse with him that nothing will be more pleasing to us. This will be the result of our patience, which God delights to reward in his servants.

Sometimes this kind of disposition results from some sin we have committed. In this case we must express great sorrow before God and deplore our misery, for this is usually what Jesus is expecting before he does good for a sick soul and repairs in it what human weakness has made it lose. Watch, then, so that your failures will not cause God to withdraw his graces from you.

### 71.3 Third Point

To bring about a cure of our spiritual paralysis, it is not enough for Jesus to tell us to rise. We too must will this, except when this paralysis is entirely a trial from God and with no culpability on our part. In that case God has only to command, and he will be obeyed. But if anything in us has brought on this infirmity or has contributed to it, we also must play a part in our cure.

Spiritual maladies differ from corporal ones. To heal corporal maladies, it is enough for Jesus to say a word or simply to will it, but in the case of maladies of the soul, we must on our part will to be cured. God does not constrain our will, although he does exhort and urge us. It is up to us to welcome his grace, to put it into effect, and to support his goodwill to cure our spiritual ailments.

Thus, when your movement toward God is, as it were, suspended, be prompt and responsive to his voice. Rise up[6] at once when he calls you, and *walk*, that is, resume the practice of virtue that you might find difficult, mortify your passions, and strive to overcome them. Be faithful, especially, to open your heart completely to your Director; this will, as a rule, prevent you from succumbing to this kind of weakness.

Finally, go straight home,[7] that is, live in seclusion, recollection, and silence. Be constantly devoted to prayer, to the other exercises of piety, and to the exact observance of the Rule of the community. They are the sure means to restore in your soul the good movements that have been interrupted.

---

1. Mt 9:2
2. Ps 51:12
3. Mt 9:6
4. Mt 9:6
5. Mt 9:6
6. Mt 9:6
7. Mt 9:6

# Nineteenth Sunday After Pentecost

## GOSPEL: SAINT MATTHEW 22:1-14

*That many are called but few are chosen to live in community*

### 72.1 First Point

In today's Gospel Jesus Christ tells us that many are called but few are chosen.[1] He says this in reference to heaven, but this truth is no less applicable to communities. Although a great number of people enter them, only a few remain faithful to the grace of their vocation, take on the spirit of their state, and remain faithful after being committed to it.

The first thing we have to do when we enter a religious community, if we wish to be chosen by God, is to learn well how to pray and to devote ourselves well to this exercise. For there is no other profession in which we are more tempted by the devil, because in community we have a sort of guarantee of salvation if we faithfully practice the Rule prescribed for us. Thus we have a great need for strength to withstand the attacks that the tempter will inflict on us there.

The second thing is to make serious efforts to become faithful to the Rule in community, for this fidelity is the principal means God gives us to be saved in community. The more exact we are in this, the more, as Saint Peter says, we make sure of our vocation and election through the good works[2] proper to our state.

But because there are but few in community who acquit themselves faithfully of this double duty, there are some who do not have the graces necessary to maintain themselves in their vocation and to keep the spirit of their state. In the end they belong only bodily to the community, or we might be obliged to cut them off from the community as depraved members who are capable only of corrupting others.

### 72.2 Second Point

The second reason why there are few chosen in community is that there are few who have a true and complete submission to their superiors. Nevertheless, obedience is the first virtue we must have for community and the main one among those that help us to persevere in it. As soon as we fail against obedience, we are abandoned to ourselves, without strength and vigor; consequently, we are incapable of doing the good proper to our state. This is why we do not persevere or why, if we do remain, that we become useless or even harmful to others, like branches that no longer are connected to the stem, which is Jesus Christ, and draw the sap necessary for them to produce.[3]

We hold on to Jesus Christ, like branches on a tree, only insofar as we are united with our superiors and act with an entire dependence on them, for, according to Saint Paul, when we are subject to them, *we are obeying God and Jesus Christ.* We must obey them, not just wishing to please men but doing the will of God with a good heart[4] as members and servants of Jesus Christ.

Superiors have a right to command us only because they speak in the name of Jesus Christ and as representatives of his person. We ought to obey them only because, according to the expression of Saint Paul, they are laboring for the perfection of the saints and the building up of the Body of Jesus Christ, who is our Head.[5] Thanks to the submission rendered to him in his ministers, he joins and unites all the parts of his body in proper proportion[6] to make one and the same body. By practicing this virtue, then, you will become one of those truly chosen by God in your community.

### 72.3 Third Point [7]

Another reason why few are chosen to live in community is that few open their hearts entirely to their superiors. Without this openness, it is impossible to avoid the evil consequences that result from the violent temptations with which the devil assails those who are called to live a community life.

Such temptations, as a rule, get more and more violent as these people make progress in virtue. For when they labor fervently to attain the perfection of their state, the devil knows that they will persevere and do him much harm by their good example and by the graces they will obtain for others by their prayers. Thus he constantly besieges them, as Saint Peter says, seeking an opportunity to make them fall.[8]

This is why Saint Dorotheus says that the devil is filled with joy when he finds some who wish to guide themselves and who do not allow themselves to be guided by their superior, because he knows that they will fall like leaves from a tree. They are acting, says this saint, in alliance with the devil and are enemies of their own salvation.

The saint even adds that he does not know any other reason for the fall of those who live in community than this confidence they have in their own lights. He concludes that there is nothing more criminal or more pernicious in a community than such conduct and that there is no other way to bring about our salvation than openness of heart.

Oh, how few there are, in spite of this, who have this spirit completely! Some say, What will my superior think if I tell him everything? But if you fail to do so, he will soon find out that you are unfaithful.

Others object, I would not dare to reveal everything to him, for I would afterward be embarrassed to appear before him.

Others say, It is enough to tell my faults in Confession. No doubt, but your superior is better placed than anyone else to give you the remedies.

Others think, He is only a Brother like me. This is true, but he has been commissioned by God to help you achieve your salvation.

Make use, then, of the means that God offers you for this purpose; otherwise, you will soon fall away from the spirit of your state, and although you were once called, you will not be among the number of God's chosen ones.

---

1. Mt 22:14
2. 2 Pt 1:10
3. Jn 15:4
4. Eph 6:5–7

5. Eph 4:12, 15
6. Eph 4:16
7. See the note on Meditation 19.
8. 1 Pt 5:8

# Twentieth Sunday After Pentecost

## GOSPEL: SAINT JOHN 4:46–53

*That we must not expect God to perform miracles to please us*

### 73.1 First Point

A courtier, having gone to Jesus, begged him to come to his house to cure his son, who was at the point of death. Jesus answered him, Unless you see miracles and wonders, you do not believe.[1] This Gospel can be very well applied to many people living in community, who frequently and inappropriately would like to see miracles in order to believe that they ought to do the good that is their duty.

First, they wish to see miracles and wonders in their superiors in order to believe them, regard them as such, and obey them. They would like to see their superiors without fault; otherwise, they criticize their actions, murmur against them, and complain about them, saying that it is very easy for superiors to give orders.

They seem to demand as much perfection in their superiors, so to speak, as they might encounter in Jesus Christ.

All this happens only because they do not obey in a spirit of faith, and they look upon their superior as only a man, not as the minister of God and the one who visibly takes his place in their regard. They do not know how to distinguish in him two kinds of people: the person of Jesus Christ, who is without any defects and whose place he takes, and the person of a man, who can be subject to many imperfections. They do not realize that when they address themselves to him as their superior, they ought not to consider anything in him but God, who is commanding them through the voice of a man.

Try to adopt this attitude of faith, and try to be well penetrated with it before you go to speak to your superior. Be faithful to make acts of faith on this point, so that you can obey him as you would obey God.

### 73.2 Second Point

A number of others would also like to see miracles and prodigies in their Brothers, in that they would like to suffer nothing on their account, which is impossible. For it is a law of God and consequently an obligation that when people live together, they suffer from one another. Saint Paul teaches us this by the words, *Bear one another's burdens*, that is, one another's defects, and so you will fulfill the law of Jesus Christ.[2]

This, then, is a law of Jesus Christ, which we must observe; to support one another is a charity that everyone is obliged to practice toward his Brothers if he wishes to preserve union with them and to show by his conduct that he forms one and the same Society with them. It follows that each Brother shares in all that his Brothers suffer.

We are not exempt from suffering from others, because it is not possible for two people to live together without causing suffering to each other in some way. Because we make others suffer, it is only right that we suffer from them in our turn. This burden that God has imposed on all people helps them to be saved. In this way *the yoke of Jesus Christ is light,* because he helps us bear easily the burdens and troubles of this life[3] rather than have them feel like something oppressive.

Do not, then, be so foolish, so unreasonable, and so unchristian as to expect to have nothing to suffer from your Brothers, for this would be to ask for a most extraordinary and unheard-of miracle. Do not expect it, then, to happen anytime during your life.

### 73.3  Third Point

Finally, there are a great number who demand miracles and prodigies from themselves. They would like to do everything well and without reproach but do not want to take the trouble for this. They would like very much to please their superiors, and they would ask nothing better than to be very closely united with their Brothers. They have a great desire to be faithful observers of their Rule, for they understand well that the Rule is a great means for them to be holy that God provides for them.

But whenever they have to do violence to themselves to realize this grand plan, they lose their breath, so to speak, at the first step they take in the path of perfection. They would want God to carry them without their having to advance and to make any move to go from one spot to another. That certainly would be a great miracle.

Saint Paul says that it must be through many tribulations that we enter into the kingdom of God.[4] When he says *it must be,* he is telling us that it would be asking God for a miracle to expect God to have us enter heaven without taking the only road that is necessary to arrive there.

So, then, without waiting for such a miracle, take the true path to heaven, which is the path of suffering. This is the narrow gate; do all you can to enter it,[5] and Jesus Christ will not fail to give you his hand to help you enter.

---

1. Jn 4:46–48     3. Mt 11:28–30     5. Lk 13:24
2. Gal 6:2        4. Acts 14:22

# Twenty-First Sunday After Pentecost

## GOSPEL: SAINT MATTHEW 18:23-35

*The obligation of people living in community to put up with the defects of their Brothers*

### 74.1 First Point

A ruler, having canceled a debt of ten thousand talents owed to him by one of his servants, because the servant had begged him for time to pay off the debt, was then much astonished when he was told that this servant had had one of his companions thrown into prison because of a debt of a hundred denarii, even though his companion had earnestly pleaded for a little more time. You wicked servant, said the ruler, Ought you not to have had compassion on your fellow servant even as I had compassion on you?[1] God has forgiven you a huge debt; he certainly expects you also to forgive those of your Brothers who owe anything to you.

It is impossible for several people living together not to have to suffer from one another. One will have a touchy disposition; another will have a contrary spirit; another, bad manners; another will be disagreeable; another will be too prone to give in; another will say what he thinks too quickly; another will be too reserved and secretive; another will be too critical.

It is rare that all these various dispositions and all these different spirits do not cause difficulties among the Brothers. If grace does not come to the rescue, it is almost impossible that they live in harmony with one another and that charity does not suffer severely.

The way to maintain union in a community in spite of all these different personalities is to bear up charitably with the defects of one another, to be ready to make allowances for others just as we want others to make allowances for us. This is what we necessarily commit ourselves to do when we decide to live in a community. Pay serious attention to this today and for the rest of your life.

### 74.2 Second Point

This charity that is required of us presupposes a patience that is proof against everything. Everyone has defects, and we bring them with us everywhere we go; consequently, it is only by overlooking them among ourselves that we can maintain peace and union, even in the most select societies. This is why Saint Paul has said that charity endures all things.[2] So that we might be convinced that he was not mistaken and that he did not say this thoughtlessly, he said it twice.

Some will say: This I will endure from my Brother, but as for that, I cannot bring myself to put up with it, or again, My disposition is too incompatible with his. You do not want to have any charity for your Brother or establish any union with him if there is anything that you are not prepared to suffer from him, for charity endures all things.[3]

Think seriously about this. If you believe that you have come to community without being obliged to suffer the defects of your Brothers, you are deceived, and you made a mistake in coming here. Take proper measures in this regard for the future and for the rest of your life.

### 74.3 Third Point

Another thing that ought to lead you to bear up with the defects of your Brothers is that God has imposed this on you as an obligation. When God placed you in community, he gave you responsibility for a burden that is difficult to bear. What is that burden? It is the defects of others. However heavy the weight of this responsibility might be, Saint Paul wants us to carry it if we wish to fulfill the law of Jesus Christ.[4] Do you understand this lesson well? Do you grasp it well? Then practice it.

God gives you the example for this by putting up with so much from you and by still suffering so much from you every day. You have committed a great many sins against God, although you are indebted to him for so many graces. Nonetheless, provided that you have recourse to God, he will pardon you everything, but only on this condition, he says, that you too pardon your Brother of everything[5] and have no resentment toward him for all the trouble he has given you and will give you. This is what God tells us in today's Gospel; this is its prelude and its conclusion.

If you are unwilling, then, to suffer anything from your Brothers, God will not endure anything from you, and he will punish you severely for what you have done against him. On the contrary, if you endure everything from your Brothers, God will pardon you everything you have done against him. You will be measured, he says elsewhere, by the same measure you use to measure others.[6]

---

1. Mt 18:23–35
2. 1 Cor 13:7
3. 1 Cor 13:7
4. Gal 6:2
5. Mt 6:14
6. Mt 7:2

# Twenty-Second Sunday
# After Pentecost

## GOSPEL: SAINT MATTHEW 22:15–21

*That we must not have human respect in our conduct*

### 75.1 First Point

The Pharisees and the Herodians, as today's Gospel relates, approached our Lord, praising him because he taught the way of God in truth without considering who a person is and without paying attention to a person's status.[1] Those who live in community especially ought to imitate our Lord in this, because having renounced the world, they must act only in view of God and without worrying at all about what people might say about them.

This is, first of all, what superiors ought to do. Because they are the only ones who deal with everyone both within and outside the community, they are also the ones about whose conduct people often try to find something to criticize.

Those in the community who like to be independent sometimes find that the superior is too exacting and too troublesome. If he is discreet and serious, they say he is too sedate. If his appearance is pleasant and winning, they say that he is too open and too accommodating. If he admonishes frequently and does not let anything slip by, they say that he is too severe. If he tolerates some defects in some of them, they say that he is allowing total relaxation. If he does well in the minds of some, he does badly according to others. Thus, hardly any of his actions will not be blameworthy.

All a superior must do in this matter is not to let himself be worried by what might be said about him. Still, he must keep watch over himself not to do anything that could give bad example or anything contrary to the duties of his ministry. He must not have any particular affection for anyone, and he must become a model for others by his piety and his observance of the Rule.

### 75.2 Second Point

Inferiors, on their part, must also act without human respect, for this is one of the things that most often corrupts human actions. Because God has created us only for himself, he does not want consideration of any other creature to motivate us to act. This is why God regards all actions performed for some created purpose as offensive to him. God has no regard for all the good that might be the apparent effect of such action.

If it happens, then, that one of your Brothers has not been faithful to the Rule, do not imitate him out of human respect. The law of God and his will must be your rule, not the example of others or the natural and human consideration you have for them. If you perform your actions to please others, you will receive no reward for them except what people will give you,[2] which is very low, very fragile, and very fleeting.

Above all, do nothing and omit nothing to please people of the world. Saint Paul speaks of such people when he says, If I were pleasing people, I would not be a servant of Jesus Christ.[3] If you were of the world, Jesus Christ says, the world would love those who belong to the world, but because you do not belong to the world, for this reason the world hates you.[4]

Because it is a necessity, according to Jesus Christ and to Saint Paul, not to please people of the world and even, instead, to be hated by them, you ought to do nothing with the intention of pleasing them. In addition the habits and the views of people of the world are quite different from those you ought to have.

So when the thought of human respect crosses your mind, remember the words of Saint Paul: If I were pleasing people, I would not be a servant of Jesus Christ.[5]

### 75.3 Third Point

It is not enough to avoid acting to please other people; you are required to act with the single view of pleasing God and of being agreeable to him.[6] As Saint Paul says, you must perform your actions and do everything in a manner worthy of God,[7] and for this purpose, walk in the way of God and do this in such a way that, as the same Apostle says elsewhere, you may follow it always and progress more and more. For, he adds, the will of God is that you be holy and pure,[8] meaning that your actions ought to be pure, having no other motive than to please God.

This will be the true and surest means to walk in the way of God and to make more and more progress. Because God in the next life is the purpose and the goal of all your actions, he ought to be the same also in this life, especially in your state, which demands of you a high degree of perfection. For God did not call you, says Saint Paul, to be impure, that is, to do things unworthy of your state, actions degraded and corrupted by the bad ends you will give them; rather, he has called you to be holy.[9] Therefore, whoever does not apply himself to do his actions with a view to God is despising God, not man.[10]

---

1. Mt 22:16
2. Mt 10:41
3. Gal 1:10
4. Jn 15:19
5. Gal 1:10
6. Col 1:10
7. 1 Thes 4:1
8. 1 Thes 4:3
9. 1 Thes 4:7
10. 1 Thes 4:8

# Twenty-Third Sunday After Pentecost

## GOSPEL: SAINT MATTHEW 9:18-26

*That several in community have left the world but not its spirit*

### 76.1 First Point

When Jesus entered the house of a chief of the synagogue to raise his daughter to life, he made a crowd of people get out, saying that the girl was not dead but asleep.[1] In like manner it can be said of several people who have left the world and entered a community that they are not dead but are only sleeping, because, they have left the world but not completely renounced it. They show this clearly enough by their conduct.

In the first place, their senses are not dead. True, some appear recollected when in the presence of their superiors; others, when they are with their Brothers in the house and during the exercises of piety, but if they go out into the streets, they have to see everything that goes on.

Others appear to be more restrained, but if something extraordinary happens, they open their eyes to see. If they travel in the country, they turn aside from their route, if necessary, to satisfy their curiosity and to see things of interest on the way, such as beautiful churches, houses, and gardens.

Others seem to be quite mortified in eating and drinking. They eat whatever is given them, with great indifference, without complaining in any way, but when traveling, they manage to eat all the best food available. If they are ill, it is very difficult to please them. Their senses are not dead but only sleeping, and that is why they are readily awakened.

Do not behave like the Israelites, who, having left Egypt by God's special protection, no longer remembered the sufferings they endured there but longed for the onions of Egypt.[2]

### 76.2 Second Point

The passions of such people are not dead either. Some accept everything of a humiliating nature that is said to them in the streets, but in the community if someone reproves them, advises them of their defects, or humiliates them on some occasion, they are very upset.

Others do not wish to suffer anything, either within or outside the community. They murmur, shake their heads, make signs to show their dissatisfaction, or even utter threats.

Others support their superiors and externally accept their penances quite well, but if one of their Brothers says a harsh word to them or someone does something to displease them, at once they are disturbed. Sometimes, when teaching, they become angry at the students and strike them, which often leads to unfortunate consequences that are difficult to remedy.

The passions of such people are not dead but only sleeping for a time, after which they awaken with much vitality in some, in others a little more moderately, in some more often, in others more rarely.

You ought to have left the world only to make your passions die entirely; otherwise, you will never attain true virtue. Apply yourself seriously to this with all the attention you can.

### 76.3 Third Point

Several, even after leaving the world, are not dead to what is in the world. To be entirely dead to it, we ought no longer to find anything there either beautiful or good. Still, some willingly seek the company of people of the world, and when they cannot be among them, they satisfy themselves by talking about them, eagerly listening to news about them, or being preoccupied with them.

Others are very pleased to have and to display clothing, garments, shirts, hats, stockings, shoes, and so forth that resemble what people of the world usually wear, or if they cannot have such things, they try to dress in a way or to put on an appearance one way or another that reflects a worldly manner.

Others read good books at times, but they will freely read others that deal with matters that are not bad but that are trivial. There might even be found some who, in spite of the prohibitions of superiors, are so unfaithful to the Rule as to read daily newspapers, to use snuff, and even to procure such things for themselves by illicit means.

All such behavior is totally out of place in people who have consecrated themselves to God, have given up all dealings with the world, and have entered a state that binds them to live a life in community according to a Rule. Although such people might devote themselves to the exercises of piety in the community and to their duties, it can be said rightly that their conduct shows that they are not dead to the world but only asleep as regards worldly living.

Nevertheless, it is only in order to die to the world and to renounce everything that goes on in the world that a person comes to live in community. Think seriously about this, and in the future live only with this intention and for this purpose.

---

1. Mt 9:24         2. Nm 11:5

# Twenty-Fourth Sunday After Pentecost

## GOSPEL: SAINT MATTHEW 24:15–35

*That sin and disregard for the Rule in a community are the abomination of desolation in the holy place*

### 77.1  First Point

In today's Gospel Jesus Christ says that when the abomination of desolation will be in the holy place, let those who are in Judea flee to the mountains.[1] No one can question that a community is a holy place. We can without doubt say of a community where God is faithfully served what Jacob says in Genesis, that the Lord is truly in this place and that this place is the house of God and the gate of heaven.[2]

If we consider its institution and its purpose, we can say of it what is said of the Temple built by Solomon, that God has chosen this dwelling and that he has sanctified it, so that his name may be blessed there forever.[3] This is true, for his name is so often invoked there, and those who dwell there are, or ought to be, together only to save themselves through the sanctification of their souls. In this way this place is the gate of heaven, because it enables us to take the path leading to heaven and prepares us to enter heaven.

This is the first purpose you ought to have had when you entered this community and what ought to keep you here. This is the end for which we live withdrawn from the world and why we commit ourselves to all kinds of exercises of piety. How little sense you would have had if you had come here with any other purpose, for as the Royal Prophet says, it is very proper and even just that holiness be found in the Lord's house.[4] For he is infinitely holy, and it is altogether right that those who live there be holy by sharing his own holiness.

Have you come to this house as to the house of the Lord? Did you come here to sanctify yourself? Is the main effort you make in this house to take the means to become holy? Often reflect on what Saint Eucherius, bishop of Lyons, says, that living in a holy house is the source of either sovereign perfection or absolute damnation.

### 77.2  Second Point

We might certainly say to several who live in community what, on entering the Temple, Jesus Christ says in the Gospel to those who were buying and selling, that his house is a house of prayer and that they are making it a den of thieves.[5] Although people ought to enter a religious community only to apply themselves to prayer and other exercises of piety, they neglect all these holy actions and fill their minds with external and secular things, take on the spirit of the world, and then fall into disregard of the Rule. Unless they change their ways, they often end up committing serious sins. Of such people it can truly be said that they are bringing the abomination of desolation into the holy place.[6]

Is it not an abomination, indeed, to find that sin and disregard for the Rule exist in a house where the Spirit of God ought to be the only guide and where people who ought to breathe only God and think only of pleasing God, because they have consecrated themselves to his service, neglect him or abandon him entirely out of boredom to satisfy their inclinations or even their passions? What desolation this brings about in a community, for there is no union or peace where God is not found!

Those who behave this way are thieves,[7] to use our Lord's expression in the Gospel, because they steal the bread they eat and occupy the place of others who prefer to live according to the spirit and the Rule of this community. Take care not to fall into such an evil.

### 77.3  Third Point

Notwithstanding the disregard for the Rule in communities, God always keeps in them faithful servants who preserve its spirit. He always reserves there for that purpose some who, as he told Elias, do not bend their knee before Baal;[8] that is, they are on their guard against the spirit of the world, and they observe their Rule and the practices of their community as well as they can.

They are the ones who still maintain the fear of the Lord, and they are the reason why God does not destroy this community, as he destroyed Sodom and Gomorrha, which would have been spared the terrible effects of his anger if he had found in them ten just people,[9] as he told Abraham.

They are the people in today's Gospel whom Jesus Christ tells to flee to the mountains,[10] that is, to avoid the company of the others in order not to share in their disregard for the Rule and not to be led astray by the contagion of their bad example. They must rise up to God by prayer.

Pray God to preserve his Holy Spirit always in your community, and often say to him with David: Do not reject us, my God, from your presence, and do not take your Holy Spirit from us.[11]

---

1. Mt 24:15–16
2. Gn 28:17
3. 2 Chr 7:16
4. Ps 93:5
5. Lk 19:46
6. Mt 24:15
7. Lk 19:46
8. 1 Kgs 19:18
9. Gn 18:32
10. Mt 24:16
11. Ps 51:13

# PART TWO

——— ✦ ———

# Meditations
for the Principal Feasts
of the Year

# January 1

## THE CIRCUMCISION
## OF OUR LORD JESUS CHRIST

### 93.1 First Point

In his circumcision Jesus Christ submitted to the Law, which required that all male children be circumcised on the eighth day after their birth,[1] although he was exempt from and superior to all law, being the sovereign Legislator.

This law applied only to sinners; because he was incapable of sin, Jesus Christ was in no way subject to it. What admirable humility on the part of Jesus, making himself resemble sinners even though he was not one. Totally innocent though he was, he took on the burden of our sins when he came into the world, for he came only to make satisfaction for them.[2]

Let us today admire the obedience and the humility of our Savior in this mystery. He came into this world, as he says, not to abolish the Law but to fulfill it.[3] Learn from him to submit to those whom God has given you as your superiors, to be humbled on the occasions that will arise, and to be circumcised with a true circumcision not made by human hands,[4] as Saint Paul says, but which consists in stripping off your carnal body, that is, your sins, passions, and inclinations. For, as the same Apostle remarks elsewhere, true circumcision is not performed on the flesh, which is only exterior, but rather on the heart and performed by the Spirit.[5]

For this reason, because you belong to Jesus Christ, mortify your flesh with its passions and disorderly desires,[6] as Saint Paul says, and Jesus Christ will make you live again with him, even though your flesh has not been circumcised, and he will totally abolish the decree of your condemnation.[7]

### 93.2 Second Point

In this mystery Jesus Christ carried out his function and his role as Redeemer of all by shedding his blood out of the love he has for us. By this outpouring of his blood, he showed that he was beginning to take on the burden of our sins and to appear on earth as a sinner: first, because under the Old Law, circumcision was established only for sinners; second, because Jesus Christ, appearing in this world as the high priest of future blessings,[8] according to Saint Paul, offered himself to God in the Temple on this day as a spotless victim to purify our consciences from dead works, so that in the name of all of us, he might offer to the living and eternal God an act of true worship in his role as Mediator of the New Testament.[9]

Is there anything that could be more humiliating for the Son of God than to appear as a sinner, although he is holy, the Just One par excellence? Yet Jesus Christ, although exempt from sin, suffers on this day in his sacred body the pain that we would have been obliged to endure as sinners, while we who have offended God so much consider ourselves and wish to be considered as innocent and just. We seek and think we have a right to our comfort; we give all our attention to avoid work and suffering.

Feel sentiments of humility, and be ashamed when you see how you avoid occasions of suffering, whereas Jesus Christ sought them for love of you. Thank him for such great goodness shown to you in his circumcision.

### 93.3 Third Point

The Eternal Father having informed the Most Blessed Virgin by the angel who announced to her the mystery of the Incarnation of his Son, whom she is to call Jesus,[10] on this day she and Saint Joseph gave him this name, which means Savior. It was quite proper that when Jesus Christ began to suffer and to shed his blood for our sins, this name be given to him at the same time, so that from this moment he has the name so admirably suited to him according to the ministry assigned to him. At the same time, he offers himself exteriorly and publicly to God, his Father, to fulfill this ministry, so that he might not seem to have this adorable name in vain.

Is it only in vain that you have the name of Christian and minister of Jesus Christ[11] in the work you do? Do you live in a manner that befits these glorious names? Do you instruct those for whom you are responsible with the attention and the zeal God asks of you in so holy a work? By your good conduct, be worthy of this distinguished role. Act in such a way that your life may begin today to be holy and edifying and continue to be such in the future.

---

1. Lv 12:3
2. Heb 10:5–7
3. Mt 5:17
4. Col 2:11
5. Rom 2:28–29
6. Gal 5:24
7. Col 2:13, 14
8. Heb 9:11
9. Heb 9:14–15
10. Lk 1:31
11. 2 Cor 5:20

# January 3

## SAINT GENEVIEVE

### 95.1[1] First Point

Saint Genevieve was so filled and endowed with grace that she consecrated herself to God from her tenderest years, with the advice of Saint Germanus, bishop of Auxerre, who approved her plan to make a vow of virginity, which she did later in the presence of the bishop of Chartres. Then she devoted herself entirely to works of piety, especially to prayer, so that her entire life was almost one continual prayer. She prepared to celebrate Sunday well by spending the entire previous night in the exercise of prayer and by stirring up in herself an extraordinary fervor that she tried to maintain throughout this day and on all feast days.

Such is the practice of the saints, which is to avoid conversation with people and to love conversing with God. Do you feel inclined to this practice? Your duty is to pray diligently and affectionately to draw down on you a great number of graces that you need in your state, both for your own sanctification and for the sanctification of others.

Be assured that the more you devote yourself to prayer, the more you will also do well in your work. Because you are not able to do anything well for the salvation of souls, you must often turn to God to obtain what your profession obliges you to give to others. For God, says Saint James, is the Father of lights, and from God every perfect gift comes down.[2] This includes everything that is given and is needed to procure our salvation. Earnestly beg of God this spirit of prayer.

### 95.2 Second Point

Prayer has little efficacy if it is not strengthened by mortification. Saint Genevieve joined the one to the other, which is why she readily obtained from God what she asked of him. As a rule, she took food only twice a week, never ate meat, and often spent entire nights in prayer. Her austerities were so great that it seemed that she no longer had a body, so much did she neglect it.

We cannot strengthen ourselves in piety except insofar as we mortify ourselves. Because our senses constantly incline us to seek their pleasure, we cannot live according to the Christian spirit unless we hold them in check and even oppose their inclinations.

For, according to Saint Paul, the desires of the flesh are contrary to those of the Spirit; they are opposed to each other.[3] This is why we often do not do the things we would want to do. Because we ought to live by the Spirit, says the same Apostle, we must also be led by the Spirit,[4] not by our senses.

Is this your concern and preoccupation? Do you take the means to be the master of your senses? If you give in to them, it will be quite difficult for you to control them later. Therefore, watch over them constantly, because no one can be sensual and Christian at the same time.

### 95.3 Third Point

The reward Saint Genevieve received in this life for all her great deeds and her exercises of piety was long and frequent illness, considerable suffering, and persecution throughout her whole life. To these were added some altogether extraordinary calumnies. After the example of Saint Paul, she responded only with acts of thanksgiving and prayers to God for those who persecuted and calumniated her,[5] because she knew that this is the reward God gives to his saints in this life, as Jesus Christ testifies in the holy Gospel, saying that this ought to make them happier[6] than the possession of all imaginable treasures. This too is what consoles God's servants, because they find in these states a conformity with Jesus Christ and his saints.

To be treated this way is all we must expect in this world after spending our life for God. This is what will help us find and possess God and his holy peace within us, just as the saint whose feast we are celebrating possessed him in the midst of all her trials.

Often testify to God that it will be a pleasure for you to suffer all the troubles he will want to send you. Do not complain in the least about what people may say or do against you. Show by your silence and patience that you are content and that you accept all willingly for the love of God. One of the best means for acquiring and preserving this divine love is to suffer much and to suffer with joy.

---

Genevieve (ca. 420–ca. 512) was born at Nanterre, a village close to Paris, and at an early age consecrated herself to virginity, with the approval of Saint Marcellinus, bishop of Paris (meditation for November 3). For a while she was a center of controversy, because of the miracles and predictions attributed to her, but she later became a patron of Paris through the friendship of Saint Germain, bishop of Auxerre (meditation for May 28) and her success through prayer in protecting the city from the invasion of the Franks under Childeric and of the Huns under Attila. Later, when Clovis was besieging the city, she led a convoy of boats bringing food to the city. After Clovis became a Christian, he and his wife, Saint Clotilda, showed great respect for

Genevieve. She was buried in the church of Saints Peter and Paul, which Clovis had built, but her remains were destroyed by fire during the French Revolution in 1793.

---

1. The 1882 edition of the meditations, the numbering of which has become standard, includes a meditation on the Holy Infant Jesus, put together from excerpts from De La Salle's *Explication de la Méthode d'Oraison*. That meditation was number 94 and is not included here, because it was not part of the original edition from which this translation has been made.
2. Jas 1:17
3. Gal 5:16–17
4. Gal 5:25
5. 1 Cor 4:12–13
6. Mt 5:11–12

# January 6

## THE ADORATION
## OF THE KINGS

### 96.1 First Point

We cannot sufficiently admire the faith of the holy Magi, for nothing was found in Israel, as Saint Bernard says, to match the faith shown by these admirable Gentiles. They behold a new, extraordinary star. At this sight they leave for a distant land to seek one whom they do not know, who is not known even in his own land.

Enlightened by this star and even more so by the light of faith, they go to announce a new Sun of Justice[1] in the place where he was born. They surprise everyone with the proclamation of this news. They are not surprised by it because they are enlightened by the true Light and because it is by faith alone, according to Saint Paul, that we make our way toward Jesus Christ.[2]

The star did not appear to them in vain, for this sight caused them to receive the grace of God, and it made this day a day of salvation for them[3] because they showed themselves most faithful to the divine inspiration.

Are we attentive to the inspirations we receive from God? Are we as quick to follow them as these holy Magi were in letting themselves be led by the star that guided them? Frequently the salvation and the happiness of a soul depend on this prompt fidelity to grace.

God graciously spoke to Samuel because, three times in a row as soon as he heard God's voice,[4] he presented himself to listen to God. Saint Paul merited to be entirely converted because he was immediately faithful to the voice of Jesus Christ, who called him.[5] You ought to do just as they did.

### 96.2  Second Point

When the Magi entered Jerusalem and Herod's palace, they asked, Where has the King of the Jews been born?[6] What a question to ask in the palace of the prince! It is true, says Saint Augustine, that several kings had been born in Judea and that Herod, who was then on the throne, had several children. However, it was not to adore or to acknowledge as king any of these that the Magi had come, because it was for none of them that heaven had brought them. It is true, Saint Fulgentius says, that a short time earlier, a son had been born to Herod in his palace. They had placed him in a silver cradle, and all Judea paid him homage, but the Magi disdained him and did not even mention him in the king's palace.

What holy audacity in our Magi, to enter the capital and to make their way even to Herod's throne! They feared nothing because the faith that inspired them and the grandeur of him whom they were seeking caused them to forget, even to scorn, all human considerations. They considered the king to whom they were speaking to be infinitely beneath the one announced to them by the star.

We cannot admire too much how these Gentiles, brought up in the errors of paganism, had such a lively faith and how they were so faithful to follow its lights. Their faith was much increased and strengthened when Herod gathered all the princes of the priests and the scribes of the people and found out from them where the Christ was to be born. They told him, in Bethlehem.[7] Thereupon he told the Magi that when they found this Child whom they were seeking, he too would go to adore him.[8]

But the Magi then left without concerning themselves any further about King Herod. So too must faith make you despise all that the world esteems.

### 96.3  Third Point

The Magi left the city of Jerusalem and proceeded to the poor village of Bethlehem to find there the King whom they were seeking. They were led there by the star, which moved ahead of them until it reached the place where the Child was and stopped there.[9] Then the Magi entered the stable and found a little Child wrapped in poor swaddling clothes in the company of his mother, Mary.[10]

At this sight, how could the Magi not fear to have been deceived? Are these the marks of a king? asks Saint Bernard. Where is his palace, his throne, his court? The stable, the saint says, is his palace; the crib serves as his throne, and his court is the company of the Most Blessed Virgin and Saint Joseph. This stable does not appear to the Magi as deserving of disdain. These poor swaddling clothes are not shocking in their eyes. They feel no disappointment at seeing a poor child being nursed by his mother.

They prostrate themselves before him,[11] says the Gospel. They honor him as their King and adore him as their God. Behold the faith that profoundly filled their spirit and caused them to respond in this way.

Recognize Jesus beneath the poor rags of the children whom you have to instruct; adore him in them. Love poverty, and honor the poor, following the example of the Magi, for poverty ought to be dear to you, responsible as you are for the instruction of the poor. May faith lead you to do this with affection and zeal because these children are members of Jesus Christ.[12] In this way this divine Savior will be pleased with you, and you will find him because he always loved the poor and poverty.

———

This feast, now generally celebrated on the Sunday between January 2 and January 8, is known as the Epiphany because it originated in the Greek-speaking Near East, where the word means a showing or a manifestation. It is the feast of the manifestation to the world at large, in the person of the three Wise Men, of the majesty and the divinity of the newborn Savior.[13]

———

1. Mal 3:20
2. 2 Cor 5:7
3. Is 49:8
4. 2 Kgs 3:3–15
5. Acts 9:4–5
6. Mt 2:2
7. Mt 2:4–6
8. Mt 2:8
9. Mt 2:9
10. Mt 2:11
11. Mt 2:11
12. 1 Cor 12:27
13. This note and many of those on the following meditations rely on W. J. Battersby, *De La Salle - Meditations,* Longmans, Green, and Co., 1953.

# January 17

## SAINT ANTHONY, ABBOT

### 97.1 First Point

When Saint Anthony heard the following words of the holy Gospel read in church, If you wish to be perfect, go; sell all you have, and give it to the poor,[1] he immediately began to carry out this invitation as though it had been addressed to him personally, convinced that this was what God was asking of him.

Let us admire this saint's fidelity to the first suggestion of grace and his promptness in following the inspiration God gave him. Are we as faithful to God's inspirations as Saint Anthony was? Are we as quick to do what grace asks of us?

We made a profession, just as he did, to renounce everything when we left the world, but have we earnestly given up everything? Are we no longer attached to anything? We know this if we are glad to be poor and if we do not want to have comfortable things for ourselves or possess anything at all.

### 97.2 Second Point

After he gave away all his possessions in favor of the poor, Saint Anthony withdrew to the desert, where he labored manually to earn a livelihood and to help the poor. To his labor he joined constant prayer.

If we wish to give ourselves to God, it is not sufficient to abandon all that we possess and all exterior things; we must also strive to attain inner perfection and to renounce our passions and our own inclinations.[2]

By withdrawing from the world, we gain this advantage. For it is impossible to overcome ourselves unless we know ourselves, and it is very difficult to know ourselves while living in the midst of the world. Do we profit by the advantage we have of living in seclusion in order to study how we can completely avoid following our natural inclinations?

### 97.3 Third Point

Saint Anthony acquired perfection in the desert and became filled with the Spirit of God.[3] He then left the desert, for a time, on account of the persecution that was raging, in order to encourage the martyrs and to strengthen the Christians in their faith. His own sanctification had kept him in solitude, but the zeal he had for the salvation of his brothers withdrew him from it. Still, distrustful of himself, once the persecution was over, he went back to the desert and lived there with more fervor than ever before.

Such also ought to be your conduct. You ought to love seclusion, where you can labor effectively at your own perfection, but you must leave it when God asks you to work for the salvation of the souls he has entrusted to you. As soon as God no longer calls you there, when the time of your work is over, you must, after the example of Saint Anthony, return to your solitude.

---

Anthony (ca. 251–ca. 356) is called the father of monasticism. The story of his life, written by his contemporary and friend, Saint Athanasius (meditation for May 2), is considered to be the first formal biography of a monk. It was widely imitated, beginning with Saint Jerome's stories of the monks Paul, Hilarion, and Malchus. (De La Salle has a meditation on Saint Jerome for September 30). Anthony was born in Upper Egypt and at an early age became a disciple of the hermit Paul of Thebes. He later founded two monasteries in the mountains near the Nile, one of which, Der Mar Antonios, still stands in the Eastern Desert between the Nile and the Red Sea. His temptations are described in great detail by Saint Athanasius and have been the subject of famous masterpieces by such artists as Bosch, Grünewald, and Ernst. During the time of the Arian controversy, Anthony left his solitude to help Saint Athanasius in his conflict with Arius and the Roman emperors.

---

1. Mt 19:21        2. Gal 5:24        3. Acts 2:4

# January 19

## SAINT SULPICE

### 98.1 First Point

Even from his childhood, Saint Sulpice always showed such a great inclination to virtue that he was given the name of pious, and his bishop obliged him to join the ranks of the clergy. Oh, what a very advantageous thing it is to practice virtue early in life![1] By this means we acquire a great facility for its practice, and we perform acts of virtue as though naturally.

This is also the advantage of those who live in communities secluded from the world. Those who love their state find nothing there but pleasure and satisfaction in all the exercises of piety practiced there, because they have acquired a habit that the fervor of grace and the love of God have made pleasing and agreeable to them. Are you so disposed? Do you love, above all things, your state in life and what is practiced in it?

### 98.2 Second Point

This saint's piety brought him such a great reputation that the king wished to have him in his company. Although it is difficult to preserve the spirit of religion in the midst of a court, this saint, nevertheless, behaved there in such a prudent manner that he radiated about him an atmosphere of piety that made him honored by everyone.

Your work requires you to have some communication with neighbors outside the community. Take care never to be among others without giving edification; be so well-mannered, reserved, and self-controlled that you may be looked upon as spreading the fragrance of Jesus Christ.[2] So act that all your exterior appearance, all your words, and all your actions may inspire virtue. This is why God wishes you to be among others; therefore, prepare in seclusion to cooperate with his intentions.

### 98.3 Third Point

When the archbishopric of Bourges became vacant, the king named Saint Sulpice to fill it. His piety caused him to be chosen in preference to all the others who were seeking this dignity. His piety also made him labor with zeal and success for the salvation of souls. Oh, how true it is, as Saint Paul says, that piety is useful for all things[3] and produces great blessings, not only in those people who possess it but also in those who see them, speak with them, and receive their instructions. Everything in them preaches piety.

Can the same thing be said of you, who ought to communicate this spirit to the children whom you have to guide? Is it enough for them to see you to be well behaved themselves? Is your behavior sufficient to encourage them to practice virtue? Does everything you tell them produce in them the spirit of piety and religion? This is the main benefit that you must impart to them, the best gift you can give them when they leave you.

---

Saint Sulpice, bishop of Bourges (died ca. 592), was called Sulpicius Severus. He was admired by Saint Gregory of Tours (538–594), who in his history of France says that Sulpice belonged to a senatorial family of Gaul. We know little else about this saint beyond what De La Salle mentions in his meditation. Jean-Jacques Olier was pastor of the twelfth-century church in Paris in honor of Saint Sulpice; nearby he founded the Sulpician seminary, where De La Salle went to study for the priesthood in 1670. The feast of Saint Sulpice in the Roman Martyrology is January 29.

---

1. Sir 6:18      2. 2 Cor 2:15      3. 1 Tim 4:8

# January 25

## THE CONVERSION
## OF SAINT PAUL

### 99.1 First Point

Saint Paul was so zealous for the observance of the Old Law that with written orders from the High Priest, he went throughout Judea, wherever he knew there were any Christians, in order to persecute them. God, who knew the ardor of his zeal, wanted to employ him in the cause of Jesus Christ, whom he was persecuting in his members and in his disciples. In a flash he threw him to the ground and enlightened him with a light from heaven.[1] How fortunate this saint was to be forestalled by grace and changed in an instant from a persecutor to an Apostle and a preacher of the Gospel.

Rejoice with this saint over the special favor he received from God, and thank God for the grace he has given you in withdrawing you from the world and calling you to such a holy work of instructing children and leading them to piety.

### 99.2 Second Point

From the moment that grace came to Saint Paul, he was faithful to it. Jesus Christ made known to him by a voice from heaven that it was he whom Paul was persecuting[2] in the Christians. Heeding this voice that spoke to him to deliver him from his blindness, he humbly asked Jesus Christ what orders he wished to give him and what he wanted him to do for him.

Jesus Christ has called you to fulfill his ministry and to teach the poor. Are you as faithful to God's voice as Saint Paul was? Do you correspond as promptly as he did to all the movements of grace? Are you as zealous as he was to fulfill the duties of your work? Do you say with Saint Paul, Lord, what do you want me to do?[3] Are you as prompt to do everything that you learn about what God is asking of you?

### 99.3 Third Point

Although God had begun to enlighten Saint Paul by an extraordinary light and had called him by a miraculous voice, he did not yet want to make known his divine will to him. He sent Paul to Ananias, to whom he had revealed what he wanted Paul to do; he wanted Ananias to speak to Paul in God's name.[4]

This is how God wishes you to act when he inspires you with something good to do. By these lights from heaven, he simply wants you to understand that he is asking you to do something that you are not doing, but he does not wish you to proceed on your own, guided solely by these lights from heaven. He wants you to have recourse to your Director and to your Superior, whom he takes care to instruct and has charged to inform you of what you must do. Never trust your own inspirations or those that seem to come from God; explain them to those who guide you, and submit to their advice.

---

Originally this feast was a celebration of the transfer of the body of the Apostle from the Appian Way to the Ostian Way or, more likely, the transfer of a relic of the Apostle to some church in Gaul around the tenth century, when the feast was first celebrated. Apparently the notion of the change from one place to another became the idea of Paul's conversion on the road to Damascus. From the beginning, this celebration has been near the feast of Saint Peter's Chair in Rome, a fact that is not without significance.

---

1. Acts 9:3          3. Acts 9:6          4. Acts 9:3–6, 10–17
2. Acts 9:5

# January 27

## SAINT JOHN CHRYSOSTOM

### 100.1 First Point

Saint John Chrysostom, predisposed by grace, left the world at a time when he could have lived there with considerable honor because of his eloquence, which was admired by everyone. He withdrew into solitude, where he devoted himself to the study of Holy Scripture, which gave him great insight and a profound religious spirit.

You have the happiness and the advantage to be separated from the world and to read and to listen to the reading of Holy Scripture frequently. As a result, you ought to learn from this source the science of salvation and the holy maxims that your profession obliges you to practice and to teach to others. Meditate on these truths from time to time, and take them as the usual topic of your conversation.

### 100.2 Second Point

The bishop of Antioch obliged this saint to preach the Gospel, which he did so successfully and with such remarkable eloquence that he charmed all who heard him and at the same time drew their hearts to God. This is how someone filled with God in solitude can boldly and effectively speak of God and make him known to those who are buried in sin and ignorance and live in a state of blindness that is hidden from them.[1]

Because it is your duty to teach your disciples every day to know God, to explain to them the truths of the Gospel, and to train them in their practice, you must be entirely filled with God and burning with love for his holy law, so that your words may have their proper effect on your disciples. Preach by your example, and practice before their eyes what you wish to convince them to believe and to do.

### 100.3 Third Point

Having been made Patriarch of Constantinople in spite of his own resistance and at the request of the emperor, Saint John was zealous in undertaking a general moral reform and in tolerating no disorders. This led to strong confrontation with the empress, whose behavior in many respects was not Christian. Before long this brought great persecution on the saint, and he was several times driven from his see.

That is how people are treated who by their blameless life and their sound doctrine uphold the Gospel and the cause of religion. The demon, unable to endure their progress in virtue and the good they do for souls, never ceases to harass them by his own efforts or by those of his agents. If you live holily, says Saint Paul, expect to be persecuted.[2] Such will be your lot and your destiny as long as you live in this world.

---

Saint John (ca. 349–407) earned the name Chrysostom, which means golden mouth, because of his eloquence. He was born at Antioch, in

Syria, son of a commander in the imperial army, and was trained as a lawyer. After his conversion to Christianity, he withdrew into solitude with some friends and began the work of writing treatises that have earned him the title of Doctor of the Church. Later, as Patriarch of Constantinople, he was sent into exile by the empress; on the way, partly as a result of the rough treatment given him, he died. He can be considered a martyr, although he did not shed his blood. Saint Innocent I (Pope from 401 to 417) inscribed his name among the saints in 407. He is buried in Saint Peter's Basilica in Rome. His feast is now celebrated on September 13.

1. Eph. 4:17–18      2. 2 Tim 3:12

# January 29

## SAINT FRANCIS DE SALES

### 101.1 First Point

What is admirable in Saint Francis de Sales is that while he was living an ordinary life exteriorly, he practiced constant mortification of his senses, granting them only what was necessary and never satisfying them fully. He ate so little at meals that his life may be called a continual fast. This obtained for him to an eminent degree the virtue of chastity, which he had vowed when still a youth.

If you wish to possess the purity that your state requires, watch over your senses so well that, if possible, you do not lose control of them on any occasion. This is one of the chief means you can use to mortify you, and it is very appropriate in your vocation.

### 101.2 Second Point

This saint had such gentleness and tenderness toward his neighbor and tried so earnestly to suppress in himself even the slightest movements of anger that after his death, no bile was found in his body. When someone once urged him to yield to impatience, he asked whether she wished him to lose in a moment what he had spent his whole life acquiring.

Learn from this saint to overcome your passions, and never allow any emotion to appear in your words or in your actions. Humility will help you much in doing this, as well as silence on all the occasions when others will cause you some trouble.

### 101.3 Third Point

This gentleness and tenderness for his neighbor made it possible for Saint Francis to convert so many souls to God. It has been estimated that as many as seventy-two thousand heretics were won back by him from their errors. This virtue won the hearts of all those with whom he dealt, and the affection they felt for him was a means he used to bring them to God. One apostate even confessed that it was the saint's gentleness and patience that made him come back to the bosom of the Church.

Do you have these sentiments of charity and tenderness toward the poor children whom you have to educate? Do you take advantage of their affection for you to lead them to God? If you have for them the firmness of a father to restrain and to withdraw them from misbehavior, you must also have for them the tenderness of a mother to draw them to you and to do for them all the good that depends on you.

———

Francis de Sales (August 21, 1567–December 28, 1622) was born of a noble family at Annecy, in Savoy (southeastern France, bordering on Switzerland). While studying in Paris at the Jesuit College of Clermont, he made a vow of chastity, which is mentioned in De La Salle's meditation. He studied law at the University of Padua from 1586 to 1591, earning a Doctor's degree. Overcoming his father's opposition, he became a priest in 1593 and six years later was appointed coadjutor to the bishop of Geneva, not far from his birthplace in Annecy. In due course he became bishop of Geneva. He was highly regarded for his wisdom and kindness. Both virtues are illustrated in his renowned book, *Introduction to the Devout Life,* published in 1609, in which he shows how ordinary life can be holy. Although addressed to all people, the book was especially meant for the busy and the well-to-do. His kindness is mentioned by De La Salle in the second and third points of this meditation, especially as instrumental in winning back to the Church the numerous Calvinists in his diocese. He also guided Saint Jane Francis de Chantal in founding the Order of the Visitation, where the charity and gentleness of Jesus Christ are guiding virtues for the Sisters and where the weak, the infirm, the sick, and the poor are primary concerns of the congregation. Francis was canonized in 1665 (when De La Salle was 14 years old), named a Doctor of the Church in 1877, and, in 1923 declared by Pope Pius XI patron of all Catholic writers, especially those who explain or defend Christian doctrine by publishing newspapers or journals. His body was transferred from Geneva to Annecy on January 29, which is the reason why his feast was once celebrated on that day. It is now celebrated on January 24.

# February 1

## SAINT IGNATIUS, MARTYR

### 102.1 First Point

Saint Ignatius was one of the first disciples and one of the most worthy successors of the Apostles. He preached the Gospel and did much to spread religion with a most astonishing zeal and courage. The more opposition he met with, the more active he became, without any human respect or fear, not even of the emperor, whom he vigorously withstood, caring nothing for either threats or promises.

With this kind of truly Christian firmness and generosity, you ought to uphold God's cause, which is what you are obliged to do in your work. You fulfill one of the main functions of the Apostles by educating in faith and in religion these new believers, that is, the children who only recently have been filled with God's Spirit in Baptism. Following the example of the holy Apostles, be worthy of so holy a ministry[1] by seclusion and by application to prayer.

### 102.2 Second Point

This saint was so filled with the Spirit of Jesus Christ and with his holy love that he very often had our Lord's holy name on his lips. In this way he shared his love with those he instructed and with whom he conversed. Because he belonged entirely to Jesus Christ and had consecrated himself to him to preach the Gospel, he also wanted the Christians to whom he taught his doctrine to be attached only to Jesus and to work only for him.

If you love Jesus Christ well, you will try in every possible way to enkindle his holy love in the hearts of the children you are forming to be his disciples. See to it that they often think of Jesus, their good and only Lord, that they often speak of Jesus, and that they long only for Jesus and desire only Jesus.

### 102.3 Third Point

Having been condemned to be devoured by lions, Saint Ignatius said that it was then that he was beginning to be a disciple of Jesus Christ, because he no longer desired anything in this world and feared none of all the torments that tyrants could invent to maltreat his body. He even longed that his body might be delivered over to the cruelest torments as quickly as possible, so that he might all the sooner enjoy the possession of Jesus Christ.

Admire this saint's yearning to suffer and die so that he would be sacrificed to God as a victim holy and pleasing in his sight.[2] Think, as he did, that you will truly become disciples of Jesus Christ only when you love him and are ready to suffer for his holy love.

———

Ignatius (died ca. 107), bishop of Antioch, is thought to have been a disciple of the Apostle John. He was martyred during the reign of the emperor Trajan. Our knowledge of him comes from seven letters he wrote to different churches while he was on his journey to Rome to be devoured by wild animals in witness to his faith. In these letters he speaks of faith in the Holy Eucharist and of the role of the bishop, and he makes the first use in Christian literature of the term Catholic Church. In his letter to the Romans, he urges them not to interfere with his martyrdom. "Allow me to be eaten by the beasts," he writes, "through whom I am to come to God. I am God's wheat to be ground by the teeth of beasts in order to become the pure bread of Christ. I long . . . to be crushed . . . that I may come to Jesus Christ." His feast has been transferred to October 17.

———

1. 1 Cor 4:1–2      2. Rom 12:1

# February 2

## THE PURIFICATION
## OF THE MOST BLESSED VIRGIN

### 104.1[1] First Point

The Blessed Virgin went to the Temple to be purified at the time prescribed by the Law.[2] She submitted to this Law and did not wish to claim any exemption, even though she was not obliged by it because she was the mother of God's Son, whom she had conceived and brought into the world without losing her virginity.

Admire Mary's humility in this mystery, for she appears here as an ordinary woman although she is far superior to all others by reason of her two roles as virgin and mother. Learn from her not to want to be distinguished from others, not to ask for or to seek any exemptions in the practice of your Rule.

The more faithful and exact you are to observe this Rule, the more God will fill you with his grace and the more joy he will give you in your state.

## 104.2  Second Point

While going through the ceremony of purification, *the Most Blessed Virgin*, in order to obey the Law to its fullest extent, offered her Son to God because he was her firstborn.[3] The eternal Father, who willed that this dear Son be one day immolated on the cross to expiate our sins, returned him for the time being to the authority of his holy mother after she had bought him back by the offering prescribed by the Law.[4]

This offering that the Son of God made to his Father was at that moment only an interior one, although it was made exteriorly on the part of the Most Blessed Virgin. Jesus was waiting to make the exterior offering of himself on the tree of the cross before the eyes of all the world.

You offered yourself to God when you left the world. Did you hold back anything at that time? Did you give yourself entirely to him? Have you taken back nothing of the offering you made to God at that time? You must not be content to have made this offering to God once. Renew it daily, and consecrate all your actions to him by not performing any of them except for him.

## 104.3  Third Point

In appreciation for the offering that was made of Jesus Christ and that he made of himself in this mystery and for the humility shown by the Most Blessed Virgin, God inspired a holy old man, Simeon, to proclaim publicly the greatness of Jesus, declaring that Jesus had come to be the Light that would enlighten the Gentiles and be the glory of the people of Israel.[5] He then invoked all blessings on his holy Mother.

Oh, how good it is to give yourself to God! Even in this life, he rewards and fills with very tangible consolations the soul that consecrates itself to him. He causes others to esteem and to honor those who are happy in humiliations. The more you give to God, the more he will bless you; the more you are despised by others, the greater you will be before God.

---

Today this feast is referred to as the feast of the Presentation of the Lord, which was the original focus of the celebration. As such, De La Salle's meditation corresponds well in the second and third points. The day has also been called Candlemas Day from the time of the tenth century, because this was the day when candles were blessed and carried in procession, possibly a devotional practice based on

Simeon's words in the Gospel that Jesus is the light that reveals God to all nations.

---

1. Number 103, one of the six meditations in the *Additions*, is found at the end both of the original edition and of this edition.
2. Lk 2:22
3. Lk 2:23
4. Lk 2:24
5. Lk 2:32

# February 7

## SAINT ROMUALD

### 105.1 First Point

Saint Romuald lived in the world for twenty years, which seemed very long to him because all he found there was misery and reasons for leaving it. He then lived a hundred years in solitude, which seemed very short to him because of the consolations that God gave him to enjoy during all that period. Saint Lawrence Justinian says that if the world knew the pleasure found in seclusion, cities would become deserts, and deserts would soon be populated.

If you wish to live happily, love seclusion. The more you keep away from the burden of the world, the more you will have peace of mind and conscience. How happy we are when we keep our mind detached from everything and our conscience pure and clean. The less we have to do with people of the world, the more fully we will possess this advantage.

### 105.2 Second Point

It is admirable that Saint Romuald, who lived for 120 years, spent 100 of them in very great austerities, wearing a hair shirt, eating only three times a week a bit of bread and some beans, and drinking only water. After that, who will dare say that austerities shorten life? Several saints lived a very austere life and yet lived much longer than most other people.

But even if austerities do shorten our days, they procure for us a great benefit by purifying both soul and body, for they weaken our passions and deliver the body from all corruption.

### 105.3 Third Point

After living for 100 years in solitude and having led a very penitential life, this saint said that the more he thought of death, the more he feared not dying well. This is because he knew that God will require such an exact account on the Day of Judgment that the just themselves will scarcely be saved.[1] According to the words of the Prophet, God will judge justice.[2]

If this saint so deeply feared the judgment of God, how fearful must you be if, perhaps, you are spending your life in neglect of the duties of your state? If, then, you wish to avoid the rigors of God's judgments and to die with peace of mind, be the judge of your actions in advance[3] during your life; condemn and punish everything in you that might displease God.

---

Romuald (ca. 950–1027) was born at Ravenna of a noble family. His father quarreled with a relative and killed him in a duel. Romuald was so shocked by this that he entered a Benedictine monastery to do forty days of penance. This led to his joining the monks, but some bad example among them led in turn to his becoming a hermit. Eventually he founded the Camaldolese, an order that combines both the community life and the eremitic life. De La Salle's belief that Romuald lived to be 120 years old is not accepted today. February 7 is the day his body was transferred to Fabriano, Italy. His feast is now celebrated on June 19.

---

1. 1 Pt 4:18        2. Ps 75:3        3. 1 Cor 11:31

# February 22

## THE CHAIR OF SAINT PETER AT ANTIOCH

*The submission we owe to the Church*

### 106.1 First Point

Oon this day Saint Peter, after the dispersion of the Apostles, established his see at Antioch and was recognized by the faithful as the Vicar of Christ. This was the occasion when those who had embraced the faith began in this city to adopt the name of Christians.[1] The Church has instituted a special feast to commemorate and honor this event, giving us an opportunity to consider with special attention the submission we owe to the Church and to the one who is its head.

The Church is our mother; to her we must be united in every way, and on her we must depend in everything concerning religion. We must be submissive to all her decisions and listen to them as oracles. The Church makes the truth known to us. We must accept it from her mouth without any hesitation and without examination. All we have to say in answer to what the Church proposes to us is, "I believe," without hesitation and with no doubt whatsoever.

Moreover, we ought to welcome everything the Church proposes to us and to do so with great docility. Jesus Christ has given the Church his power and authority over us, and he tells us that anyone who does not listen to the Church must be regarded by us as a pagan and a publican.[2] This caused Saint Augustine to say that he would not believe the Gospel if he were not bound to do so by the authority of the Church.

You are obliged in your work to teach children the truths of our holy religion. By necessity you must also be outstanding in your simple and humble submission to all the decisions of the Church. Is this your position?

### 106.2 Second Point

The Pope, being the Vicar of Jesus Christ, the visible head of the Church, and the successor of Saint Peter, has wide authority over the entire Church. All the faithful who are members ought to regard him as their father and as the voice God uses to give his orders to them. He possesses the universal power of binding and loosing[3] that Jesus Christ gave to Saint Peter; to him Jesus Christ has committed the responsibility first given to this holy Apostle of feeding his flock.[4]

Your role, then, is to work to increase and to take care of this sheepfold; therefore, you must honor our Holy Father, the Pope, as the holy shepherd of this flock and the High Priest of the Church. You must respect his every word. It ought to be enough that something comes from him for you to be infinitely attentive. Is this how you have acted up to the present? Adore God's authority in this sovereign Shepherd of souls, and in the future, look upon him as the great teacher of the Church.

### 106.3 Third Point

The bishops have been established by God to be the defenders of the Church. They are also, says Saint Paul, the first ministers of Jesus Christ and the dispensers of the mysteries of God.[5]

You must, therefore, honor them, respect their words, and be submissive to them in everything that concerns the care of the souls that have been entrusted to you. Because bishops have been appointed by God to watch over the doctrine and the morals of those who labor under their ministry and are in charge of the entire spiritual guidance of their diocese, all those who are employed in this labor to procure the salvation of souls must do so only in dependence on them. By this means they will draw down upon themselves and on their work the blessings of God. Acknowledge that God established this hierarchy, and submit to it.

---

It is significant that De La Salle wrote this meditation during the time when the Pope's authority was being seriously challenged over the issue of Jansenism, especially in France. Six different Popes issued no less than twelve decrees, over a period of 60 years, against the adherents of this doctrine. The final condemnation came in the Bull *Unigenitus* from Pope Clement XI in September 1713. Cardinal Noailles of Paris led several bishops in opposition to this condemnation and appealed to a general council over the head of the Pope. De La Salle was greatly disturbed by this, as he indicated in a letter to Gabriel Drolin. The firm support of the Pope, illustrated by this meditation, is one of the chief characteristics of De La Salle's teaching to the Brothers and, through them, to the students in the Christian Schools. Regarding the original title of this feast, the Chair of Saint Peter at Antioch, Saint Gregory the Great (on whom De La Salle wrote a meditation for March 12) says that Saint Peter was regarded as the head of the Church in Antioch for seven years prior to going to Rome. The feast is now called simply the Chair of Peter. It was celebrated as early as the fourth century in Rome.

---

1. Acts 11:26
2. Mt 18:17
3. Mt 16:19
4. Jn 21:15–17
5. 1 Cor 4:1

# February 24

## SAINT MATTHIAS, APOSTLE

### 107.1 First Point

Judas sold and betrayed Jesus Christ, his Lord and God, to the Jews, so that they might put him to death. Then he gave himself to the devil by dying in despair. After the Ascension of Jesus Christ into heaven, the Apostles assembled in a house to pray and to prepare themselves to receive the Holy Spirit. At Saint Peter's request, they chose Saint Matthias to take Judas' place.[1] This holy disciple was admitted among the number of the Apostles only after a common prayer was recited publicly by Saint Peter in the name of all the Apostles and disciples, who were praying together in the same place.[2]

This shows us that in all we do for the glory of God and the salvation of souls, we ought to undertake nothing without praying to ask God for the light and the grace we need to succeed in whatever we undertake for him in this holy ministry, which can succeed only insofar as we are aided by his help and directed by his Holy Spirit.

### 107.2  Second Point

In choosing Saint Matthias to take Judas' place, the Apostles were not content to pray; they consulted among themselves in order to decide nothing in this matter except through consultation. They were convinced that if they joined counsel to prayer, God would make known to them his will regarding the choice which they had to make of one among those present who had accompanied Jesus Christ and would now become one of them to share in the holy ministry of the apostolate.[3]

This is how God wishes you to act in your own conduct and in your ministry. You ought to do nothing and to be involved in nothing except on the advice of your superiors, for it is up to them to let you know what God is asking of you and how you must carry it out, with respect both to you and to the good of those for whom you are responsible. Be assured that by these two means you will make great progress and that God will not allow you to go astray.

### 107.3  Third Point

In the choice they made of Saint Matthias to fill Judas' place, the Apostles were not influenced by any human consideration; they even preferred him to a relative of Jesus Christ. They paid attention to two things only. First, he had always been with Jesus Christ from his Baptism to his Ascension into heaven,[4] so that he would be perfectly instructed in the teaching of Jesus Christ and would be able to preach it with assurance. Second, he had to be able to witness to the Resurrection of Jesus Christ,[5] for if this mystery were to be proclaimed with certainty, it had to have eyewitnesses who were beyond question.

This ought to lead you to realize that to carry out your ministry properly, you must have in it no human considerations, and you must not be concerned about anything that cannot help you bring about the salvation of the souls for whom you are responsible. This is the purpose of your state and of your work. Is this how you are acting?

---

The only reliable information about Saint Matthias is found in the Acts of the Apostles. According to the Greeks, he brought Christianity to Cappadocia and was crucified there. It is said that he was buried in Jerusalem until Saint Helena (about whom De La Salle writes in the meditations for May 3 and September 14) brought his relics to Rome. His feast is now celebrated on May 14.

---

1. Acts 1:14–26         3. Acts 1:21–26         5. Acts 1:22
2. Acts 1:24–25         4. Acts 1:21–22

# March 7

## SAINT THOMAS AQUINAS

### 108.1 First Point
Saint Thomas is one of the greatest Doctors of the Church, which he enlightened by the quite extraordinary and almost miraculous learning that God gave him. This saint studied as much at the foot of the crucifix as he did in books. Because he excelled so greatly in the science of theology, he is considered the Angel of this sacred school, surpassing all other theologians. In all the difficulties he met while studying or writing, he had recourse to prayer, and when this did not suffice to give him an understanding of what he wanted to know, he added fasting. By these two means, he acquired such great knowledge and became a miracle of learning.

It is true that what you need to learn are the ordinary things about religion and salvation. Still, it will be difficult for you to possess them perfectly unless you employ the three means that Saint Thomas used to become learned; I mean books, prayer, and mortification. By these three means, God wishes you to learn in your state what you need to know and to teach others.

### 108.2 Second Point
In all his studies and all his writings, Saint Thomas had no other purpose than the glory of God and the building of the Church. Be-

cause of this he merited to have Jesus Christ give him this praise: Thomas, you have written well of me; what reward do you wish me to give to you for the great good you have done for the Church? But this saint had worked with such great disinterestedness for the good of the faithful, especially those who have to teach others, that he made no other reply than this, that he wanted no other recompense than God.

Your profession commits you to teach children the science of salvation, and you are bound to do this with total disinterestedness. Do you do this with the sole view of procuring the glory of God and your neighbor's salvation? Declare to God that you will never have any other intention than that.

### 108.3 Third Point

This saint, who had such eminent knowledge, excelled so much in the virtue of humility that he refused all the honors of the Church that were offered to him, and he regarded himself as the least among his brothers in community. As a result, in spite of his great activity, he served them as a companion.

Although his learning won him great renown and caused him to be looked up to and honored by the whole world, he managed not to draw attention to himself outside his community. His whole aim in study was to use his learning for the purpose proper to it and for which God asked him to labor and to study.

The admirable thing is that although he was so learned, he had no desire to be esteemed by others. This led him often to thank God that he had never had any thought of vanity that would make him deserving of blame. Oh, how rare it is to find a man who excels in anything and who does not on that account have a higher opinion of himself!

Try to share in this saint's humility, for you have nothing in you except what is lowly and humbling. To acquire this virtue, love humiliations a great deal, for they are the means, the most apt ones, to procure it.

———

Thomas Aquinas (1226–1274) was born in the castle of Rocca Secca, near Naples. He began his education at the nearby abbey of Monte Casino and later attended the University of Naples. His decision to become a Dominican, then an Order not yet 30 years old, shocked his noble family, and he was kidnapped by his brothers and tempted to violate his chastity. However, he escaped and continued his studies as a Dominican under Saint Albert at Cologne and with Saint Bonaventure in Paris, where he also taught philosophy and theology. His

*Summa Theologica,* published after his death along with his other writings in 17 volumes, earned him the title of Doctor of the Church in 1567. Pope Leo XIII declared him the patron of all Catholic schools. He died on March 7, but his feast is now celebrated on January 28, the day his body was transferred to Toulouse in 1369.

# March 12

## SAINT GREGORY THE GREAT, POPE

### 109.1 First Point

Saint Gregory was destined by his father to succeed him in his position as a senator in Rome, but this saint, still young when his father died, built several monasteries and withdrew to one of them, leaving the world and all his wealth in order to live a life of obedience. This saint condisered submission to be the greatest benefit in life, because it is the most fitting attitude for a creature, the one that makes humans most pleasing to God and draws down the most graces. This is why he believed himself happier to be hidden from all and to submit to a superior than to possess all the wealth and honors on earth.

Is this how you esteem the state in which God has placed you? Do you think you are most fortunate to be there? Do you prefer it to all that you could have and desire in this world? You are unworthy of so holy a state if you do not have this disposition. If you do not feel it, at least try to acquire it.

### 109.2 Second Point

Saint Gregory suffered throughout his life with extreme patience. First, he practiced excessive austeries as a religious. Second, the pains of gout made his body so emaciated that it was difficult to recognize him. Third, he suffered from persecution; Emperor Maurice, who had been his close friend, became a cruel enemy and wished to deprive him of his title of Universal Patriarch of the Church.

In all this Gregory imitated the holy man Job, whose spirit he had thoroughly absorbed while writing a commentary on the Book of Job. The only remedy he used in all this suffering was recourse to prayer,[1] in which he found great support; God became his protector in his sufferings and in the opposition he met.[2]

Do you love the sufferings found in your state? Do you endure them with as much patience as Saint Gregory loved and suffered his? If you truly possess the spirit of your state, God will make you discover in it all sorts of consolations, even in your suffering.

### 109.3 Third Point

When this saint was elected Pope, he immediately took to flight but finally accepted the responsibility of head of the Church in spite of his feelings. Nevertheless, with unflagging zeal and in spite of his great infirmities, he worked to procure the good of the Church by his preaching, his writings, and his constant attention.

He had not been able, prior to his elevation to the Sovereign Pontificate, to labor in person for the conversion of infidels, something to which his zeal inspired him. After he became Pope, he sent out evangelical laborers to preach the faith to them and to instruct them in our religion. By such conduct this saint showed that it was only his humility that made him flee the papacy, because once he had accepted his election, his zeal led him to accomplish great things for the cause of religion.

You do not have infidels to convert, it is true, yet you are obliged by your state to teach children the mysteries of religion and to give them the Christian spirit. Because this task is no less important than the conversion of infidels, do it with all possible care and attention.

---

Pope Gregory (ca. 540–604) was born in Rome of a patrician family and became prefect of the city, following his father's public career. When his father died, he inherited vast estates, but in 574 he resigned from office and became a Benedictine monk. In 578 he was ordained a priest by the Pope. In 590, when Pope Pelagius II died, Gregory was elected to succeed him. He wrote numerous books and sermons, which won for him the honor of being regarded as one of the four great Doctors of the Church. He did much to reform the morals of his day and the liturgy of the Church. Gregorian chant is named for him. He is also the Pope who sent Saint Augustine of Canterbury to England to restore the faith there among the pagan Angles and Saxons, who had destroyed the earlier Christian culture in Britain. He died on March 12, but his feast is now celebrated on September 3, the day he became Pope.

---

1. Job 1:6–2, 10     2. Ps 37:39–40

# March 19

## SAINT JOSEPH

### 110.1 First Point

Because Saint Joseph was made responsible by God for the care and external guidance of Jesus Christ, it was important that he have the qualities and virtues necessary to fulfill worthily so holy and ex-alted a ministry. The Gospel tells us about three, all very fitting for the responsibility entrusted to him: he was just; he was very submissive to God's orders,[1] and he had a very special solicitude for the education and the protection of Jesus Christ.[2]

The first quality that the Gospel attributes to Saint Joseph is that he is just. This is also the main virtue he needed in order to be able to provide guidance to Jesus Christ. Because our Lord is God and holy, it would not be fitting that the person in charge of guiding him not be holy and just before God.

It is even entirely proper that Saint Joseph be, after the Most Blessed Virgin, one of the holiest people to be found in the world at that time, so that he might have some conformity with Jesus Christ, who was entrusted to him and confided to his care. The Gospel also says of him that he is just before God, that is, holy in every way. We even have grounds to believe that Saint Joseph, thanks to a special privilege, was entirely exempted from sin.

You also have been charged, very much like Saint Joseph, with a holy work, a work that is very similar to his and requires that your piety and your virtue be more than ordinary. Take Saint Joseph as your model, for he is your patron, and strive to be worthy of your ministry and to excel in virtue by following the example of this great saint.

### 110.2 Second Point

The second virtue that the Gospel points out to us in Saint Joseph is his holy and entire submission to God's orders. God in-structed him by an angel to remain with the Blessed Virgin when he was questioning whether he ought to leave her; at once he banished the thought of leaving her from his mind. After the birth of the Child Jesus, God warned Joseph during the night to take the Child to Egypt to save him from the persecution of Herod; at once he arose and de-parted to bring the Child and his virgin mother to Egypt.[3] After Herod's death, God told Joseph to come back to Judea, and he re-turned there without delay.[4]

Oh, how admirable is this prompt and simple obedience in this great saint! He does not hesitate a single instant to carry out what God desires of him! Do you have as much at heart to do God's will as this saint did?

If you want God to bestow many graces on you, both for you and for the Christian education of the children you have to protect and to guide, you must imitate this saint in his love for and in his fidelity to obedience, which of all the virtues is the one most appropriate for you in your state and in your work and the one that will bring you the most grace.

### 110.3 Third Point

The Gospel also makes us admire in Saint Joseph the care he has for the holy Child Jesus, which he showed in the promptness with which he took him to Egypt[5] when God told him to do so; in the precaution he took, on leaving Egypt, not to take him to Judea, for fear of Archelaus, who then occupied the throne of his father, Herod,[6] and in the sorrow he felt at having lost Jesus when they were returning from Jerusalem, as the Most Blessed Virgin testified in these words: Your father and I have been searching for you in great sorrow and in great affliction.[7] Two things inspired the great solicitude that Saint Joseph felt for Jesus: the commission that the eternal Father had given him and the tender love Saint Joseph had for Jesus.

You must have a similarly great attention and affection for preserving or procuring the innocence of the children entrusted to your guidance and for keeping them away from whatever might interfere with their education or prevent them from acquiring piety, just as Saint Joseph had for all that could contribute to the welfare of the Child Jesus. For you have been made responsible for these children, just as Saint Joseph was made responsible by God for the Savior of the world. This is also the first care you ought to have in your work if you wish to imitate Saint Joseph, who had nothing more at heart than to provide for the needs of the Child Jesus.

—————

De La Salle had a special love for Saint Joseph, developed undoubtedly as part of his training in the seminary of Saint Sulpice. The first seal of the Institute, of which we have samples on obediences as early as 1707, depicts Saint Joseph with the Child Jesus, and this special devotion to the Infant Jesus and Saint Joseph is mentioned in the Bull of Approbation. This meditation explains the several reasons why such a devotion was considered by the Founder as most appropriate for the Brothers. The original morning and evening prayers of the Brothers included a special prayer to Saint Joseph, also a litany to

Saint Joseph after the midday recreation, before returning to school. The Rule of 1705 states: "At one o'clock the Brothers will assemble in the oratory to recite the Litany of Saint Joseph, Patron and Protector of the Community, to ask for his spirit and his assistance in the Christian education of children" (CL 25:100). *Pratique du Réglement Journalier,* the original text for the order of the Brothers' day, lists the feast of the Great Saint Joseph as one of the special days for a holiday. On this day in 1719, De La Salle was able to say his last Mass with the Brothers at Saint Yon, an event that was regarded as a special favor from Saint Joseph. The Founder died less than three weeks later, on April 7.

---

1. Mt 1:19
2. Mt 1:20–24
3. Mt 2:13–14

4. Mt 2:19–21
5. Mt 2:14
6. Mt 2:22

7. Lk 2:48

# March 20

## SAINT JOACHIM

### 157.1[1] First Point

Together with the Church, let us admire the honor that God paid to Saint Joachim by choosing him to be the father of the Most Blessed Virgin and to prepare the way for the mystery of the Incarnation. He was fittingly named Joachim, which means preparation for the Lord. With the Church, let us recognize that God's choice of this saint was for him a most extraordinary favor. With Saint Epiphanius, let us acknowledge that all people are greatly indebted to this holy Patriarch for giving to the world the most excellent of all gifts, the purest and most exalted of all creatures, the Most Blessed Virgin, mother of Jesus Christ.

Let us honor this saint as one who contributed to the forming of the Church and to whom the Church owes what she is, because he fathered the Most Blessed Virgin, mother of him from whom the Church was born. Consider, moreover, that if we are children of the Church and members of Jesus Christ,[2] it is Saint Joachim who procured this benefit for us.

God has given you no less an honor than he gave Saint Joachim by placing you in the work you have, for he has destined you to be the spiritual father of the children whom you instruct. If this saint was chosen to be the father of the Most Blessed Virgin, you have been destined by God to produce children for Jesus Christ and even to produce and engender Jesus Christ in their hearts.[3] Can you say that you have fully embraced God's designs on you in this ministry?

### 157.2 Second Point

His constant fasting and prayer won for Saint Joachim the favor of being the father of the Most Blessed Virgin. For this saint, seeing that his wife, Saint Anne, was sterile, devoted himself so intensely to fasting and prayer that he, in some way, forced heaven to grant Saint Anne the gift of fecundity, which both of them ardently desired. This is why Saint Epiphanius called the Most Blessed Virgin the child of fasting and prayer.

We cannot sufficiently admire the marvelous results produced by prayer and by the privation of sensual pleasures, because they contributed so much to the coming of Jesus Christ on earth and to the birth of the Most Blessed Virgin, his mother. Nor can we go too far in making use of these two remedies against the sorrows and the temptations that sometimes overwhelm us in this life.

By these two means, God will grant us all the graces we need. This is why you are obliged in the work you do to have recourse to them as often as possible, especially when you have something to beg from God for those who are in your care. You ought to be their intercessors with God to obtain for them by your prayers the piety that you cannot procure for them by all the care you take to teach them, for it belongs to God alone to give true wisdom,[4] which is the Christian spirit.

### 157.3 Third Point

Saint Joachim was fully aware of this special grace that God had given him to be the father of the Most Blessed Virgin. As soon as she was old enough to live in the Temple, he willingly deprived himself of her presence and offered her to God as one who had come from him and belonged to him. He spent the rest of his life separated from her, although he loved her very tenderly.

Then, having consecrated to God the daughter whom God had given him, he considered that he no longer needed his wealth beyond what was required to live frugally. Wishing to live a poor life, he offered to God the greater part of his possessions, devoting a share of them to the upkeep of the Temple and the rest to feeding the poor and the pilgrims.

In this way Saint Joachim teaches you to be detached from the love of creatures and to do all you can, so that those whom God has entrusted to you may be fit to be presented to him, not showing affection for them except to lead them to his holy love and to fill them with his Spirit. In the future, therefore, show no partiality for any of them, admiring only their piety without paying attention to anything in them that is agreeable or attractive in their appearance.

---

In De La Salle's time, the feast of Saint Joachim, father of the Most Blessed Virgin, was celebrated on this day between the feast of Saint Joseph and the feast of the Annunciation. The Eastern Rite celebrated the feast many centuries before it became a part of the Roman Liturgy in the sixteenth century. It was moved to August 16 by Pope Pius X when he revised the calendar of feasts in 1913–1914, but it was joined to the Feast of Saint Anne (July 26) in the reform of the liturgy after Vatican II. The details of Saint Joachim's life cited by De La Salle in the third point of his meditation are known only through the apocryphal gospel of Saint James.

---

1. The edition of 1882, from which the official numbers of the meditations are taken, transfers this meditation from March 20, when it was celebrated in the time of De La Salle, to August 16; therefore, it is out of order in the present enumeration.
2. 1 Cor 6:15
3. Gal 4:19
4. Prv 2:6

# March 21

## SAINT BENEDICT

### 111.1 First Point

When Saint Benedict was a student in Rome, he left the city in order to avoid the bad example of his fellow students and withdrew to a very wild solitude where he practiced continual prayer and very great austerity. By doing this he prepared himself to become the father of a great number of religious to whom he gave a very wise Rule that insists a great deal on seclusion and leads a person to great perfection. By this holy Rule and by his exact and faithful guidance, he drew a great number of souls to God, separating them from the world and from all human conversation, so that they might be in a position to converse with God alone.

This is, indeed, one of the greatest advantages you can possess in this life and one of the main means you can use to give yourself to God. The more faithful you are to the Rule, the more you will acquire the perfection of your state. The less you communicate with people, the more God will communicate with you.

### 111.2 Second Point

This saint exercised such great vigilance and attention over himself to preserve purity that when he felt subject to temptations, he practiced great mortifications to help him overcome them. Once, when harassed more violently than usual by these temptations, he even rolled himself over thistles and thorn bushes with such violence that his body was all covered with blood. He avoided any conversation with women to such an extent that however holy his sister, Scholastica, was, he saw her only once a year, and even then he remained only a short time with her and spoke only about God.

If you wish to be as pure as your state requires, mortify your mind and your senses, and use them only when necessary. Above all, have a fear of all familiarity with women, and speak to them only when obliged to do so by necessity.

### 111.3 Third Point

The education of children was regarded of such great importance by this saint that he educated and cared for a great number of them in his monasteries. He took care to have them instructed in learning and in piety. He also put in his Rule a number of practices that he wanted to see observed in receiving and guiding them.

He welcomed Saint Maurus, who was only eight years old at the time, and a number of others at an early age. These children were brought up with so much care and attention that they were never allowed to go anywhere alone; a religious accompanied them at all times. As a result, they acquired more of the purity of angels because they knew less about the evil of humans.

Are you careful to keep your students away from whatever might corrupt their morals, especially bad company, and do you inspire them with a horror of such companions? Are you so vigilant over their conduct that you prevent them from doing the least thing wrong when they are in your presence? Do you show them how to avoid all occasions of evil when they are no longer under your supervision? Learn from Saint Benedict how to bring up properly the children whom you have to guide. Act so as to obtain from him by your prayers the grace of guiding them well.

Benedict (ca. 480–ca. 547) was born at Nursia, in Umbria, and educated in Rome. He began at an early age to lead the life of a hermit in a cave at Subiaco, on Monte Calvo, about 35 miles from Rome, probably in reaction to the corrupt morals he had witnessed as a student in the imperial city. Others eventually joined him, and he set up small hermitages for them, but he was led to leave this way of life with several companions and establish a new kind of community monasticism on Monte Cassino. There he composed his Rule, which influenced the entire monastic movement for the next six centuries, earning for him the title of Patriarch of Western Monasticism.

The Benedictine way of life influenced De La Salle in his development of the Institute and of the Rule of the Brothers, particularly with respect to silence, obedience, penance, and attention to detail. He was inspired by Saint Benedict's insistence on fraternal union, stability, and the common sense that Saint Benedict taught to temper everything, so that the strong would have something to long for and the weak would not draw back in alarm. There is also a touch of irony and kindly humor in Saint Benedict's Rule; there are similar traces in De La Salle's letters. The feast of Saint Benedict is now celebrated on July 11, the day that the Benedictines have traditionally celebrated to commemorate the transfer of the saint's relics from Italy to France in the seventh century, although this event is under dispute.

# March 25

## THE ANNUNCIATION
## OF THE MOST BLESSED VIRGIN

### 112.1 First Point

Let us give thanks with the whole Church for the honor that the Most Blessed Virgin received on this day, to become the Mother of God. This is the greatest honor any mere creature can ever receive. Saint Ambrose declares that it was the greatness and the excellence of Mary's faith that procured this favor for her.

In this role she has become an object of veneration for the angels themselves, who, although much higher by nature, nevertheless, are far beneath her in view of the dignity she received on this day.

Still, this dignity only leads her to humble herself, for when the angel declares to her that she is the Mother of God and honors her as such, this admirable virgin has no reply except that she is the servant of the Lord.[1] Saint Ambrose cannot help marveling at such a response in the mouth of this holy virgin at the very moment when she is chosen to be the Mother of God.

Let us profit today from such a great example. May all the graces that God gives us, no matter how remarkable they might be, incline us also to humble ourselves below everyone else.

### 112.2  Second Point

God's goodness shines out in this mystery no less than the Most Blessed Virgin's humility. The Son of God, says Saint Paul, possesses divine nature and takes nothing from God by regarding himself as God's equal; nevertheless, he empties himself on this day and takes on the nature of a slave, making himself like us except for sin.[2]

This was, as the angel says to the Most Blessed Virgin, so that he might deliver his people from their sins,[3] as he committed himself by clothing himself with human nature. Seeing that holocausts, which were the most excellent sacrifices of the Old Law, were not sufficiently pleasing to God to take away our sins, Jesus offers himself in sacrifice and says to his eternal Father, Today I come into the world to do your holy will[4] and to accomplish all justice.[5] For this purpose, the Prophet Isaiah says, he bore all our sins and took upon himself all our weaknesses.[6]

Let us do what we can by irreproachable conduct to achieve what the Son of God in this mystery did for all people, which is to destroy sin entirely.[7]

### 112.3  Third Point

If God gives us so many signs of his goodness toward us on this holy day, we also have the advantage of receiving a great number of graces. Jesus Christ says in the Gospel that he came into this world only to give us life and to give it to us in abundance.[8]

*By him and in him,* says Saint Paul, a general reconciliation of all things with God has taken place. By the blood that Jesus shed on the cross, peace has been restored in heaven and on earth.[9]

He also, according to the same Apostle, although we had strayed far from God and had become his enemies, has reestablished us in grace to make us holy, without blemish, and without blame before him.[10]

He too, according to the same Apostle, has made us worthy to share the lot of the saints.[11]

This day, therefore, is a day of joy and blessings for us, for it was on this day that God, *who is rich in mercy,* as Saint Paul says, out of the infinite love with which he has loved us, sent his own Son, even when we were dead by our sins and by our crimes, to give us new life in Jesus Christ, to manifest to future ages the magnificence of the riches of his grace through the goodness he has had for us in Jesus Christ. If, then, we enjoy such abundant graces to save ourselves[12] and to become perfect saints,[13] as Saint Paul says, we are indebted for all this to what Jesus Christ did for us on this day by becoming man out of love for us.[14] Let us show him our gratitude by the holy use we make of these graces.

———

The date of this feast was determined by the relation between the feast of Christmas and the visit of the Angel Gabriel to Mary, a period of nine months. From its inception, this feast was the celebration of the Incarnation of Christ rather than the honor of the Most Blessed Virgin. This explains in part why De La Salle focuses in his meditation more on the mystery of the Incarnation than on Mary.

---

1. Lk 1:38
2. Phil 2:6–7
3. Mt 1:21
4. Heb 10:8–9
5. Mt 3:15
6. Is 53:4
7. Rom 6:6
8. Jn 10:10
9. Col 1:20
10. Col 1:21–22
11. Col 1:12
12. Eph 2:4–7
13. Eph 1:4
14. Gal 4:4

# April 2

## SAINT FRANCIS OF PAOLA

### 113.1 First Point

Saint Francis of Paola had an altogether extraordinary humility, which is the reason why he never took Holy Orders, judging himself entirely unworthy. He also gave the name Minims to the religious of his order, wanting them to consider themselves as the least of all, with no one below them. He knew how to practice this virtue very well, for he served his brothers at table and washed their feet, including those of the novices. Because God usually raises up those who humble themselves,[1] God honored him with the gifts of miracles and of prophecy that spread his reputation everywhere.

You have the happiness to labor for the instruction of the poor and to be engaged in a work that is esteemed and honored only by those who have a truly Christian spirit. Thank God for having placed you in such a sanctifying state, one that provides for the sanctification of others but that, nevertheless, has nothing attractive to others and even gives those who labor in it frequent occasions to be humiliated.

### 113.2 Second Point

This saint had a very tender love for all his brothers. He greatly encouraged them to practice this virtue because he wished charity to be the characteristic of his order. He wanted very much that his religious be taught to do everything out of charity. How happy are they who apply themselves to this virtue with all possible care!

Outside of obedience, the virtue that ought to stand out most in community is charity and union of hearts. Because we ought not to be here except to bring one another to God, we must especially strive to be united in God, to have but one and the same heart, and to have one and the same mind. What ought to inspire us most to achieve this, as Saint John says, is that those who live in love live in God, and God lives in them.[2]

Are you united with your Brothers? Do you speak to them and treat them with love? Do you not pay too much attention to your dislikes and antipathies? Deepen within you the conviction that in community you ought to live anew the spirit of the first Christians, who were all of one heart and one mind.[3]

### 113.3 Third Point

This saint, if we may say so, brought the practice of austerity in his order to excess. When he was thirteen, he withdrew to a deserted place where he gave himself over to fasting, to spending entire days and nights in prayer, and for a space of six years in privations that are hardly believable. As a rule, he walked barefoot, slept on the ground in all kinds of weather, ate only a little bread, and drank only a little water once a day after sunset. He obliged his religious by vow never to eat anything other than Lenten fare except when ill. A person must feel great hatred for the body to treat it with so much rigor.

Are we, then, to complain if we live a poor life after Jesus Christ has given us the example of such a life and after so many great saints have practiced such extreme austerities? The austerities that we read about in their life and that we see practiced by those whom they have left after them ought to encourage us to imitate them in accord with the spirit of our Institute.

Francis (1416–1507) was born at Paola, in Calabria, and became a hermit at an early age, perhaps as young as 15. Eventually, as a result of his reputation for holiness and wisdom, he attracted others to his way of life and founded the Minims of Saint Francis of Assisi. *Minimi* in Latin means the least members (of God's household). Pope Sixtus IV sent him to France, at the request of Louis XI, to assist the king on his deathbed.

One Minim who had considerable influence on De La Salle is Nicolas Barré of Rouen. The Founder consulted him on the decision to give up his patrimony. Father Barré organized a community of women, *Maîtresses des Écoles chrétiennes et charitables du Saint-Enfant Jésus*. He also encouraged Adrien Nyel to organize a similar group of men. He sent two of his women teachers to Reims in response to a request from Canon Nicolas Roland, so that Roland could start a community of women in Reims. This was the community, the Sisters of the Infant Jesus, that Roland asked De La Salle to care for as the executor of his will, thus beginning De La Salle's involvement with Adrien Nyel and the work of the Christian Schools.

---

1. Lk 14:11          2. 1 Jan 4:16          3. Acts 4:32

# April 11

## SAINT LEO THE GREAT, POPE

### 114.1 First Point

The gentleness and wisdom of Saint Leo were admirable and won for him the esteem and veneration of infidels, even the most uncivilized. These qualities of the saint had led the Pope and the emperor to make use of him in settling a dispute between two generals of the Roman imperial army, a mission that he concluded successfully. Later, when Leo became Pope, the emperor begged him to meet and to plead with Attila, King of the Goths, encamped before Rome and ready to besiege it, in order to convince him to give up his plan. The saint acquitted himself of this mission with so much wisdom, eloquence, and success that this barbarian prince was led to withdraw and to leave Italy in peace.

Is it in this way, by your gentleness and your wisdom, that you lead those entrusted to your care to give up bad habits and disorderly conduct and to devote themselves to piety? These two means, joined to prayer, are often more effective on souls than any other method you could imagine.

### 114.2  Second Point

Saint Leo's zeal for strengthening the Church and for defeating her enemies and the heresies that arose in his time manifested itself in an extraordinary manner. He was eminently successful in this; having assembled several Councils, especially the Fourth General Council, he confirmed the faith of the entire Church in the mystery of the Incarnation.

When we are called to an apostolic work, if we do not know how to join zeal to action, all we do for our neighbor will have little effect. In your work you ought to devote your effort to oppose the interior and exterior enemies that would prevent the progress of your disciples in piety, mainly, their wayward companions and their own evil inclinations. There is no means you must fail to use to prevent your students from being corrupted by either one of these enemies.

Is this what you try especially to do to procure the good of their souls? Often reflect that it is for this purpose that God has commissioned you.

### 114.3  Third Point

This saint forbade religious to concern themselves with secular matters. Be convinced that it is for you, more than for any others, that he issued this prohibition.

First, because you scarcely have the time you need both to devote to the exercises that contribute to your own sanctification and to carry out properly the duties of your ministry for the instruction of children, it would be shameful for you to spend any part of your time on matters that do not belong to you, for God obliges you to consecrate all your time to him.

Second, exterior matters distract your mind a great deal and make you incapable of concentrating on the exercises that require your mind to be fully occupied with God, because these exercises are aimed entirely at his service and at the care and guidance of souls in order to direct them on the road to heaven.

---

Leo the Great (Pope from 440 to 461) was probably born in Rome, but we do not know the date. As Pope he wrote so brilliantly in defense of the faith, especially against the Pelagian and Eutychian heresies, that he was declared a Doctor of the Church in 1754. He also earned the title of the Great because of his courageous confrontations: with Attila, in 452, which spared the city of Rome from the Huns, and with Geneseric, three years later, which won mercy from the Vandals. He died on November 10; his feast was transferred to that day in the revision of the liturgy following Vatican II.

# April 21

## SAINT ANSELM

### 115.1  First Point

When he was fifteen, Saint Anselm resolved to devote himself to God and asked to be given the religious habit; however, the abbot of the monastery to which he applied, fearing that the youth's father might object, refused his request. This discouraged the young man so much that he took on the spirit of the world and abandoned himself to dissolute living. Oh, how little it takes to change the goodwill of children and young people!

This example teaches those who are young that when they wish to consecrate themselves to God in the way of virtue, they must not be discouraged by any obstacles and difficulties that they encounter. After they have committed themselves and made it known to those who are responsible for them, those in charge must act so wisely in their regard that nothing in them or in their conduct is able to give these youths any dislike for the service of God or to cause them to deviate even slightly from their duties.

Is this one of your main concerns in your work? The progress your disciples can make in piety and the benefit you can derive from instructing them depend very much on this kind of care.

### 115.2  Second Point

When this saint grew older, he gave up his dissolute manner of living and followed a powerful inspiration from God to become a religious. He made such progress in three years' time in the practice of virtue and in the mortification of his passions that he was chosen prior and then abbot of his monastery.

Let us understand from this that God does not altogether abandon those who have a good heart. From time to time, he takes care to favor them with his graces; however, it is important for them to correspond faithfully to these graces and to follow inspirations when God sends them. But they ought to do so only after consulting with their superiors, as Saint Anselm did, and then follow their advice. On this fidelity the salvation of many people often depends.

Are you especially faithful to the inspirations that God gives you? Before acting on them, do you consult your superiors, so that they can see whether they come from God and then help you to take all the measures necessary to render them useful to you?

### 115.3 Third Point

After becoming a superior, this saint endeavored to guide his religious with so much gentleness and charity that he won all their hearts. He took such tender care of a young religious who was ill, who had found it difficult to submit to his guidance and to recognize him as his superior, that he moved the young man by his charity and won him over to return to his duties. Observing a certain abbot treating some young gentlemen rigorously, Saint Anselm told him that when you guide young people with so much rigor, you do not have any success at all instructing them.

By reason of your state, you are responsible for the instruction of children. Profit by the words and the wise conduct of this saint, because all your care must be to procure for them the Christian spirit. You must consider the obligation you have to win their hearts to be a principal means to lead them to live in a Christian manner. Often reflect that if you fail to use this means, you will drive them away from God instead of drawing them to him.

---

Anselm (1033–1109) was born at Aosta, in Piedmont. After a period of neglect of religion, he entered the Benedictine Order at the monastery of Bec, in Normandy, the center of the monastic revival in that part of France. In time he was chosen abbot and became famous as a teacher. William of Normandy conquered England in 1066, and under his successor, William Rufus, Anselm reluctantly became the archbishop of Canterbury. His career as archbishop was contentious, partly because of his own lack of diplomacy but also because of the king's intransigence and, at times, his irreligious spirit. Nonetheless, Anselm is a Doctor of the Church because of his writings in philosophy and theology and because of his spirituality, which focuses on the sufferings of Christ. No doubt this orientation, which affected subsequent Cistercian spirituality, was reflected in the gentle and compassionate nature of Anselm, which De La Salle mentions in this meditation.

# April 25

## SAINT MARK, EVANGELIST

### 116.1  First Point

Saint Mark, a disciple of Saint Peter, accompanied him in his travels and in preaching the holy Gospel. He was so faithful to Saint Peter and so beloved by him that this saint joins Mark's name to his own in the greetings he addresses in his first Epistle. He calls him his son,[1] as having begotten him in Jesus Christ[2] and as having raised him in the faith and in the practice of Christianity.

How fortunate this saint was to be instructed by so well-qualified a teacher! How clearly did his conduct show how much he profited by such an advantage, for he always remained an exact observer of the doctrine of this holy Apostle, which was none other than that of Jesus Christ.

You can have the advantage of being instructed by the same teacher as Saint Mark if you often read the Epistles of Saint Peter and faithfully put into practice the holy maxims contained there, which are so consoling and instructive.

### 116.2  Second Point

Saint Mark wrote his Gospel while living in Rome. He was urgently requested to do so by those who had been converted by Saint Peter, because they desired to have in writing what this holy Apostle had taught them by word of mouth. When Saint Peter had read the Gospel, he approved it and ordered it to be read in the public assemblies that were held in the Church; this produced much good.

Because you are bound to teach every day the doctrine of the holy Apostles and of Jesus Christ, you are obliged to learn it so well that you possess it perfectly and by this means make your students true disciples of Jesus Christ. Are you careful to learn thoroughly the holy maxims contained in this saint's Gospel and to meditate on them often, so that you will be able to inspire them in those for whom you are responsible? Your primary concern for them ought to be to make sure that they grasp fully the doctrine of the holy Apostles, to give them the spirit of religion, and to make them practice what Jesus Christ has left us in the holy Gospel.

### 116.3 Third Point

Saint Mark, having been formed by Saint Peter in the apostolic ministry and having written his Gospel based on what he had learned from this holy Apostle, was sent by him to preach in Egypt. Because he joined example to his words and his behavior was most exemplary, in a very short time a great number of people, after hearing and observing him and being inspired by his holy life, embraced the Christian religion.

He led them to such great perfection that they imitated the first Christians in Jerusalem, as described in the Acts of the Apostles. They gave up their properties and put everything they had in common, to be distributed to each according to his needs.[3] They had but one heart and one soul.[4] They gathered every day to pray in one spirit and to receive the Body of Jesus Christ, and they encouraged one another in the practice of good.[5] Their conduct even proved a subject of admiration for infidels and pagans.

This ought to be the model of our perfection. Would we want to have less perfection than these first Christians, who lived in the world with much greater detachment and perfection than many religious who live in seclusion and are obliged by their profession to renounce the world?

---

Mark, also called John Mark in the Acts of the Apostles, was a cousin of Saint Barnabas and the son of the Mary in whose home the Christians gathered and to which Saint Peter went when he had been rescued from jail by the angel (Acts 12:12–17). Mark was a companion to Saint Paul on the latter's first missionary journey, but he refused to go with him when they started to travel north. Paul did not take him on his second journey, but he subsequently was with Paul in Rome. Mark was also in Rome with Saint Peter and probably wrote his Gospel there as the interpreter of Peter, according to early tradition. It is also a tradition that Mark was the founder of the church in Alexandria and that he was martyred there during the persecution of Trajan. Yet another tradition has it that his body was brought to Venice in the ninth century and is buried there under the high altar of the church dedicated to him.

---

1. 1 Pt 5:13
2. 1 Cor 4:15
3. Acts 2:44–45
4. Acts 4:32
5. Acts 2:42

# April 29

## SAINT PETER, MARTYR

### 117.1 First Point

We cannot sufficiently admire the faith of the martyr, Saint Peter, for he possessed it perfectly, even from his childhood, and he died in its defense.

This saint was born of Manichean parents, yet they never could convince him by promises or threats to follow their false religion, nor could his childhood companions, who were heretical. He was only seven years old when his uncle asked him what he had learned in school. He replied that he had learned what to believe about God, and thereupon he recited the profession of faith of the Catholics. When his uncle rejoined that he must not believe any of this, he answered, I will believe it unto death, and nothing will ever prevent me from believing it!

Is it not amazing to find such strong faith in a seven-year-old child? Do you have such faith that nothing can prevent you from professing by your actions the truths and maxims of the Gospel?

### 117.2 Second Point

This saint's great faith led him to become a religious of Saint Dominic, because this saint had founded his order to give the Church preachers to combat heretics, who at that time were seriously disturbing the Church. Saint Peter was fortunate to receive the habit from the hands of Saint Dominic.

On one occasion in community, he displayed his faith and confidence in God. Two women saints came from heaven to visit him in his cell, and he was accused of having allowed worldly women to visit him. As a result, the prior of the monastery had him put in prison. The saint endured this calumny, founded on a false and rash judgment, without offering any defense and without saying a single word. But God, who protects those who are unjustly persecuted, made his innocence known to his fellow religious.

Do you keep silence in a like manner when you are reproved for faults that you did not commit? What you ought to do on such occasions, and what you perhaps fail to do, is to say nothing in defense and, instead, to profit by the humiliation.

### 117.3 Third Point

This saint displayed his faith openly by preaching against the heretics and by making a great many outstanding converts among them. God gave to his words, inspired by faith, a very great holiness, and the crowds of people who came to listen to his sermons were so large that he had to be carried into the church on a litter.

All these conversions, together with his preaching and the fact that the Pope named him Inquisitor of the Faith, caused heretics to hate him so much that some of them set out to waylay him. They caught up with him on the road and struck him a blow on the head with a sword. He had just time enough before he died to repeat his profession of faith and to write with a finger dipped in his own blood: I believe in God.

Do you have a faith as lively as that of this saint? You are bound to excel in the spirit of faith, for you have to teach children the maxims of the holy Gospel and the mysteries of our religion. Often say to God, with the holy Apostles: Lord, increase our faith![1]

---

Peter, Martyr (1205–1252), although he was born of heretical parents, somehow grew up as an orthodox Catholic and entered the Dominican Order. He became a successful preacher in Lombardy and was appointed Inquisitor General for the territory around Milan by Pope Gregory IX in 1234. His zeal in this position aroused hostility and led to his assassination while he was traveling from Como to Milan. His murderer repented and died as a Dominican Brother. De La Salle was attracted to Saint Peter, Martyr, as a model of the spirit of faith.

---

1. Lk 17:5

# April 30

## SAINT CATHERINE OF SIENA

### 118.1 First Point

Saint Catherine had such a special love for purity that she made a vow of virginity when only seven years old. To do that is to be specially favored by grace and to perform heroic acts of virtue even in childhood. With time this virtue grew so strong in her that when her parents proposed to her a very advantageous marriage, she refused and never wanted even to hear it mentioned again. This angered her parents against her so much that they obliged her to do all the lowliest and most difficult household chores. She was very happy about this and endured with the greatest patience all the ill-treatment they inflicted on her at the time. She contented herself with setting up a kind of little oratory in her heart, where she withdrew to console herself with God.

If you were to suffer insults and scorn because you aim to do good and to work for your perfection, would you be ready to put up with such treatment patiently? On such occasions we see whether our virtue is solid.

### 118.2 Second Point

This saint made use of austerity to help her preserve the treasure of her purity. Her austerity was so extraordinary that she can be said to have carried it to excess. For three years she spoke to no one except to her confessor. Every day she took the discipline for an hour and a half. She wore an iron chain on her body, slept sitting in a chair, never ate meat, and drank only water. On one occasion she did great violence to herself by sucking the pus that came from the sore of a sick person. She endured patiently a calumny spread by an invalid woman whom she nursed. When Jesus Christ asked her to choose between a gold crown and one made of thorns, she chose the thorns.

Would you make a similar choice? When will you love mortification and suffering as this saint did?

### 118.3 Third Point

To reward her for so many trials and so much mortification, God favored Saint Catherine with such consolations that it can be said of her that having participated in the sufferings of Jesus Christ, she merited to have some share in his glorious life[1] even in this world. When her parents maltreated her and kept her in a state of humiliation, she enjoyed the happiness of conversing interiorly with God and of being consoled by him. During the time of her profound silence, Jesus Christ often came to visit her and talked familiarly with her. After she had sucked the pus out of the sore, as we mentioned, Jesus Christ allowed her to drink a sweet liquor flowing from the wound in his side. After that, she was almost constantly caught up in ecstasy.

This is how God gives even in this life the hundredfold of what we do for him.[2] Oh, how this ought to spur you on to suffer willingly for the love of God!

---

Catherine (1347–1380) was born in Siena, the daughter of a wealthy wool dyer, Giacomo Benincasa. In adolescence she was drawn to prayer and solitude and became a problem for her mother by resisting any suggestion either of marriage or of becoming a nun. A compromise was reached when she joined the Third Order of Saint Dominic at the age of 16. The rigorous, humble life of prayer on which De La Salle focuses in his meditation drew a large following of people, including priests. This became the foundation for an extraordinary life of extensive public influence. Catherine convinced Pope Gregory XI to leave Avignon in 1376 and to return the papacy to Rome, although this led the French cardinals to revolt and caused the great Western Schism, which lasted for 70 years. She lived only 33 years, but her influence was exceptional. Her writings, including over 400 letters, earned for her from Pope Paul VI in 1970 the title of Doctor of the Church. Her feast is now celebrated on April 29.

---

1. Phil 3:10    2. Mk 10:29–30

# May 1

## SAINT JAMES AND
## SAINT PHILIP, APOSTLES

### 119.1  First Point

Saint James was so devoted to prayer that Saint Chrysostom says of him that his forehead had become hardened like a stone because he always kept it pressed to the ground when he prayed. This great application to prayer is shown in the Epistle he wrote to all the faithful; he states at the beginning that *we ought especially to ask God for true wisdom and piety,* that *God's liberality toward us is great,* and that *we ought to pray with faith.* He explains the main reasons why we do not receive what we ask of God.[1]

Learn from this holy Apostle, from his example as well as from his words, the love you must have for prayer, the great benefit it produces in you, and the attention you ought to give to this holy exercise.

### 119.2  Second Point

This saint, having been chosen to be the first bishop of Jerusalem, labored much to establish the Church there. By his instructions and his holy life, he brought about the conversion of a very great number of Jews and pagans. This is what led to his death, for the Jews threw him down from the roof of the Temple.

How fortunate we are when we have the advantage of suffering and dying, as this saint did, because we have labored to win souls to God! This is what you ought to expect as your reward for the care and work of your ministry.

Study also the admirable instructions that this saint set forth in his Epistle. They will help you very much to be sanctified and to form the Christian spirit in those for whom you are responsible, for it is impossible for these truths not to make holy those who put them into practice.

### 119.3 Third Point

When Saint Philip was called to the apostolate by Jesus Christ, he immediately showed such great zeal for leading souls to God that he brought Nathanael to Jesus Christ[2] in order to make him know Jesus and by means of Jesus to engage Nathaniel to take the true path of salvation.

It seems that Jesus Christ also gave this saint a special grace, namely, that of tenderness and an engaging manner to bring others to know and to love Jesus Christ, for Jesus Christ addressed Saint Philip when he was thinking of feeding the great multitude of people who had followed him.[3] Again, when several Gentiles who had come to Jerusalem were eager to see Jesus, they asked this saint to introduce them to him.[4]

In your work you have a special need for zeal for the salvation of souls. Ask this earnestly of God by the intercession of Saint Philip, who will help you very much to obtain it.

———

De La Salle considers that the Apostle James, son of Alpheus, is the same James who was the first bishop of Jerusalem, martyred in 62 A.D. and the author of the Epistle. Some scholars, however, hold that the Apostle bishop and the author of the Epistle are two different people, but there is no confusion about Philip as one of the first Apostles called by Jesus. The feast of these two Apostles was transferred to May 3 by Pope Pius XII in 1956 to allow for the feast of Saint Joseph the Worker on May 1. The feast of the other Apostle James, son of Zebedee, is on July 25.

———

1. Jas 1:5–7        3. Jn 6:5            4. Jn 12:20–22
2. Jn 1:43–50

# May 2

## SAINT ATHANASIUS

### 120.1 First Point

Saint Athanasius was one of the principal defenders of the Church against Arius and those of his sect, who denied the divinity of Jesus Christ. He always opposed them and silenced them everywhere by the holiness of his life, the wisdom of his conduct, and his excellent writings. Even before he was made a bishop, he attended the Council of Nicea, where he displayed his deep learning and opposed Arius so forcefully that he proved to him as well as to all the others present that his teaching was false and heretical. Throughout the years of his episcopate, he always fought all the partisans of this heretic.

Although you do not have sufficient learning to defend the Church against heretics, you are obliged in your ministry to have enough learning to teach the children in your care the good and sound doctrine of the Church. Is one of your main concerns, then, to learn these teachings and to possess them well? God will ask you to give an account of this responsibility. Failure in this would make you unworthy of your state.

### 120.2 Second Point

The Arians always regarded Saint Athanasius as their enemy and always opposed him, first, at his election, which they tried their best to prevent because they could not tolerate that the one who had so strongly opposed their leader might be in a position to halt the progress of their heresy. This he would quite easily be able to do, clothed with the authority of a bishop and especially as Patriarch of Alexandria.

It is impossible to work for the destruction of erroneous teaching without gaining the enmity of those who maintain it. If no heretics oppose you, because there are perhaps none in the places where you teach, still you can be sure that as long as you have a solid piety and keep your distance from the world, dissolute and worldly people will speak out against you. But just as Saint Athanasius always had God as his protector, do not doubt that God will take your side and will be your defender.

### 120.3 Third Point

It is surprising how far the enemies of Saint Athanasius carried their anger against him. There were no calumnies, injuries, deceptions, persecutions, evil treatments, and tribulations that the Arians did not try to use to destroy him. They accused him of all kinds of crimes, murder, violence, and injustice, but all these charges were completely and publicly dismissed in the presence of his accusers, who were put to shame because of all their lies.

Be ready to endure injuries, outrages, and calumnies in return for all the good you have tried to do for others.[1] This is the main reward that God promises in this world and often the only one we receive from the poor in compensation for the good we do for them. Prepare your heart to accept these trials with love.

---

Athanasius (ca. 295–May 2, 373) was born in Alexandria and received an excellent education in the classics and in the Scriptures. He also spent some time as a hermit, becoming a close friend of the abbot Saint Anthony (see De La Salle's meditation for January 17). As De La Salle mentions in his meditation, Athanasius was very influential in opposing the heresy of Arius at the Council of Nicea, when Athanasius was only 30 years old. Later, as Patriarch of Alexandria, he continued his staunch defense of the true faith and endured exile three times. He wrote the *Life of Saint Anthony*, which had a great influence on the development and spread of monasticism. He is a Doctor of the Church, but his feast was not introduced into the Roman liturgy until the late Middle Ages.

---

1. 2 Tim 3:12

# May 3

## THE FINDING
## OF THE HOLY CROSS

### 121.1 First Point

Saint Helena, mother of Emperor Constantine, had such great zeal for religion and profound respect for the cross on which Jesus Christ was nailed that she traveled to Jerusalem to try to recover this sacred wood. The great faith of this saint did not allow her to grow discouraged in the face of the many difficulties she encountered in the execution of her project. She took so much trouble that at last she found the true cross and arranged to have it displayed for the veneration of the faithful.

It is not enough to adore the cross, says one Father of the Church; we must carry it. Nor do we need to go very far looking for it. The cross, says the author of the *Imitation,* is always ready wherever we are and wherever we might look: above, below, outside, and within. On all sides, the same author says, you will find the cross. Prepare today, then, to love the cross, because you will always have it.

### 121.2 Second Point

The crosses of the two thieves were also discovered with that of Jesus Christ, but the cross of Jesus was recognized by several miracles that took place when it was touched, especially by the resurrection of a deceased person. According to Saint Paulinus' account, this corpse had shown no sign of life when touched by the other two crosses.

In this world there are crosses of thieves and those of Jesus Christ. Those of the thieves have no grace attached to them and impart no movement of life in those who endure them, because these people carry them with the wrong dispositions. The crosses of Jesus Christ are those that often work miracles, procure a good spirit of self-denial, inspire the practice of other virtues, and sometimes even revive the dead by giving an aversion and horror for sin.

Is the cross you carry the cross of Jesus Christ? How do you recognize this? Do the difficulties you suffer lead you to practice many virtues? Pay attention to this: if these crosses turn you away and make you complain, they are the crosses of thieves.

### 121.3 Third Point

Having discovered and verified the true cross of Jesus, Saint Helena distributed parts of it to many churches, so that throughout the world the cross might be acknowledged and honored by all the faithful. As a consequence, Emperor Constantine by edict forbade the use of crucifixion ever after as a means of executing any criminal, and this has always been observed in Christian lands.

It was because the true cross was discovered and honored in the Church that the feast we are celebrating today was instituted. Do you honor the cross when you have the advantage of carrying one? Do you thank God for the honor he does you? On such occasions do you show that you glory only in the cross of Jesus Christ?[1] Does the cross become a punishment for you, rather than a sign of honor, because you regard it only as something that makes you suffer and that crucifies you, instead of welcoming it with affection and respect as a gift from God and an honor he does you? This is how you must embrace the cross if you wish to suffer as a Christian.

---

There were originally two feasts of the Holy Cross, the Finding by Saint Helena on May 3 and the Exaltation on September 14. Today there is only the one feast, the Exaltation, which celebrates the rescue of the Cross from the Persians by the Christian Emperor Heraclius on May 3, 629. The Finding, which took place in 320, was originally celebrated on September 14; history has worked a strange shift of the dates. Both meditations by De La Salle dwell on the same theme, that the way to honor the cross is to carry it patiently.

---

1. Gal 6:14

# May 4

## SAINT MONICA

### 122.1 First Point

In her youth Saint Monica had a special attraction to prayer, and her greatest pleasure was to spend days and nights in prayer, avoiding the company of those who might turn her attention away from God. Having learned some prayers from her mother, she never gave up reciting them. What a blessing it is to be brought up in piety from our youth! This makes it easier to preserve that spirit throughout life. Saint Monica had this advantage, and it contributed a great deal to the conversion of her husband and of her son.

Do you take care to educate the children confided to you in a Christian spirit? Do you try, above all else, to inspire them with recollection in their prayers and with love for this holy practice? You, on your part, ought to pray much for them to obtain for them from God the gift of piety, something God alone can give them.

## 122.2 Second Point

Saint Monica's husband had an unpleasant and irritable disposition. When her neighbors wondered how she could put up with him, she told them not to be surprised, because from the moment she accepted him as her husband, she had submitted herself to him, and she respected him as much as she was able. Still, by her prayers and tears, she converted him and led him to become catholic and to change his disposition.

This saint teaches us that when we have to live or to deal with someone who has a disagreeable disposition, we must do two things: first, arm ourselves with patience and be accommodating; second, often ask God in prayer to give the other person a more accommodating spirit and to grant you the grace to put up with him. Is this how you act when you happen to be in such a situation?

## 122.3 Third Point

Saint Monica's son, Saint Augustine, abandoned himself to a dissolute life in his youth and even fell into the heresy of the Manichees. She did everything she could to withdraw him from his evil ways and to bring him to life in Jesus Christ.[1] He says that his saintly mother experienced a much more difficult time giving him birth in the spirit than she had bringing him bodily into this world. She never stopped praying and weeping for his conversion. She even crossed the sea and undertook long journeys to keep him from being altogether lost. Finally, after so much suffering, she had the joy of seeing him change his life completely.

When you see those confided to you inclined to a dissolute life, do you do all you can to win them over to God? Is there anything you would not do for them to eliminate in them the evil to which they are inclined? Do you have recourse to God to procure for them a change in conduct? Because you are responsible for their souls, you must use every possible means to put them on the road to heaven.

———

Monica (ca. 332–387) is the mother of Saint Augustine. De La Salle's meditation is based on the facts of her life that Saint Augustine makes known in the ninth book of his *Confessions.* Her feast was set on May 4 because the conversion of Saint Augustine was celebrated on May 5 by the Canons Regular of Saint Augustine in Belgium, where her body was brought in 1162. The feast of Saint Monica is now held on August 27, the day before the feast of her son.

———

1. 1 Cor 4:15

# May 5

## THE CONVERSION OF SAINT AUGUSTINE

### 123.1 First Point

God, all good and merciful, for a long time and in many ways, urged Saint Augustine to be converted and to change his manner of living radically, yet for many years this saint led a disorderly life. He was not always resisting grace, but he was not consenting to its movements, and he was constantly hesitating to follow them. Now he wanted to change; now again he no longer wanted to change. He remained for a considerable length of time in this disturbed state of mind, and he was surprised to see himself so indecisive. On the one side, his disorderly behavior, and on the other, the strong urging of grace, made him shed tears in abundance. The effect this produced made him still more irresolute and unsettled. As he said, vanities and trifles held him back and prevented him from giving himself entirely to God.

Is grace not urging you to live according to the perfection proper to your state? Do you not have, from time to time, a strong inspiration to do violence to self, to practice some significant act of virtue? Do you not find it difficult to follow these calls? Do you not sometimes even resist grace?

### 123.2 Second Point

The day finally arrived when God, having gradually softened Saint Augustine's heart, caused him to hear a voice saying to him clearly, Take and read. Upon opening a book of the Epistles of Saint Paul, he was moved and converted by the reading of a single passage. It poured into his heart, he says, like a light that filled it with a deep peace and scattered all the darkness of his doubts. From that moment he renounced forever all worldly aspirations, and he suddenly found inconceivable joy and pleasure giving up the pleasures of worldlings and all their vain amusements.

Have you been thoroughly converted to God? Have you renounced the world entirely? How often has God made you hear an inner voice, loud enough to impress you, but you have not listened to it? Oh, how many people consecrated to God have not given themselves entirely to him and live in laziness and negligence! At least say with David, today I wish to begin to belong entirely to God.[1]

### 123.3 Third Point

So faithful was Saint Augustine to grace from the instant of his conversion that henceforth he made it a point not to follow in any way the movements of nature. At first he endeavored to give up the pleasures of the senses, which are the gateways through which sin enters our souls and which readily soil them, no matter how little our senses have influence over our souls. That is why Saint Augustine took care to allow his senses only such use as was necessary for his bodily needs.

Next, he took great care to give up all study prompted by mere curiosity and whatever served only to satisfy his mind. He cut himself off from all that is human and natural, affirming in this way that the happiness of man consists only in the true joy that is found only in God.

Have you taken the same steps that Saint Augustine used to go to God and to put himself in a condition to be attached to God alone? Be convinced that you will not acquire solid piety except by these same means.

———

Augustine (354–430) describes the moment of his conversion in the eighth book of his *Confessions*. He was struggling to make a definite break with his past, when he heard children singing in Latin, *Tolle, lege* (take and read). At once he picked up the book of the New Testament and read at random from Romans 13:13, ". . . not in carousing and drunkenness, not in sexual excess and lust, not in quarreling and jealousy. Rather, put on the Lord Jesus Christ, and make no provision for the desires of the flesh." In that instant his hesitation ceased. His friend, Alypius, who was nearby and going through the same turmoil, picked up the book and read the next sentence, which converted him: "Extend a kind welcome to those who are weak in faith."

———

1. Ps 77:2 (Vulgate)

# May 6

## THE MARTYRDOM
## OF SAINT JOHN THE EVANGELIST

### 124.1 First Point

When the mother of Saints James and John asked Jesus Christ *to seat her two children, one on his right and one on his left, in his kingdom,* Jesus Christ asked them if they were able to drink the chalice that he would drink. He then told them that they would drink it,[1] to show them that both of them, by proclaiming his name, would suffer violent torments difficult to endure. This is indeed what happened to Saint John on several occasions, even though he did not die as a result of the violent tortures that he suffered. Today the Church honors these sufferings and has established an important feast to commemorate them.

Regard Saint John as having been an Apostle by his sufferings as well as by his words and by preaching the holy Gospel. Thank God for sharing his chalice with him as with his beloved disciple and for thereby treating him as a true friend.

### 124.2 Second Point

What Saint John suffered to honor Jesus Christ and his religion includes the following: not long after the descent of the Holy Spirit, he was put into prison with Saint Peter;[2] after getting out, he was condemned by the Jews to be cruelly scourged.[3] Later on, when he was preaching the Gospel at Ephesus, he was brought to Rome by order of Emperor Domitian, who condemned him to be cruelly scourged, as the Romans customarily did before putting criminals to death. Then he was cast into a cauldron of boiling oil, from which he emerged, says Tertullian, stronger and in better health than when he entered it.

Such were the sufferings of Saint John that are honored today by the Church, especially those he endured at Rome and the great miracle that occurred on that occasion. The feasts of the martyrs, says Saint Cyprian, are exhortations to martyrdom. Celebrating Saint John's martyrdom ought to spur us on to suffer, after his example, gladly and for the love of God.

### 124.3 Third Point

When Saint John endured this martyrdom, God preserved his life by a miracle because he wished to purify John by fire and thus prepare him to receive the great revelations he needed in order to write his prophecy, the Apocalypse. He did this on the island of Patmos,[4] to which the same emperor exiled him.

Do not be surprised if God often sends you occasions to suffer. The more he sends, the more he shows that he loves you,[5] and the happier you ought to be, because it is by suffering that God purifies you, so that you may be more pleasing in his eyes. These trials make it easy for you to avoid sin and to receive the graces of God in abundance. Act so that you will derive this benefit from the trials you experience.

---

Tertullian (ca. 160–ca. 230) gives an account of the martyrdom of Saint John at Rome. The feast, celebrated in the Basilica of Saint John at the Latin Gate, where the martyrdom was said to have occurred, is no longer observed.

---

1. Mt 20:21–22
2. Acts 4:3
3. Acts 5:40
4. Rv 1:9
5. Prv 3:12

# May 8

## THE APPARITION OF SAINT MICHAEL

### 125.1  First Point

Today the Church celebrates the memorial of the apparition of Saint Michael on a mountain in Italy to let it be known that this place was under his protection and that God wished it to be consecrated in honor of Saint Michael and the holy angels. For this reason, the bishop went in procession with all the clergy and the people to consecrate a church there under the name and patronage of Saint Michael. On several occasions, this saint has appeared in a striking manner to show that he took under his protection places and people whom he honored by his presence.

We cannot do better than to entrust ourselves to this saint in all that concerns our salvation, for he will help us a great deal to achieve it. Once, by God's command and acting out of zeal for God's glory, he overcame and hurled into hell Lucifer and his followers.[1] He is still always ready to oppose him and to help us fight against him and overcome the temptations that he suggests to us.

Have recourse, then, to this holy Archangel; beg him to help you in the struggles you may have to endure in your state and to guide you directly to God with certainty in the path marked out for you by your Rule. Be faithful to it, and this saint will protect you.

### 125.2 Second Point

You enjoy something similar to the apparitions of Saint Michael in the inspirations that come to you to renounce the world and to give yourself entirely to God, for these lead you to rise above all created things and to be devoted to God alone.

The name Michael tells us that nothing is like unto God. It was given to him to indicate that this holy Archangel was destined by God to defend his glory and to exalt his infinite excellence above all creatures.

We must believe that all the inspirations that come to us to consecrate ourselves to God with an entire disengagement from all creatures are given to us from God through the ministry of Saint Michael. His role in our regard is to detach us from all things and to induce us to give ourselves entirely to God.

So, then, when you feel your mind filled with worldly thoughts and you experience distaste for your state and your spiritual exercises, beg Saint Michael to help you realize that the God whom we serve is superior to all else and that nothing outside of him truly deserves our affection. Let us also pray to this saint to inspire us with horror for the world, which wishes to take God's place in our hearts, and to banish from our minds all worldly ideas by those awesome words he spoke in his combat against Lucifer, Who is like unto God?

### 125.3 Third Point

The first effect that ought to be produced in us by the inspirations God gives us through the ministry of Saint Michael is to have an entire detachment from all the things of earth, which comes from the contempt we have for them through a deep understanding of their emptiness and of the limited quality and permanence of the pleasure found in them because they are nothing and God is everything.

Another effect these inspirations ought to produce in your soul, following from the first, is an interior taste for God. This leads you to seek only God and to give yourself entirely to him, because he is the only being worthy to be adored and loved. If there is anything lovable in creatures, it comes only from their relationship with God and as an overflow of God and his perfection.

From this day on, let this be your disposition, to desire only God and to belong entirely to him, for our hearts, says Saint Augustine, can be at rest only when they rest in God.

Have you no attachment to anything, so that you can say that you would have no trouble to give it up? Do you have more esteem for one creature than for another? When you are deprived of something of finer quality and given something else less fine, are you satisfied? By such experiences you can judge whether you are attached to anything and whether you have contempt for all creatures.

Do you have a taste for prayer and the interior exercises because they bring you to God? Are you gladly occupied with thoughts of God and with conversation about God? Is there anything besides what concerns God that matters to you and that touches you? Does a sin, however slight it might seem, cause you more grief than anything you could suffer? In your work do you prefer the task of inspiring piety in the children above everything else, no matter what? By such indications you will know whether you seek only God and whether you seek him in truth.

---

This feast was established to celebrate the dedication of the shrine in honor of Saint Michael the Archangel on Mont Gargano. The feast has been suppressed in favor of the feast of Saint Michael on September 29 (*Meditations,* 169).

---

1. Rv 12:7–9

# May 10

## SAINT GREGORY OF NAZIANZEN

### 126.1 First Point

While a student at Athens, Saint Gregory applied himself more to the perfection of his soul than to learning literature. He had such great concern to avoid sin that he paid special attention to shun bad companions and particularly people of the opposite sex. He felt sure that this is one of the occasions that contributes the most to make us sinners. At this period he gladly spent much time with Saint Basil, with whom he formed such a close friendship that when Saint Basil retired into the solitude of a hermitage in Pontus, Saint Gregory went to find him there and lived with him an angelic life.

How fortunate you are when you are far from occasions to offend God! This is an advantage. You ought, therefore, to thank God frequently, even daily, for this grace, because it is one of the principal means of salvation.

Bad companions are so dangerous, especially in youth, that there is nothing to which you must pay more attention than to prevent those you teach from keeping such company. Nor is there anything you ought to recommend more strongly to them than to become close friends with the best of their companions, the most pious and the best behaved.

### 126.2 Second Point

This saint, having been chosen to govern the Church of Constantinople, suffered a great deal from the opposition of the Arians, who persecuted him viciously in various ways. They accused him of being an idolater who wanted to introduce several gods. At this the people wished to stone him, and he was brought before judges who had been stirred up against him to have him condemned.

Yet he always remained a firm and indomitable defender of the true faith. He preached with so much zeal and so effectively that during the three years he lived in that city, he converted a large number of heretics. By the time he left the city, it was purged not only of Arianism and all the other errors with which it had been infested on his arrival but also of many vices that had reigned there previously, as this saint testifies.

Such are the usual consequences of persecutions suffered by those who labor for the salvation of souls. The more they are burdened by difficulties in their apostolic labors, the more conversions God brings about through their ministry and the more effectively they procure the salvation of souls.

Do not be surprised, therefore, if in doing your work, you meet with difficulties and contradictions. The more you suffer, the more you ought to be encouraged to fulfill your duties well, because then you can be sure that God will pour out abundant blessings on the work you are doing.

### 126.3 Third Point

This saint resigned his bishopric not long after he had entered it, in order to calm down the trouble caused by the Arians concerning his election. He withdrew entirely from contact with the world and applied himself diligently to prayer, which became his main occupation. He lived austerely in constant mortification, especially of his tongue, because he recognized that this is one of the most necessary mortifications. He even says, out of humility, that his tongue escaped him so readily that he experienced much trouble restraining it and that for this purpose he took great care to watch over it. Once he even imposed on himself a penance of not talking for forty days because he thought he had spoken too much.

The work you do during the day does not prevent you from living in seclusion. Love this seclusion, and willingly preserve it, after the example of this saint, who sanctified himself by means of it. It will help you very much to acquire the perfection of your state and to procure piety for your disciples. But if you do not appreciate a secluded life and if you rarely pray, you will not possess the fervor necessary to inspire your students with the Christian spirit.

Also, control your tongue; such self-control will make it easy for you to practice recollection and to remember the presence of God. It will also be an excellent means for you to keep silence, order, the exact practice of your spiritual exercises, the faithful observance of your Rule, self-control, tranquility, and peace. These great advantages ought to induce you not to give free rein to your tongue.

———

Gregory Nazianzen (ca. 329–390) was born at Arianzus, in Cappadocia, the son of the bishop of Nazianzus, when it was normal for clergy to be married in that country. He studied in his native land, in Palestine, in Alexandria, and for ten years in Athens, where he formed a close friendship with Saint Basil. (See De La Salle's meditation for June 14). He spent time as a hermit in the desert with Basil, but he left it to help his aging father. He accepted ordination as a priest with great reluctance, but he wrote a beautiful treatise on the priesthood as an apology for his reluctance. He was by nature too gentle to become assertive in his administration as a bishop, which marred his friendship with Basil and led him to resign from his later role as bishop of Constantinople. However, he did oppose the Arian heresy with vigor, and his writings have earned for him the title of Doctor of the Church. His feast has now been joined with that of Saint Basil and is celebrated on January 2. During his lifetime he was called "The Theologian" because of his learning and eloquence.

# May 19

## SAINT PETER CELESTINE

### 127.1 First Point

From his youth Saint Peter Celestine was drawn to solitude. He therefore withdrew to a lonely mountain where he lived for three years, mortifying his body in order to resist the temptations that bothered him. His penances were carried to such an excess that when he slept, he used a stone for a pillow. Silence was his element; a daily use of the discipline was his recreation; his belt was an iron chain. So diligently did he devote himself to prayer that it became his main exercise. Thus, seclusion, mortification, and prayer were the means this saint used to sanctify himself.

You too can easily use these means to go to God, for these exercises are the usual practices you have in your Institute. Be faithful to them, and be convinced that you will do good for souls only in proportion to the love you have for these three things and your practice of them.

### 127.2 Second Point

The outstanding holiness of this great servant of God was the reason why the cardinals, in his absence, chose him to govern the Church. As soon as the saint heard of this, he took to flight, but he was later obliged to accept this dignity. However, he maintained a religious humility in the midst of it. All he had to ride on was an ass. Once crowned as Pope, he did not give up any of his austerities, and even in his elevated position, he preserved the same spirit of seclusion. This is how a person must act in the world, if he wants to save himself there and maintain himself in piety.

In your work you are obliged to have some contact with the world. Take care not to acquire its spirit; maintain your reserve and a certain air of self-control, which will help you avoid being corrupted. This will edify your neighbor and inspire piety in those whose education has been entrusted to you.

### 127.3 Third Point

This saint had accepted the papacy with reluctance and felt completely out of place in that role. He thought only of his place of solitude and constantly longed for the seclusion there. He felt nothing but distaste for the pomp of the Roman court. His duty as Sovereign Pontiff, which obliged him to attend constantly to external business, put him into a situation totally opposed to the inclination for solitude that he had had from his childhood. This led him to request permission from the cardinals to withdraw and to resign the dignity of Sovereign Pontiff.

Although it is by the will of God that you exercise the external functions of your work and although you find therein the means to be sanctified, these duties must not make you lose the spirit and the love of seclusion. Be devoted to your work, then, in such a way that as soon as you are no longer needed there, you return home as to your place of refuge and find all your consolation in attentiveness and application at your spiritual exercises.

———

Peter Celestine (ca. 1210–1296) was born in the Abruzzi region of peasant stock; while still very young, he retired to solitude. Despite his desires, he was surrounded by followers and ended up founding the hermits of Saint Damian, also known as Celestines (later incorporated with the Benedictines). In 1274 their Rule was approved by Pope Gregory X and as many as 36 monasteries came under the direction of Saint Peter. However, he resigned and became a solitary hermit until forced by the cardinals to accept the papacy in 1294 in an effort to settle a two-year stalemate over filling the vacancy of the Holy See. It was a mistake; because he had no talent for the job of Pope, many abuses ensued. Finally, he resigned in favor of his successor, Boniface VIII. He wrote a Bull to justify his resignation, citing past examples. Boniface became fearful of a schism and arrested Peter, keeping him in a rather rough imprisonment until he died on May 19, 1296. Clement V canonized him in 1313, at the request of Boniface's enemy, Philip of France. His feast is no longer listed in the Roman liturgical calendar.

# May 20

## SAINT BERNARDINE

### 128.1 First Point

From his earliest youth, Saint Bernardine had such great prudence and self-control that the most disorderly of his fellow students were prudent and reserved in his presence and did not dare to speak of anything that was the least bit unbecoming. When they saw him coming from a distance, they said to one another, "No more of this talk; here comes Bernardine."

Are you likewise equally self-controlled and reserved in the presence not only of your Brothers but also of your students? Do you give them a similar example of proper behavior? Does what they observe in you make such an impression on them that it alone is able to make them behave properly? This is the good effect that your position as their teacher ought to produce in those under your guidance.

There is no one to whom you cannot and must not try to be helpful by the example of your virtues. This was the first way Saint Bernardine practiced his zeal. It is also the way you are obliged to preach to everyone and the principal apostolic function you must exercise.

### 128.2 Second Point

This saint wished to become a religious, but he did not know which order to join. He thought that he could not take any better means to find out than to have recourse to prayer, which is what he did. Kneeling before a crucifix, he earnestly begged God for the grace to learn what his vocation was. At once he heard a voice, which said to him, "You see me entirely naked on this cross. If you love me and seek me, you will find me here, but strive to be empty and crucified." This convinced him to join the Order of Saint Francis. After selling his property and giving the money to the poor,[1] he exercised his zeal by crucifying himself, for he was at first subject to violent temptations. He fasted continually, slept on the floor, spent nights in prayer, and labored without ceasing. When he went begging, little children often threw stones at him, and he suffered disgraceful calumnies.

Is prayer the first means you use to know God's will? When you are in doubt, do you resolve to do what is most likely to crucify you[2] and to make you die to self? These are two sure ways to know God's will and to do it.

### 128.3 Third Point

This saint was assigned to be a preacher. In this function he showed so much zeal that he preached every day without dispensing himself from choir or the other religious exercises, even though he continued to preach for 28 years. Through his sermons he converted a great number of people by inspiring them with devotion to the Holy Name of Jesus.

He brought so much renown to his religious family from all those he attracted to it, as much by the example of his holy life as by the efficacy of his words, that when he took the religious habit, there were only twenty monasteries and some three hundred religious belonging to his order in all Italy, but when he died, he left 250 monasteries and over 5,000 religious.

Do you exercise your zeal for your neighbor in such a way that all you do to help others sanctify themselves does not prevent you in any way from being exact and diligent at all the exercises of your community? Are you convinced that God will bless your labors for your neighbor only to the degree that you are faithful to your Rule, because you will not obtain any graces to contribute to the salvation of others except insofar as you are faithful to grace and have the true spirit of your vocation?

———

Bernardine (1380–1444) was born of the noble Sienese family Albizeschi at Massa Marittima, where his father was governor. Orphaned at the age of six, he was raised by aunts. At school in Siena, he was outstanding for his intelligence, his goodness, and his popularity. At the age of 17, he began a life of service to the poor and a quiet spirituality. Four years later, he joined the Franciscans and became active in the reform group of the Order. Ordained in 1404, he led a hidden life for 12 years and then began a career of itinerant preaching. He was Vicar General of the Order from 1430 to 1442. At the same time, he traveled much, usually on foot, and was the most popular preacher of his time in Italy. He is remembered especially for his talks on penance and for his devotion to the Holy Names of Jesus and Mary. He was canonized only six years after his death.

———

1. Mt 19:21          2. Gal 5:24

# May 27[1]

## SAINT MAGDALEN DE PAZZI

### 130.1  First Point

This saint excelled in her ardent love for God. From her earliest youth, she spoke only of God and devoted herself a great deal to prayer, convinced that having been created only for God, she would find nothing outside of him deserving of her attention and affection. Her love for God and for what concerned his service led her to withdraw from the world soon after making her first Communion. She took a resolution to become a religious, and, although only ten years old at the time, she consecrated herself to God by a vow of virginity.

You often have time set aside for prayer and have the happiness of being able to converse with God. Are you careful to profit by this opportunity? In your conversations with your Brothers, are you faithful to speak only of God, of what concerns him, and of what can give you eagerness for his holy love?

### 130.2 Second Point

The great love she had for God led her, above all, to receive Holy Communion often, so great was her desire to unite herself intimately with Jesus Christ, our Lord. This is why, when she was still only a small child too young to receive Communion, she would draw near to her mother when she communicated and not leave her all day long because of the pleasure she had being near and touching a person who had received the precious Body of Jesus Christ. Because of this, her confessor allowed her to receive Communion at the age of ten. When she became a religious, she chose the Order of Carmelites because the reception of Holy Communion was more commonly practiced there than in many other orders.

Do you also make it a point to receive Communion often? This is an advantage you enjoy in your Institute. Do you conform in this matter to the established practice? Is it because of a tender affection for Holy Communion that you receive it? Consider this the greatest advantage and the greatest happiness you can enjoy in this world.

### 130.3 Third Point

This saint also showed her great love for God by suffering very much for him. Her deepest desire was to imitate in every way the life and the Passion of Jesus Christ. When only twelve years old, she made a sort of crown with very thorny orange branches, fixed it on her head, and spent the whole night in great pain. She often took the discipline with metal chains, and she wore a rough hair shirt with a girdle made of sharp points. She also endured severe temptations and intense interior suffering.

Do you love to suffer this way for God? Know that what shows best the love you have for him is when you take pleasure in suffering something in order to be more like Jesus crucified and to please God. This is also what will be most capable of drawing down God's abundant graces on you.

———

Mary Magdalen of Pazzi (1566–1607) was baptized Catherine and belonged to a noble Florentine family. She became a Carmelite nun at the age of 17 and took the name Mary Magdalen. She served as mistress of novices and was elected prioress. De La Salle was 19 years old when her name was added to the Roman Liturgy in 1670. The feast is now celebrated on May 25, the day she died, although it was originally assigned May 27. It was for a time appointed to May 29 by Leo XIII, which permitted the feast of the Venerable Bede, Doctor of the Church, to be observed on May 27.

---

1. The date of this meditation in the original edition appears more like the number 25 than 27, which might account for its being placed ahead of the following meditation, dated May 26.

# May 26

## SAINT PHILIP NERI

### 129.1 First Point

Saint Philip Neri had a great love for chastity. Once, a shameless woman pretended to be sick, and when she called him to her room and to her bed on the pretext of comforting her in some way, he resisted her courageously. This led God to reward his great courage and zeal for this virtue and to give him the grace not to feel the least stirring of the flesh.

One of the best ways to acquire and to preserve chastity is to flee from the initial assaults of the demon of impurity and to do great violence to self to gain victory on some occasion or notable temptation. This is also what has drawn down abundant graces and procured outstanding chastity for many saints.

Because this virtue is one of the most necessary and most important in your state, there are no means you ought to fail to use in order to preserve it. Those that will help you most are a horror of the world and a very great recollection. Acquire these virtues, then, with all possible care.

### 129.2 Second Point

This saint devoted himself so strongly to prayer that he sometimes spent 40 hours uninterruptedly at it. His heart became so inflamed that he had to throw himself on the ground and to bare his chest to cool the heat. Because God usually gives much consolation to those who love this holy exercise, this saint sometimes felt so overcome by joy and consolation that he was constrained to cry out,

Enough, Lord, enough! One day he experienced such a great assault of the love of God that his heart was all on fire. As a result, his ribs spread apart, and from that time on, they never returned to normal; this caused him to have heart palpitations for the rest of his days.

The duty you have of obtaining grace, not only for you but also for others, and of learning how to touch hearts ought to make you devote yourself especially to prayer, which is the exercise designed for you by God to procure his graces. Is this, then, what you have most at heart? Try to perform all your actions in a spirit of prayer, one of the best ways to sanctify them.

### 129.3 Third Point

This saint had a very great devotion to the Passion of Jesus Christ and to the Most Blessed Virgin. He could not think or speak of the sufferings of Jesus without weeping, because he considered himself to be the cause. This made him sometimes say that the wound in Christ's side was very large, but if God did not restrain his hand, he would make it even larger. He also sometimes spent entire nights conversing with the Most Blessed Virgin.

These two loves, for Jesus Christ and for the Most Blessed Virgin, have, as a rule, been the principal devotions of the greatest saints. Saint Bernard and Saint Francis found their greatest pleasure meditating on the Passion of Jesus Christ. They had such a very tender devotion to the Most Blessed Virgin that they chose her as the protectress and support of their orders.

Consider her in the same way as the protectress of your Institute, and because the Passion and death of Jesus Christ are the means to sanctify all the world, often ask God to apply the merits of Jesus generously both to you and to the children entrusted to you.

———

Philip Neri (1515–1595) was born in Florence and from boyhood was noted for his combination of goodness and joy. He gave up a business career with an uncle in Naples after only a few months and traveled on foot to Rome. At first, he led a quiet life of prayer, study, and penance, during which he had a mystical experience alluded to by De La Salle. While praying to the Holy Spirit on Pentecost, he felt a ball of fire enter his heart; after his death it was discovered that two of his ribs over the heart were broken. Philip is best known for founding the Congregation of the Oratory, which grew out of his use of a room for prayer and for jovial entertainment of the young people of Rome. The musical term *oratorio* derives from this. Cardinal Newman became a member of the Oratory in Rome and founded two houses in England.

Saint Philip wanted the members to be secular priests without any further vows, bound together by fraternal love, the apostolate of preaching, and the administration of the sacraments. He said Mass and heard Confession on May 25, but he became quite ill early the following morning and died after blessing the community.

# May 27

## SAINT GERMAIN,
## BISHOP OF PARIS

### 131.1  First Point

Saint Germain was saved from death in his childhood, and even before his birth, by very special acts of the Providence of God, who had destined him to labor much for the good of his Church. Providence gave him the advantage of living with one of his uncles, a man of great piety, who took very great care of his education. He instructed him and formed him in the knowledge and practices of solid virtue; as a result, Germain achieved a great degree of holiness.

Adore God's fatherly Providence in your regard. He withdrew you from the world in order to prepare you to acquire the virtues you need to do your work well and to educate a great number of children in the Christian spirit. Do you correspond with God's designs for you? Do you strive in your state of life to achieve such a level of holiness that you can make holy those for whose guidance you are responsible?

### 131.2  Second Point

This saint was ordained a priest, although still very young, and displayed such great wisdom in his conduct and led such a holy life that not long afterward he was chosen to be the abbot of a great number of religious in the monastery that today bears his name. There he guided his Brothers with untiring zeal and fervor, which made him their model in all the practices of the Rule. His nights of prayer, his other prayers, and his mortifications were continual.

Are you completely faithful to the Rule in your community? This is the sure way to draw down on you the graces of God that you need to fulfill the duties of your state and of the ministry to which God has called you. The more exact you are in observance of the

Rule, the more you will be able to lead children to God and to procure for them a true and solid piety. Because this is the purpose of your state, take the means that are most appropriate for you and that God requires of you in order to succeed.

### 131.3 Third Point

When Saint Germain's great holiness and the great number of miracles he performed led to his being chosen bishop of Paris, he omitted none of his exercises of prayer and mortification. He spent entire nights praying to God in various churches. He wore the same clothes winter and summer, and his biographer says that because there was no one to make him suffer martyrdom, he practiced such great mortifications that he martyred himself.

All these practices of piety that he performed gave his instructions a special power to convert people. It was said of him that he was like the Apostles, not only because of the great number of miracles he performed but also because of the amazing effects of his instructions.

You have a work that might appear of little consequence, but it has the same purpose as that of this saint. Imitate him by taking the same means he used to be successful. If they are the same means, they will be as effective for you as they were for him.

––––––––

Saint Germain (ca. 496–576) was born in Autun and raised by his uncle, a priest, as De La Salle notes. Ordained in 530, he became the abbot of the monastery of Saint Symphorien near Autun. Later he was made bishop of Paris at the request of King Childebert. He worked strenuously, often without success, to establish peace among Childebert's successors and is one of the most revered saints of France. He had King Childebert build a large church in honor of Saint Vincent, which was renamed in his own honor after his death, the church of Saint-Germain-des-Prés in Paris. His feast is celebrated on May 28, the day he died, although the date in the book of De La Salle's meditations is May 27.

# June 6

## SAINT NORBERT

### 132.1 First Point

From his youth Saint Norbert was brought up at the emperor's court; however, he was specially favored by grace and felt himself touched by an extraordinary movement of the Spirit of God. Leaving the court, he withdrew entirely from the world to enter the ecclesiastical state. There he devoted himself to preaching, even more by his example than by his words. Because of this, his preaching was very effective and won many people to God.

Because you are obliged by your state to instruct children, you must be powerfully motivated by the Christian spirit in order to procure this spirit for them. Your conduct must be very edifying, so that you are able to be a model for those whom you are appointed to teach. They must be able to learn from your recollection the self-control that they ought to practice. They must see in your wisdom how they ought to behave. Your piety must be a guide for them to follow in church and during prayers.

### 132.2 Second Point

The Spirit of God, which inspired this saint, led him to give up the income he was receiving from his ecclesiastical position, to sell his inheritance, and to give the proceeds to the poor. He also led an extremely austere life. With a few companions whom he had chosen, he went about preaching from town to town and from village to village, as the 72 disciples of Jesus Christ had done.[1] They all, like him, lived a life of great austerity and bodily mortification. They went about barefoot, ate but once a day, and observed perpetual abstinence. The sum of their exercises was to obey, to devote themselves to prayer, to mortify themselves, and to preach the holy Gospel. Thus it was that Saint Norbert formed his order and that it had a great number of religious who did great good in the Church.

You have a purpose that strongly resembles what this saint had in mind in founding his order, which was to teach the truths of the Gospel to the poor. So make use of the same means he used to succeed in this task, namely, prayer and mortification.

### 132.3 Third Point

The extraordinary fasting and the eminent virtues of Saint Norbert led to his being chosen bishop in spite of his reluctance. In this position he could not tolerate vice, and he denounced it boldly in all those who were scandalously abandoning themselves to its practice. On this account some people were offended and looked for a chance to kill him. How true it is that the impious and the dissolute cannot tolerate anyone who opposes their disorderly life.

Saint Norbert escaped this danger; then he fought a heretic who denied the presence of the body of Jesus Christ in the Holy Eucharist, and he destroyed the error. Is this not the function of a bishop, to oppose vice and to maintain the faith in its vigor and strength?

This is also what you cannot dispense yourself from doing if you wish to fulfill well your ministry, to prevent your students from abandoning themselves to vice and to dissolute conduct, and to impress firmly and solidly on their minds the truths of our faith, which are the foundations of our religion.

---

Norbert (ca. 1080–1134) was born at Xanten, near Cologne, and brought up as a member of the imperial court, where he lived a worldly life in spite of his ordination to the subdiaconate and his plans to become a priest. He was thrown from his horse one day by a thunderstorm and thereupon underwent a spiritual experience of conversion, alluded to by De La Salle, which is sometimes compared to the conversion of Saint Paul. He founded a monastery at Prémontré, near Soissons, and an order of Canons Regular (Premonstratensians, or Norbertines, sometimes called White Canons from the color of their habit). Their purpose was to combine community life and the ministry of the priesthood. In 1126 he was made archbishop of Magdeburg, and he helped Saint Bernard correct the schism of the antipope of his day. He accompanied the true Pope, Innocent II, when he returned to Rome in 1133.

---

1. Lk 10:1

# June 10

## SAINT MARGARET, QUEEN OF SCOTLAND

### 133.1 First Point

This queen had a very special virtue and piety. Her conduct was so reserved, wise, and serious that no one could look at her without being inspired with respect for her. Her love for prayer was so great that we might say that her principal occupation was to pray. Every night, after taking a little rest, she would go to spend much time in church, where she would not allow anyone to speak to her of any business matters. Oh, how solid piety is when it is based on virtue, and how genuine and true virtue is when it is accompanied by piety!

In your state of life, you enjoy several means for practicing virtue and developing piety. You have the opportunity to pray often and the ability to pray well. Do you use all these means that God gives you to save yourself and to acquire the perfection of your state? If you are not faithful to them, you deserve severe punishment from God for such negligence.

### 133.2 Second Point

Saint Margaret's principal care was to govern her household properly and to make sure that all who belonged to it revered and loved God. She even became the teacher for her children, teaching them herself to read. She devoted herself to their education as her supreme duty, regarding it as the most pleasing thing she could do for God. For the same reason, this was likewise the first object of her prayers.

This saint is a great example of what you ought to do for the children God has entrusted to you. This queen made her primary work to do what is essential in your state. Consider this an honor for you, and regard the children whom God has entrusted to you as children of God. Have much more solicitude for their education and instruction than you would have for the children of a king.

### 133.3 Third Point

Her love for the poor was extraordinary. Every morning, Saint Margaret spent time instructing poor children and afterward gave them food to eat. Because she honored Jesus Christ in them, she knelt to serve them. She and her husband fed three hundred poor people in their own dining room. It is also said that she frequently got money from her husband, the king, to give alms and that he gladly gave it to her. She often sent him out into the countryside to become informed about the sad state of the poor, so that he could direcct all his efforts to help them.

You are by your state obliged to instruct poor children. Do you love them? Do you honor Jesus Christ in their person? With this in mind, do you prefer them to those who have a certain amount of material wealth? Do you have more concern for the former than for the latter? This saint gives you an example of this and teaches you how you ought to regard the poor.

Margaret of Scotland (ca. 1046–1093) was born in Hungary, where her father, Prince Edward of England, was in exile. At age 12, she returned with her widowed mother to England when Saint Edward Confessor was king but went into exile again, this time to Scotland, at the time of the Norman Conquest in 1066. King Malcolm III of Scotland fell in love with her and dissuaded her from entering a convent as a nun. She had considerable influence on her husband and was able to resolve the differences between the Celtic church and Rome, thus avoiding a schism. She is also responsible, together with her sons, for infusing much of medieval culture into Scottish life, creating a golden age in Scotland that lasted two hundred years after her death. De La Salle stresses the influence she had on her eight children. She was canonized in 1250, and in the seventeenth century (at the time De La Salle was studying for the priesthood), Pope Clement X made her Patroness of Scotland. Her feast is now celebrated on November 16.

# June 11

## SAINT BARNABAS

### 134.1 First Point

Saint Barnabas was one of the first to join the Apostles after our Lord's Ascension, and he showed a very great detachment from the goods of this earth. As we learn from the account given by Saint Luke in the Acts of the Apostles, he sold his property, which was considerable, and brought the money to the feet of the Apostles.[1] For this reason, from then on he was held in special esteem by the disciples and all the faithful. He was set apart for great things in the Church, not only by the Apostles but also by the divine will, which made itself known in his regard.[2]

It is difficult to realize how much good a detached person is able to do in the Church. The reason for this is that detachment shows a deep faith. A person who abandons himself to the Providence of God is like a sailor who puts out to sea without sails or oars.

Beg God through the intercession of Saint Barnabas for the disinterestedness that is so necessary in your profession, and on your part, strive to make this virtue your own.

### 134.2 Second Point

This detachment of Saint Barnabas procured for him so great an abundance of faith and of the spirit of religion that Saint Luke, praising him in a few words, says that he was a man full of goodness and filled with the Holy Spirit and faith.[3] This goodness in him and the tenderness he felt for his neighbor led the Apostles to appoint him, along with Saint Paul, to distribute the alms sent from Antioch to Jerusalem during a great famine.[4] Faith and the Spirit of God, which inspired him, enabled him to perform several miracles that led people to regard him, along with Saint Paul, as a god.[5]

Do you act in such a way that you have as much kindness and affection for the children you instruct as Saint Barnabas had for the people for whose conversion and salvation he was working? The more tenderness you have for the members of Jesus Christ and of the Church who are entrusted to you, the more God will produce in them the wonderful effects of his grace.

### 134.3 Third Point

Saint Barnabas was not one of the 12 Apostles; nevertheless, he possessed fully the grace of the apostolate. According to Saint Luke's account, it was the Holy Spirit who, when some of the disciples were offering sacrifices to the Lord and fasting, told them to set apart Saul and Barnabas to carry out the work for which he had called them. This led the disciples to lay hands on him as well as on Saint Paul.[6]

Thus sent by the Holy Spirit, Barnabus produced such great results in Antioch through the preaching of the Gospel, as Saint Luke declares, that a great many people there were converted to the Lord, and it was at Antioch that the disciples were first called Christians.[7] Along with Saint Paul, Saint Barnabas was also the first to preach the Gospel to the Gentiles.

If, like Saint Barnabas, you are filled with faith and the Spirit of God, as you ought to be in your work, you will be the cause that those whom you instruct will not be Christians in name only. They will also have the spirit and the conduct of Christians, which will cause others to admire them for their piety.

———

Barnabas is first mentioned in the fourth chapter of the Acts of the Apostles for his generous act of selling the farm he owned and donating the proceeds to the first Christian community in Jerusalem. In Acts he is described as a Levite from Cyprus, named Joseph, and given the new name of Barnabas, which means son of encouragement. He was an encouragement to Paul when Paul first came to Jerusalem and needed someone to vouch for his conversion before those in the Christian community who still feared him (Acts 9:26ff). Later, when Barnabas was sent to Antioch to encourage the early Christians (some of whom were from Cyprus and were inviting Greeks into the community), Barnabas asked Paul to come there to help him (Acts 11:22ff). They worked together there for a year. Later, they were sent with relief funds from Antioch to Jerusalem, where they were joined by a cousin of Barnabas, the Evangelist Mark. The three of them undertook the first missionary journey (Acts 13 and 14). From that time on, there is no mention of Barnabas, except in a passing reference in Paul's First Letter to the Corinthians (9:5). His role in the Church, it seems, was to launch Paul on his great mission to the Gentiles. Tradition has it that Barnabus continued his own missionary work and was martyred at Salamina, on his native Cyprus, around 70 A.D.

---

1. Acts 4:36–37
2. Acts 13:2
3. Acts 11:24
4. Acts 11:28–30
5. Acts 14:2–13
6. Acts 13:2–3
7. Acts 11:24–26

# June 13

## SAINT ANTHONY OF PADUA

### 135.1 First Point

This saint, while still very young, left the world to enter the Order of Canons Regular; however, he often had visits from his relatives in the house where he lived. Because he did not want to have these visits, to avoid them he withdrew to another monastery a long way off, where he led a much more secluded life.

You need to live in seclusion to learn the knowledge of salvation[1] that you must teach others. This is the benefit that you ought to receive from this kind of life. In this way you must learn how to speak about God and be able to speak about him effectively. Be convinced that it is in seclusion and in silence that you learn how to speak well. The more you enjoy seclusion and silence, the more you will be able to fulfill your ministry on behalf of your neighbor.

### 135.2 Second Point

This saint had such a great zeal for religion and for making God known to the infidels and such a great desire for martyrdom that when he saw five of Saint Francis' friars go off to preach the Gospel to the Moors and heard later that they had been martyred, the desire to imitate them, not only in their preaching but also in their martyrdom, led him to plan to enter the Order of Saint Francis. No sooner had he finished his novitiate than he obtained permission to go to Africa to labor for the conversion of infidels.

You are obliged in your work to teach the truths of faith to your disciples and to instruct them in their religion. To fulfill well this duty, you ought to consecrate yourself entirely and even, if necessary, to give your life. Is this how you act? Do you have this generous disposition?

### 135.3 Third Point

When this saint was put to the work of preaching by the order of Saint Francis, it became apparent that God had placed his holy word in his mouth, for when he preached, all his hearers were filled with admiration, and he brought about altogether surprising conversions.

He succeeded so well in this holy ministry because he had prepared for it by seclusion and prayer, undertaken it only through obedience, and always stayed in humble work until his superior ordered him to preach.

It ought to be only in response to the order of God and in submission to your superior that you work for the salvation of souls. This will be the way to sanctify you in this work and to procure the sanctification of others.

------

Anthony of Padua (1195–1231) was born of noble parents in Lisbon, Portugal, and entered the Canons Regular of Saint Augustine in that city at the age of 15. De La Salle mentions his desire for separation from his relatives. During the eight years that Anthony spent in the more secluded monastery at Coimbra, which was a renowned center for biblical studies, he became a profound scholar. But the martyrdom of five Franciscans whom he had met at Coimbra on their way to Morocco made him lose interest in theology and gave him a great desire for martyrdom. With the permission of his provincial, he reluctantly withdrew from the Augustinians and joined the Franciscans. He was no sooner in Morocco, however, than he fell sick and was forced to return. Circumstances again intervened when a storm drove his ship to Sicily. From there he went to Italy, where at first he was assigned to menial tasks in a little hospice in Forli. Called from the kitchen to deliver an extemporaneous sermon because no one else was willing, he astonished everyone with his wisdom, power, and eloquence. Thereupon he began ten years of extensive and vigorous preaching throughout Italy that culminated in exhaustion and death on June 13, 1231, at the age of 36. One biographer notes the irony in his popularity today as a meek and sweet patron of petitions to recover lost articles, which disguises his life as a remarkable scholar, a powerful preacher, and a worker of extraordinary miracles.

---

1. Lk 1:77

# June 14

## SAINT BASIL

### 136.1 First Point

Brought up in piety by his grandfather, Saint Basil received instructions from this saintly old man that made such an impression on his mind that he renounced the world entirely and withdrew to a place of solitude where he built a monastery. He gave very wise rules to the religious who came there to place themselves under his direction. There he took on a life of such privation that by the end of his days, his body fell into a very great exhaustion brought on by the austerities that he continually practiced. By these two means, solitude and fasting, this saint prepared himself to do great good in the Church.

If you want to do much good for souls through the exercise of your ministry, nothing will help you more than separation from the world and the practice of temperance. Temperance helps a great deal to preserve purity, and separation from the world draws down on a soul the grace of God in abundance, not only for ourselves but also for others.

### 136.2 Second Point

The spirit of religion, which this saint had acquired in solitude, enabled him as bishop to inspire such good behavior and piety in those who were in his presence in church that when the emperor came there, he was highly edified by the reserve and the silence of the clergy and all Catholics, who seemed to be angels singing God's praises on earth, and by the good order in the ceremonies and in the chanting of the Psalms. He went away marveling, and he sent rich presents to the church.

This is how it ought to be with you. Filled with the spirit of piety as a result of being thoroughly devoted to prayer and to recollection, you ought to inspire this spirit in your disciples so well that people who see them will admire their good behavior and their self-control in church. On the contrary, fear that their lack of self-control would reflect on you and arouse the anger of heaven against you for being the cause by the lack of recollection you show in the holy place where you have to keep watch over them.

### 136.3 Third Point

When this saint was a bishop, he also had such great zeal to uphold and to defend the Church that he was one of its most notable champions against the Arians. He strove with all possible care to unite the minds of the people in one faith and their hearts in the same spirit of charity and religion.

All his efforts for the peace of the Church caused him to be persecuted by the heretics and even by the emperor, who, urged and importuned by their demands, decided to send Saint Basil into exile. But when this prince was about to sign the edict of condemnation, his hand could not write a single word. This is how God protects those who defend his cause.

Do not tolerate the dissolute among those whom you teach. Make piety be their characteristic as well as yours. The world will persecute you,[1] but God will be your defender.

––––––

Basil (329–379) was born in Caesarea, the capital of Capadoccia, into a family of saints: not only the venerable grandfather mentioned by De La Salle but also a canonized grandmother, mother, father, two brothers, and one sister. He also became a close friend of Saint Gregory Nazianzen while a student in Athens. With a desire to lead a monastic life like his sister, he traveled widely to study existing monasteries and then founded his own, not far from his sister's, and drew up the Rule that became the model for the Orthodox churches of the East, from which Saint Benedict borrowed for his Rule for the West. In 370 Basil became archbishop of Caesarea and was both a leader for his own people and a champion of orthodox faith for all Christendom against Arianism. This won for him the title of the Great and also of Doctor of the Church. He died on January 1, which is the day on which the Eastern Churches celebrate his principal feast. His feast is now celebrated in the Roman calendar, along with that of Saint Gregory Nazianzen, on January 2.

––––––

1. Jn 15:20

# June 22

## SAINT PAULINUS, BISHOP OF NOLA

### 137.1 First Point

Saint Paulinus displayed a great detachment from the pleasures and comforts of life and from all the goods of the world. No sooner was he married than he persuaded his wife to preserve celibate chastity with him, so that they lived together like brother and sister. Then they sold all their property and distributed most of the proceeds to the poor. The remainder they used to build a church in honor of Saint Felix, where Saint Paulinus prayed every night for the rest of his life.

Made prisoner by the Goths, who threatened to kill him unless he gave them all his treasure, he begged God not to allow him to be tortured for the sake of gold and silver, for God knew where he had put all his wealth. From this Saint Augustine took occasion to remark that all Saint Paulinus' wealth was in God because he did not want to possess anything except God. No doubt it was his renunciation of all things that had given him this disposition.

You have renounced the world exteriorly and all that people seek in it for their contentment. Take care that this renunciation also be interior and procure complete detachment for you. Ask for this through the intercession of Saint Paulinus.

### 137.2 Second Point

This saint's love for the poor was so admirable that even though he had become poor for the sake of Jesus Christ, he never refused to give alms. One day a poor person came to his door, and the saint ordered that he be given the last bit of bread that they had. His wife, however, did not wish to do this, fearing that they would be left in extreme need. But God provided for them, because when mealtime came, several barges full of wheat arrived for him. At the same time, he was told that one barge loaded with grain had been lost. This gave him the chance to say to his wife that she ought to have had more trust in God and that because she had not wanted to part with one loaf, God had made them lose that one barge full of wheat.

Is this how you love the poor? God asks you to give them not material but spiritual alms, which is all the more important, for the life of the body is nothing compared to the life of the soul, which is immortal.

### 137.3 Third Point

This saint was not satisfied with this charity toward the poor, rare as it was. He carried it to excessive lengths, as we can see in the instance related by Saint Gregory the Great. A mother came to him desolate because the Vandals had taken her son prisoner and their king's son-in-law had made him his slave. In her distress the woman could think of nothing else to do except to have recourse to Saint Paulinus. He had nothing to give her, so to obtain her son's release, he became a volunteer slave and took the place of the son of this widow. God blessed this unparalleled act of charity to such an extraordinary degree that Saint Paulinus soon afterward was sent back to his bishopric with great honor, accompanied by all the captives from his diocese, who were turned over to him and granted freedom.

You are committed to God in place of those whom you instruct. By taking upon yourself the responsibility for their souls, you have, so to speak, offered to him soul for soul.[1] Have you sometimes reflected on the commitment that you have made (to be responsible for those whom God has entrusted to you), in order to be faithful to it? Do you care as much for their salvation as you do for your own? You must not only take all possible care of them but also consecrate your life and self entirely to procure salvation for them.

---

Paulinus (ca. 353–431) was born in Bordeaux, France, of wealthy parents. He married a Spanish lady in 378. After he and his wife became Christians, in 389, he was ordained a priest, in 394 or 395, and settled in Nola, Italy, as head of an informal monastery that he had established. He corresponded with the leading churchmen of his day: Saint Jerome, Saint Augustine (who addressed to him his treatise on the Care of the Departed), and Saint Sulpice. He was also a guest of Saint Ambrose. In 409 he was chosen bishop of Nola. Two of his poems and 51 of his letters have survived.

---

1. Ex 21:23

# June 24

## THE NATIVITY OF SAINT JOHN THE BAPTIST

### 138.1 First Point

Saint John enjoys this special privilege, that his birthday is honored in the Church as is that of Jesus Christ. Saint Bernard says that the reason for this honor is that he was holy from his birth, for he was sanctified in his mother's womb by Jesus Christ when the Most Blessed Virgin went to visit Saint Elizabeth.[1]

Because he was closely united to Jesus Christ, having been chosen by the eternal Father to be his precursor,[2] it was most fitting that he be raised to a level of grace above that granted to other people and that his holiness be manifest at his birth. This is why Jesus Christ said that among all people there was none greater than John the Baptist.[3]

With the Church, let us honor the birth of Saint John as the beginning of his sanctity and of the sanctification of so many others.

Because we were not born saints, let us pray that the second birth that we received when we withdrew from the world may be for us the beginning of our sanctification. In the words of Saint Leo, let us pray that we not do fall back into the degradation of our first birth by conduct inconsistent with the state we have embraced.

### 138.2 Second Point

Saint John was holy also by the life he led. When he could barely walk, he went into the desert[4] to live there separated from all contact with others. Although his father and his mother were so holy and separated from the world, their piety did not seem to him an adequate model of what God asked of him. He needed to go out and to discover from God, in seclusion and through the practice of prayer, what manner of life ought to be his. He needed to practice altogether extraordinary austerities, living only on locusts and wild honey,[5] to attain the sanctity God asked of him. In this way he prepared to preach penance.[6] The infallible way to preach penance successfully is to practice it.

The Church, in his Office for the day, gives us another reason for the seclusion and the mortification of this Saint, namely, the fear of staining his soul with the slightest sin. Those are also the two reasons that ought to engage you to live apart from the world and to maintain wise and regulated behavior.

### 138.3 Third Point

By living a penitential life in the desert until he was thirty years old, Saint John prepared to preach in a holy manner. Then, says the Gospel, the Lord put his words into John's mouth, and at once he went out to all the country around the Jordan, preaching penance for the remission of sins.[7] All the people came to him, even publicans and soldiers, and he told them what they needed to do to be saved.[8] A great number of those who went to him followed his advice and were converted to God. The example of his secluded and austere life enabled him to win people's hearts easily and to convince them to do penance for their sins.

By your vocation you are obliged to announce the truths of the Gospel every day. Practice those that are required of all Christians before you undertake to teach them to others. Although you do not have the grace, like Saint John, of being the precursor of Jesus Christ, you do possess the grace of being a successor in his ministry. Be assured, however, that you will make this effective for others only insofar as it has produced its effect in you. See that it does so without delay.

---

On June 24 the summer solstice was celebrated in ancient times by lighting fires to honor the sun. (Tthe summer solstice is generally reckoned on or about June 22.) The Church put the feast of Saint John on this day apparently because Jesus Christ called him a burning and shining light (John 5:35), and the Church wanted to substitute the celebration of John's birthday for the pagan rites. The only other saint whose birthday is a feast of the Church is Mary, Mother of God.

---

1. Lk 1:39–44
2. Lk 1:17
3. Mt 11:11
4. Lk 1:80
5. Mk 1:6
6. Mk 1:4
7. Lk 3:2–3
8. Lk 3:10–14

# June 29

## SAINT PETER

### 139.1 First Point

It ought not to be surprising that Saint Peter was so dearly loved by Jesus Christ and that our Lord established him as the head of his Church.[1] His great faith won for him this honor, the faith that led him to renounce all things to follow Jesus Christ[2] and to give himself to him completely. It is true, as Saint Jerome says, that Saint Peter gave up little, if we consider what he possessed; he left only a fishing boat and some nets. But if we pay attention to the fact that he gave up at the same time the desire to possess anything, he did indeed give up much, as this saint observes, because he renounced what is most important in this world, what is most capable of attracting and absorbing people's hearts.

The faith with which he was already filled enabled him to make this generous act. Because Jesus Christ was then just a common man in the eyes of the world, without any acclaim, nothing but a strong faith could have enabled anyone to leave everything to follow him, because to all appearances there was nothing to be hoped for from him.

Have you truly renounced everything with all your heart's desire? Have you put yourself under the protection of God alone, with an entire abandonment to his Providence? Make this generous act in imitation of Saint Peter and through his intercession.

### 139.2 Second Point

His great faith led this holy Apostle to follow Jesus Christ always. Of the three who were with Jesus Christ in the principal occurrences of his life, Peter is named first in the holy Gospel.[3] He is also the first of all the Apostles to go to the sepulchre to look for the body of his beloved Master,[4] which illustrates the great attachment he felt for him. His faith shone out above all the other Apostles so strongly that when Jesus questioned them to learn what people were thinking about him and then asked them what they thought of him, Saint Peter, enlightened as he was from above, as Jesus Christ declared, by a light incomprehensible to the human mind and that could come to him only from heaven, replied, You are the Christ, the Son of the living God![5] This led Jesus Christ to entrust to him the care of his Church.

Be convinced that you will contribute to the good of the Church in your ministry only insofar as you have the fullness of faith and are guided by the spirit of faith, which is the spirit of your state and by which you must be inspired.

### 139.3 Third Point

Another effect of Saint Peter's extraordinary faith was that as soon as all the Apostles had received the Holy Spirit on Pentecost, he preached with so much energy and power that an innumerable multitude of those present from all kinds of nations, each hearing him speak in his own native tongue,[6] were so amazed by what he told them (although he spoke in very simple terms) that three thousand of them were converted on the spot[7] and embraced the faith of Jesus Christ. A few days later, five thousand more[8] did the same. This great faith of Saint Peter also enabled him to perform a large number of miracles, which made his words effective and enabled even his shadow to heal the sick.[9]

Do you have faith that is able to touch the hearts of your students and to inspire them with the Christian spirit? This is the greatest miracle you can perform and the one that God asks of you, for this is the purpose of your work.

---

De La Salle meditates on Saint Peter as a model of faith and, in the following meditation, on Saint Paul as a model of zeal, because he wants to associate the twofold spirit of his Institute with these two great saints of the Church. Both saints are now celebrated on June 29.

| | | |
|---|---|---|
| 1. Mt 16:15–19 | 4. Jn 20:3–8 | 7. Acts 2:41 |
| 2. Mt 19:27 | 5. Mt 16:16 | 8. Acts 4:4 |
| 3. Mt 17:1 | 6. Acts 2:5–7 | 9. Acts 15:15 |

# June 30

## SAINT PAUL

### 140.1 First Point

The most admirable trait in Saint Paul is his all-embracing and ardent zeal, which he first showed by defending the faith of Moses, in which he had been very well instructed.[1] Because he was very knowledgeable and saw that the Christian religion was beginning to spread throughout Judea by the preaching of the Apostles, he took every possible step to oppose and to destroy it. As a consequence of his zeal, he took part in the stoning of Saint Stephen,[2] even though he was a relative. Then, having done all he could against the faithful in Jerusalem, he took steps to secure authorization to persecute those in the city of Damascus.[3]

His zeal for the law of God made him undertake all these travels and all these persecutions against the Christians,[4] but he did all this out of ignorance,[5] as he states. This is why God did not leave him in error but enlightened him in a completely miraculous manner.

You have the advantage of knowing the truth and the happiness of having been born and brought up in the Christian religion. You must necessarily consider it your first duty to uphold it. Are you as zealous in this respect as Saint Paul was to preserve the Jewish law? You have an easy means of doing so by instructing children, teaching them the truths and the holy maxims of the Gospel, and strongly opposing everything that the spirit of immorality is able to inspire in them to the contrary.

### 140.2 Second Point

After Jesus Christ had converted Saint Paul and had taught him his religion with the help of no one,[6] this saint preached with so much zeal and so much success that he labored more to spread faith in Jesus Christ, as he says, than all the other Apostles did.[7] His entire effort was to procure the conversion of souls, especially *the Gentiles,* for whom *God,* he says, by his power had established him as their Apostle.[8]

His efforts brought about important results, for he preached in many provinces and performed all sorts of prodigies and miracles to establish Christianity. This made the people want on one occasion to offer a sacrifice to him, as though he were a god who had come down from heaven and taken the form of a man.[9] He led a life more heavenly than human, for he thought only of drawing souls to God and of instructing, strengthening, and consoling them.

God, by his power and very special goodness, has called you to give the knowledge of the Gospel to those who have not yet received it. Do you regard yourselves, then, as ministers of God? Do you fulfill the duties of your work with all possible zeal and as having to give an account of it to him?

### 140.3 Third Point

Zeal cannot be more genuine and more firm than when it continues in the midst of the greatest sufferings and the most cruel persecutions. In this way Saint Paul's zeal was put to the test. Several times he was thrown into prison; he was wounded frequently; often he was almost at death's door because of the beatings given him. Five times he was cruelly scourged; three times he was beaten with rods; once he was stoned. He was shipwrecked three times, and he spent a day and a night adrift on the sea. He was in danger of falling into the hands of robbers. Those of his own nation laid ambush for him, as did the Gentiles also. He endured afflictions and sorrow, lengthy nights of prayer, hunger, thirst, and cold;[10] in the midst of all these ordeals, his zeal never slackened.[11]

In your ministry you need much zeal. Imitate the zeal of this holy Apostle, so that neither insults, injuries, calumnies, nor persecutions of whatever kind may be able to diminish your zeal in the slightest or to force a single complaint from you. Consider yourselves very happy to suffer for Jesus Christ.[12]

––––––

De La Salle meditates on Saint Peter as a model of faith in his meditation for June 29 and on Saint Paul as a model of zeal in his meditation for June 30 because he wants to associate the twofold spirit of his Institute with these two great saints of the Church. Both saints are now celebrated together on June 29.

1. Acts 22:3
2. Acts 7:58
3. Acts 9:1–2
4. Acts 26:11
5. 1 Tim 1:13
6. Gal 1:11

7. 1 Cor 15:10
8. Gal 2:8
9. Acts 14:11–13
10. 2 Cor 11:23–27
11. 1 Cor 4:11–13
12. 2 Cor 12:10; Acts 21:13

# July 2

## THE VISITATION
## OF THE MOST BLESSED VIRGIN

### 141.1  First Point

Let us admire the promptness with which the Most Blessed Virgin went to visit her cousin, Saint Elizabeth, as soon as she learned the will of God. She undertook this journey without delay, in spite of the difficulties of the road, which was mountainous.[1] She had nothing in view except to do what God desired of her; this was what she had most at heart. Her promptness drew down God's blessings on her visit and was a cause of the great things that God performed through her.

We must consider ourselves blessed when we are visited by God through his inspirations. Let us be faithful to them, for to this fidelity God usually attaches a great number of graces. He does this only insofar as we do what he shows us that he wants us to do when he gives us his inspirations. God sends us his holy inspirations only to make us prompt to put them into practice with the intent to accomplish his holy will exactly.

### 141.2 Second Point

God urged the Most Blessed Virgin to go to visit Saint Elizabeth because he wished to sanctify John the Baptist by the presence of Jesus Christ, his Son, and to deliver him from original sin while he was still in the womb of Saint Elizabeth, his mother.

Because Saint John the Baptist was destined to be the precursor of Jesus, it was quite fitting that he be sanctified in advance by a very special grace of Jesus Christ, who was necessarily to be the Savior of all[2] and whose coming John was to proclaim.

For this same reason, God inspired the Most Blessed Virgin, as soon as she had conceived, to go without delay to visit her cousin, so that Jesus Christ might make known his coming to Saint John and thus perform for his precursor his first miracle while still enclosed in Mary's womb.

God also wanted Saint John to pay homage to Jesus by leaping for joy[3] at the approach of his Savior.

Let us beg Jesus to be willing to visit us and to perform a miracle of grace in our favor by encouraging us to do significant violence to ourselves in order to practice a virtue for which we experience much repugnance.

### 141.3 Third Point

In this visit God was not content to confer an extraordinary grace on Saint John, thanks to the presence of Jesus, his only Son. He also wished by means of the presence of the Most Blessed Virgin to give himself to Saint Elizabeth in such a way that she also would be at once filled with the Holy Spirit[4] and know that Mary is the Mother of God.[5] This made Saint Elizabeth realize how great a happiness she enjoyed and how much she had reason to be surprised that the Mother of her Lord had come to visit her.[6]

Admire how advantageous this visit of the Most Blessed Virgin was to Saint John and to Saint Elizabeth. Because you have the honor of being visited by God every day in prayer and often by Jesus in Holy Communion, make sure that their visits to you are not without effect but that both procure for you abundant grace, which will help you advance in virtue every day and tend in some particular way toward perfection. Do not fail to examine from time to time what benefit you have derived from these visits.

---

This feast was originally and appropriately part of the Advent period and seems, by being moved to May 31 (in the present calendar of the Church), to have been placed in relationship with the celebration of the birth of Saint John the Baptist on June 24. The Franciscans apparently began observing the feast in the thirteenth century; it was only about one hundred years later that it became part of the liturgy of the universal Church. Saint Francis de Sales wanted his Order of the Visitation to take our Lady's visit to her cousin as the model for their service to the poor in their homes, but he was ahead of his times, and the Church insisted that his nuns stay cloistered. De La Salle's emphasis on fidelity to the inspirations of God, which he stresses in this meditation, is a significant component of his spirituality.

---

1. Lk 1:39–40
2. 1 Tim 4:10
3. Lk 1:44
4. Lk 1:41
5. Lk 1:42
6. Lk 1:43

# July 14

## SAINT BONAVENTURE

### 142.1 First Point

This saint had such a great love for poverty that he wrote a book, which he entitled *The Apologia of the Poor,* to make known the excellence of this virtue. In it he demonstrates that voluntary poverty is the foundation of Gospel perfection, because by renouncing all things and the desire to have anything, which is called poverty of spirit, we cut off and tear out the root of all evils, which is concupiscence,[1] as Saint Paul declares.

This is why, says Saint Bonaventure, when Jesus Christ wished to lead his disciples to perfection, he began by making them understand the happiness that the truly poor in spirit enjoy.[2] Then he urged them to practice poverty, telling them that if they wished to be perfect, it was necessary for them to sell all that they had and to give it to the poor.[3] In this book Saint Bonaventure taught only what he practiced, because he chose the poorest order in the Church when he became a religious.

Let us enter into the sentiments of this holy doctor and imitate his example.

### 142.2 Second Point

Poverty deserves little esteem unless it is accompanied by humility. Accordingly, Saint Bonaventure tried especially to acquire this virtue. No sooner had he entered the novitiate than his greatest pleasure was to sweep the house, wash the pots, and devote himself to the lowliest chores in the monastery.

This same virtue led him to refuse the archbishopric of York in England and made it necessary for the Pope to give him a specific order to accept the position of Minister General of his order. In this work, in spite of its exalted character, he behaved with such great simplicity that he could be distinguished in nothing from the other religious. Similarly, when chosen to be a cardinal, he lived without any ostentation and in the practice of religious humility.

In return God rewarded him with the wisdom of the Holy Spirit, by whom he was singularly favored.

The more humble you are, the more graces you will receive. This is one virtue you need very much in your state.

### 142.3  Third Point

What makes a religious most commendable is great exactness in observing the Rule. That is what this saint practiced more than anything else. He even wrote books about the observance of the Rule, in which he wanted the smallest details to be respected and none of them whatsoever to be omitted. He even adds that these details might appear as small, even as mere trifles, to those who do not understand what the religious life is. In it nothing is small if everything practiced there is considered with the eyes of faith.

Is this how you look upon your holy practices? The more you are commited to what in your Rule seems least important in the eyes of the public, the more consolations you will have in your state and the more love you will feel for what the Rule prescribes for you. The more you act with simplicity in regard to what is to be observed, the more the practice of it will become easy for you.

---

Bonaventure (1221–1274) was born at Bagnorea, near Viterbo, and was baptized Giovanni, the son of Giovanni and Ritella de Fidanza. He joined the Franciscans, received the name Bonaventure, and while still a young man, was sent to the University of Paris for his education. There he met Saint Thomas Aquinas as a friend and a teaching colleague. He was elected Minister General of the Franciscans at the age of 36, in 1257, a post he held for 16 years. He managed to do much to reconcile the two factions of his order, the *Spirituales,* for the strict observance, and the *Relaxati,* who wanted mitigations. In 1260 he gave his Order its first constitutions and was untiring in visiting all the provinces to see that this legislation was observed. He was also a popular preacher and found time to write both spiritual and theological treatises. His emphasis was on the mystical dimension of the Christian life. He grounded this movement of Franciscan spirituality on a solid theological and psychological basis while curbing the excesses of those who lacked a proper balance. Although he refused appointment as archbishop of York in 1265, he accepted the Pope's request to become the Cardinal bishop of Albano in 1273. He died on July 14, 1274, while attending the Ecumenical Council of Lyons. His canonization was delayed by dissension among the Franciscans until 1482. He was declared a Doctor of the Church in 1588. Dante gives him a prominent place in *Paradiso* (XII, 127ff), where he tells the story of Saint Dominic and criticizes some of his relaxed followers. His feast is now celebrated on July 15.

---

1. 1 Tim 6:10          2. Mt 5:3          3. Mt 19:21

# July 17

## SAINT ALEXIS

### 143.1 First Point

Saint Alexis' break with the world and with the pleasures of the flesh was altogether extraordinary. This saint was married against his inclination and out of pure obedience to the will of his parents, who committed him to it because he was their only son. But he regretted this step the very day of his marriage and, touched by a powerful movement of grace, secretly left his father's house and went to a far distant country. He lived there unknown for seventeen years, spending his time in constant prayer and living in a most austere manner. He would have always remained there had the renown of his holy life not made him known and obliged him to leave the place where he was.

You who have left the world, have you renounced it with as much enthusiasm as Saint Alexis did? Was it your intention then, and is it still at present, never to have any more dealings with the world and to live in it totally unknown? If so, you will be in a position to labor usefully in your work.

### 143.2 Second Point

This saint was not satisfied to live unknown in the world; he also wished to live in poverty. After giving away all he had to the poor, he put on a poor man's garb and resolved to spend the rest of his life in the practice of voluntary poverty. He did this to such an admirable degree that having returned to his father's house, he continued to live there as a pauper amidst riches and was regarded as a beggar in the midst of the wealth that belonged to him.

This was acting as Jesus Christ had done when he lived on this earth; even though everything belonged to him, he remained like a stranger and a poor man, living on alms and never wishing to possess anything as his own.

Because you have the advantage of working especially for the instruction of the poor, you must, according to the spirit of your Institute, have a much higher regard for them than for the rich. You also ought to live as the poor do, detached from everything in order to have some conformity with them. Have, then, as much love for poverty as people of the world have for riches.

### 143.3 Third Point

This saint loved contempt no less than poverty. Having come back to Rome, he asked his father, who did not recognize him, to accept him in his house as a poor person. He lived there for seventeen years, always hidden, unknown, living on the scraps they gave him out of charity, abandoned by all. The house servants despised him and sometimes made fun of him on account of his poverty and misery, the way he appeared exteriorly in the midst of so much insult and contempt. He was glad to be humiliated in this world for the love of Jesus Christ.

How could he have remained for so long in his own father's house in such poverty and humiliation without wanting to make himself known and in this situation always appearing content without showing the least displeasure exteriorly? Oh, a person must be quite humble and love contempt to be able to endure constantly this burden of mortification!

You have a work that is honorable only in the sight of God because it seeks to spread his kingdom. Do you accept with joy the contempt that comes to you from people? The kingdom of God, which you serve and in which you hope, is not of this world.[1]

---

Alexis (fifth century) is known through stories coming to Rome from the Middle East in the ninth century. They were preserved and embellished by Saint Adalbert, a monk who lived in the tenth century. De La Salle bases his meditation on these legends. The feast is no longer celebrated in the Church.

---

1. Jn 18:36

# July 22

## SAINT MARY MAGDALEN

### 144.1 First Point

One cannot admire too greatly the tender love that Saint Mary Magdalen had for Jesus Christ. Attracted by the sight of his miracles and by his very moving discourses, she left the world in which she had been involved and gave herself entirely to Jesus Christ. Nothing held her back, neither human respect, which might have made her think of what people would say about the sudden change in her conduct, nor her attachment to the pleasures and comforts of life, nor her concern for status (Jesus Christ's followers were, for the most part, drawn from the outcasts of the people). She had so strong a thought to follow him that she renounced at once everything else for love of him and without regard for any human considerations.

You who have left the world, have you renounced it in such a way that you no longer think of it at all? Are you completely disgusted with everything that makes up the pleasure of people living in the world? Are you no longer attached to anything?

### 144.2 Second Point

This love she had for Jesus Christ so filled her heart that once she was converted, she resolved never to abandon him again. She was one of the holy women who followed him everywhere on his journeys and supplied his needs and those of his disciples.[1] At a banquet held in Bethany, where Jesus was present a few days before his death, she poured a fragrant ointment over his feet[2] and later accompanied him even to Calvary, where she saw him die.[3] She did all this to show that she could not leave Jesus Christ, so deeply did she love him.

Are you as faithful to follow Jesus Christ when he causes you to suffer as when he showers you with his blessings? Alas! As soon as someone says something to you that causes you some pain or you are given some reproof, do you not show your resentment? On occasions such as these, you must show that you follow Jesus Christ and are one of his disciples.

### 144.3 Third Point

When love is ardent, it is even stronger than death.[4] This is clear in Saint Mary Magdalen's love, which was so great that when Jesus Christ was buried, she stayed near the sepulchre.[5] Then she bought a great quantity of perfumes to embalm the body of Jesus and returned to the tomb early on the morning of the Resurrection with the other holy women.[6] Seeing that the stone which had closed the tomb had been rolled away, she ran to tell Saint Peter and Saint John that someone had removed her Lord.[7]

Because she loved him so tenderly, she remained close by the sepulchre, weeping.[8] She looked here and there until she saw two angels, who assured her that Jesus Christ had risen.[9] By her faithfulness at the tomb of Jesus Christ, this saint merited to be the first one to whom he appeared after his Resurrection.[10] After consoling her, he ordered her to go and to tell his Apostles that he was risen, which she did at once.[11]

By the kindness he showed to Mary Magdalen, Jesus Christ has made it clear how good God is to those who love him and with what tenderness he rewards, even in this life, the love they have for him.

You ought to show the great love you have for Jesus by being eager to talk with him in prayer and by your desire to receive him as often as possible in the Eucharist.

————

Mary Magdalen is identified in the Latin Church as the Mary present at the crucifixion and the Resurrection, also as the Mary of Bethany, sister of Martha and Lazarus, and also as the sinner who came to Jesus when he was a guest of Simon the Pharisee. In the Greek Church, these three are considered as three separate people. De La Salle follows the Roman tradition in his meditation. The devotion to Mary Magdalen in France was enhanced by the belief that her body, with that of Lazarus, was brought to Provence in the ninth century. In 1713 De La Salle, discouraged by the turn of events in Marseille, made a retreat in the monastery of Saint Maximin, near the Sainte Baume grotto of Saint Mary Magdalen, about 30 miles from Marseille.

————

| | | |
|---|---|---|
| 1. Lk 8:2, 3 | 5. Mt 27:61 | 9. Lk 24:4–6 |
| 2. Jn 12:1–3 | 6. Lk 24:1 | 10. Mk 16:9 |
| 3. Jn 19:25 | 7. Jn 20:1–2 | 11. Jn 20:17–18 |
| 4. Song 8:6 | 8. Jn 20:11–12 | |

# July 25

## SAINT JAMES THE GREATER

### 145.1 First Point

Although all the Apostles were well loved by Jesus Christ as his dear disciples to whom he entrusted his mysteries,[1] Saint James was one of those he loved the most and to whom he confided his secrets most openly. It was Saint James' happiness to be present at the Transfiguration of Jesus Christ[2] and to see his glorious body, although a momentary glory, a favor granted only to his brother, Saint John, and to Saint Peter.[3] He also had the privilege of *accompanying Jesus Christ in the garden of Gethsemani,* where he was betrayed by Judas to the Jews who arrested him.[4]

Are you as satisfied to follow Jesus Christ to Calvary as you are to Tabor? Most people, even those who seem dedicated to God, are very glad to share in the consolations of Jesus Christ, but there are very few who are willing to take part in his sufferings. This, however, is what Saint Peter exhorts us to do. Rejoice, he says, when you share in the sufferings of Jesus Christ. Let this be the main cause of your joy.[5]

### 145.2 Second Point

Besides being especially loved by Jesus Christ, Saint James was also one of those most respected by the Apostles. In one of his epistles, Saint Paul informs us that Saint James is considered one of the pillars of the Church.[6] Saint Paul, although chosen and enlightened by Jesus Christ in a miraculous manner, had a similarly high esteem and great respect for Saint James.

It is, therefore, quite proper that you pay him very special honor as one of the Apostles who was most enlightened about our holy religion. Because you have to instruct the children under your guidance concerning religion, ask through the intercession of this holy Apostle for the grace to understand it well.

### 145.3 Third Point

A further proof that Saint James was among the most zealous workers for the progress and the support of the Christian religion is the fact that Herod had him beheaded, persuaded that this would please the Jews. This did, in fact, please them[7] because they feared that establishing the Christian religion would do much to destroy their own. It is believed that Saint James was the first Apostle to shed his blood for the faith of Jesus Christ.

You have been appointed by God to succeed the holy Apostles in teaching the doctrine of Jesus Christ and in confirming his holy law in the minds and hearts of those whom you instruct when you teach catechism, which is your principal function. Consider yourselves very fortunate and highly rewarded to be overwhelmed with insults and to suffer all kinds of outrages for the love of Jesus Christ.[8] If dissolute people take pleasure in causing you to suffer, let it be a great satisfaction for you to endure, because it will help you die to yourselves.

James the Greater is the brother of Saint John the Evangelist, often singled out by Jesus for special favors, along with Peter and John. He was put to death by Herod around 42 A.D (Acts 12:2). He is the Patron Saint of Spain, probably as a result of a legend that his body was discovered through a star that appeared over a field. His shrine became known as Campostella (field of the star).

1. Mk 4:11
2. Mt 17:1–2
3. Mt 26:37

4. Jn 18:2–12
5. 1 Pt 4:13
6. Gal 2:9

7. Acts 12:2–3
8. Acts 5:41

# July 26

## SAINT ANNE, MOTHER OF THE MOST BLESSED VIRGIN

### 146.1 First Point

According to Saint John Damascene, Saint Anne, the wife of Saint Joachim, was childless for twenty years. In this way God wished to make her understand that the child she would bring into the world would be a gift of grace. She spent these twenty years in all sorts of exercises of piety, and, as far as she was able, she gave generous alms to the poor, so that sterility of her soul would not be added to that of her body. This is the concern of a soul who wishes to receive an abundance of grace.

Take care not to remain in a sterility that can rob you of a taste for prayer and an attraction for God. See that your days are full,[1] as Holy Scripture says, by practicing good works of the kind God asks of you in your profession. This is the way to be happy in it and to please God.

### 146.2 Second Point

During all the years of her sterility, Saint Anne devoted herself very much to prayer to obtain from God the grace of being freed from this condition. By her diligent prayer, she merited to bring into the world the Most Blessed Virgin, Mother of our Lord Jesus Christ.

Let us admire the great honor God paid her by choosing her to be the mother of so holy and distinguished a daughter and thereby to become the first person to take part in the great mystery of the Incarnation.

This was the effect of her fervent and continual prayer. It led Saint John Damascene to say that as the former Anna conceived Samuel by her prayers,[2] so Saint Anne by her diligent prayer became the mother of the Most Blessed Virgin.

God has chosen you to teach others to know him. He also wishes you to bring forth, so to speak, the Most Blessed Virgin in the hearts of those whom you instruct, by inspiring them with a tender devotion to her. This spiritual vitality of yours must be the effect of your fervent prayers, of your love for the Most Blessed Virgin, and of the zeal you show in your instructions to have her loved.

### 146.3 Third Point

Saint Anne, after bringing the Most Blessed Virgin into the world, offered her child to God as belonging to him because the child had come from him and had been born to belong most especially to the Son of God as his mother. Saint Anne rightly judged that because she had been honored by such a great favor, she must show her gratitude to God by offering him what she had received from him.

She also offered herself to the Lord and consecrated to him the remainder of her days, for God had chosen her in preference to all the other women in the world to bring forth the holiest and purest of all creatures. It was only right that after offering her most holy daughter to God, she would also consecrate herself to him and devote herself henceforth entirely to his service.

You received great graces from God when he withdrew you from the world and called you to a ministry devoted entirely to the salvation of souls. Are you consecrated to God in such a way that you have given up everything to think only of him and of the duties of your work? Do this from now on, at least, to be able to fulfill well so holy a ministry.

---

Saint Anne, the mother of the Blessed Virgin Mary, was honored, probably along with Saint Joachim, her husband, as early as the sixth century in Constantinople. Devotion in Rome can be traced archeologically to the eighth century. The feast was not established in the Roman Liturgy until 1584 by Pope Gregory XIII. When the liturgy was revised after the Second Vatican Council, the celebration of Saint Joachim's feast was transferred from August 16 and joined with that of Saint Anne on July 26.

---

1. Gn 25:8          2. 1 Sm 1:20

# July 29

## SAINT MARTHA

### 147.1  First Point

It was Saint Martha's privilege to be greatly loved by Jesus, as the Gospel testifies; for this reason Jesus honored her several times by lodging with her and being her guest at table. This was also the motive that led Jesus to go to Martha's home, although a long way off, to bring her brother, Lazarus, back to life.[1]

We can scarcely measure how much this saint profited by the frequent visits of Jesus. We could say that after the Most Blessed Virgin, Saint Martha is one of the people most honored during the life of Jesus, because she often welcomed into her home the same Son of God[2] whom the Most Blessed Virgin bore in her womb and from her resources gave food to the One whom Mary nourished with her milk.

You can enjoy an even greater honor than this saint, whenever you wish, by receiving Jesus Christ within you in Holy Communion. Purify your heart to prepare to receive him often and to profit by so great a favor.

### 147.2  Second Point

This saint was very grateful for such great favors, and every time that Jesus did her the honor to visit her, she devoted herself to prepare his meals and to serve him with all possible affection. So great was her eagerness to offer Jesus Christ this service that she even complained once that her sister, absorbed in listening to Jesus, did not bother to help her.[3] She had nothing more at heart than to serve Jesus well. She even had such great esteem and such deep respect for Jesus that when he came to raise Lazarus to life, she went out quite a distance to welcome him.[4]

Are you as eager for Communion as Saint Martha was to welcome Jesus into her home and to give him food from her resources? The respect you ought to show him when he comes to you consists in not tolerating in your heart any imperfection and in preparing your soul for him ahead of time with great devotion.

### 147.3  Third Point

Nothing is more admirable than the faith Saint Martha showed when Jesus raised Lazarus to life. She told Jesus that if he had been with her when her brother was ill, he would not have died, that she knew that God would grant him all that he would ask, and that if he wished to bring her brother back to life, he could easily do it. But when Jesus told her that her brother would indeed rise again, she declared that it was true that he would rise at the time of the general resurrection. When Jesus added that he was the resurrection and the life and that those who believed in him would live and never die, he asked her if she believed this, and she answered, yes, that she did believe that he was the Christ, the Son of the living God who had come into this world.[5] This answer, which was the same answer of Saint Peter that Jesus Christ had so highly praised,[6] deserves very special veneration because of the great faith it shows.

Especially in your actions, your faith ought to be seen by your performing them only with the spirit of faith, as you are obliged according to the spirit of your Institute.

———

Martha, the sister of Mary and Lazarus of Bethany, who was the busy hostess when Jesus visited them, was not honored in the liturgy until about the fifteenth century.

———

1. Jn 11:18–23
2. Lk 10:38
3. Lk 10:39–40
4. Jn 11:20
5. Jn 11:21–27
6. Mt 16:16–17

# July 31

## SAINT IGNATIUS OF LOYOLA

### 148.1 First Point

Once converted to God, Saint Ignatius first led a very secluded life in a hospital in Manresa, where he practiced very great austerities. He accustomed himself to eat but once a day only bread given him in alms. He drank nothing but water and took the discipline three times a day. He continually wept over his sins and spent seven hours a day on his knees. That is how this saint made his novitiate in the spiritual life. On one occasion he even spent seven days without eating, praying unceasingly and without interruption to be freed from certain spiritual afflictions.

Was it by experiencing austerities that you began to give yourselves to God? This is the time, above all, when we ought to practice them, even though we need them all our life to preserve ourselves in piety. For this purpose, do at least some small part of what this saint practiced so fervently.

### 148.2 Second Point

This saint's zeal for the salvation of souls was so ardent that to do this work with greater skill and success, he began to study at the age of 33. He was living in a hospital all this time, begging alms and teaching catechism to children and the poor. So generous was his zeal that he traveled one time from Paris to Rouen to help one of his companions who had stolen from him and then had fallen ill.

On another occasion, after he had noticed the hour when a dissolute young man used to satisfy his passion, he threw himself into a freezing pond and cried out that he would not get out unless the young man gave up his evil plan.

Your work will be of little value if you do not have as your purpose the salvation of souls. Does your zeal for the poor lead you to seek ways as effective as those used by Saint Ignatius? The more ardently you pray for the good of the souls entrusted to you, the more God will help you find the skill to touch their hearts.

### 148.3 Third Point

After this saint had been working for the glory of God with so much piety, poverty, humility, and zeal, others joined him and under his guidance labored effectively for the good of the Church. They made great progress in virtue and vowed to give up all their property, to dedicate themselves solely to the conversion of souls and to their own spiritual advancement, and to submit themselves entirely to the Pope to do whatever he would judge most timely for the spiritual good of their neighbor.

That is how Saint Ignatius began to establish his Company, which is of such great benefit to the Church, for it has spread to all the countries where the Christian religion is practiced and has brought about the establishment of the Church in several places where God was not known.

Because the end of your Institute is the same as that of the Institute founded by Saint Ignatius, which is the salvation of souls, and because God has called you to educate children in piety, just as he called the disciples of this saintly founder, live in as great a detachment and show as great a zeal to procure the glory of God as this saint did and as the members of his Company do. Then you too will do great good for those whom you instruct.

--------

Ignatius (1491–1556) was born at Loyola, in Calabria, the Basque hill country of Spain. He spent his early years in court and as a soldier. While he was recovering from the fracture of his thigh inflicted in battle, he read the lives of the saints and was moved to dedicate his life to God. He made this dedication at the shrine of our Lady at Montserrat and then took up hospital work in the nearby town of Manresa. Here he was inspired to compose the Spiritual Exercises, in which he describes the principles by which a Christian chooses to dedicate his life to the greater glory of God *(Ad Majorem Dei Gloriam)*. After making a pilgrimage to the Holy Land, Ignatius, at the age of 30, began his education in Salamanca. Seven years later, he went to Paris and the Sorbonne, where he met the first companions with whom he began the Society of Jesus. Later, he was ordained to the priesthood and in Rome drew up the Rule for his Order, adding to the three customary vows of the religious life a vow of obedience to the Pope. He died in Rome and was canonized in 1622. De La Salle found much inspiration in the founder of an apostolic order dedicated to education and vowing the highest regard for the Pope. Some elements of the Brothers' Rule were adapted from the Rule written by Ignatius.

# August 1

## SAINT PETER IN CHAINS

### 149.1  First Point

This feast was instituted to thank God for the grace he gave the Church when he delivered Saint Peter from the prison where Herod Agrippa had put him, planning to put him to death a few days later.[1] Herod wanted to destroy the Christian religion from its beginning by condemning to death the one who was the leader. This prince took such great care to have Saint Peter guarded in the prison that he gave the assignment to a squad of sixteen soldiers, divided into the four watches four at a time.[2]

But what does anyone need to fear who has God for a protector?[3] Kings have power over men and can dispose of their life only if God allows them.[4] Thus, since the newborn Church still needed Saint Peter, he remained in Herod's hands for only a few days, even though Herod had him chained and guarded with what seemed so much security,[5] for God wanted to make use of all this to strengthen and to uphold the newly established Church.

Let us adore God's power, which makes sport of that of men when he pleases,[6] for men have no power, except insofar as he lets them share in his.

### 149.2 Second Point

While Peter was so closely guarded in prison, the Church raised prayers for him to God without ceasing, which were finally heard. The very night before Herod had determined to send Saint Peter to his punishment, this holy Apostle was sleeping between two soldiers, bound with two chains, while guards stood watch at the prison door. Suddenly, an angel appeared, filling the place with light. Tapping Saint Peter, he woke him and told him to rise promptly. At that same moment the chains fell away from his hands. This angel led Saint Peter past the first and the second guard and by the gate of iron, which opened by itself. At the end of the street, the angel left him. Then Saint Peter, who up to this point had thought all these happenings to be a dream or a vision, realized that God, in fact, had sent his angel to deliver him from the hands of Herod and from all the expectations of the Jewish people.[7]

Let us thank God with the Church for having freed Saint Peter in this way, so that he would have the chance to preach the Gospel and to increase the flock of Jesus Christ.[8]

### 149.3 Third Point

Having gone to a house where several people had gathered and were praying, Saint Peter told them how God had freed him from prison.[9] At this all thanked God for the goodness he had shown him. The chains that had bound Saint Peter have always been preserved in the Church with great veneration as precious relics and have performed many miracles.

The greatest miracle that they ought to produce in our hearts is a love for suffering and insult, for we cannot go to heaven except by following the path of tribulation.[10] We must, says Saint Paul, glory in the cross of Jesus Christ,[11] that is, in the cross Jesus Christ has sanctified by carrying it and which is our life and our salvation because it is the source of these blessings.

As we, along with all the Church, pay homage to the chains that Saint Peter bore, let us also honor those that God has placed on us. Let us ask him that just as the two chains of this holy Apostle miraculously became one, so too our sufferings may be so closely united to his through grace that we will share in the desire he had to suffer for Jesus Christ.

---

This feast is no longer celebrated, but veneration of the chains of Saint Peter was widespread as early as the fifth century. Similarly, there was devotion to the chains of Saint Paul. Peter's chains are still venerated in the Roman Basilica of San Pietro in Vincoli (where tourists may also see Michelangelo's famous statue of Moses). What are believed to be Saint Paul's chains are also preserved in the basilica near his tomb on the Ostian Way.

---

1. Acts 12:3
2. Acts 12:4
3. Ps 27:1
4. Jn 19:11

5. Acts 12:6
6. Ps 2:4
7. Acts 12:5–11
8. Jn 21:15–17

9. Acts 12:12–17
10. Acts 14:22
11. Gal 6:14

# August 4

## SAINT DOMINIC

### 150.1 First Point

In his youth Saint Dominic attained such great perfection that his bishop, desiring to reform his cathedral chapter and to make it more faithful to its regulations, named him a canon and, later, an archdeacon. In these two positions, he led a very exemplary life and gave proof of extraordinary fervor.

One of his main virtues was his compassion for his neighbor, especially for the poor. This virtue led him to do penance for the sins of others as well as for his own. It likewise led him to sell all his property to assist the poor, and when he was unable to assist them any further, he wept with compassion. Seeing a woman who was in great sorrow because her son had been captured by the Moors, he offered himself to her to be sold or exchanged for her son.

You know that you are responsible for the instruction of the poor. Imitate the tenderness of this saint toward them, and overcome nature when it suggests that you ought to have more consideration for the wealthy. Jesus Christ will look at the good you do to the poor as done to him.[1]

### 150.2 Second Point

The love this saint had for his neighbor led him to have ardent zeal for the instruction and the conversion of those who were living a disorderly life. This was why he gave up his position as a canon, in which he felt he was of little use to the Church. The Albigensian heresy had started up, and he did all he could to destroy it, sparing neither travel, nor meetings, nor preaching, nor writing; he also suffered all sorts of difficulty and fatigue. To this great zeal he joined fervent prayers, continual and abundant weeping, and great mortification to procure the conversion of these heretics. These means that he employed succeeded so happily that he converted over 100,000 heretics.

It is your duty in your state to combine a life of seclusion and of mortification with zeal for your neighbor's salvation, because the purpose of your work is to labor continually for the Christian education of children. Do this work with all possible care, because if you do, you will be unable to count how many you have gained for God and made true Christians.

### 150.3 Third Point

This saint's zeal did not stop short at what he personally could do for the glory of God and the salvation of souls. When some companions had joined him, he asked the Pope to establish a religious order whose members would have as their purpose to preach the Gospel everywhere.[2] This is what his disciples have done and continue to do.

One of their main practices for promoting piety among the faithful is to inspire them with devotion to the Most Blessed Virgin, especially to her rosary, which they recite daily in choir with much piety.

How fortunate you are to have for your purpose to teach children their religion and to do so by teaching them catechism every day! One of the best means you can use to succeed in your work is to have a very special devotion to the Most Blessed Virgin and to communicate this devotion to the hearts of those entrusted to you. Do you recite the rosary every day? Do you lead your students to do the same? With what piety do you recite it and have them recite it? Do you offer this prayer as a tribute that we in our Institute pay to the Most Blessed Virgin and as a powerful way to draw down her help and protection on our Institute and on your work?

---

Dominic (1170–1221) was born at Calaruega, in Castile, Spain. He studied for ten years at the University of Palencia, and at the age of 24, he joined the reformed canons regular at Osma, eventually becoming the prior. In 1206 Pope Innocent III commissioned him and his bishop, Diego, to the work of preaching against the Albigensian heretics in the South of France. After much hardship, with six companions in 1215, he organized the Friars Preachers, also called the Dominicans. Their constitution was approved a year later by Pope Honorius III, and the Order spread rapidly to such faraway countries as England, Denmark, Hungary, and Greece. Dominic died in Bologna on August 6, 1221, and was canonized in 1234. His feast is now celebrated on August 8.

---

1. Mt 25:40          2. Mt 24:14

# August 5

## OUR LADY OF THE SNOW

*Devotion to the Most Blessed Virgin*

The feast that the Church celebrates today originated in the very special devotion to the Most Blessed Virgin professed by a Roman gentleman and his wife. Because they had no children, they dedicated all their wealth to her and earnestly asked her to show them how she wished them to use it. This prayer was answered by a very remarkable and extraordinary miracle, for on the fifth of August (a time when the heat in Rome is excessive), the spot in the city where the Most Blessed Virgin desired a church to be built in her honor was covered with snow. The Pope went there in procession along with all the people and marked out the area where the church was later built at the expense of this noble and generous family. The great devotion of these two illustrious people, the gratitude that the Most Blessed Virgin showed them for it, and the complete confidence we must have in her make up the subject of our prayer today.

### 151.1  First Point

We are not in a position to offer temporal gifts to the Most Blessed Virgin, for we have renounced the world and left all to consecrate ourselves to the service of God.[1] All she asks of us, the reason why the Church seems to have instituted this feast today to honor the holy Mother of God, is to encourage us to have a very special devotion to her and to procure it for those whose guidance God has entrusted to us. The Church calls your attention to the great grace she gave on this day to these two people who were so eager to promote her honor, which was that she willed that they be remembered in the Church and that what they did to honor her, and what she did in their favor, be proclaimed until the end of time by all the faithful.

Let us be convinced that everything we do to honor the Most Blessed Virgin or to cause her to be honored will be very richly rewarded by God through her. Let us always acknowledge her as our good Mother, for Jesus Christ gave her as such to all those who would be devoted to her. He did this in the person of Saint John, when, at the point of death, he said to him, My Son, behold your Mother.[2]

### 151.2 Second Point

What must oblige us most especially to have a great devotion to the Most Blessed Virgin is the fact that she is so highly honored by the Eternal Father. He has given her a position above all pure creatures because she bore in her womb the One who is equal to him and who is one in nature with him. She is exalted above all creatures because of the abundance of grace bestowed on her, which surpasses that given to anyone else, and because of the purity of her life, which no one has equaled. This led Saint Anselm to declare that it was only right that Mary be clothed in great glory and lifted high above all creation, because, after God, no one is superior to her.

Is it not to be incomparably raised above all creatures to have become the temple of the living God when she conceived the Son of God? For this reason, we apply to her the words of Psalm 132: God has chosen her to make his dwelling in her,[3] and these other words from Psalm 65: Your temple is holy.[4] Abbot Rupert goes even farther; he says that once the Holy Spirit had visited the Most Blessed Virgin to make her conceive the Son of God, she became totally beautiful with a divine beauty. This made Saint Bernard say that we ought to honor the Most Blessed Virgin with the tenderest of devotions because God placed the fullness of all good in her when he enclosed the divine Word in her womb.

But what ought to encourage us most especially to cultivate such a devotion is the great good that we will receive from it. The same saint says, Let us have a great veneration and a most tender devotion to the Most Blessed Virgin, because it is through her that we receive the benefits that God wishes us to have. Entering into detail concerning these benefits, he explains as follows: The Holy Spirit distributes all his gifts, graces, and virtues to whomsoever he pleases, when he pleases, and in the manner and the amount he judges proper, through the ministry of the Most Blessed Virgin. Saint Anselm, to stir up our trust in her, adds that when someone invokes the name of the Mother of God, even if the one who has recourse to her does not deserve to be heard, the merits of this most holy Mother of God still suffice to win from God's goodness whatever that person asks. Let us, then, have confidence, as Saint Bernard continues, that if we have true devotion for the Most Blessed Virgin, nothing we need for our salvation will be lacking.

### 151.3 Third Point

It would be of little use to us to be persuaded of our obligation to have a special devotion to the Most Blessed Virgin if we did not know what this devotion includes, if we did not possess it effectively, and if we did not show it on the appropriate occasions. Because she is superior to all creatures, we must have a greater devotion to her than to all other saints, whoever they may be. We show our devotion to the saints at certain times and on certain days of the year, but the devotion we ought to have for the Most Blessed Virgin must be continual.

This is why it is of Rule in our Institute (1) not to let a single day go by without reciting the rosary and to say it while walking in the streets; (2) to celebrate all her feasts with great solemnity; (3) to uncover our heads and bow every time we hear her name or pass in front of her image, as this devotion requires; (4) considering her as the principal patroness of our Society, we place ourselves daily under her protection at the end of our prayer in the morning and in the evening and after each exercise; we have recourse to her, placing in her, after God, our entire confidence; (5) we invoke her in our most pressing needs as our primary advocate, after Jesus Christ, before God.

Are we faithful to all these practices of devotion toward the Most Blessed Virgin? How well do we perform them? Is it in the spirit we have proposed above? Let us not fail in this if we wish to receive a great abundance of grace through the merits of the Most Blessed Virgin.

---

The format of this meditation (with its introductory explanation) and the style do not seem typical of De La Salle; should this meditation have been placed with the other six in the *Additions* of the original editions?

The feast celebrates the dedication of the Basilica of Saint Mary Major, on the Esquiline Hill in Rome, the oldest church in honor of our Lady, dating back to the fifth century. While the legend described in the introduction to the meditation is said to have occurred in the fourth century, it was Pope Sixtus III (432–440) who built the great basilica there to celebrate the Council of Ephesus, which in 431 declared Mary to be the Mother of God. Over many centuries, of course, the building has been restored and extended a number of times.

---

1. Mt 19:27      3. Ps 132:13      4. Ps 65:5
2. Jn 19:27

# August 6

## THE TRANSFIGURATION OF OUR LORD

### 152.1 First Point

Jesus came upon this earth to make satisfaction for our sins[1] and was always considered as the man of sin by his Eternal Father because he was burdened by the sins of the whole world,[2] even though he never did and never could commit any sin. For that reason he remained on earth, subject to all the sufferings of this life and to all the miseries that are the consequence of sin. Because of this, he always appeared as an ordinary man and kept hidden from the rest of the world the glorious state his holy soul enjoyed, which his sacred humanity had a right to enjoy from the moment of his conception. He was even willing to be mocked, scorned, and insulted by those who did not live according to his teaching.

In fulfilling the obligation he had taken to satisfy for us the justice of his Father,[3] he considered himself, according to the prophetic expression of David, the most despised of men and the outcast of the people,[4] even though he was the King of glory.[5]

We, who were born in sin and have lived in sin, must be conformable to Jesus Christ[6] in this life and suffer with him if we wish to have him for our head, to be one of his members, and to destroy sin in ourselves.[7] As Saint Paul teaches us, neither afflictions nor disappointments, neither hunger nor nakedness, and neither dangers nor persecutions ought to be able to separate us from the love of Jesus Christ. If we are put to death for his sake, the same Apostle says, and if we are considered only as sheep destined for the slaughter, amidst all these evils, we will remain victorious,[8] inspired by the example of him who has loved us so much and who delivered himself up to death for love of us.[9]

## 152.2 Second Point

Although the purpose that the Son of God set before himself on coming into this world was to suffer for us,[10] he willed to show for a short time, as it were in passing, some rays of his glory to three of his Apostles.[11] With this in view, he led them to a solitary place on a high mountain.[12] There he first gave himself to prayer and, while praying, was transfigured in their presence. His face became as bright as the sun, his garments all shining with light and as white as snow.[13]

Saint Peter, who was present at this mystery, when giving testimony to what he had seen, says, We ourselves were witnesses of the majesty of Jesus Christ, for he received from God the Father a testimonial to his honor and glory when we were together with him on the holy mountain.[14] Moses and Elias also were there and joined with him to do him homage.[15]

Because Jesus Christ always possessed this glory within himself, when he was transfigured, the change that appeared in him was only external. It is not the same with us. The change that must take place in us is interior; we must be entirely transformed by the light and the fulness of grace and by the possession of the Spirit of God. If there were to follow, later on, some change in our exterior, this would come about only as an overflowing of the happiness that we enjoy in the depths of our soul, because we will then be taken up with God alone and with what we must do for love of him.

## 152.3 Third Point

It was while he was in seclusion and during prayer that Jesus Christ was transfigured. The topic on which he conversed with Moses and Elias during his transfiguration was what would be accomplished in him during his Passion and death, which he was going to suffer on a cross outside the city of Jerusalem[16] as he desired. While Jesus Christ was speaking about his sufferings and death, a luminous cloud appeared and covered him and Moses and Elias. From that cloud, where the glory of God appeared, a voice came forth that spoke these words: This is my beloved Son; listen to him.[17] Relating what happened in this mystery, Saint Peter says that they heard this voice coming from heaven.[18]

All this ought to make us understand (1) that it is only in seclusion and prayer that a soul can attain a true transfiguration or, rather, a transformation of itself and be enlightened by God, and (2) when the soul is transfigured in this way with Jesus Christ, it must be willing to meditate on his Passion and cross to show that all its desire is to become like Jesus Christ[19] in his sufferings. The Eternal Father will not recognize us as his well-beloved except insofar as we love suffering and give proof of this love by practice and by daily living this spirit. We must remember these words of Jesus Christ, that we must bear our cross daily to be his disciples.[20]

---

This feast was extended to the universal Church in 1457 by Pope Calixtus III to commemorate the victory of Saint John Capistrano over the Turks near Belgrade. It was earlier celebrated in the liturgy of the second Sunday of Lent.

---

1. 1 Jn 3:5
2. 2 Cor 5:21
3. Is 53:6; 2 Cor 5:21
4. Ps 22:7
5. Ps 24:7
6. Rom 8:29
7. Eph 4:15; 1 Cor 6:15
8. Rom 8:35–37
9. Eph 5:2
10. Heb 10:5–7
11. Mt 17:1–2
12. Mk 9:1
13. Lk 9:29
14. 2 Pt 1:16–18
15. Mt 17:3
16. Lk 9:29–31
17. Mt 17:5
18. 2 Pt 1:17–18
19. Rom 8:29
20. Lk 9:23

# August 7

## SAINT CAJETAN

### 153.1  First Point

What Holy Scripture tells us about the ancient Patriarchs can also be said of Saint Cajetan, namely, that his days were full and that he died full of days,[1] for as soon as he had received Holy Orders, he devoted himself to procure the salvation of souls in such a way that the day and the night did not seem enough for him to do his work, so ardent and so all embracing was his zeal for his neighbor. He spent all day administering the sacraments, visiting and encouraging the sick, and in other acts of piety; then he spent nearly all night in penance, study, and prayer. In this way what he did at night helped him to prepare for what he had to do during the day.

Because you are obliged to work for the salvation of your neighbor, bring to the exercise of your work the same preparation that Saint Cajetan brought in order to fulfill well his ministry. Therefore, study your catechism, read good books, pray fervently, and in accord with the spirit of your Institute, mortify your mind and your senses. You must learn the truths of religion thoroughly by study, for ignorance in you would be criminal, because it would cause ignorance in those who are entrusted to you. Prayer and mortification are needed for you to draw down the graces of God on you and on those whom you instruct.

### 153.2 Second Point

This saint saw that one of the most common and most telling reproaches that the heretic Luther leveled against the Church was the disorderly life of priests. He believed that the best way to silence this apostate was to found an Order of Clerks Regular, whose members would be able by their regulated conduct and disinterestedness to serve as an example for priests as much by their regulated conduct as by their perfect disinterestedness in the exercise of their duties. He gave up an important position he held, and with three companions, one of whom was a bishop who resigned his see, he founded this order that is a great edification to the Church.

These two things are necessary for you in your Institute: a regulated life and disinterestedness. They are also the two most appropriate ways to do good for souls. By a regulated life you will edify your disciples and be for them a constant model of self-control, wisdom, and piety. This will be a very moving lesson for them, and with disinterestedness you will do everything by grace and for God alone. As a result, God will infallibly bless what you are doing.

### 153.3 Third Point

In his order this saint promoted detachment from everything to such an excess, if we can speak this way, that he not only did not allow those in his order to possess any revenue or regular income, either in common or individually, but also forbade them to ask for alms, either in person or through others. They were to abandon themselves for food, clothing, and all bodily needs to God's Providence alone. They were to base themselves on these words of Jesus Christ in the Gospel: Do not be worried about what to eat and what to drink and about all the necessities of life, because if you seek first of all and even uniquely the kingdom of God, all these things will be given to you in plenty.[2] God did not leave them in want; several times he came to their help in an extraordinary fashion.

You cannot carry disinterestedness too far in your work. You have to teach poor children; instruct them by your example. To teach them to love poverty, let your disinterestedness lead you to practice it as far as it pleases God.

You know too that you are committed to keep schools gratuitously and to live on bread alone, if need be, rather than accept anything. Be on your guard, therefore, never to receive anything whatever, either from the students or from their parents. Ask for this spirit of disinterestedness through the intercession of Saint Cajetan.

---

Cajetan (1480–1547) was born in Vicenza, Italy, and studied at Padua. After earning his doctorate in civil and canon law, he was ordained in 1516 as a member of the Roman Oratory of Divine Love, a confraternity pledged to deep spiritual life and works of charity for the poor. Later, in 1524, he founded a Society of Clerks Regular with the help of a friend, Gian Pietro Carafa, who later became Pope Paul IV. The group became known by the name Theatines, taken from the title of Carafa when he was bishop of Chieti (*Theatinus* in Latin). They vowed to live entirely on Providence, even prohibiting themselves any asking for alms. In this De La Salle saw a model for the Brothers' commitment to gratuitous teaching and total trust in God. Cajetan died in Naples on August 7, 1547, and was canonized in 1691 by Pope Innocent XII. De La Salle was 40 years old at that time and passing through a most critical period in his work to found the Institute.

---

1. Gn 25:8      2. Mt 6:31–33

# August 10

## SAINT LAWRENCE

### 154.1 First Point

It is impossible to understand how much Saint Lawrence loved and esteemed the poor. His love for them was such that when Saint Sixtus, whose deacon he was, was being led to martyrdom and told him to give to the poor all the wealth he had placed in his hands, he executed the assignment and completely emptied the treasury of the Church.

Again he showed his extraordinary regard for the poor when the emperor, having learned that he had been given charge of all that belonged to the Church, demanded that he hand over the treasure entrusted to him. The saint gathered all the poor and presented them to the emperor, telling him, Here are the treasures of the Church.

Let us admire how great the faith of this saint was, for it led him to look upon the poor as the treasure of the Church, that is, as being the most precious and most valuable part in the Church, having the closest relationship with Jesus Christ. Let us share this saint's attitude, we to whom God has entrusted the most valuable portion of his treasure.

### 154.2 Second Point

We cannot praise too highly the desire this saint had for martyrdom. This was apparent when Saint Sixtus was being led away to be martyred. As Saint Ambrose relates it and as it is expressed in the Church's Office, Saint Lawrence said to him: Where are you going, holy Father, without your son? Are you going to offer yourself in sacrifice unaccompanied by your deacon, without whom you have never been willing, up to now, to offer the sacrifice of the Body and Blood of Jesus Christ on the holy altar? Is there something in me that has displeased you? Have you found me unworthy of my ministry? What! You trusted me to distribute the Blood of Jesus Christ, yet you will not allow me to accompany you when you are about to shed your own. This saint had an even greater ardor in his heart than in his words. Nothing could stop him except the response addressed to him by Saint Sixtus, who assured him that in three days he too would suffer very cruel torments.

When will we have as great a desire for suffering as this saint had for martyrdom? Ask this of God through the intercession of Saint Lawrence.

### 154.3 Third Point

This saint clearly gave witness that his desire to suffer was genuine by the joy he showed when he was made to suffer in his martyrdom. The emperor considered that Saint Lawrence's action when he presented the poor as the treasure of the Church was an insult of the grossest kind. He had him tortured with pincers and iron claws, and red-hot iron plates were applied to his sides. Seeing that he remained unmoved and ever joyful in the midst of his sufferings, the emperor had him stretched out on a gridiron to roast his body by a slow fire to see whether by such means he could shake his constancy. But this fire, on the contrary, made him rejoice all the more and increased the interior flame that consumed him so strongly that when half of his body was roasted, he told the tyrant to have him turned over on his other side, so that being roasted completely, he could make a good meal.

What can we say of such constancy? Will it provide us with an incentive to encourage us to love suffering? We are born to suffer; we must live in suffering and die suffering. Let us beg this saint to obtain these holy dispositions for us from God.

Lawrence was a martyr during the persecution of the Emperor Valerian, probably in the year 258, and became one of the most famous of all martyrs. His popularity may be credited to the fourth-century story of his being roasted to death on a gridiron by the emperor. There are inconsistencies in this story that raise questions about its historical accuracy. It is probable that Lawrence was one of the seven deacons of Pope Sixtus II, who were all martyred in 258 by decapitation, which raises the question of why Lawrence was singled out to be ranked with the Apostles Peter and Paul among the early Christian martyrs.

# August 13

## SAINT CASSIAN,
## BISHOP AND MARTYR

### 155.1 First Point

The zeal shown by Saint Cassian cannot be praised too much. The Emperor Julian the Apostate had forbidden any Christian to teach youth. Saint Cassian, nonetheless, thought that he could not take on a work more useful for the Church and better able to promote religion than that of a schoolteacher. He devoted himself with all possible care to instruct children, and while teaching them reading and writing, he trained them in piety and educated them in the fear of God.

The emperor, for his part, was working to destroy religion by destroying schools; this saint, on the contrary, was trying to establish religion through the instruction and education of the young.

Oh, how often it happens that the work which people consider lowly produces much more good than the most brilliant work! Value your work as one of the most important and most excellent in the Church, for it is one that is most able to strengthen it by giving it a solid foundation.

### 155.2 Second Point

The patience of Saint Cassian was indeed admirable. He was denounced to the judge as being a Christian and was found in his school teaching children the mysteries. When pressed to declare his religion, he admitted that he was a Christian, and his instructions made this amply clear. On the spot he was judged and condemned, and the sentence was executed. He was delivered over to the hands of his own students, who put him to death by stabbing him with the iron styluses they used for writing. This martyrdom was all the more cruel because the children had less strength to strike him. What patience this saint must have had to suffer for so long and with such constancy from the ones for whom he had gone to so much trouble!

You have this saint as your patron, and you have succeeded him in his work, but do you imitate his patience? How often do you let yourselves be carried away by an initial impulse, either by hitting the students, something that is against your Rule and all good order, or by correcting them perhaps improperly or without reflecting? You cannot instruct them better than by edifying them and by controlling every angry impulse.

### 155.3 Third Point

The martyrdom endured by Saint Cassian was the only reward he received from his students for the care he had taken of them. He considered himself fortunate when those to whom he had tried to give life in Jesus Christ[1] brought about his death. Seeing himself about to die from the wounds he received from them, he desired that his blood, spurting out upon them, might give life to their souls.

The only thanks you ought to expect for instructing children, especially the poor, is injury, insult, calumny, persecution, and even death.[2] This is the recompense of saints and apostolic people, as it was for our Lord Jesus Christ. Do not expect anything else if you have God in view in the ministry he entrusted to you. This is also what ought to encourage you to work at it with all the more affection, and this will give you the way to do more good. The more faithful you are to God on occasions of suffering, the more God will pour out his graces and blessings on you in the exercise of your ministry.

———

Cassian (martyred around 363) is known through an account of his life by the Christian poet Prudentius (348–410). There is a short biography of Saint Cassian, based on Prudentius' poem, in the appendix of De La Salle's *Meditations*. In this meditation on Saint Cassian, De La Salle reflects on his being a teacher and on his martyrdom by his students. He speaks of Cassian as a patron for the Brothers, especially in his patience with students. It is an historical error to call Cassian a bishop; this probably resulted from confusing him with another martyred Cassian who was bishop of Todi. Cassian may well be the first teacher but not the last to suffer a slow martyrdom from his students. His feast is not in the current liturgical calendar. In the Rule of 1718 (CL 25, p. 134), the feast of Saint Cassian was moved to Thursday and treated as an all-day holiday for the Brothers.

---

1. 1 Cor 4:15        2. 1 Cor 4:11–13

# August 15

## THE ASSUMPTION
## OF THE MOST BLESSED VIRGIN

### 156.1  First Point

The Most Blessed Virgin, filled with the love of God throughout her life, remained on earth only with reluctance and solely through submission to God's will. For this reason, death appeared to her pleasant and desirable, and because her soul held on to her body so lightly, as it were, she died without pain. The extreme joy she felt at that moment, caused by the desire to see God, who possessed her, filled her soul with such consolation that she easily went from earth to heaven without any struggle. What blessed detachment from the bonds of her body in the soul of Mary, already detached from whatever could have attached her to earth!

Because we have left the world, nothing ought to be able to attach us to it. We must always be ready to die. This is the consequence of detachment from all things. We find it hard to die because we find it hard to leave what we love and what holds on to us. Strive, then, to imitate the Most Blessed Virgin in her total detachment, and ask God through her intercession for the grace of a happy death.

### 156.2  Second Point

The Most Blessed Virgin did not remain in the tomb for long; a few days after her death, she rose. It was quite proper that God granted her such a favor, for without doubt it would not have been fitting that the flesh from which the flesh of Jesus Christ came would suffer corruption. It was, moreover, worthy of God's goodness that the very special purity of the Most Blessed Virgin would be rewarded by so great a favor.

How, O my God, could you have allowed that the body of the Most Blessed Virgin, which had been the tabernacle of your Incarnate Word, the Temple of the Holy Spirit,[1] and the sacred ark of a soul filled with your grace, would be for a long time separated from that soul and not be honored even after death with all the favors it could possibly receive?

The special grace we ought to ask of the Most Blessed Virgin on this day is to be removed and to be freed from the corruption of the world[2] and especially to have great purity, which is the true incorruptibility that we ought to procure for our body. Because the Most Blessed Virgin possessed this virtue in all its perfection, she can help us very much to preserve it.

### 156.3 Third Point

The greatest favor that the Most Blessed Virgin received after her death and that the Church honors especially on this day is that she was taken, body and soul, to heaven by the angels. It was quite right that her sacred body, which, as Saint John Damascene says, was a living heaven, be placed in heaven as soon as she left this world and that she who was the Mother of the Incarnate Word would be immediately raised up by him to be placed near him and to receive the honor deserved by this admirable privilege. For this reason she was elevated far above all the blessed spirits, who honor her as their sovereign.

It was also right that because the Most Blessed Virgin had received an abundance of graces and had always been faithful to them, she would be filled with glory and that her body, having been spiritualized by her renunciation of the pleasures of the senses, would die only to fulfill the common law and would follow her soul to heaven.

If we detach ourselves entirely from our body, we will lead a heavenly life on this earth, and when we die, our body, having already acquired a sort of incorruptibility, will live forever before God by the transformation that will have been wrought in it by grace. Pray to the Most Blessed Virgin to obtain this favor for you today, that your body, sharing in the life of your soul by mortification of your senses, may no longer take pleasure in anything on this earth but may live in some way as though it were in heaven.

---

In 1950 Pope Pius XII defined the doctrine of our Lady's Assumption, saying that the Immaculate Mother of God was assumed body and soul to heavenly glory. This statement embodies the two bases for the doctrine: her Immaculate Conception and her dignity as Mother of God. From earliest Christian times, even before the Council of Ephesus in 431, at which the doctrine of her being the Mother of God was defined, the *Dormitio Sanctae Mariae* was celebrated with the greatest solemnity by the Church. The term *dormitio* suggests a belief that Mary did not die (separation of body and soul) but only slept while body and soul were taken to heaven. De La Salle, however, accepts the fact of her death. Some theologians agree with him. The feast's stational church is the Basilica of Saint Mary Major. At different times over the centuries, the Feast has been celebrated with a vigil and with a procession from the Forum.

1. 1 Cor 6:19        2. 2 Pt 1:4

# August 20

## SAINT BERNARD, ABBOT

### 158.1[1] First Point

Saint Bernard was brought up so well by his mother that in a short time he acquired a solid piety and displayed all sorts of virtues, especially chastity, which he possessed to such an eminent degree that once, because he had looked too closely at a very attractive woman, he immediately threw himself naked into a freezing pond to take vengeance on and to punish himself for the fault he had committed. When a shameless woman entered his room to tempt him, he immediately cried out, Robber! By his cries, he prevented her from robbing him of his chastity.

By such heroic actions, by generous resistance to occasions of sin, and by a holy violence, the saints acquired this virtue. They are also the same means that you must use to preserve it. By your great recollection, above all, you will make it easy for you. For as you see, Saint Bernard suffered an attack against his virtue by looking too closely at a woman.

### 158.2 Second Point

This saint attained such great chastity and reached such a high degree of modesty and self-control by means of a complete mortification of his senses that after spending a year in the monastery of Citeaux, he did not know whether the dormitory ceiling was made of stone or of wood. Likewise, after walking along the shore of a lake all day long, he had not seen it. He was so mortified with regard to drink that he once drank oil, believing that he was drinking water, and he had accustomed himself to fasting and taking so little food that eating, as he says, had become a torture for him. That is how this saint learned to die to himself and to become a perfect religious, appearing no longer to have any use of his senses.

When will you be entirely detached from the pleasure you find in using your senses? Detachment requires you to watch closely in order to be mortified in some way on every occasion. Be faithful to this practice.

### 158.3 Third Point

The astonishing virtues of Saint Bernard, as well as the great number of his miracles, made him known throughout the whole Church and won for him the respect of everyone. So high was the esteem he enjoyed that as Abbot of Clairvaux he was followed by a great crowd of people who came to place themselves under his direction. His abbey numbered as many as 700 religious, and there was an almost incredible number in the other monasteries he founded whom he helped to live in great perfection.

This made him so venerated by bishops, princes, and the people that as a result, no one undertook any important project without coming to him for his advice and judgment. The more this saint tried to keep hidden, the more people came to him either to embrace the austerities of his Order or to answer to the needs of the Church.

Virtue cannot hide. When it is seen, it is attractive, and the example it gives makes such a strong impression on those who witness it practiced or who hear it talked about that most people are led to imitate it.

Is this the effect that your good behavior and piety produce in your students? It is the main means you ought to use to win them over to God.

———

Bernard (1090–1153) was born near Dijon, France. At the age of 22, he became a Benedictine monk at Citeaux, the austere abbey of the Cistercian reform. He did not join alone, however, but brought thirty others with him, among whom were relatives, a testimony to his extraordinary influence on others even at that early age. The abbey flourished and sent out groups to make other foundations, one of which was led by Bernard and settled at what became known as Clairvaux. It became the center of the Cistercian reform for all of Europe. His influence extended farther and farther as mediator and advocate in the reform of the whole Church. At the same time, he did not neglect the training of his own monks at Clairvaux and wrote many beautiful mystical and theological treatises. He was largely responsible for preaching the Second Crusade, at the request of the Pope, and was greatly saddened by its failure. He died on August 20,

1153, was canonized in 1174, and named Doctor of the Church in 1830.

---

1. Number 157, on Saint Joachim, is on March 20, between 110 and 111 in the present edition. It received its number from the 1882 edition, whose numerical designation has become standard for references.

# August 24

## SAINT BARTHOLOMEW, APOSTLE

### 159.1 First Point
Saint Bartholomew had the honor of being one of the Apostles chosen by Jesus Christ.[1] To fill himself entirely with the Gospel truths, he always carried the Gospel of Saint Matthew with him on his journeys. This was the treasure in which he placed all his confidence for securing the salvation of the souls whom he converted in great numbers.

It is true that he had the abundant grace of the apostolate and that this was what worked in him and drew souls to God. Because he was humble, he attributed the results of his preaching to the living and effective word of God,[2] which he drew from Saint Matthew's Gospel, much more than to anything he could say. He knew that this divine word alone is able to make the division between the flesh and the spirit[3] that is so necessary to bring about the entire conversion of a soul.

How fortunate you are to carry the holy Gospel with you at all times, for in it are found all the treasures of the knowledge and the wisdom of Jesus Christ.[4] Be faithful to this practice. From this holy book, you must draw the truths that you are to teach your disciples every day to give them by this means the true Christian spirit. For the same reason, nourish your soul daily with the holy maxims contained in this wonderful book; make them familiar to you by often meditating on them.

### 159.2 Second Point
When the holy Apostles spread throughout the whole world in order to announce the holy Gospel to all the peoples of the earth,[5] this saint was assigned to go to preach the Gospel in Armenia and in the Indies, where he did very considerable good. He persuaded the

king, the queen, and the whole royal family, along with twelve entire cities in this kingdom, to make a public profession of the faith and the law of Jesus Christ. This won for him the esteem and the veneration of all these people, who always regarded him as an extraordinary man whom God had sent to withdraw them from their blindness and ignorance[6] and to procure their salvation.

This is what the saint did through the preaching of the word of God and by frequent and diligent prayer, which he offered to urge God to touch their hearts. Because this saint knew that he could not succeed in apostolic work without the special help of God, he applied himself very faithfully to prayer, so that God would give to all these people confided to him the grace to be docile to the word of Jesus Christ.

You have the advantage of sharing in the duties of the Apostles by teaching catechism daily to the children under your guidance and by instructing them in the maxims of the holy Gospel. You will not do them much good, however, if you do not possess in full measure the spirit of prayer, which gives a holy fervor to your words and makes them able to penetrate very effectively the depths of the hearts of your students.

### 159.3  Third Point

The great number of conversions brought about by this saint drew down on him a great persecution by the priests of the idols, who were very opposed to the establishment of the Christian religion and less inclined to listen to the word of God and to profit by it. This led them to incite the king's brother in this nation to make an attempt on the life of Saint Bartholomew. They were certain that if they caused this saint to die, they would destroy Christianity, but because this was God's own work, all their projects were ineffectual.[7]

This prince, filled with hatred for Saint Bartholomew, was so inhuman that he caused him to be flayed alive; then he cut off his head. We cannot conceive how much this Apostle suffered in his martyrdom, because to flay a person alive is one of the cruelest torments that can be inflicted. Yet this saint endured it with such patience that he seemed to be dead and no longer to have feeling, for he was so filled with the Spirit of God that the interior feeling that enlivened his soul continually raised him to God and seemed to deprive his body of the feeling natural to it.

You have to suffer a constant martyrdom that is no less violent for the spirit than Saint Bartholomew's was for his body. You must, so to speak, tear off your own skin, which Saint Paul calls the old man, in order to be clothed with the Spirit of Jesus Christ, which is, according to the same Apostle, the new man.[8] Let this, then, be your effort throughout your life, so that you may truly become disciples of Jesus Christ and imitators of this holy Apostle in his martyrdom.

———

Bartholomew, identified with Nathaniel, the friend of the Apostle Philip, was called by Jesus to be among the first Apostles (John 1:45ff). He is also mentioned in the account of Jesus' appearance to the Apostles by the side of the lake after the Resurrection (John 21:2). He came from Cana, which might explain why he asked, Can anything good come from Nazareth? (John 1:46). Tradition has made him the Patron of Armenia, where he is said to have been martyred. His relics were transferred to Mesopotamia in the sixth century and from there to Beneventum in the ninth century. There is also a church in Rome that claims his relics.

———

1. Jn 1:43ff
2. Heb 4:12
3. Heb 4:12
4. Col 2:3
5. Mk 16:15
6. Eph 4:18
7. Acts 5:39
8. Eph 4:22–24

# August 25

## SAINT LOUIS, KING OF FRANCE

### 160.1 First Point

Saint Louis, King of France, whom the Church honors today, was as eminent in virtue as in dignity. First of all, he had an extreme horror for sin, which his mother, a very virtuous princess, had instilled in him from the time he reached the use of reason. He always had held this sentiment so deeply in his heart that he often said he would prefer to lose his kingdom rather than to commit a single mortal sin.

He even had such a great spirit of religion that in memory of the honor he had received by being baptized at Poissy, he often called himself Louis of Poissy and signed his name this way out of esteem and respect for that sacrament.

He also heard two Masses on his knees every day, deeply penetrated by the spirit of faith. So great was this virtue in him that one day, when someone came to tell him that a child was appearing in the host at the Sainte Chapelle, he did not take a single step, saying that he did not need to see the miracle in order to believe in the presence of Jesus Christ in the Eucharist, for faith alone made him believe this.

He recognized and adored Jesus Christ in the poor. He invited three poor people to dine with him every day, besides feeding 120 others with the same food that was given to his servants.

Do you have as much horror for sin and as much of the spirit of religion as this holy king? Make a frequent examination on these two points. Be convinced that you will preserve your piety and procure it for your students only insofar as you fully possess these two qualities. Without them your soul will be like a city without walls and fortifications, always open to the attacks of your enemies.

### 160.2  Second Point

Because mortification supports piety, this saint's practice of it was unusual. His austerities were very extraordinary for a person of his rank. He fasted every Friday of the year and ate no meat on Wednesday and, often, on Monday. When fasting, he ordinarily ate but one meal, which usually consisted only of bread and water. Every Friday, after going to Confession, he took the discipline of little iron chains at the hands of his confessor.

In a spirit of humility and mortification, every Saturday he washed the feet of the three poor people who had eaten with him, and he did this on his knees. Also, one of the practices of mortification of this prince, who was so filled with the Christian spirit, was to wear clothes made of ordinary, rough material, such as coarse wool or similar cloth, in order to be able to give to poor people the money he would have spent on costly attire.

What was even more mortifying for such a great king was the patience he always had in suffering everything that was said against him without ever complaining or letting it disturb him, for he was mindful of what Jesus Christ had suffered for him.

The more you accept mortification, whether external or internal, especially the latter, the more you will possess the Christian spirit and the spirit of your state. Hence, make the practice of mortification something usual and ordinary in your life. Spend no day without training in one mortification that you prefer and that you put into practice.

### 160.3  Third Point

This saint's zeal for the good both of the Church and of his country was so admirable that it is difficult to be able to describe it. This holy zeal led him to wage war against infidels to destroy the empire of the devil in their country and to establish the reign of Jesus Christ there.

In the first journey he made to recover the Holy Land, he was made prisoner; during the second journey, he died of the plague. When the Saracen deputies came to Paris, he declared to them that his only desire was for them to profess the Christian religion. He built a great number of churches and monasteries, and he loved members of religious communities very much because of their piety and because they are the ones who do much to strengthen the Church.

He brought back to France a great number of relics, among others, the crown of thorns of our Lord and a large portion of the Holy Cross. He loved his subjects tenderly. After he had worked with wonderful care to procure peace and tranquility for them, he gave them good laws and regulations to guide them to God. Before he died, he gave his son instructions that are so wise and so Christian that they are able to teach kings how to govern their kingdoms in a very saintly manner.

In your work you ought to unite zeal for the good of the Church with zeal for the good of the nation of which your disciples are beginning to be and one day ought to be perfect members. You will procure the good of the Church by making them true Christians, docile to the truths of faith and to the maxims of the holy Gospel. You will procure the good of the nation by teaching them how to read and write and everything else that pertains to your ministry with regard to exterior things. But piety must be joined to exterior things; otherwise, your work would be of little use.

––––––––

Louis (1214–1270) was born at Poissy and became heir to the throne of France at the age of 12, under the regency of his devout mother, Queen Blanche of Castille. At the age of 19, he married Marguerite of Provence and had numerous children by her. He was a wise ruler of his kingdom, an example of justice, mercy, simplicity, and peace. He was, however, luckless in the crusades, defeated in the first (1250) and dying of illness in the second, on August 25, 1270. His devotion to the Passion has been enshrined in the beautiful Sainte Chapelle, in Paris, which he caused to be built to house the relics of the Crown of Thorns and the True Cross.

# August 28

## SAINT AUGUSTINE, BISHOP

### 161.1  First Point

Once Saint Augustine had been converted to God through the prayers of his holy mother and the powerful and effective instructions of Saint Ambrose, he withdrew to the countryside, where for three years he led an extremely solitary and penitential life. Here he learned to enjoy the presence of God and to practice with perfection the rules of the holy Gospel, which were the subject of his meditation. Here he often poured out his heart in the presence of his God.

He could not console himself at the thought of his former disorderly life. Whenever he considered the enormity of his sins, he became so overwhelmed by the love of God for him that he could not sufficiently admire and give thanks for the extraordinary goodness that this God of love had shown to him. Sometimes deeply touched by the greatness and the incomprehensibility of God and of God's gifts to all people, his heart would melt and soften, then burst forth in leaps of love for his God.[1]

In holy seclusion this saint became a new man, a man of God; there, after being converted, he prepared to labor effectively for the conversion of others.

You cannot become capable of laboring usefully in your work except in seclusion and in prayer. These are the two means at your disposal by which you can become entirely free from the world and from inclination to sin and be consecrated entirely to God.

### 161.2  Second Point

This saint was ordained priest, despite his reluctance, by the bishop of Hippo, who decided that he was able to do great service for the Church. Along with several other clerics, he then led a very regulated life, separated from all dealings with the world. In this way he acquired a great reputation, not only because of the eminent virtue that he practiced while living in community with much edification but also because of his great knowledge, the soundness of his mind, and the marvelous power with which he fought the Arians, Manicheans, and other heretics, both in his sermons and in his writings. Just as grace had done much in him for his own conversion, so it likewise brought about through him surprising results in the conversion of others. This grace, combined with his natural intelligence and his profound learning, silenced all the arguments of the most obstinate heretics and those most capable of giving some semblance of truth to their opinions.

In your work you do not have to war against heretics but against the immature inclinations of children that urge them strongly to evil. You will not overcome these by merely natural learning but by the Spirit of God and the fullness of his grace. You will not draw this grace on you except by the power of prayer. Be very faithful to prayer, then, so that enlightened by the graces of the Holy Spirit, you will silence the evil inclinations in these little souls and drive far from them all the suggestions of the devil.

### 161.3 Third Point

Having become bishop of Hippo, Saint Augustine devoted himself with all possible zeal to the guidance of his diocese, but God did not restrict his zeal to so limited a field. Because God had given his spirit a generosity at least equal to the depth of his knowledge, God made him useful to the whole Church. Saint Augustine was consulted by Popes and Councils and by nearly everyone in the world, even by several unbelievers to whose conversion he contributed a great deal. From all sides, people came to him to ask for clerics formed under his guidance to become pastors of the Church.

Yet, so holy a manner of life was strongly opposed and condemned by the heretics, who considered him as their greatest enemy, the one among the Doctors of the Church whom they feared the most. They said everything they could against him to ruin his reputation, but because it was founded on the solid base of piety and humility, they were never able to do him any harm. He showed, in fact, extraordinary humility in leaving an account of his sins to posterity.

Our Community can be very useful to the Church, but be convinced that it will be so only to the degree it is based on these two foundations, piety and humility, which will make it indestructible.

------

Augustine (354–430) was born at Tagaste, in Numidia, now called Souk-Ahras, in Algeria. It is believed that his parents were Berbers. His father, Patricius, a pagan, was a small landowner and town councilor who was converted at the end of his life by Saint Monica, his wife. De La Salle has also written a meditation on Saint Augustine's conversion (May 5) through the prayers of his mother. His Baptism was postponed to avoid the risk of post-baptismal sin. He was eventually baptized by Saint Ambrose after his conversion at the age of 32. He has described his wayward life prior to Baptism in his *Confessions,* which he wrote to give praise to God. After returning to Africa from Italy, he was ordained a priest at the age of 37 and was consecrated bishop of Hippo four years later. He labored during the next 35 years as a devout bishop for his people, as the leader of a community of priests, monks, and nuns (for which he wrote the Rule of Saint Augustine), and as a profound theologian, writing and debating powerfully against the Manichean, Donatist, and Pelagian heretics. He died on August 28, 430.

---

1. Lam 2:19

# August 29

## THE BEHEADING
## OF SAINT JOHN THE BAPTIST

### 162.1 First Point

Because the purpose of the sojourn of Jesus Christ on earth was for the sanctification of all people, it also seems that the purpose the Savior had in choosing Saint John the Baptist as his prophet and precursor was to bring about the destruction of sin. In this sense the saint came to prepare the way for Jesus Christ.[1] Because we cannot be sanctified except after sin has been destroyed through sorrow for it and through penance, that is what Saint John the Baptist did.

To enable him to do this as much for himself as for others and to fulfill in this his ministry more effectively and solidly, Jesus Christ began by visiting him before his birth, while Jesus was still in his holy mother's womb.[2] He delivered John from original sin, something which can only be accomplished by the unaided grace of Jesus Christ, without any action by the one afflicted with this sin. Jesus Christ wanted Saint John to come into this world free from sin, so that he might be able all the more easily to destroy it in those for whose conversion he would labor.

Although you have not come into this world exempt from sin like Saint John, at least you ought to have made it a point to be free of it since your spiritual birth and your consecration to God. Since then, have you not committed a great number of sins, even some of considerable gravity? Is this how you have been faithful to Jesus Christ, who did you the honor of calling you to his service and withdrawing you from the abyss of the world and of sin?

### 162.2 Second Point

Saint John, strengthened by the grace he had received from Jesus Christ while still in the womb of his holy mother, seems to have lived for no other purpose than to destroy sin. From his childhood he took all possible precaution not to fall into sin. While still very young, as the Church sings in his honor, he withdrew to the desert[3] to put himself in a state not to commit the least sin. It was, no doubt, for the same reason that he was clothed, as the Gospel tells us, in a garment made of camel's skin, wore a leather belt about his waist, and ate only locusts and wild honey.[4]

This is a great way to destroy sin in ourselves, living a poor and penitent life and avoiding all contact with people as this saint did during all the time he lived. What a grace it was and what an advantage for this saint to have always lived in innocence! This is what made Jesus Christ say of him, that among all people there was none greater than John the Baptist.[5]

This saint was not content with destroying sin in himself; he also worked all his life to destroy it in others. They came to him in crowds from all over Judea; he preached to them in the desert and baptized them in the Jordan.[6] He converted a very great number of them, and everyone had an altogether special veneration for him.[7]

Pay attention to Saint John's manner of life and to his zeal. Reflect that like him, you are obliged to prepare the way for the Lord in the hearts of your disciples and to destroy the reign of sin in them. To obtain this grace from God, which requires great purity of heart, avoid the least sins, and for this purpose make use of the same means he did: seclusion from the world and a poor and penitent life.

### 162.3 Third Point

The courageous and tireless zeal demonstrated by Saint John to do away with sin was finally the cause of his death. Herod, the Tetrarch of Galilee, having taken the wife of his brother, Philip, and having committed many other crimes, Saint John reproached him forcefully, which is why Herod had him arrested and put in prison. Yet he did not dare put him to death, because the people regarded this saint as a Prophet,[8] and Herod considered him to be a saint and had much respect for him.

However, having given a banquet for the leading men of his court and the daughter of the adulterous woman having danced before him, Herod was so pleased, as were those who were with him at table, that he promised with an oath to give her whatever she would ask. Her mother at once advised her to ask the king for the head of John the Baptist, which he agreed to do on the spot, although regretfully, only because of the oath he had taken and out of consideration for those whom he had invited. When the order for the execution was given, one of the guards went to cut off Saint John's head in prison and brought it to the king on a platter.[9] Such was the consequence of this great saint's zeal and of his preaching.

Is this the reward you hope for in your work? Do you desire to suffer much in it, to be greatly persecuted for it, and in the end to die in it after having worked with all the energies of your soul for the destruction of sin?

---

This feast has been celebrated since the fifth century. De La Salle focuses on Saint John's death in the third point of his meditation. The first two points resemble the reflections he makes in the meditation he wrote for the feast of the Nativity of Saint John (June 24).

---

| | | |
|---|---|---|
| 1. Lk 1:76 | 4. Mt 3:4 | 7. Mt 14:5 |
| 2. Lk 1:41–44 | 5. Mt 11:11 | 8. Mt 14:3–5 |
| 3. Lk 1:80 | 6. Mt 3:1, 5–6 | 9. Mt 14:6–11 |

# September 8

## THE NATIVITY
## OF THE MOST BLESSED VIRGIN

### 163.1 First Point

Let us honor the Most Blessed Virgin on her birthday and join in the quite extraordinary joy felt by the entire Church, which today solemnly celebrates this happy day when God brought into this world the woman who initiated the salvation of all people. God, who conducts all things with wisdom, having the plan to save his people[1] and to be born like them, chose by preference a virgin who was worthy to be his temple and his dwelling place. To prepare her just as he wished her to be, he adorned her by the power of the Holy Spirit with all the natural and supernatural qualities fitting for the one who would be the mother of God.

It was necessary for this purpose that the body of this holy Virgin would be so perfectly formed and so well functioning from the time of her birth that it was able to contribute to the holiness of her soul. In this way the Holy Spirit, coming upon her, put her in a state to find favor before God and to be the object of his delight.[2] He gave her such inner strength that she was able to resist all the attacks of the evil spirit that might have corrupted, or at least diminished, the purity of her heart.

Oh, how very right it is that she who was destined to form a man-God would be entirely the work of God and the most perfect of pure creatures!

### 163.2 Second Point

Let us admire with how many graces God adorned the soul of the Most Blessed Virgin at the moment of her birth. She was so filled with grace[3] that no pure creature has ever been like her or ever will be. The Holy Spirit, giving her a share in his fullness, communicated all his gifts to her and took up his dwelling in her, from that time on, to prepare her to receive and to contain in her womb the Son of God made man. He also gave her a heart so filled with God's love that she lived only for God. Everything in her related to God alone; her mind was occupied only with God and with what God helped her to know that would be pleasing to him. All the faculties of her soul had no other function except to give homage to God.

Even her body served as an instrument for the holy actions that took place within her and that helped to spiritualize her body as far as possible and to make it a holy sanctuary where Jesus Christ some day would enter and there offer himself interiorly to God, as a victim without blemish,[4] to perfect the purification of the soul of this holy Virgin, whom the Holy Spirit had possessed from her birth.

Oh, how happy this day was for Mary and also for all people who find their refuge in her because of the treasure of grace God placed in her at the moment she appeared in the world!

### 163.3 Third Point

It is impossible for us to believe how great was the cooperation of the Most Blessed Virgin with all the graces she received from God at the moment of her birth. By a special privilege, she already enjoyed the use of reason and made use of it to adore God and to thank him for all his goodness. From that time on, she consecrated herself entirely to God to live and to act only for him during the rest of her life.

She professed her nothingness profoundly in the depths of her soul, acknowledging that she owed everything to God. She admired interiorly what God had done in her, saying to herself what she later declared in her Canticle, God has done great things in me.[5] As she looked at herself and contemplated God in herself, she was altogether amazed to see the generosity of God in his creature. She was convinced and thoroughly aware that everything in her must pay honor to God. With David she continually said that her very bones were so indebted to God that they could not refrain from crying out, Who is like unto God?[6]

If Mary received an abundance of grace,[7] it was to share it with all those who have recourse to her. By your care for her and your recourse to her, gain the help you can receive from her.

---

De La Salle took his inspiration for this meditation from the liturgy of the feast as it was celebrated in his time, borrowing thoughts from the Lessons of the Nocturnes, the Collect, and the Gradual of the Mass. The celebration of Mary's birthday probably began in the Near East. It was introduced in the West during the eighth century.

---

| | | |
|---|---|---|
| 1. 1 Tim 2:4 | 4. Heb 9:12, 14 | 7. Lk 1:28 |
| 2. Lk 1:30, 35 | 5. Lk 1:49 | |
| 3. Lk 1:48–49 | 6. Ps 35:10 | |

# September 12

## SUNDAY IN THE OCTAVE OF OUR LADY'S NATIVITY: THE HOLY NAME OF MARY

### 164.1 First Point

Today the Church celebrates the feast of the holy name of the Most Blessed Virgin to teach us how useful and advantageous it is for us to invoke her holy name in our needs. The name Mary, by which we honor the Most Blessed Virgin, means star of the sea. It is, says Saint Bernard, very well given to her, because she is indeed a star that enlightens, guides, and leads us to a harbor in the stormy sea of this world. This holy Virgin, says the same saint, is for us the star that rose out of Jacob,[1] whose ray, which is Jesus Christ, enlightens the whole world,[2] for she conceived him in her virginal womb like a star that sends forth its rays without any corruption and enlightens all the world, as Saint Bernard expresses it, following Saint John's Gospel. She is this clear and brilliant star, says Saint Bernard, rising above this great and spacious sea, shining by her merits, and enlightening by her example.

You have, without doubt, a need for light in this life, where you are always as if upon a stormy sea at the risk of your salvation. Have recourse to Mary. She will enlighten you and help you know God's will for you, because she shares in the light of Jesus Christ, her Son, who came into this world to enlighten everyone (even though many did not recognize him).[3] She is a light shining in the darkness.[4] Ask her often, then, to enlighten your mind and to make it docile to the truth. Because she knows the truth perfectly, it is easy for her to instruct you in the truth and to make you understand what you, who are only in darkness, cannot understand.

### 164.2 Second Point

The road you must follow through this life being so dangerous, you need a guide to walk safely. You cannot have a better guide than the Most Blessed Virgin, because she is most pure within and without, because the saints call her the treasurer of the graces that God has given to her to share them with you, and because she knows all the paths and means to keep you safe amid the dangers you will encounter. This is why it is most advantageous to allow yourselves to be guided by her, because, says Saint Bernard, when we follow her, we cannot go astray; when we think of her, we cannot wander from the right path; when we pray to her, we can never despair of reaching the place where we intend to go; when she helps and upholds us, we cannot fall; when she protects us, we can fear nothing, and when she guides us, we cannot grow weary.

In dangers and in narrow, perilous paths, think of Mary. Invoke her sacred name, and at once you will find comfort and deliverance from all your troubles. Oh, how happy you are, if you are devoted to the Most Blessed Virgin, to have easy recourse to her holy name and by this invocation alone to be safe in the midst of all the problems of so difficult a journey!

### 164.3 Third Point

It is not enough to sail securely. You must reach the harbor; otherwise, all the distance you have covered will be of no avail, because it will not be the goal you set out to attain. This star of the sea, the Most Blessed Virgin, will guide you there without difficulty, because she knows very well where you are going and is familiar with the way you must follow to arrive there. She knew for herself the road to reach the goal, and she has arrived there. Because she had a perfect understanding of the ways of God and was so abundantly prepared by his grace, this set her on the path and made her understand how happy a person is when carried by the grace of God, as the author of the *Imitation of Jesus Christ* says very well.

We are in this world only to save ourselves, and we will find all the means we need for this in the womb of the Most Blessed Virgin, where Jesus Christ lived and which he sanctified by the dwelling he made there. He also left there an abundance of grace able not only to fill totally the soul of the Most Blessed Virgin but also to enlighten, enliven, and inflame the hearts of those who have recourse to her by invoking her holy name. Adopt this devotion; ask God for it on this holy day. Remember her name, and invoke it often with all the respect and veneration it deserves.

―――――

For a time this feast was celebrated on the Sunday after the feast of the Nativity of Mary. It was inserted into the liturgy by Pope Innocent XI in thanksgiving for the Christian victory over the Turks at Vienna on September 13, 1683. The date of September 12 was fixed during the reform of the liturgy under Pope Pius X (1903–1914). This feast is not in the current liturgical calendar.

―――――――――――

1. Nm 24:17        3. Jn 1:9–11        4. Jn 1:5
2. Jn 1:9

# September 14

## THE EXALTATION
## OF THE HOLY CROSS

### 165.1 First Point

The feast celebrated by the Church today was originally established when Saint Helena, the mother of the Emperor Constantine, discovered the Holy Cross and when it was presented with great honor and received with much glory throughout the world by all Christians. However, this feast became much more important when the Emperor Heraclius brought this Holy Cross back in triumph, carrying it on his shoulders and placing it in Jerusalem on the same spot of Calvary where Jesus Christ was attached to it.

We ought to unite ourselves with the joy that the Church displays on this day by the great solemnity with which she honors this sacred wood. At the same time, we ought to enter into the sentiments of Saint Paul when he says that we must glory in the cross of Jesus

Christ.[1] It is indeed in this cross that we must place all our glory, says the same Apostle, casting our eyes on Jesus Christ, our divine Master, who placed his glory and all his happiness in suffering and dying on this cross, despising the shame and ignominy[2] that accompanied the cross. For this Holy Cross (which has since become so venerable to Christians) was, as the same Apostle says, a cause for scandal to the Jews and a folly to the Gentiles.[3]

The Apostles, according to the expression of the same Saint Paul, made it an honor for them to preach Jesus Christ crucified throughout the world,[4] because they professed to know nothing but the same Jesus crucified,[5] quite far from voiding the cross of Jesus Christ,[6] which is for us the virtue and the power of God.[7] Let us, therefore, spend this day and the rest of our life in great respect and profound adoration before this sacred mystery, which, as the same Saint Paul adds, was hidden before Jesus Christ for our glory. The princes of this world did not have the advantage of knowing it,[8] although the Cross is the instrument of our salvation and has procured for us the life of grace and our resurrection.

### 165.2 Second Point

It is not fitting that the honor we must pay to the cross of our Lord be limited to showing it respect and to adoring it. Rather, we must love it with all the affection of our heart and desire to die attached to it as Jesus Christ our divine Master desired. For, as the author of the *Imitation* says, those who embrace the cross of Jesus Christ with a good heart need not fear the dreadful sentence of damnation. Because we have been freed from sin by means of it, we must not doubt (and we ought to have this confidence) that if we love the cross in union with Jesus Christ, who loved it tenderly and bore it with extreme joy, all the miseries of this life will become pleasant and agreeable to us. In this way we will be truly happy, having found our paradise in this world, because we will have entered into the sharing of the suffering spirit of Jesus Christ, who has reconciled us by his death on this holy cross, as Saint Paul says, and made us holy, pure, and beyond reproach before God.[9]

Let us, then, consider attentively how much we owe to this sacred wood for having contributed this way to our sanctification. By a zeal of ardent love, let us raise it up to Jesus Christ to unite it to him, for he still loves it now, as he loves our salvation, and is glad to have borne it for our sanctification. Therefore, when you have some trouble, unite with Jesus suffering. Love his cross, because you are one of his members;[10] this union and love will soothe your pains and make them much more tolerable.

### 165.3 Third Point

All the external and internal honors we can pay to the Savior's cross will be of little use to us unless we honor it in another way, by bearing constantly,[11] as a good and faithful servant, the cross[12] that the same Jesus, our Master, wishes to give us, who remember that he was quite willing to be crucified for love of us. As Minucius Felix so well says, although Jesus Christ requires that we adore his Holy Cross, this is not what he asks the most. It is that we drink cheerfully of his sacred chalice if we desire to be his friend and to have a place with him in his kingdom.[13]

Let us, then, like Saint Paul, place all our glory in bearing in our bodies the sacred wounds of the suffering Jesus,[14] so as to make ourselves conformable to Jesus crucified and to honor his Holy Cross in the manner that will be most pleasing to him and most efficacious and advantageous for us. We judge well that the entire life of Jesus was nothing but a cross and a constant martyrdom. We will never appear better as his servant, his friend, and his imitator than by imprinting on ourselves the sign of his Holy Cross and by suffering pain like his.

How could we dare look for another way to please God, to honor God, and to offer an agreeable sacrifice except by the way of the blessed cross. Jesus, our Savior, did not spend a single hour of his life without suffering in order to honor his Father, and no saint has ever lived in this world without suffering and without the cross.

---

The feast of the Triumph of the Cross, as it is called today, focuses less on the occasions of its origin (the Finding by Saint Helena, around 320, and the Exaltation, or rescue, of the Cross from the Persians by the Emperor Heraclius, in 629) and more on the mystery of the Cross in the work of salvation. As in his meditation for May 3, De La Salle stresses the importance of carrying the cross of suffering daily out of love for Christ.

---

1. Gal 6:14
2. Heb 12:12
3. 1 Cor 1:23
4. 1 Cor 1:23
5. 1 Cor 2:2
6. 1 Cor 1:17–24
7. 1 Cor 1:24
8. 1 Cor 2:7–8
9. Col 1:22
10. Eph 5:30
11. Lk 9:23
12. Mt 25:21
13. Mt 20:22
14. Gal 6:17

# September 16

## SAINT CYPRIAN

### 166.1 First Point

Saint Cyprian, one of the principal Fathers of the Church, was most zealous for her discipline and for upholding the doctrine and maxims of Jesus Christ. He had been a pagan and a most learned one. He was converted by a priest named Cecilius, whom he loved tenderly and ever afterward honored as his father. Even before receiving Baptism, he studied Holy Scripture. Filled with the truths he learned there and with the Catholic spirit, he was admitted to the sacrament. As soon as he was baptized, he sold all his possessions, distributed the proceeds to the poor,[1] and resolved to practice celibate chastity.

In this way, from the moment he became a Christian, he lived stripped of all his wealth and freed from affection for all the goods and all the pleasures of the earth. That was how it was to live as a perfect Christian. It seems quite clear that this saint was altogether virtuous from the very beginning and had a heart fully imbued with the Spirit of Jesus Christ. With this disposition he could not but practice great virtues. He gave edification to everyone by his holy life, just as he won admiration by his talent and knowledge of literature. That is what enabled this saint to render great benefits in the Church.

You are in a state where you must know well the maxims of the holy Gospel, both to work at your own sanctification and to procure that of others. Do you practice these maxims as this saint did? Have you, like him, renounced the goods and pleasures of life?

Often you do not enjoy the goods and comforts of life because you cannot have them. Often those who lack them the most also desire them most eagerly. Are you not of this number? It is not enough to be deprived of such things unless it is done willingly and with affection. That is why Jesus Christ says that not only the poor but also the poor in spirit are blessed.[2] This spirit of poverty is often no less rare in religious communities than it is in the world.

### 166.2 Second Point

Saint Cyprian, living such a holy life, was soon made a priest and, almost as quickly, bishop of Carthage by the choice of all the people. To avoid being bishop, he fled, but he was compelled to accept the dignity. Once installed as bishop, this saint enlightened the entire Church by his excellent writings, and during persecution he worked forcefully to uphold those who were wavering in their faith. He displayed admirable zeal for the instruction of his people, and he had, above all, a special care for the poor. When people make themselves voluntarily poor to imitate Jesus Christ, they also love, as he did, those whom God has made poor.

Every day you have poor children to instruct. Love them tenderly, as this saint did, following in this the example of Jesus Christ. Prefer them to those who are not poor, for Jesus Christ does not say that the Gospel is preached[3] to the rich but *to the poor.* These poor children are also the ones whom God has entrusted to you and to whom you are obliged to proclaim the truths of the holy Gospel. The poor were the ones who most frequently followed Jesus Christ, our Lord. They are also the ones most disposed to profit by his teaching, because in them it meets with fewer external obstacles.

Everyone agrees that this saint surpassed all the other bishops of his time in knowledge and eloquence as well as in wisdom and humility. Following his example, you must know your religion well, but you must also show how well you possess it by your wise conduct and your piety.

### 166.3 Third Point

This saint worked very hard for the Church; he also endured an infinite number of evils because of his zeal and the attachment he had for her. A furious persecution broke out against the faithful, and the pagans demanded that Saint Cyprian be thrown to the lions. At once he was denounced, and at the same time all his goods were confiscated. He went into hiding to continue to be of service to his people and to the Church. During this cruel persecution, it seemed important that he keep alive in order to strengthen his people. He remained in hiding for two years, ministering without interruption to the needs of his diocese and writing treatises and letters filled with the love of God. After two years of seclusion, the Emperor Decius having died, he returned to Carthage. But not long after this, the Emperors Valerian and Gallian exiled him. When he came back from this exile, the proconsul condemned him to be beheaded. That is how this saint left the exile of this life after suffering for a considerable time to defend the Church of Jesus Christ.

One of the things that contributes most to impress the truth of the Gospel in people's hearts and to make them appreciate it is when those who teach this truth, as ministers of Jesus Christ and dispensers of his mysteries,[4] willingly endure persecution and practice what Saint Paul says, We are cursed, and we bless; we are persecuted, and we suffer it; we are insulted, and we respond with prayers;[5] we are regarded as the refuse of the world, but we are not disheartened.[6] Do you have this disposition? It is necessary for you if you wish to do good in your work.

---

Cyprian was an African who practiced law and taught rhetoric before his conversion to Christianity. His considerable talents and learning became, after his conversion and ordination to the priesthood, the reason for his being chosen as bishop of Carthage by the priests of that diocese. In this role he was zealous for orthodox belief and purity of morals among his priests and people during years of both peace and persecution. On September 14, 258, Cyprian was beheaded on orders from the Emperor Valerian.

---

1. Mt 19:21
2. Mt 5:3
3. Mt 11:5
4. 1 Cor 4:1
5. 1 Cor 4:12–13
6. 2 Cor 4:8

# September 21

## SAINT MATTHEW, APOSTLE AND EVANGELIST

### 167.1 First Point

The most admirable trait in the life of Saint Matthew is that he faithfully followed Jesus Christ as soon as he was called. He lived in Capharnaum, a city of Judea,[1] where he was a collector of the imperial tax. Jesus Christ, who was preaching his Gospel there, one day passed by the gate where Saint Matthew stayed, and the saint immediately left his counting house and all he had and followed Jesus Christ.[2]

To show the joy and gratitude he had toward Jesus Christ because of his conversion, he invited him to a great banquet in his house, where several publicans and sinners were present.[3] These, says Saint Jerome, were converted by our Lord.

Saint Matthew's conversion is quite extraordinary and shows the power of grace and the effect it produces in a soul. It is true that the word of Jesus Christ is efficacious[4] in the calling of his first Apostles, but as most of them were poor fishermen, it is not so surprising that they at once followed Jesus Christ, whereas Saint Matthew had property and lived comfortably.

Were you as prompt to follow Jesus Christ as Saint Matthew was: on the spot, at the first word, not taking time to settle his affairs, and without even asking for a delay in order to do so? How many times has Jesus Christ perhaps called you? Have you not, like Saint Augustine, often replied: Tomorrow, tomorrow I will be converted? Do you not still say as much every day? Have you renounced all things from the bottom of your heart? Perhaps some of us had nothing to renounce, like the first Apostles. For them it was quite easy. Still, do we not seek our ease and comfort? That is something unworthy of a servant of God, who is obliged to give up the world and all things.[5]

### 167.2  Second Point

After his conversion, Saint Matthew remained faithfully attached to Jesus Christ until the end of his life, as Saint Jerome tells us. This is why he was chosen to be one of Christ's Apostles, to preach his Gospel with him and after him and to be the first to write the Gospel, in the same language in which Jesus Christ had preached it, Syriac, which was a corrupt Hebrew.

It is inconceivable how much Jesus Christ loves those who give up everything for him and how many graces he gives them both for themselves and for others. Because their hearts are empty of the things of this world, God fills them with his Holy Spirit, as he did the heart of Saint Matthew. For the more we give up exteriorly, the more God gives us interiorly.

Be attached only to Jesus Christ, his doctrine, and his holy maxims, because he has done you the honor of choosing you in preference to a great many others to announce these truths to children, whom he loves so especially.

Think highly of your work, which is apostolic, and carefully study the Gospel of Saint Matthew, in which we find proposed the holiest maxims of Jesus Christ and the fundamental truths of Christian piety. The more you study this, the more learned you will become in the science of the saints, and the better prepared you will be to instruct others.

### 167.3  Third Point

This holy Apostle set out at the same time as the others to preach the Gospel; his assignment was Ethiopia. There he made great progress, converting to the faith the king and his entire family. When this king died, the prince who succeeded him wished to marry the daughter of his predecessor, named Iphigenia. Because she had made a vow of chastity, she refused him. This king wanted to force Saint Matthew to persuade this princess to marry him despite her vow, but Saint Matthew, on the contrary, urged her to remain firm in her resolve. As a result, this barbarian put him to death, despite the fact that he had converted almost the entire country to the faith of Jesus Christ. This led to the saint's being called the victim of virginity.

When attempts are made to entice your students to do evil, strengthen them in doing good. Do not expect any other rewards when you do the duties of your work well than to suffer *persecution, injuries, insults, and curses and to have people accuse you falsely of all sorts of evil,* as Saint Matthew wrote and as he put into practice. Rejoice when this happens, adds the same saint, and leap for joy, because a great reward is reserved for you in heaven, for it was in this way that they persecuted the Prophets before you.[6] Be convinced that such persecutions will draw down on you the grace of God in abundance and his blessings on your work.

---

The only certain facts about Saint Matthew are those found in the Gospel. The details used by De La Salle concerning his mission and martyrdom are not historically certain.

---

1. Capharnaum is in Galilee.
2. Lk 5:27–28
3. Lk 5:29
4. Heb 4:12
5. Lk 14:33
6. Mt 5:11–12

# September 29

## SAINT MICHAEL THE ARCHANGEL

### 169.1[1] First Point

Saint Michael the Archangel was the leader of all the angels who remained faithful to God. He it was who, through zeal for the glory of God, joined with all the holy angels to fight against Lucifer and his adherents,[2] who were dazzled by the perfections and graces God had placed in them and revolted against him, being unwilling to submit to God's orders because they did not sufficiently consider how much the One who had created everything great in them was above them and infinitely more worthy than they of honor and glory. They were even so blind that they resisted Saint Michael, who had been commissioned by God to enlighten them by his wisdom and to show them that nothing can be compared to God and, as Saint Paul says, that to him alone is due all honor and glory forever and ever,[3] that all creatures, such as they are, are nothing in themselves and must abase themselves and acknowledge their nothingness before God in the sight of his glory and majesty. This was the ray of light that God had impressed on Saint Michael. The mere appearance of this archangel silenced those miserable angels, who became creatures of darkness and were banished to a place of darkness because they did not want to open their eyes to the true light.

Will we always resist the light of grace, which tells us that we must leave all for God and that only in God will we find our true happiness even in this life?

### 169.2 Second Point

Saint Michael, inspired by this attitude of faith, which served as his shield[4] against the evil angels, was victorious over them by these words: Who is like to God? At the same time, he gave glory to God with his followers as they cried out, You are worthy, O Lord, our God, to receive all glory, all honor, and all power, because you have created all things.[5] Now salvation and power and the reign of our God have been established, because the accuser of our brothers, who day and night accused them before our God, has been thrown down from the heights of heaven.[6] At that moment all these holy angels were confirmed in eternal glory, from which they have never fallen and which can never have the least alteration in them. What happiness for this holy archangel: to be the first of these blessed spirits who devote themselves entirely to praise God in heaven and, by his zeal and respect for God, to have contributed the most to start bringing others to heaven!

Honor this great saint as the first to give glory to God and to cause him to be glorified by his creatures. Pay him the honor he deserves for having been so loyal to God. Join with him and with all the blessed spirits who are with him in heaven, and regard them as the models of what you ought to do for God. Often recall those words that inspired them in the fight and that supported them against the devils: Who is like unto God? So that these words may strengthen you in your temptations when you are under attack, say, Is the pleasure I would have by yielding to this attraction of concupiscence to be compared with the joy I have from God?

### 169.3 Third Point

Saint Michael gives glory to God even now, day after day, by the good that he does for Christians and by the graces he obtains for them, because he has been chosen by God to be the protector of the Church, which he upholds and defends against her enemies. Was he not the one, in fact, who was sent by God to help King Ezechias kill 180,000 men in Sennacherib's army,[7] who, according to Saint Jude, struggled against the devil to have control over the body of Moses[8] and who even, as the Church chants, has been appointed by God to welcome the souls of the just when they leave their bodies and to bring them to heaven? He, likewise, defends the Church, as the well-beloved of God, against schism and heresy, which from time to time oppose her holy teaching and disturb her.

Let us, then, join with this holy leader of the angels to share in his zeal, both for our own salvation and for that of all Christians. Let us abandon ourselves completely to his care and have confidence in his help. Let us be docile to his interior voice, so that all the means that God offers us through him for our salvation may be effective in us and that we on our part may not place any obstacle to their action.

Often pray to Saint Michael to have the goodness to protect this little family and this church of Jesus Christ,[9] according to the expression of Saint Paul, which is our Community, to give it the means of preserving within it the Spirit of Jesus Christ, to give all its members the graces they need to persevere in their vocation, and to procure the Christian spirit for all those who are under their guidance.

---

The Archangel Michael was honored by the Jews as a special protector of Israel (see Dan. 10:13) and became for Christians a special protector of the Church (see Jude 1:9 and Rev. 12:7–9). Originally, September 29 was the feast of the Dedication of the Basilica of Saint Michael on the Salarian Way, but since the reform of the liturgy by Vatican II, the feast is celebrated in honor of the three principal archangels, Michael, Gabriel, and Raphael. De La Salle has another meditation on Saint Michael, May 8, number 125.

---

1. Number 168, one of the six meditations in the *Additions,* is found at the end both of the original edition and of this edition.
2. Rev 12:7
3. 1 Tim 1:17
4. Eph 6:16
5. Rev 4:11
6. Rev 12:10
7. 2 Kgs 19:35
8. Jude 9
9. Rom 16:5

# September 30

## SAINT JEROME

### 170.1 First Point

Saint Jerome was gifted with an excellent mind and extraordinary learning. At first he devoted himself to humane learning, but having perceived that this turned him away from God instead of giving him appreciation for him, he gave this up and spared no pain, labor, money, or effort to be instructed in Holy Scripture and to reach a perfect understanding of all the mysteries it contains. In these sacred books, the outpouring of all the treasures of God's knowledge and wisdom are found.[1] As the Prophet expresses it, they are the divine books that the true servants of God must devour and be filled with[2] in order to communicate their secrets and to expound them in God's name to those whom they are bound to instruct and to form in the Christian spirit.

This is what Saint Jerome did, for he was consulted by people from all over the world concerning difficulties in Holy Scripture, which he studied so well and resolved so well that he left no doubt in those who had appealed to him regarding their questions. In this way Saint Jerome enlightened the Church with the understanding he had received from God. To possess this gift even more fully, he withdrew from the world, so that secular concerns would not prevent him from deepening his grasp of the sacred truths that God wished to make known to his people.

If you wish to be filled with the mind of God and entirely fit for your work, make the sacred books of Holy Scripture your special study, particularly the New Testament, so that it serves as a rule of conduct for both you and those whom you instruct.

### 170.2 Second Point

Saint Jerome traveled over almost all the world in order to be able to consult with the greatest men of his time, especially those most versed in the science of Holy Scripture. In Athens he met Saint Gregory of Nazianzen, who told him that to understand well the meaning of Holy Scripture, it is necessary to begin by putting it into practice. This is why he followed the advice of this great saint, whom he began from that time to look upon as his teacher, and went at once into the Syrian desert to live there a holy and penitential life. As soon as he arrived there, he devoted himself to prayer, meditation on

Holy Scripture, and the practice of all it teaches, spending nights in prayer and constantly fasting, separated from all contact with the world.

There he came to understand thoroughly what Saint Paul says, that knowledge sometimes puffs up, but charity edifies, and that if anyone thinks he knows something, he has not yet learned what he must know, but if anyone loves God, he is known and loved by God.[3] Of what use, says the author of the *Imitation,* is knowledge without the fear of God? Of what use is it, he adds, to speak profoundly about the mystery of the most Holy Trinity if the person is displeasing to God for lack of humility? In the solitude where Saint Jerome lived as though in a paradise, he learned to despise himself and to place no value on anything whatsoever on the earth.

You must have knowledge in order to teach, but be convinced that you will know the Gospel better by meditating on it than by committing it to memory.

### 170.3 Third Point

Saint Jerome vigorously devoted himself to work against heretics in order to make himself the defender of the Church. It is true that he was such a humble a priest that he did not dare perform any of the priestly functions, considering himself altogether unworthy. Nevertheless, in his quality as God's minister, he made himself very useful to the Church, protecting it in the assaults that its enemies delivered against it, who plotted all the more actively for its destruction because it had not yet attained the growth and the external glory that it has had since then.

This saint showed such vigor, zeal, and even grace in combating heretics that they considered him their scourge. They did not dare to contend with him, because the reasons he brought out to refute their teachings were so accurate and so strong that he easily convinced them of their error.

Penance and prayer, joined to the penetrating quality of his good mind, put him in this position. In this way Saint Jerome exercised his ministry as a priest of Jesus Christ. *Although there is only one and the same Spirit, who imparts his graces to all,* says Saint Paul, there is, however, a diversity of graces. Although there is only one and the same God, who works all things in all, there is a diversity of supernatural operations. One receives from the Holy Spirit the gift to speak with high wisdom; another, the gift to speak with knowledge; another, the gift of prophecy; another, the discernment of spirits; another, the gift to speak in different tongues; another, the interpretation of tongues; another, the gift to govern; another, the gift to assist his brothers.[4] In this way those who have labored for the good of the Church have done so in various ways.

Today, ask through the intercession of Saint Jerome for some share in the grace given to him by God for the good of the Church, and prepare to labor for the Church according to the gift that is yours. Like this saint, love seclusion and prayer. They are the means that will make you useful to the Church.

---

Jerome (ca. 342–420) was born at Stridon, in northern Italy, and received a good education, both in his native city and in Rome, especially in the Latin language and polemical rhetoric. After some efforts to live in a Christian community, he settled as a hermit in the desert of Chalcis, on the island of Euboea, Greece. To fight temptations against unchaste thoughts, he took up the study of Hebrew, which later was very helpful in his study and translation of the Scriptures. He studied further in Constantinople under Saint Gregory Nazianzen, worked as secretary for Pope Damasus in Rome, and finally settled in Bethlehem, where he did his great work of translating almost the whole Bible into Latin. The translation, known as the Vulgate, became the official text of the Church. He was as severe and caustic a critic in his writings as he was austere in his personal asceticism, but he died peacefully in Bethlehem. His remains are now buried in the Basilica of Saint Mary Major in Rome.

---

1. Col 2:3          3. 1 Cor 8:1–3          4. 1 Cor 12:4–11; 28
2. Ez 2:8

# October 1

## SAINT REMIGIUS

### 171.1 First Point

Saint Remigius was born as if by miracle, his mother being beyond her childbearing years. From his youth he won the admiration of everyone as much by the liveliness of his spirit as by his good conduct and piety. To make this more firm, he left the world entirely while still quite young and shut himself up in a hermitage, where he lived a very penitential life.

This is how God leads those he is preparing for something great, by seclusion and prayer, because it is in solitude or an entire separation from creatures that we learn to have a dislike for and to separate ourselves entirely from everything that pleases people who live in the world. We then learn how to converse with God, who willingly speaks to people when he finds them detached from everything else. For God loves to speak with them heart to heart, and the more he finds their hearts empty of the things of the world, the more he makes himself known to them and fills them with his Spirit. This is what happened to Saint Remigius, who was so highly favored by God in his seclusion that the renown of his virtues won for him a great reputation.

It is not reputation that we ought to seek or to desire in this world but the fullness of the Spirit of God, in order to live rightly in our vocation and perform our work well. Be convinced that only a life of seclusion and prayer will enable you to possess this fullness of God's Spirit. This is why you must love seclusion and pray with great fervor.

### 171.2 Second Point

The great reputation Saint Remigius acquired by his piety made such an impression on the people of the area that they came to carry him off from his hermitage to make him archbishop of Reims, even though he was only 22 years old. He did all he could to oppose the choice they made of him, but the splendor of his virtue affected these people more deeply than all his objections, which did nothing to lessen their resolve.

This saint showed great zeal for the good of the Church in the administration of the duties of his episcopal function; he omitted nothing of what he though might contribute to it. It is commonly the result of true seclusion that those who become filled there with the love of God seek to share this afterward with others when God, for the good of the Church, places them in a position where they are obliged to deal with the world. Then these great saints, filled completely with God's Spirit, devote themselves with all possible care to make known and to cause others to value what they experience within themselves. Stirred up by the zeal that has hold of them, they successfully help a great number of souls to give themselves to God.

You are in a work that requires much zeal, but this zeal would be of little use if it did not have its proper effect; this, however, it cannot have unless it is a product of the love of God living in you.

### 171.3 Third Point

The greatest good that Saint Remigius did for the Church during his episcopate was to convert and to baptize Clovis, the King. In this he was helped by the prayers and the efforts of Saint Clotilda. This also procured salvation for various provinces of the kingdom. As a result, the Pope admired him and congratulated him, as did all the other holy bishops of the time.

Those who are called to procure the salvation of souls and are filled with God and his Spirit, as Saint Remigius was in his solitude, succeed in their work to the full extent of their desires. Nothing can resist them, not even God (if we may so speak), as we see in the case of Moses, who constrained God, in a certain manner, to do what he asked God to do for the people whom God had entrusted to his care.[1] What a glorious thing it was for Saint Remigius, before God and before the world, to have contributed as much as he did to lead so many of the French people to become Christians and to have caused Jesus Christ to be adored where until then he was unknown.

Your work does not consist in making your disciples to be Christians but in helping them to be true Christians. This is all the more useful because it would avail them little to have received Baptism if they did not live according to the Christian spirit. To give this spirit to others, you have to possess it well. Recognize what this requires of you; it is, without doubt, to put into practice the holy Gospel. Read the Gospel frequently, then, with attention and affection, and let this be your principal study, but study it especially in order to put it into practice.

--------

Remigius (ca. 437–530) was born in France; his mother was Saint Celinie, who had another son also a saint, Principe, bishop of Soissons. Remigius was made archbishop of Reims, according to tradition, at the age of 22 and served in this role for more than 70 years. He baptized Clovis, King of the Franks, on Christmas day in 496.

De La Salle had a special devotion to this patron of his native city. Blain tells us (CL 7: 229–30; CL 8: 281) that when he was struggling to learn what God wanted of him in the work of the Christian Schools, he would spend the whole night on Fridays and Saturdays at the tomb of Saint Remigius in the church dedicated to the saint.

--------

1. Ex 32:11–14

# October 2

## THE HOLY GUARDIAN ANGELS

### 172.1 First Point

Let us admire God's goodness and thank him for the grace he has given us in assigning an angel to take care of us, protect us, and serve us. God was not satisfied to give us his only Son to rescue us from sin and to send us his Holy Spirit to fill us with his holy grace. To omit nothing of all his care that could advance our interests and keep us in piety and in his holy love, he also sends the holy angels to be with us on earth. He sends these blessed spirits, who rejoice before him in heaven, to be near us always, to help us, and to serve us in every kind of situation. He orders them to watch over us on his behalf, to guide us, and to enlighten us in all our ways,[1] so that we may be able to go straight to heaven in safety without wandering astray.

This is truly a marvelous effect of his goodness, says Saint Bernard, and one of the greatest proofs of his love. Let us, then, show our gratitude for this by carrying out exactly what the angels inspire us to do.

### 172.2 Second Point

The help we receive from our good angels is quite considerable. They suggest to us a great number of good and holy thoughts to bring us to God. They urge us to do penance for our sins. They offer our prayers to God. They pray for us and procure for us gifts so numerous and so great that it is difficult to describe them.

The Royal Prophet speaks about them in a few words when he says, *They will bear you up in their hands lest you dash your foot against a stone,* in other words, lest your soul be wounded by the slightest sin. You will walk on the asp and the adder and trample under foot the lion and the dragon.[2] This means that under their guidance, we will remain invulnerable against all the attacks of the devil.

We ought to fear nothing, then, under the protection and guidance of these angels of God, for, says Saint Bernard, they will not allow us to be tempted beyond our strength, and in situations that are too difficult and dangerous for us, they will bear us up in their hands, to enable us to surmount trials and difficulties without being harmed[3] in any way. With what ease, then, you will overcome all that is opposed to your salvation, having the good fortune to be upheld by the hands of such defenders.

### 172.3 Third Point

How much this help we receive from our good angels ought to lead us to respect them! Must this not also inspire us with devotion toward them and with confidence in their protection? We owe them respect, says Saint Bernard, because of their presence; devotion, because of their kindness toward us; confidence, because of their care to guard us. We are also obliged to acknowledge the unbounded charity with which they obey the order to take care of us in such great and such continual need.

Every time we feel ourselves assailed by some violent temptation and threatened by some considerable difficulty, let us invoke this angel who watches over us, leads us, and gives us such generous help in our needs and difficulties. By fervent and continual prayer, let us address ourselves to our Guardian Angel, ever present and ready to defend and console us.

Often pray also to the Guardian Angels of your students, so that under their powerful protection, your students may willingly practice the good you have taught them and do so with greater ease.

———

Not until 1670 was the feast of the Guardian Angels made a celebration for the whole Church, but devotion to these protectors of individual people was a much older practice among Christians. During De La Salle's lifetime, the popularity of the devotion became widespread. That it meant much to the Founder can be noted by the fact that in two of his *Meditations for the Time of Retreat,* he calls on the Brothers to see in these angels a model for their service to the students in the Christian Schools. The school year in France began on or near October 2, a day on which, according to the Rule, the Brothers would all receive Holy Communion.

---

1. Ps 91:11   2. Ps 91:12–13   3. Ps 91:12, 13

# October 4

## SAINT FRANCIS

### 173.1 First Point

So great was the love of Saint Francis for the poor that he gladly gave them alms on every occasion and was unable to turn down anyone who asked him for anything, because he saw Jesus Christ in them and was convinced that whatever good he did for them, he did for Jesus Christ.[1]

This same love for the poor led this great saint to devote himself to instruct them, rather than the rich, because he knew that this was what Jesus Christ did when he was on earth with his holy Apostles. This led Jesus to reply to the disciples of Saint John, when they asked him what they ought to report about him to their master, Tell him that I am preaching the Gospel to the poor.[2]

Finally, this love for the poor led Saint Francis to serve them in the hospitals of the places he visited. It was to imitate Jesus Christ, who also loved the company of the poor, that Saint Francis was so strongly drawn by affection for them.

You are required by your work to love the poor, because the task you have in this work is to be devoted to their instruction. Look upon them, with Saint Francis, as images of Jesus Christ and as those who are best disposed to receive his Spirit in abundance. In this way the more affection you show for them, the more you will belong to Jesus Christ.

### 173.2 Second Point

Not content with loving the poor, Saint Francis also wanted to be poor and detached from earthly things. To accomplish this completely, one day when his father was complaining that he was giving a great deal to the poor, Saint Francis at once went with him before the bishop and, having publicly renounced his father's inheritance before this prelate, left home on the spot and never wished to live there any more.

He then also undertook to give up all the pleasures and all the comforts that a person can enjoy in this world. He always lived in this detachment, which made him often repeat these words: My God and my all, because when he had stripped himself of everything on earth, he no longer had anything but God and was able to possess him to the full.

He discovered perfect poverty and total emptying of self in Jesus Christ at his birth and in Jesus Christ suffering and dying. This is why he had special devotion to these two mysteries and every year celebrated the Nativity of Jesus Christ with very particular devotion in the desire to conform himself to Jesus Christ in the extreme poverty of his birth and death.

Learn from this saint to love poverty and to live in detachment from all things. The more detached you will be from creatures, the more you will possess God and his holy love. What! Will you keep on saying, as Saint Augustine said before his conversion, They are mere trifles that hold me back and keep me from belonging entirely to God!

### 173.3  Third Point

Love for suffering possessed the heart of Saint Francis so much, as well as love for poverty, that considering how much Jesus Christ had suffered for him, he could not be content, after he had left the world, to spend a single moment of his life without suffering. This is why Jesus Christ suffering, who has always been the model of those who willingly suffer for the love of God, gave such delight to his heart that he could neither keep nor satisfy himself from the contemplation of Jesus in this state.

He fasted very rigorously almost all the year round. In winter he wore very little clothing, which made him suffer very much from the cold. He often spent his nights in prayer and took very severe disciplines. He practiced very harsh austerities, and he could say with Saint Paul that he was attached to the cross with Jesus Christ.[3] For this reason, one time when he was at prayer, a Seraphim imprinted on his body the sacred stigmata of the Passion. He received this favor only after he had devoted himself to continual mortification.

Imitate this great saint in the love he had for suffering, and see to it that either your mind or your body is always mortified. May this mortification be so effective in you that it reproduces on your body, so to speak, the sacred stigmata of Jesus Christ crucified.

———

Francis (ca. 1181–1226) was born at Assisi, in Umbria, son of a prosperous merchant, Peter Bernadone. Led by a deep religious experience, he abandoned a military life and the wealth of his family at the age of 28 or 29, embraced a spirit of utter simplicity for the love of Christ, and, with the approval of the Pope, led a small group of followers in a life of poverty and itinerant preaching. He also inspired Saint Clare to found a religious group, the Poor Clares. His followers soon became very numerous, and he was forced to write a Rule and to delegate the administration of the Brothers to others. He was saddened by the departure from his original simplicity necessitated by the different types of people attracted to his following. He was favored with the stigmata toward the end of his life, and he suffered also from ill health and near blindness. But his spirit of love and joy prevailed, as can be seen in the Canticle of the Sun, which he composed shortly before his death.

———

1. Mt 25:40         2. Mt 11:5         3. Gal 2:19

# October 6

## SAINT BRUNO

### 174.1 First Point

While in the world, Saint Bruno was a learned teacher who taught theology at the University of Paris and later in Reims, where he was also a canon. In the discharge of his duties in both these places, he won general approval by his wise conduct as well as by his profound learning. He also maintained a seriousness that earned him the respect of all.

Piety by itself is ordinarily useful only for the people who possess it, but when learning is united with piety, it makes for a great person very useful to the Church. Such was Saint Bruno, at once a burning and a shining light:[1] burning, because of his love for God, and shining, because of the excellent lessons he gave to others.

You must try to share the interior and exterior graces of this great saint. You will share his interior graces if you procure the piety appropriate to your state, by vigilance over self, by your good works, and by your prayers. You will share his external graces, as far as they are part of your duty, if you are dedicated to knowing thoroughly the Christian doctrine that you have to teach to your students and if you work to inspire them with piety through your sound teaching. Be diligent, then, to acquire both of these graces.

### 174.2 Second Point

Saint Bruno was not satisfied with the piety he had acquired in the clerical state, solid though it was. Because grace was urging him on to something more perfect still, he engaged six other people with whom he associated to withdraw from the world with him. Together they went to live in a wild desert spot, where they led an angelic life.

In the peace of solitude, unknown to the world and thinking only of their sins and of the means to live a holy life, people find God and strive to please him. On the one hand, there is nothing to distract them from God, and, on the other hand, there is nothing that does not encourage them to do all they can to please him. They are indifferent toward everything that concerns this life; they are no longer preoccupied about their bodies or seeking after all the comforts of life, for they have quit the world to get rid of all that.

Such was the practice of Saint Bruno and his associates, who were able to say, with Saint Jerome, that cities are as disagreeable to them as a prison and that solitude is for them a paradise.

You have quit the world as much as Saint Bruno did, although you are not in as profound and severe a solitude. But have you truly renounced the world? Do you no longer think of it or of your relatives? Are you truly disgusted with the world, because of the type of life you led there and the poor service you gave God? You must without doubt consider that you are blessed to have left it.

### 174.3 Third Point

Saint Bruno and his associates, having settled down in their desert, which is now called the Grande Chartreuse, together and by common consent chose three very sure means to go to God: seclusion for the rest of their life, almost continual prayer, and mortification in everything. United, they used these means for the rest of their life in order to labor effectively at their sanctification.

What usually leads religious astray is the frequent contact they have with the world, because this withdraws them from the union they ought to have with God. God and the world, the Spirit of God and the spirit of the world, cannot exist together,[2] as Jesus Christ says in the holy Gospel. This is why, he adds, when we have the one, we cease to have the other.

Take, then, your steps in this matter, and do not reattach your affection to what you have quit.

Prayer draws down the grace of God and keeps temptation away; it is also by prayer that God becomes our strength against the devil. You need to use all these means to be strengthened in your state, because left to yourself, you are nothing but weakness. So take care not to neglect prayer, which is so necessary to maintain you in piety and to grow in it.

Mortification subdues the body and makes it less susceptible to temptation. You must, then, use it every day as a shield against the devil. If you cannot practice these three things as constantly as Saint Bruno did, do so at least with as much fidelity and fervor.

---

Bruno (ca. 1035–1101) was born in Cologne and studied in Reims, becoming successively a canon of each cathedral. His desire for solitude led him to found a monastery, near Grenoble, in the Carthusian mountains, which became the famous Grande Chartreuse. Called to Rome by the Pope, he eventually was allowed to retire to solitude again. He founded another Carthusian monastery, in Calabria, southern Italy, where he died.

---

1. Jn 5:35          2. Mt 6:24

# October 9

## SAINT DENIS

### 175.1 First Point

When Saint Paul visited Athens, that famous city in Greece, he converted a great number of people there, among whom was Saint Denis,[1] one of the judges in that city, who was illustrious by his birth and very enlightened in matters of human learning. It is even said of him that he knew, because of the extraordinary eclipse that appeared when our Lord was suffering on Calvary, that this event happened, because the God of nature was dying.

So, when Saint Paul came and preached to them about a God unknown to them,[2] Saint Denis concluded that this must be the one whose coming and death nature had proclaimed with visible signs. Once Saint Paul made known to him who this God is and that he alone deserves homage, because, as he said, this is the One who made the whole world and everything that is in it; he is the Lord of heaven and earth and has made the human race, so that people may search for him and try to find him, and this same God is not far from them, for in him they have life, movement, and being,[3] Saint Denis promptly believed in this God and renounced the worship of the false gods.

How admirable was the conversion of this great saint, who served the Church very well both by his sublime writings and by preaching the Gospel. If Saint Paul had converted no one but Saint Denis, he would without doubt have rendered a great benefit to the Church. So it is that God, as he did in the case of Saint Denis and others, makes use of their natural intelligence and what they acquire through human learning to bring them to him.

### 175.2 Second Point

This saint, once converted, was so faithful to grace that in a short time he was able to instruct others. He, therefore, devoted himself to preach the holy Gospel and traveled to France, where he became bishop of the principal city of the kingdom and there preached with such apostolic zeal that a great number of the inhabitants renounced their false gods and believed in Jesus Christ.

How happy we ought to consider ourselves to have received through Saint Denis the beginning of the true faith and our knowledge of the God whom we must adore! What honor we must pay this saint, especially today when the Church celebrates his feast! What gratitude must we show him for having procured for us so great a blessing!

Yet it would be of little use to be enlightened by the light of faith if we did not live according to the Christian spirit and if we did not observe the maxims of the holy Gospel. The main purpose of faith is to lead us to practice what we believe. This made Saint James say that faith is dead which is not accompanied by good works. You believe, he adds, that there is one God; you do well; the devils also believe this, but we are justified by our works, not by faith alone.[4]

Be convinced that the main conversion is that of the heart and that without it the conversion of the mind is quite sterile. This is why if you strive to strengthen your faith, let it be in order to increase your piety.

### 175.3 Third Point

The reward given to apostolic people in this life is to be persecuted and to die in the defense and promotion of the faith they have proclaimed. The disciple, says our Lord, is not greater than his master, nor is the Apostle greater than the one who sent him.[5] If they have persecuted me, he adds, they will also persecute you.[6] This is what happened to Saint Denis after he had spent a long time preaching the Gospel. The devils who made themselves adored in the different idols of the false gods endured impatiently the numerous and illustrious conversions made by this apostolic man. He was arrested, cruelly flogged, and then exposed to wild beasts, which, out of respect for his sanctity, would not touch him. Finally, he was condemned to be beheaded.

Such was the end of all the labors of Saint Denis and the consequence of all he had done to procure in this kingdom the establishment of religion and the true worship of God. Because this was also the end and the consummation of the life of our Lord Jesus Christ and of all he did on earth for our salvation, it was very fitting that this saint be treated like his Master and die as he did in a cruel death. This saint was glad to shed his blood and to give witness to Jesus Christ by his fidelity in his service and in the ministry God had entrusted to him.

Like Saint Denis, you are called to announce the truths of the holy Gospel. Carry out this ministry well, and take care that those whom you guide are well instructed in the mysteries of our holy religion. After spending your life in the performance of such a holy work, do not expect to receive any other recompense than to suffer and to die as Jesus Christ did in sorrow.

In this meditation Denis (martyred around 260), bishop of Paris, has been confused with Dionysius the Areopagite in the Acts of the Apostles (17:34), a common confusion until about the nineteenth century. According to Saint Gregory of Tours, Denis, bishop of Paris, was sent to France by the Pope and martyred at a spot that was later named for him, Saint-Denis, near Paris. The Abbey of Saint-Denis became the burial place of the French kings. De La Salle opened a school in Saint-Denis in 1708; a community of Brothers is still there today.

1. Acts 17:34
2. Acts 17:23
3. Acts 17:24; 27–28
4. Jas 2:17, 19–24
5. Jn 13:16
6. Jn 15:20

# October 10

## SAINT FRANCIS BORGIA

### 176.1 First Point

Nothing is more admirable than the humility of Saint Francis Borgia. In the world he had been a great lord in the court of the Spanish king. Then, having withdrawn from the world and having entered the Company of Jesus, he desired, to the extent he had been honored in the world, to be despised now that he had renounced the world. He considered himself and on all occasions treated himself as the least and most criminal of all people. This he showed particularly on one occasion when he had to sleep next to a priest of the Company, who all night long spit in his face. He did not complain but wiped his face each time with his handkerchief. Next morning, when this priest apologized for what had happened, Saint Francis told him that he could not have spit on a dirtier place.

To act and to speak this way is to know how to join patience with humility and to carry both to the summit of perfection. This saint often said that he found no spot more appropriate for him than to place himself at the feet of Judas, but when he found Jesus Christ already there on the day of the Last Supper, he no longer knew where to place himself in order to be as low, he said, as he deserved.

See how much this saint humbled himself and to what extent he despised himself. You had, perhaps, a quite lowly place in the world, and yet do you not fear and avoid experiences of contempt more than this saint desired, sought, and ardently loved them? At least be strong enough to accept and to bear them willingly when you encounter some occasion of being humbled.

### 176.2 Second Point

In the world this saint had been immensely wealthy, yet he made himself poor, very poor, for the love of God once he had quit the world. He kept nothing of all his wealth on quitting the world, and after he became a religious, he never handled gold or silver coins, so that he entirely forgot their value. His bed, his clothes, his way of life, and his room were all characterized by great poverty.

This saint took pleasure in practicing this virtue; it seemed that the more he felt the rigors of poverty, the happier he was, because he knew that Jesus Christ had given us the example of this virtue and had practiced it to the highest degree from his birth. For this reason, he felt that it was only right that those who wish to join Jesus most closely and who had the honor of belonging to his Company ought to share in a perfect manner the love and practice he had for this virtue, which he desired to be the inseparable companion of his disciples.

This was also what this saint required of all the members of his Company when he was their General. He even wished that all the houses of professed members who belonged to the Company would have no other foundation than poverty.

Is this the sort of foundation on which you desire your community to be built? It is a sure and unfailing foundation for those whose faith is true and who are interiorly inspired by the Spirit of our Lord. You cannot do better than to base your fortune on this foundation; it is the one that Jesus Christ thought to be most solid and on which the holy Apostles began to build the edifice of the Church.

### 176.3 Third Point

What greatly helped this saint to give himself entirely to God is that even while he was still in the world, he loved to mortify himself so much that when he was obliged to appear at court functions or to attend some entertainment, he wore a hair shirt underneath his clothes in order to be able to control himself in the dangerous occasions so frequently found in such assemblies. When he went on a journey, the baggage he guarded most preciously was the one containing his instruments of penance, such as his different hair shirts and his disciplines.

He liked everything that made him uncomfortable, and he was glad to be baked by the heat of the sun in summer and chilled by the cold in winter. The most disagreeable seasons were the most pleasing to him. When he suffered great sorrows, he was joyful, and he showed no one more gratitude than the ones who persecuted him, because he considered himself very blessed[1] *in persecution,* according to the spirit of the Gospel. He even claimed that he would be very sorry at the hour of his death if he had spent a single day without suffering for the love of Jesus Christ.

We are truly Christian only insofar as we are like our Savior, and it is a love for suffering and mortification that makes us resemble him. Learn, like this saint, to spend no day without mortification through a spirit of religion in order to give witness to the one you profess.

―――――

Francis Borgia (1510–1572) was born in Gandia, Spain, of a noble, wealthy family. He married at age 19 and had eight children. He became Duke of Gandia when his father died in 1543. Gradually, he was attracted to the Jesuits, and after his wife died in 1546, he asked Saint Ignatius to accept him into the new order and joined with the Emperor's permission in 1551. He became the third General Superior of the order, in 1565. He was canonized in 1671, when De La Salle was 20 years old. The feast is not celebrated in the current liturgical calendar.

―――――

1. Mt 5:11

# October 15

## SAINT TERESA OF ÁVILA

### 177.1  First Point

Saint Teresa was so favored by grace from her childhood that at the age of seven, upon reading the lives of the holy martyrs, she felt herself inspired to suffer martyrdom for the faith. With one of her brothers, she even set out for Africa to find there among the Moors the chance to shed her blood. When they were brought back by one of their uncles, she spent her time with this brother building little hermitages in order to seclude themselves there and to pray to God.

How happy it is to begin to serve God from early life! When piety has been taken in with the infant's milk, it takes hold of the heart to such an extent that it is almost impossible to lose it entirely. It sometimes can fade away, as it did in Saint Teresa for a time, but the fundamentals always remain in the soul and revive, little by little, to produce new action, as happened in the case of Saint Teresa. In her this spirit grew day by day until the last breath of the saint's life.

This example teaches us how advantageous it is to inspire children with piety and to procure it for them, especially by making them read good books capable of making good impressions on their minds. Because God has called you to give children a Christian education, for this purpose use the same means that God employed for Saint Teresa to prepare her early with his graces.

### 177.2 Second Point

For the rest of her life, this saint continued to have a great desire to suffer, and she was not content with mere desires but wanted to put them into effect, for she practiced great austerities and almost continual penances. On his side, God supported her in the ardent love she had for suffering. For many years he tested her with very painful illnesses that gave her no respite, with very violent temptations, and with dryness in prayer very difficult to endure. Thus this saint experienced not only the tenderness but also the rigors with which God sometimes treats a soul whom he loves and whom he desires to favor with his most extraordinary and very special graces.

He also did some great things for this saint, for after difficult and long years of dryness, she received a highly elevated gift of prayer, which she describes in clear detail in her writings, which have been honored by the approbation of important people and are considered among the faithful as heavenly doctrine. God gave her this grace also, that one day while she was in prayer, a Seraph pierced her heart with a flaming arrow; as a result, for the rest of her life, she felt in her heart an ardor that kept her always attentive to God.

This is how God rewards souls who give themselves perfectly to him and who suffer much for him. If you wish to be honored with the graces that he grants only to his well beloved, be glad when he afflicts you and tries you, because, as the Wise Man says, God chastises the children whom he loves tenderly.[1]

### 177.3 Third Point

The main occupation of Saint Teresa during her life after she had consecrated herself to God was continual and sublime contemplation, in which she had no other purpose than to be closely united with Jesus Christ, her Spouse. In the midst of her greatest dryness, she was profoundly immersed in God and totally abandoned to him, in spite of the interior darkness she experienced. The more God caused her to suffer, the more she had recourse to him, because she found everything in him, no matter how hidden he was to her. Faith alone guided her in this state and provided her with light. Also, because she found everything in God, she had the happiness of finding God in everything. Wherever and in whatever condition she might be, God was her guide.

Oh, how fortunate this saint was to enjoy the presence of God! This caused her to perform all her actions in view of God, and it led her to make a vow to do whatever she knew was most pleasing to God. This is the result of frequent and fervent prayer, to enjoy God by anticipation as far as living faith can procure this happiness in this world.

If you love God, prayer will be the food of your soul, and God will enter within you and will have you eat at his table,[2] as Saint John says in the Apocalypse. You will then have the advantage of having God present in your actions and of having no other purpose than to please him. You will even have a constant hunger for him,[3] as the Wise Man says, for, according to the expression of the Royal Prophet, you will not be filled until you enjoy his glory in heaven.[4] By living a holy life, be worthy of such grace and of possessing such happiness.

---

Teresa (1515–1582) was born near Ávila, Spain, partly of Jewish descent, and grew up in a large, upper-middle-class family. When her mother died in 1528, she became a boarder in a convent school in Ávila and in 1536 entered the Carmelites there. After some years of mediocre living in the convent, she was favored with a spiritual conversion and received excellent guidance from her uncle and from Dominican and Jesuit priests. In 1562 she founded the first of her reformed convents, Saint Joseph at Ávila. She spent the next 20 years of her life in this reform movement, which included the Carmelite Friars with the help of Saint John of the Cross. Her spiritual writings, especially *The Interior Castle*, and her autobiography won for her the title of Doctor of the Church in 1970.

---

1. Prv 3:12        3. Sir 24:21        4. Ps 17:15
2. Rev 3:20

# October 18

## SAINT LUKE, EVANGELIST

### 178.1 First Point

Saint Luke was the faithful companion of the Apostles of Jesus Christ. From them he learned the mysteries of the Christian religion and the holy Gospel,[1] as he declares. How fortunate it is to draw truth from its source! This is the way to possess it well and to practice it perfectly. This is also what made Saint Luke so firm in his faith, for he found in the holy Apostles and in their teaching, which he studied with the greatest attention,[2] all that was most solid in his piety. He made his faith, his actions, and his way of life be ruled by what they had taught him.

As for his faith, it was so enlightened that he had the happiness of knowing the purest truths of the holy Gospel and of being filled with the holiest maxims found there.

As for his actions, they were so wise that they made him known and loved by everyone.

As for his way of life, it was governed so well that it served as a model for the Christians of his time.

In these three ways, you ought to be imitators of this saint. Your faith must be a light that guides you in all things and a shining beacon to lead to heaven those you instruct.

Your conduct must be so wise in their regard, as it is for you, that your students will respect it, because they will see that it is far above ordinary human behavior and free from the passions that destroy, or at least diminish, the respect due to those who are responsible for leading others.

Finally, your way of life must be a model for them, because they ought to find in you the virtues they are to practice.

### 178.2 Second Point

This saint had a very special friendship with Saint Paul, which is why in several of his epistles, Saint Paul sends to his correspondents and to others the greetings of Saint Luke as well as his own. He calls Saint Luke his very dear friend,[3] whom he has also chosen to be the companion of his travels. That was a great benefit to Saint Luke, because in this way he shared in the ardent zeal of this holy Apostle, in the many conversions he made, and in all the work he did in the long and frequent journeys he undertook to work to establish the Church.

Saint Paul had a great love for suffering and took pleasure in it; he also communicated to Saint Luke a love for mortification, which he had so much at heart that the Church writes of him that he always bore in his body the mortification of Jesus Christ. This was something he had learned from Saint Paul, who said of himself that he bore on his body the stigmata, that is, the marks of the wounds of Jesus Christ.[4]

You will establish between Saint Paul and you a close friendship, as Saint Luke did, if you often read his epistles, select and study the principal maxims contained in them, meditate on them attentively, and make it your glory to practice them. Make it a point every day to practice one of them in particular.

### 178.3 Third Point

It was Saint Luke's privilege to write the holy Gospel and in this way to be one of the secretaries of Jesus Christ. He was also the historian of the foundation of the true religion by writing the book of the Acts, which contains an account of the wonderful things accomplished by the holy Apostles in Judea after the death of Jesus Christ, before they spread out to preach the Gospel throughout the world.[5] He describes especially the principal deeds and journeys of Saint Paul.

It could be that Saint Luke did not often proclaim the holy Gospel in person, and he might not have converted a great many people by his preaching, but how many did he not bring to embrace our religion through his writings! This expression from his Gospel, Sell all you have, and give it to the poor,[6] was all that Saint Anthony needed to quit the world and all his wealth and to withdraw into the desert for the rest of his life.

Spoken words pass on and touch hearts only once and momentarily, but the good done by written words, which last forever, like those Saint Luke composed, produces results unendingly and is able century after century, even to the end of the world, to convert a great number of souls, provided they are well disposed to hear the word of God expressed therein.

Listen with docility to the word of God. Read it every day with attention, and Saint Luke will be for you an Apostle of Jesus Christ and a preacher of the holy Gospel.

---

The Evangelist Luke was probably born at Antioch, in Syria, of Greek, not Jewish, parents. As author of the Gospel bearing his name and the Acts of the Apostles, he is the largest single contributor to the New Testament. We learn about him from passages in the Acts, together with a few references to him in Paul's epistles. From the style and content of his writings, we can deduce that he was well educated and knowledgeable in geography, the administration of the empire, and medical matters and that he was concerned about historical accuracy, care for the poor, and sensitivity toward women. Moreover, he was probably familiar with the mother of Jesus or at least greatly interested in all that concerned her.

---

1. cf Lk 1:2   3. Col 4:14; Phlm 24   5. Mt 28:19
2. Lk 1:3      4. Gal 6:17            6. Lk 18:22

# October 19

## SAINT PETER OF ALCANTARA

### 179.1 First Point

When still quite young, Saint Peter of Alcantara entered the Order of Saint Francis and set about at once to imitate the Founder in the love he had for poverty. For this reason he customarily called poverty the pearl of the Gospel and caused it to flourish in the monasteries that he reformed.

The more we are poor, the more we will have the spirit of Jesus Christ, who made it his glory to be poor throughout his life and who established his religion on the foundation of this virtue. The more despoiled we are of the possessions of this world and the more we renounce the comforts of life, which are the most natural reasons why people desire and love riches, the more we will share in the possession of grace and the more pleasing we will be to God. The heart must be empty of these material creatures if we wish God to take full possession of it, as Jesus Christ said to the young man who asked him the way to be perfect.[1] This is why apostolic people who labored effectively for the salvation of souls, as this saint did, tried not only to have no attachment to possessions but even to regard them as rubbish,[2] according to Saint Paul's expression.

This is also what you need to do to be worthy of your work. Poverty ought to be so dear to you that you practice it in all things, with the result that as you hold on to nothing but God, you find in God what cannot be found in creatures. In this way you will be able to receive from God the fullness of grace, both for you and for others, especially the love of the poor and the zeal you need to bring them completely to God.

### 179.2 Second Point

It is impossible to appreciate how austerely this saint lived. For some twenty years, he wore an undergarment made of tin. He never covered his head or his feet, and in the coldest winter he never came near the fire. His cell was so small that he could neither stand erect nor lie at full length in it. He slept so little that he had almost overcome the need for sleep. By means of all these most extraordinary austerities, he became so independent of the needs of his body that it seemed he no longer had one or that it no longer belonged to him.

The passions cannot be mastered or the flesh prevented from revolting unless fasting and mortification are used to bring them into subjection. This is the way that all the saints lived in order to obtain this result; you will not find any other way than this, joined to prayer. This is what Jesus Christ prescribes for us in the holy Gospel.[3]

It is quite right that the body be submissive to the spirit, but if we wish it to be so, we must take the sure means to achieve this result. Take those of fasting and prayer, and if this saint cannot be your model in all that he did to mortify his body, imitate him at least in his recollection, which was so great that he never looked at the ceiling of the places where he was and did not know any of his religious except by the sound of their voices.

### 179.3 Third Point

This saint had a marvelous gift of prayer and spent a great deal of time in this exercise. His recollection at prayer was ordinarily so great that it obtained for him an almost continual awareness of God.

He took such delight in prayer that he had an extreme dislike for sleep, because, as he said, it was the only thing that could separate him from God's presence, something that death cannot do, because it gives us the living, effective, and eternal presence of God. This saint, considering that prayer procures this happiness, used to say that a half hour of prayer ought to be regarded as only a preparation for making it well.

Try to make interior prayer well in the same way this saint did, by the practice of interior recollection. If you persevere in it, recollection will make the practice of the presence of God easy. There is nothing you must or can procure with more care, for it is happiness anticipated in this life. It is also of great use to you in your work, because this work concerns God and aims at winning souls for him. It is, therefore, a matter of great consequence not to lose sight of God in your work. Be as faithful to this as you possibly can.

Peter of Alcantara (1499–1562) was born in the city of Spain that is part of his name. His father was a lawyer and the governor of Alcantara. At the age of 16, Peter entered a very strict house of the Observant Franciscans at Manjaretes and was ordained in 1524. Shortly thereafter, he began a series of reform efforts that became a separate Alcantarine Franciscan group, until 1897, when Leo XIII joined them to the Observants again. He also helped Saint Teresa of Ávila in her reform. He was canonized in 1669, another of the saints recognized in De La Salle's lifetime. His feast is not in the current liturgical calendar.

1. Mt 19:21        2. Phil 3:8        3. Mk 9:29

# October 21

## SAINT HILARION

### 180.1 First Point

Saint Hilarion was competent in the humanities and in literature, thanks to the keenness of his mind, but he made himself much more admirable by the purity of his life and especially by his great piety. The example of Saint Anthony, who was then famous throughout the desert, did much to help him acquire this spirit. The reputation won by this great Father of the desert induced Saint Hilarion to go out to find him. Once near him, he observed with great care Saint Anthony's way of life and his great abstinence, which no infirmity could make him quit. He also noted the saint's diligent application to prayer, his humility in dealing with his Brothers, his strictness joined to gentleness when he corrected them, and the zeal he showed for their sanctification. Later on, Saint Hilarion dedicated himself with all conceivable fervor to practice all the virtues he had observed in Saint Anthony.

Oh, what power and efficacy does example have to convert souls and to lead them to make progress in virtue! This saint lived a life of great perfection; the example of Saint Anthony led him to it.

It is mainly in communities that good example is most notable and has the most power and efficacy. All those who live there together encourage one another to practice what is most holy and most perfect in the Gospel maxims, because when someone does something good, others feel ashamed not to do it. Moreover, according to an axiom of the philosophers, both the practice and the love of what is right are easily communicated in community to those who have a little goodwill to do what is right.

Let everyone, therefore, be encouraged and motivated by the example of the more fervent among your Brothers and by those who possess most fully the spirit of your Institute.

### 180.2  Second Point

Another thing that engaged Saint Hilarion to give himself entirely to God is the fact that he had impressed so deeply on his mind the saying of our Lord in the holy Gospel, Whoever does not renounce all that he possesses cannot be my disciple,[1] that when his parents died—he was still only 15 years old—he gave away all that he had and withdrew into solitude.

Oh, how powerful the word of God is to touch hearts! It is, says Saint Paul, living and effective; it pierces the heart better than a two-edged sword; it enters and penetrates even to the secrets of the soul.[2]

How happy you would be if this divine word penetrated so deeply into your heart that you would no longer be attached to any creature! Yet you will not be worthy of your ministry except insofar as you have this disposition. This is the first thing God requires of those who wish to be his disciples. Nothing contributes more to this than solitude. Because you cannot seek anything but God there, your first thought is to empty your heart of all created things in order to be able to fill it entirely with God.

Nor is anything more consoling and more useful than to be devoted to God in your youth, because then you have the advantage of being able to establish solid piety, which becomes like second nature. If you have not had this advantage in your youth, seek through interior and continual application to your exercises to have it so deep in you that it becomes unalterable.

### 180.3  Third Point

This saint practiced most extraordinary penance and abstinence. He usually ate almost nothing. Fifteen figs a day made up all his nourishment; sometimes it was dry bread and vegetables soaked in cold water. He broke his fast only after sunset. To the day he died, he took his rest on hard ground and on a few reeds. This penitential life, combined with prayer and his gift of miracles, won him the esteem and admiration of all who lived in the area. As a result, a great many people came to him to receive encouragement. This is how those who have overcome their bodies and their passions become masters of the

elements and of all the world. This saint had made himself so independent of all creation that it seemed only proper for God to share
with him his power over his creatures to dispose of them as he
pleased.

You can perform several miracles in regard to you and your
work: in your own regard, by an entire fidelity to grace, not letting
any movement of grace go by without corresponding with it; in regard to your work, by touching the hearts of the wayward children
entrusted to your care, by making them docile and faithful to the
maxims of the holy Gospel and to their practice, and by teaching
them to be pious and recollected in church and during prayers and
devoted to the performance of their duty in school and at home. Such
are the miracles that God gives you the power to perform and that he
asks of you.

———

Hilarion (fourth century) is known to us from the biography of him
written by Saint Jerome, who learned about him from Saint Epiphanius of Salamis, who knew Hilarion personally. Hilarion was born in
Palestine and studied in Alexandria, becoming a Christian there at the
age of 15. His life was a series of moves from one place to another in
search of solitude, which was constantly thwarted by his reputation
for miracles. He eventually found peace in Cyprus, where he died at
the age of 80.

———

1. Lk 14:33            2. Heb 4:12

# October 28

## SAINTS SIMON AND JUDE,
## APOSTLES

### 182.1[1] First Point
Saint Simon and Saint Jude, seeing the miracles performed by
Jesus Christ, despised and quit the world in order to follow him and
to be numbered among his disciples. How happy you are to have the
same destiny and the advantage of having left the world! You ought to
value this grace as one of the greatest you have received in your
whole life.

Thank God for it every day, and in order to live according to the spirit of your vocation, despise the world, consider it as the enemy of Jesus Christ, and be always opposed to it and to all its maxims. Have a horror of frequenting it, and do not have communication with people who live in it, except insofar as necessity obliges you to do so. This is the way to protect against all its snares and all the dangers you meet there and to preserve the spirit of your vocation. By communicating with the world, we adopt its spirit, which is contrary to that of Jesus Christ. Because the two cannot exist together in a soul, if we fill ourselves with the spirit of the world, we necessarily lose that of Jesus Christ.

Today, ask God earnestly through the intercession of the two holy Apostles whose feast the Church is celebrating to inspire you always with more and more separation from the corrupt world and with an attraction to the holy way of the life of Jesus Christ.

### 182.2 Second Point

These holy Apostles devoted themselves to preaching the Gospel, and they converted many souls to God. The devil and the world, unable to tolerate their apostolic labors and the good they were doing to establish the Gospel, stirred up such cruel persecutions against them that they were finally put to death. For these saints, by preaching the Gospel, were destroying the kingdom of the devil and fighting against the maxims of the world.

If you carry out your ministry faithfully and work effectively and successfully for the salvation of the souls entrusted to you, persecution from the devil or from the world will always be your portion. If you hate the world and oppose its practices and maxims, be assured that it will also hate you and declare open warfare against you.[2]

Prepare to sustain this. By prayer more than by any other means, you will be able to prepare for this combat, because it belongs to God to fight in you and for you against the devil and the world. It can only be by his special help that you will overcome them both. Far from growing sad over this, rejoice because you are at war with them. When you are displeasing to men[3] will be a sign that you are pleasing to Jesus Christ, for the world can love only those who love it and have the same practices that it has.[4]

### 182.3 Third Point

These two holy Apostles had such an ardent zeal for the establishment and the progress of the Christian religion that nothing was able to stop them. All the threats that could be uttered against them and all the tortures they were made to endure could not prevent them from proclaiming Jesus Christ and making him known.

You will never do anything that can promote your own salvation and that of your neighbor without the world's opposing it. Suffer these contradictions with courage; remain steadfast in the practice of what is right, in spite of all the obstacles you may encounter. God will bless all you do with zeal for love of him, and you will be victorious over those who will oppose what you are doing for God. Do not bother to please those whom Jesus Christ could not please and who are his declared enemies. Often say with Saint Paul, If I were pleasing men, I would not be worthy to be a servant of Jesus Christ.[5]

However, it is not enough for you to be true servants of Jesus Christ; you are further obliged to make him known and adored by the children whom you instruct. The care you must have for your own perfection ought to lead you to do this.

---

Simon is unknown except for the mention of him as one of the 12 Apostles. He was called the Zealot in Luke 6:15 by Christ and in Acts 1:13, which could mean only that he was a man of zeal for the Law rather than a member of the Zealot party, as stated in Mark (3:18). There are many apocryphal stories about him, including his martyrdom in Persia with Jude. Jude cannot be positively identified as the author of the Epistle that bears this name nor as the brother of James, despite the translation of the first verse of this epistle. What is certain is that he was one of the Apostles, sometimes called Thaddeus (which might mean deep-chested). Beyond that, none of the details of his life and death, as in the case of Simon, is more than apocryphal.

---

1. Number 181, one of the six meditations in the *Additions,* is found at the end both of the original edition and of this edition.
2. Jn 15:18–19
3. Gal 1:10
4. Jn 15:19
5. Gal 1:10

# November 1

## ALL SAINTS

### 183.1 First Point

The happiness of the saints is something so great and so far above human thoughts that Saint Paul says, when he speaks of it, Eye has not seen; ear has not heard, nor has the heart of man ever conceived what God has prepared for those who love him.[1] It is, he says, the hidden wisdom of God, which he has prepared before all ages for our glory.[2] This eternal wisdom, which is filled with glory and majesty and constitutes all the glory and happiness of the saints, is hidden from us in this life and is known to us only through faith. It is just that only in heaven will we see God unveiled and entirely revealed. We know, says Saint John, that when Jesus appears, we will be like him, because we will see him as he is.[3]

What a joy for the saints to be made like God through participation in his nature and in his divine perfections![4] There God is truly in the saints by a holy sharing in his greatness, and the saints are in God, because their entire being is penetrated by God, so that they can think of and love only God.

Today, pay homage to the saints, but let it be in God, because it is in him that you find them all. Admire how great is the happiness they enjoy in heaven, how wonderful is the glory they receive, and beg them to obtain from God for you the grace to share in their glory after your death.

### 183.2 Second Point

No matter what hope you can have to share in the glory of the saints, it will have no effect unless you work to become a saint by using the same means that they used to achieve this. *They endured great combats*, says Saint Paul, in the various kinds of afflictions that suffered. They served as a spectacle to the world because of insults and ill-treatment. With joy they saw themselves despoiled of all their goods, knowing that they had more excellent goods that would never perish.[5] Elsewhere he says that they endured mockeries, scourgings, chains, and prisons; some were stoned; others, sawed in two; some were put to death by the sword; others wandered about garbed in sheepskins and goatskins, being abandoned, tormented, and persecuted; others, finally, of whom the world was not worthy, passed their life wandering in deserts and on mountains, living in dens and caves[6] of the earth. All these saints, tormented in various ways, were unwilling to rescue their present life but chose to find a better one in the resurrection.[7] This is how Saint Paul describes in admirable fashion the different means that the saints used to obtain the glory they now possess.

Because, then, Saint Paul adds, we are overwhelmed by a great cloud of witnesses who surround us, let us detach ourselves from everything that weighs us down and prevents us from raising ourselves to heaven. Let us run with patience in this race that is open before us[8] and that is the only way we will reach the happiness of the saints. For, adds the same Apostle, these are only the afflictions that produce the eternal weight of glory to which we are destined in the next life.[9]

Yearn, then, for sufferings every day, as did many of the saints, in the desire and the hope of being clothed with them one day with the immortality of heaven.

### 183.3 Third Point

What inspired the saints to suffer so much in this life in order to enjoy a blessed eternity afterward is the example of the Savior. They were convinced, as Saint Paul says, that they must always bear in their bodies the mortification of Jesus Christ, so that the life of Jesus might also appear in their mortal bodies, knowing that he who raised Jesus from the dead will also raise his elect with him and place them all in his presence.[10] Because of this confidence, continues Saint Paul, they preferred to be separated from their bodies in order to enjoy the presence of the Lord.[11]

This is why their whole ambition was to be pleasing to him, convinced that because all those whom God has predestined must in this life be conformable to the image of his Son[12] and take him as the model of their conduct, all also must appear before the tribunal of Jesus Christ, so that each one may receive what is due to the good or evil actions he performed while clothed in the body.[13] This is why, as long as the saints were in their bodies as in a tent, they sighed beneath its weight, because they desired that whatever was material in them might be absorbed in life.[14]

Take Jesus Christ as your model, then, and yearn as the saints did for the happiness that they now enjoy, considering, as Saint Paul says, not the visible things but the invisible, for the visible things are temporary, whereas the invisible ones are eternal.[15]

------

This feast was inaugurated when the Pantheon in Rome, which had originally been dedicated to all the pagan gods by the emperor Agrippa in 273 B.C., was consecrated to the worship of God in honor of our

Lady and all the Christian martyrs by Pope Boniface IV (608–615).
Pope Gregory IV (827–844) assigned the feast to November 1.

| | | |
|---|---|---|
| 1. 1 Cor 2:9 | 6. Heb 11:36–38 | 11. 2 Cor 5:8 |
| 2. 1 Cor 2:7 | 7. Heb 11:35 | 12. Rom 8:29 |
| 3. 1 Jn 3:2 | 8. Heb 12:1 | 13. 2 Cor 5:10 |
| 4. 2 Pt 1:4 | 9. 2 Cor 4:17 | 14. 2 Cor 5:4 |
| 5. Heb 10:32–34 | 10. 2 Cor 4:10–14 | 15. 2 Cor 4:18 |

# November 2

## COMMEMORATION OF THE SOULS
## IN PURGATORY

### 185.1[1] First Point

It is a holy and wholesome thought to pray for the dead that they
may be delivered from their sins.[2] This is what Judas says in the Second Book of Maccabees, chapter 12. This is, indeed, one of the best
and most holy instructions that can be given to us, because it leads us
to do what is most advantageous for the souls in purgatory. Because
they cannot help themselves and cannot secure any of the relief they
need to be delivered from their sufferings, they need to be assisted by
the prayers and good works of those who are still living.

What a painful condition it is for them to be detained in devouring flames because during this life they did not make up for some less
serious sins or for not having entirely expiated the sins that caused
them to lose sanctifying grace! This is why these holy souls, although
entirely submissive in this state to the will of God, urgently beg for
the prayers of the living, which can obtain for them, often quite easily, what is impossible for them, because God is unwilling to accept in
expiation for their sins whatever good they can do, for he gave them
enough time during life to satisfy for their sins.

Look with compassion on the state of these holy souls, who, although free from fear, yearn for their deliverance so that they will be
able quickly to enjoy God, which they await with hope in the infinite
goodness of God, assured that they will have the benefit of being delivered from their sufferings.

### 185.2  Second Point

There is for us an element of obligation to pray often to God for the suffering souls in purgatory. First, God has abandoned them to his divine justice for as long as he wills, according to the gravity of their sins and the little care they took in this world to do penance for them. God does not allow them after death any other means than the suffrages of the faithful who are still in this life, which they can apply to the holy souls by prayers, by fasting and other penances, by alms, by the holy Sacrifice of the Mass, or by any other works of satisfaction that there might be.

Second, we are united with these holy souls by an external union, because we are all members of the Church and of Jesus Christ.[3] We are also united with them in Jesus Christ through sanctifying grace, which we share with them. These two kinds of union ought to inspire us with sentiments of compassion for these suffering souls.

### 185.3  Third Point

But what makes particularly clear to us how much we are obliged to sympathize with the sufferings of these just souls in their afflictions and what ought most strongly to engage us to help them in all kinds of ways is the fact that the Church, our common Mother, overlooks nothing to inspire us with this zeal in favor of her suffering children, for whom she is full of tenderness.

We must consequently unite with her as her members to offer God our prayers and the holy sacrifice of the Mass, so that joined with her and all the faithful who are her members and who make up only one body with her,[4] we may easily obtain from God by this very intimate union and this abundance of prayers and suffrages the prompt deliverance of these suffering souls. They in their turn, once they are in heaven, will be able to secure for us many graces by their prayers, so that we too may procure this joy.

Today, then, take part in the spirit of the Church, and unite with her in all the prayers and sacrifices that she offers to God for the relief of the souls in purgatory. Implore for them the help of God with all possible fervor and earnestness in order to have the honor of being worthy members of the Church and cooperators with Jesus Christ[5] in the redemption of these captive souls.

------

This feast became part of the liturgy of the universal Church in the fourteenth century. Prior to that it was a long-standing practice of the Benedictines, begun during the tenth century at the Abbey of Cluny by

Saint Odilon. At one time it was a practice for every priest to say three Masses on this day.

---

1. Number 184, one of the six meditations in the *Additions,* is found at the end both of the original edition and of this edition.
2. 2 Mc 12:45–46
3. Eph 5:30
4. Rom 12:5
5. 2 Cor 6:1

# November 3

## SAINT MARCELLINUS, BISHOP OF PARIS

### 186.1 First Point

This saint's virtuous parents took great care of his education; consequently, because he was endowed with a good disposition, he soon acquired such piety that he was esteemed and honored by everyone. This also won him a high reputation.

What a great blessing it is to be brought up well, for in this way we acquire many virtues with great ease, because the tendencies of the young are easily guided, and they accept without great difficulty the impressions we seek to give them.

Consider, therefore, how important it is that you work as perfectly as you can to educate well all those who are under your guidance and to procure piety for them. This is the principal object and purpose of your work.

Be assured that you will succeed in this only if you are pleasing to God and that he will pour out on you and your work his abundant blessing only insofar as you make their education your principal concern.

The trouble you take to do this will in the end make your students docile and solidly submissive to their parents and those to whom their parents confide them, self-controlled and well-behaved in public, and pious in church and in all that refers to God, to holy things, and to religion.

### 186.2 Second Point

This saint was so humble, reserved, and serious that the bishop of Paris at the time admitted him into the ranks of the clergy on the sole consideration of the virtues that distinguished him. He was a source of edification and an example for all the other members of the clergy, even when he was just beginning his career as an ecclesiastic. Because all considered him their model, his bishop resolved to ordain him a priest, even though Saint Marcellinus, for his part, expressed reluctance; he considered himself unworthy of this honor and of the dignity of this sacred office.

You are in a work that by its ministry resembles that of priests more than it does any other work. Because it was the rare and extraordinary virtue of Saint Marcellinus that led to his being raised to that ministry, you, on entering your state, ought to bring and to preserve in the exercise of your ministry a piety that is more than ordinary. It must distinguish you from other people; otherwise, it will be difficult for you to carry out your ministry successfully. Because your vocation was not instituted except to procure the spirit of religion and of Christianity for those whom you instruct, it cannot achieve its purpose and enable those who are in this work to achieve their purpose unless beforehand they have worked seriously to sanctify themselves.

### 186.3 Third Point

When the bishop of Paris died, the holy life of Saint Marcellinus caused him to be chosen to replace him. In this exalted responsibility, so difficult to carry out well, he showed how great was his zeal for the salvation of souls. Besides using all the natural and supernatural talents God had given him to procure their sanctification, he did not cease to pray and keep watch to help the ones who needed conversion and to draw down on others the graces needed for them to be strong in the practice of good and to advance in virtue.

In some sense it can be said that each of you is a bishop, that is, the vigilant guardian of the flock that God has entrusted to you;[1] consequently, you are obliged to keep watch over all those who belong to it; as Saint Paul says, you have to give an account to God for their souls.[2] Do you sometimes reflect before God how fearful this account is? The soul of each one of those you guide is infinitely dear to God, and if any one of them is lost through your fault, God has said it, and he will do it: he will require from you soul for soul.[3]

You have two kinds of children to instruct: some are disorderly and inclined to evil; others are good or at least inclined to good. Pray continually for both, following the example of Saint Marcellinus, especially for the conversion of those who have evil inclinations. Work to preserve and strengthen the good ones in the practice of good; nevertheless, direct your care and your most fervent prayers to win over to God the hearts of those who are prone to evil.

---

Marcellinus (fifth century) was born in Paris and succeeded Prudentius as bishop of that city. His life was written by Fortunatus, bishop of Poitiers, and is evidently the basis for De La Salle's description of him. The part of Paris where he is buried is still called Saint-Marceau.

---

1. Acts 20:28          2. Heb 13:17          3. Dt 19:21; Ez 22:14

# November 4

## SAINT CHARLES BORROMEO

### 187.1  First Point

What was most special and most remarkable in Saint Charles was his perfect detachment from the goods of this earth. He made this quite clear while he was still very young, when he was given a rich abbey and his father wanted to appropriate the revenue. Saint Charles took the liberty of telling his father that this revenue did not belong to him but to the poor, and he took care that it was distributed to them.

He continued to act in this manner even after he became the proprietor of his estate. When he was bishop, he renounced the considerable revenues that his uncle, the Pope, had bestowed on him. He then sold all his possessions and gave the proceeds to the poor.[1]

But what is altogether extraordinary is that in a time of public emergency, during a pestilence and a famine, he even sold all his furniture and his own bed in order to assist the poor and the sick. He had nothing else left to help them, for he had given away everything he possessed and had kept nothing for his own use from the revenues of his archdiocese.

Detachment from riches and from the comforts of life is one of the first dispositions we must have to belong entirely to God and to work for the salvation of souls. This was also the first thing that Jesus Christ required of his holy Apostles and what they inspired in the first Christians.

If you wish, then, to be worthy to be employed in the salvation of souls, be detached from everything, and the grace of God will be given to you in abundance, not only for you but also for others. Say, as it is written in Genesis, Give me souls, and take all the rest for you.[2] In other words, dispose of all the rest as you please, because, except for your holy love and the salvation of souls, I am indifferent to all the rest.

### 187.2 Second Point

It is not enough to be detached to be able to work effectively for the Church and for the salvation of our neighbor. We must also stead-fastly apply ourselves to prayer and mortification. Saint Charles did so diligently, even though he was constantly preoccupied by the good of his diocese. He prayed twice a day without fail, and he was so absorbed in his prayer that when one of the disorderly religious whom he was trying to reform fired a musket at him while he was at prayer with his household, he was not in the least disturbed and continued to pray. He often grieved before God for the salvation of the people of his diocese and frequently even spent part of the night in prayer. If something important for the good of the Church arose, he prayed throughout the whole night.

Because this saint was well aware that prayer without mortification is often an illusion, he did not fail to join the one to the other. In his palace he lived like a poor man to whom alms had to be given, fasting nearly every day on bread and water and never eating meat, eggs, or fish. He wore a hair shirt and took the discipline. He often slept on straw or in a chair. He slept very little, because, as he said, a bishop who is responsible for souls must not be less vigilant than officers in the army.

Often reflect that you must be a man of prayer, because you must pray not only for you but also for those whom you have to guide and for the needs of their souls. For your prayer to be effective, you must join mortification to it.

### 187.3 Third Point

Saint Charles' zeal for the salvation of souls was incomparable; it is difficult to be able to express the lengths to which he carried it. Inconceivable as it may be, he wanted to be informed in writing every year about the conduct of every person in his diocese individually, so that he might on his part exercise all the vigilance and care possible to procure their salvation. He wanted the parish priests of his diocese to come to the assistance of the dying and to be present at their last hour, the moment when a soul has the greatest need for help.

But the zeal of Saint Charles stood out in a most surprising manner when the city of Milan was attacked by the plague. From the beginning he sacrificed himself to bring help to the victims of the epidemic. He administered the sacraments to them in spite of great fatigue and danger, constantly exposing himself to death during the whole time the pestilence lasted. On that occasion this saintly bishop showed how much contempt he felt for his own life when it was a matter of procuring the salvation of his neighbor.

Compare your zeal for the sanctification of your disciples with that of this great saint, for you ought to spend your entire life trying to make them become good Christians. Watch over them with as much attention to detail as Saint Charles did when he kept watch over all the members of his diocese.

---

Charles Borromeo (1538–1584) was born of a noble family at Arona, Italy. He earned a doctorate in canon law at Pavia in 1559 and forthwith was created a cardinal by his uncle, who had just become Pope Pius IV. He was made archbishop of Milan and Papal Secretary of State and worked strenuously for the conclusion of the Council of Trent between 1560 and 1564. After that he became the embodiment of the spirit and ideals of the Counter-Reformation inaugurated by Trent. He was strict in his efforts to reform the morals of his archdiocese but even more committed to his own spiritual life of sacrifice and prayer. He was canonized in 1610 by Pope Paul V.

---

1. Mt 19:21          2. Gn 14:21

# November 11

## SAINT MARTIN

### 189.1[1] First Point

While still quite young, Saint Martin became a soldier, and he remained one until he was 40, but he had even more care to enroll in the Christian militia than in that of the emperor. Although born of a pagan father, he had his name entered in the Church on the list of catechumens when he was only eleven years old. Afterward he devoted himself entirely to piety and to the service of God in such a way that he was admired for his virtue even among those who had already received the grace of Baptism.

He had especially such great tenderness for the poor that when he was still in the military and had come upon a naked man who begged him for something to cover himself, Saint Martin cut his own mantle in two and gave the beggar half. This led Jesus Christ to let him know that he acknowledged this gift as made to himself. He appeared to him the next night, wearing the half-mantle and saying, Martin, although he is only a catechumen, clothed me with this mantle.

You, enrolled in the army of Jesus Christ, are in his service and, as it were, on his payroll. Do you have the service of God as much at heart as Saint Martin did? Are you also as charitable toward the poor as he was, even though he was still only a catechumen? Every day you are with the poor, and you are commissioned by God to clothe them with Jesus Christ and with his Spirit. Have you been careful, before undertaking such a holy ministry, to be clothed with him[2] in order to communicate this grace to them? *For*, says Saint Paul, *no one knows who God is except the Spirit of God, and this Spirit of God*, he adds, penetrates everything, even the deepest and most hidden mysteries in God.[3]

Pray, therefore, to the Spirit of God to make known to you the gifts that God has given you,[4] as Saint Paul says, so that you may announce them to those whom you are commissioned to instruct, not with discourses that use human wisdom but with what the Spirit of God inspires in his ministers.[5]

### 189.2 Second Point

Having left the army, Saint Martin went to find Saint Hilary, bishop of Poitiers, and built a monastery near that city, where he withdrew with many religious. There he lived with them a very austere life in such great piety and separation from the world that it seemed they no longer had any contact with the world, except that some of them went out for the ordinary needs of life, and this as rarely as possible. In this seclusion Saint Martin gave himself entirely to God, devoted himself to prayer with much fervor, and acquired a great habit of remembering the presence of God.

In seclusion we learn to find God. There we come to enjoy God through the ease we have to practice prayer after we have severed all communication with the world. Also by these means, Saint Martin prepared to do great things, especially by filling himself with the Spirit of God and with zeal, which was necessary for him to labor as usefully as he did for the salvation of souls.

Because you need both these things, you also need seclusion and separation from the world, for neither of these things can be found in the world. The world, as Jesus Christ says, cannot receive the Spirit of God, because it does not know him[6] and because the maxims and practices that the Spirit of God inspires are entirely opposed to those of the world.

### 189.3 Third Point

The result that seclusion produced in Saint Martin was that God destined him, and the clergy and people of Tours chose him, to be their bishop. In this holy office, he exercised his zeal for the destruction of the worship of idols, which was still prevalent in France, whose kings had not yet become Christian. But because he knew that it was up to God to establish his religion and that people are only God's ministers to preach it and make it known, he devoted himself constantly to fasting and prayer without ever losing his attention to God.

This saint had a tireless vigilance for all the needs of his church, considering himself responsible before God to provide what was needed. He knew that a bishop must do two things: beg God for the salvation of souls and carry out God's commands in order to procure this salvation. For this reason, Saint Martin divided his time between these two things:

1. A great part of the time, he kept his hands lifted up to heaven to draw down the grace and blessing of God for the conversion of souls.

2. He devoted himself to this task with such zeal and diligence that even at the hour of his death, in the ardor he had for the salvation of souls, he told God that if he were still needed by his people, he would not refuse the work.

Let all your time, following the example of Saint Martin, be spent in these two things: asking God insistently for the salvation of those who are under your guidance and seeking and helping them use these means.

---

Martin (ca. 315–397) was born at Salaria, in Hungary, and became a catechumen at an early age, despite the fact that his father was a pagan. Conscripted in the Roman army, he became a Christian after a vision of Christ rewarding him for his generosity to a poor beggar needing warm clothing. He left the army after a miraculous victory over the barbarians in which, unarmed, he led the Romans. Coming under the guidance of Saint Hilary of Poitiers, he built a monastery near that town. Later he was chosen to be bishop of Tours. Sulpicius Severus (360–406) wrote a biography of Saint Martin, which has preserved the details of his life.

1. Number 188, one of the six meditations in the *Additions,* is found at the end both of the original edition and of this edition.
2. Rom 13:14
3. 1 Cor 2:10–11
4. 1 Cor 2:12
5. 1 Cor 2:4, 13
6. Jn 14:17

# November 19

## SAINT ELIZABETH OF HUNGARY

### 190.1  First Point

The piety of Saint Elizabeth was so great that from the age of five, she took no pleasure except to be in church or in her room in order to pray there to God. This led her to speak rarely, because she knew that it is easy to converse often with God when we talk rarely to people and that silence is one of the best means to avoid sin and to keep ourselves in fervor.

So that her children might belong entirely to God, she had the custom of taking them in her hands, as soon as they were born, to offer them to the Lord with fervent prayer. Although married, she got up every night for prayer. Early in the morning, she went to church, where, kneeling on the ground, she remained in prayer for a long time. By these practices this saint was a model of piety and virtue in her family and in her dominion. Also in this way *this saint showed by her good deeds,* as Saint Paul requires of women, the piety of which she had made profession.[1]

Following this saint's example, let us practice piety, for, says Saint Paul, *Piety is a great wealth, and it is useful for everything;* to it the good things of this life and those of the future life have been promised.[2] Act, then, to procure these benefits by using this means, which is very sure and without which you cannot succeed in possessing the true goods that alone ought to be the object and the goal of all your desires.

### 190.2  Second Point

This saint was also very mortified. Every day she took the discipline, even to blood, and when her own strength failed, she begged her attendants to give her the discipline and not to spare her at it.

When the king, her husband, was away, she wore a hair shirt continually. When she went to church, she knelt with both her bare knees on the ground, because she wanted mortification to accompany all her actions. In a spirit of mortification, she also took great pleasure serving lepers; the more their flesh was decomposed, the more she cherished them. In a spirit of penance, she also wore simple clothing made of very ordinary material.

There are many people who would like to have piety, and they often pray to God even with affection and fervor, but they have to have all their comforts. If they have something to suffer, right away they complain, and everyone must commiserate with them and become involved to search for some way to comfort them. How can such people desire so much to suffer nothing, seeing a queen love so firmly to mortify herself?

Withdrawn as you are from the world, you ought to consider mortification as an obligation for you. Let it serve as a seasoning for all that you do for God, and make a habit of practicing it. Be assured that to live without the spirit of penance and without mortification is not to live as a true Christian, much less as a religious.

### 190.3 Third Point

What makes the glory of Saint Elizabeth stand out the most is the great love she had for humiliations. Having founded hospitals, she served the poor patients herself. She dressed their sores and rendered them all kinds of service, even the most humiliating. This drew down on her the criticism of a great number of people who considered such actions unbecoming a person of her rank. But the desire she had for being humbled led her to pay little attention to these complaints.

The occasion when she showed the most how deeply she had at heart to be humiliated was after the death of her husband, the king, when she was driven out of her palace at ten o'clock at night with her three children and her maids. She found no place where she could spend the rest of the night and went to a stable. At midnight she went to the monastery of the Franciscans to have a *Te Deum* chanted to thank God for the disgrace that had happened to her. Later, she took up residence in a poor cottage that a priest offered to her in charity. There she worked at spinning to earn what was needed to live and to feed her children. Was this not great patience for a queen?

Try to imitate her, and when occasions of humiliation happen to you, receive them as sent by God and as one of the greatest honors and main advantages that you can have in this world. In this way no matter what happens to you, you will always be satisfied.

Elizabeth of Hungary (1207–1231), the daughter of King Andrew II of Hungary, was married at the age of 13 to the saintly Louis of Thuringia, Germany, for whom she bore a son and two daughters. As queen she combined great solicitude for the poor and an austere life for herself. When her husband was killed in Sicily on his way to a crusade, her brother-in-law, Henry, usurped the throne and expelled her. Eventually, she was restored as queen, and her son, Herman, succeeded to the crown. She, however, continued her life of prayer and poverty, dying at the age of 24. The feast is now celebrated on November 17.

---

1. 1 Tim 2:10    2. 1 Tim 4:8

# November 21

## THE PRESENTATION
## OF THE MOST BLESSED VIRGIN

### 191.1 First Point

It is not without reason that holy Church has made a great feast of the Presentation of the Most Blessed Virgin, for it was on this day that she consecrated herself to God to be entirely devoted to him for her whole life. She did this not only to separate herself from the corruption of the world but also to avoid all occasions for her mind to be taken up with vain thoughts of the world and to keep her heart from placing its affections on created things, for her heart had been created only to love God and to give itself totally to him. For this purpose, it is believed on the testimony of a pious and ancient author, inspired not only by grace but also by her understanding, although she was still quite young, she made a vow of perpetual chastity, so that, as Saint John Damascene says, with her body totally free from all the pleasures of this life, she could preserve her soul in great purity.

By withdrawing from the world, you are consecrated to God to live in this Community with a complete detachment from everything in the world that is able to satisfy your senses. To settle down in this Community, you ought to consider the day you made this move as the one on which your happiness on earth began, to be completed one day in heaven. But it was not for that day alone that you ought to have consecrated yourself to God, for you made a consecration of your soul on that occasion. Because your soul will live forever, your dedication to God must be forever. If you have begun this on earth, it ought to have been only to carry out here on earth a kind of apprenticeship for what you will do eternally in heaven.

### 191.2 Second Point

The Most Blessed Virgin dedicated herself entirely and without any reservation to God on this holy day. Her parents, who had accompanied her for this holy action, left her in the Temple to be brought up in its precincts with other virgins and to devote herself there to the practice of all kinds of virtues. It was quite right that God, who one day would want to make of Mary a temple for his divinity, would do something great for her from her childhood by the eminence of the grace with which he would honor her and by the excellence of the virtues he would produce in her. This is why a pious author says that she constantly occupied herself in the Temple in the service of God and in the holy exercise of fasting and prayer, which she practiced day and night. In this way the all-pure virgin lived a holy life during the entire time she spent in the Temple.

You have the happiness of being in God's house, and you are bound there to his service. You must be filled with graces by the holy practice of prayer and strive to practice the virtues that are most fitting to your state. By these holy exercises, you will be able to fulfill your duties well, for you will not fulfill them as God requires of you except insofar as you are faithful to and diligent at the holy practice of prayer. By this means *the Holy Spirit will come to you and will teach you,* as Jesus Christ promises his holy Apostles, all the truths[1] of religion and the maxims of Christianity that you must know and practice perfectly, because you are obliged to inspire them in others.

### 191.3 Third Point

The sojourn of the Most Blessed Virgin in the Temple resulted in making her heart a holy temple for the Lord and a sanctuary for the Holy Spirit.[2] This is also what the Church sings about her on this holy day, that she is the temple of the Lord and the sanctuary of the Holy Spirit. Because of this she is the only one who has pleased God in so perfect and exalted a manner that there never has been any creature who has been like her. She is that daughter whom the Lord, according to the words of Genesis, prepared for his Son as the day of the Lord drew near,[3] as told by a Prophet. This is why God prepared her beforehand and made her a holy victim whom he consecrated to himself.

As it says in the Apocalypse, she fled into the desert,[4] that is to say, the Temple, a place separated from the usual activities of people, where she made for herself a seclusion that God had destined for her. It was fitting to the Son of God, before making his dwelling in her, that she no longer have external dealings with ordinary people but that all her dealing would be in the Lord's Temple. There she usually would be conversing even more with the angels than with her companions to make herself worthy to be greeted by an angel on behalf of God.[5]

Honor the Most Blessed Virgin today as the tabernacle and the living temple that God built,[6] adorned by God's own hands. Pray to her to obtain for you from God the grace that your soul may be so well adorned and so well disposed to receive the word of God and to communicate it to others that you may become through her intercession a tabernacle of the divine Word.

---

This feast is based on a tradition that is without any biblical foundation for its historicity. It was first celebrated by the Pope when he was at Avignon in 1372, although the Eastern Church had celebrated it many centuries before. Pope Sixtus made it a feast for the universal Church in 1472. Pope Pius V (1566–1572) suppressed it, but Pope Sixtus V (1585–1590) restored it to the Roman breviary.

---

1. Jn 16:13
2. 1 Cor 3:16
3. Gn 3:15

4. Is 13:6
5. Rev 12:6
6. Lk 1:28

7. 2 Cor 6:16

# November 25

## SAINT CATHERINE,
## VIRGIN AND MARTYR

### 192.1  First Point

Converted to the faith in her early youth, Saint Catherine found a solid way to preserve her faith by reading holy books, and she devoted herself to this practice in such a way that she mastered them perfectly. As a result, when some people wanted to dissuade her from practicing the religion she had embraced, none of them ever succeeded. She was even so strong in her faith that after she was arrested by order of the emperor and he saw how she spoke with such energy concerning her religion, he assembled the philosophers and the most learned people in Alexandria to refute her. But all they got out of the arguments they had with her was the embarrassment of being overcome by a young woman.

See how important it is for you to know Holy Scripture well, because Saint Paul assures us that whoever ignores it will be ignored[1] and that this knowledge makes a person strong in the faith and in the practice of good. As the same Saint Paul says, this is what teaches salvation through faith in Jesus Christ, what is inspired by God and useful for instruction, reproof, correction, and for training in piety and justice, so that the man of God may be perfect and well equipped for all sorts of good work.[2]

This was the benefit Saint Catherine drew from reading Holy Scripture. It is important that you obtain the same benefit from the same source, for you are commissioned by God to instruct, reprove, correct, and lead to piety the children who are entrusted to you. Read Holy Scripture frequently, then, and let this holy reading fill you so fully with the Spirit of God that it will enable you to do all these things with ease.

### 192.2 Second Point

Once she had filled herself with the Christian spirit and had been well grounded in the faith, Saint Catherine withdrew entirely from the world to devote herself in a very special way to prayer. She spent much time at this, applying her mind and heart to meditation on the holy truths that she had learned in the divine books and training herself in their practice. She looked upon the poor, whom she frequently served, as being Jesus Christ.

What an admirable thing it is, of what great help to those who wish to live in piety and in the practice of virtue, to meditate often on the holy and exalted maxims contained in Holy Scripture! They are far above all that the human mind can conceive by itself. Holy Scripture enlightens the mind with divine light,[3] *which,* Saint John says, enlightens everyone who comes into this world.[4] Because, according to Saint Paul, the precepts of the Lord are in Holy Scripture,[5] meditation on them inspires us to practice them.

Following Saint Catherine's example, make use of this means to be sanctified. Often meditate on the words of Holy Scripture to be encouraged to do what is right and to be guided according to the spirit of your state. The word of God contained in Holy Scripture has this effect, according to Saint Paul, because it is living and effective and penetrates more deeply than a two-edged sword. It enters, continues the same Apostle, and penetrates even to the most hidden depths of soul and spirit.[6] Make use of it, then, for this purpose because it procures such great benefits.

### 192.3  Third Point

This saint was accused of being a Christian before the Emperor Maximian, who was then at Alexandria. Seeing that he had not been able to engage her by argument to change her religion and to take up the cult of the false gods, the Emperor wanted to try gentleness and promises to win her over and to bring her to do what he desired. When he found that all the means he used were futile and incapable of moving the heart of this saint, whose constancy was unbreakable, he had her cruelly scourged, put her in prison for twelve days, and gave her almost nothing to eat. He then had her put on wheels designed to break her body into bits, but because, by the help of grace, she suffered no harm from all these tortures, the emperor had her head cut off.

Seclusion, prayer, and reading Holy Scripture usually serve, as they did for Saint Catherine, to prepare us to suffer with courage all that God wills us to suffer. When we have prepared ourselves by these three means, it often happens that we become, as it were, insensible to sufferings, because we accept them as sent by God and as a means of uniting ourselves closely to him and possessing him. Like this saint, you will be contented and comforted by God in your sufferings if you prepare for them as she did.

———

Catherine (fourth century?), according to the legend written about her, was beheaded after an unsuccessful attempt to kill her on a spiked wheel (the Catherine wheel) during the reign of the Emperor Maxentius (306–312). (In the third point of this meditation, De La Salle places her martyrdom during the reign of the Emperor Maximian.) The story of her refuting 50 philosophers has led to her becoming the patron of Christian philosophers and being venerated as one of the Fourteen Holy Helpers. She was popular among the crusaders, who did much to spread devotion to her. She is included in the Litany of the Saints. Saint Gertrude (1256–1301) saw her on a throne in heaven. Saint Joan of Arc (1412–1431) heard her voice.

———

| | | |
|---|---|---|
| 1.  1 Cor 14:38 | 3.  1 Cor 2:14 | 5.  2 Tim 3:16 |
| 2.  2 Tim 3:15–17 | 4.  Jn 1:9 | 6.  Heb 4:12 |

# November 30

## SAINT ANDREW, APOSTLE

### 78.1[1] First Point

Saint Andrew, who was for a time a disciple of Saint John the Baptist, became a follower of Jesus Christ when our Lord, passing along the shore of the sea, called him with his brother, Saint Peter, and told them to come with him and he would make them fishers of men. Saint Andrew left everything at once and followed Jesus Christ.[2] He had the advantage of knowing Jesus sometime previously, because Saint John the Baptist had pointed him out to him, and from that moment he followed him.[3] That is how this saint had the honor of being the first disciple of Jesus Christ, who always showed him very special affection and often had him as his companion.

The way to be specially loved by Jesus is to be attached to him, to give up everything for him and without hesitation, and to do everything he asks and everything he inspires in us as soon as we hear his voice.

You have the advantage of being placed in the following of Jesus Christ and of being withdrawn from the world. Have you left everything for him? Have you no longer an attachment to anything? Are you faithful to follow God's voice when he speaks to you in prayer? Do you not often neglect his holy inspirations? As the Prophet King says, do you not harden your heart[4] and make it unresponsive when grace inspires you to carry out what God asks of you? What happens when you act this way? God withdraws his grace and abandons us to ourselves and to our own weakness. Then, without the grace of our state, we can no longer maintain ourselves in it.

### 78.2 Second Point

Saint Andrew faithfully carried out what Jesus Christ had predicted to him when he called him to the faith, namely, that he would be a fisher of men,[5] that is, he would win others to God and would attract them to Jesus Christ by the net of the apostolic grace that he would give him. He even had a share in this grace, as soon as he knew Jesus, and brought his brother, Saint Peter, to our Lord.[6] This made Saint Peter Damian say that from the start of his apprenticeship in Christianity, this saint had already applied himself to effect good in souls and had already become a preacher of the truth, although he was barely a listener. This new disciple, not satisfied with taking care of his own salvation, was already trying to bring others to become disciples with him. After the descent of the Holy Spirit, this saint continued to exercise his zeal in many countries, because he knew that Jesus Christ had left his Apostles on earth for no other purpose than to preach his doctrine everywhere.[7]

You have been called, just as the holy Apostles were, to make God known, and you need great zeal for this. Ask God for a share in the zeal of Saint Andrew. Regard him as your model, and proclaim Jesus Christ and his holy maxims without growing weary. For this purpose, you need to have learned these truths from Jesus Christ by often being in his company through your diligence in prayer. This is where, after you have studied your responsibility to instruct others, you must not spare anything in you to procure the glory of God in every kind of way.

### 78.3 Third Point

After preaching in Achaia, Saint Andrew was brought before Aegeus, the proconsul of this province, who forbade him to preach the Gospel to the people, but prohibitions like this did not keep him from fulfilling his ministry. He considered that Jesus Christ was much more to be respected than this proconsul. As Saint Peter had said to the prince of the Jewish people, it was more correct to obey God rather than men.[8] This saint continued to speak so forcefully about Jesus Christ, his humiliations, and the cross on which he died that this judge condemned him to die on a cross just like his Master, Jesus Christ. Before attaching him to it, he had him cruelly scourged.

As soon as the holy Apostle saw the cross that was prepared for him, he cried out that this cross was very dear to him, that he had for a long time desired it, and that he had, in fact, even looked forward to it with much eagerness. He then asked the cross to receive him tenderly, as it had received Jesus Christ, who felt honored to die on it and had made it something lovable and honorable. Surprisingly, the zeal of this holy Apostle was so ardent that he was not able to give up, even in death. It happened that while he hung on the cross, where he remained for two days, he did not stop preaching and instructing the people who were present.

Do you have as much love for suffering as Saint Andrew had in his suffering for the cross on which he died? Do the pains, sufferings, and persecutions that you have to endure in your ministry, instead of wearing down your courage, serve to increase your zeal and inspire you all the more to make Jesus Christ known and loved?

———

Andrew, as the Gospel tells us, was the brother of Saint Peter, one of the first to be called by Christ, a fisherman by trade. He was the one who told our Lord about the boy with the five loaves and two fish and about the Gentiles who had come asking to see Jesus. There are many conflicting stories about his mission after Pentecost. He has become patron of Russia and Scotland. The tradition of the X-shaped cross of Saint Andrew, part of Scotch heraldry, does not seem to have been associated with him before the fourteenth century. His cult began in the fourth century in Constantinople, one place where his body is said to be buried. His relics are said to have been transferred to southern Italy in 1210; his head, to Saint Peter's, Rome, in 1462.

---

1. This number and the numbers of the succeeding meditations follow the 1882 edition, which makes November 30 the beginning of the liturgical year for the feasts of the saints; the original edition begins the feasts of the saints with January 1.
2. Mt 4:18–20
3. Jn 1:35–40
4. Ps 95:8
5. Mt 4:19
6. Jn 1:41–42
7. Mk 16:15
8. Acts 4:19

# December 2

## SAINT FRANCIS XAVIER

### 79.1 First Point

After Saint Francis Xavier joined Saint Ignatius and made a spiritual retreat under his direction, he resolved to give himself entirely to God. He had a great love for suffering, especially the mortification of his body and his senses. This spirit led him to undertake extraordinary penances.

From time to time, he went three or four days without eating, and when he did eat, he abstained not only from meat and wine but also from wheat bread, and he was satisfied with the coarsest kind of food used by the poor. To mortify his body, he used a discipline made of metal, and he beat himself so roughly that blood flowed freely from the wounds he made. He slept very little, lying on a bit of straw on the ground. On one occasion among others, he tied cords so tightly around his body and left them there so long that they entered his flesh. The infection this caused him was judged to be incurable, but he was miraculously healed through the prayer of his companions. Once he sucked an ulcer full of pus that made him nauseous.

By a life mortified like this, the saints who worked the most for the salvation of souls prepared and conditioned themselves to achieve very great results in this ministry.

Because God has called you to such an exalted work, if you cannot practice these great mortifications, at least you ought to mortify your senses and your own spirit, which must no longer live in you, for God asks you not to live and to be guided except by his divine Spirit.

### 79.2 Second Point

This saint, by whom God planned to do such great things, had his heart set on the love of humiliations, knowing that it is to the humble that God gives in greatest abundance the grace[1] to convert souls. Jesus Christ makes this clear enough when the only thing he gives as a lesson to be learned by his holy Apostles is that they be humble of heart.[2] In this way he shows them what would make them most capable in their ministry for the conversion of souls.

In this spirit of humility, Saint Francis Xavier always traveled on foot, no matter how lengthy the journey, except when he had to cross the sea. In the same spirit, he usually stayed in hospitals, and during one long sea voyage, he acted as a servant toward everyone. Later, he served for two months as a domestic servant for a Japanese soldier. He wrote on his knees to Saint Ignatius, his superior.

That is how this saint prepared for the conversion of a great number of souls, for God usually acts this way with those who serve him with humility, as the Most Blessed Virgin testifies in her canticle that God acted in her regard. The more humble people are, the more God accomplishes great things through them.[3]

Do you wish to convert your disciples and easily win them over to God? Be children like them, not in prudence, says Saint Paul, but in evil.[4] The more you become little, the more you will love to be considered as such. The more you cherish the persecutions and humiliations that people direct against you, the more you will touch the hearts of those whom you instruct and engage them to live as true Christians.

### 79.3 Third Point

It is inconceivable how many souls Saint Francis Xavier converted to God, once he had filled himself with the spirit of God before going off to preach the holy Gospel. It is estimated that he converted several hundred thousand in India and in Japan. He baptized several princes and even several kings. He spent his time preaching, catechizing, confessing, and visiting hospitals. Finally, his zeal was so extraordinary that he was ready at all times to exercise his apostolic functions. Nothing, no matter how humble, was beneath him when it was a question of converting souls. This saint especially had such great zeal for the instruction of children (which had been inspired in him by Saint Ignatius) that he went about in the streets ringing a little bell to call them to catechism, and he devoted himself to teaching them the principal mysteries of our religion.

How happy you must be at having been called to exercise this function in the Church, by which this great saint felt he was so honored! Desire to share in his zeal for so great a work, and take the means this saint used to prepare to bring about so many conversions.

---

Francis (1506–1552) was born at Xavier, in the Spanish kingdom of Navarre. He was educated in Paris and became a professor of philosophy at the College of Beauvais. At the University of Paris, he met Ignatius of Loyola, a fellow Basque, and became one of the first Jesuits, in 1534. In 1542 he was sent to India as Apostolic Nuncio to the Far East. Seven years later, after having labored ardently in the south and in Malacca, he carried the Gospel to Japan. He died in 1552, at the age of 46, while waiting for permission to enter China. He was canonized with Saint Ignatius in 1662 by Pope Gregory XV and is the Patron of Catholic Missions. The feast is now celebrated on December 3.

---

1. Jas 4:6; 1 Pt 5:5   3. Lk 1:48–49   4. 1 Cor 14:20
2. Mt 11:29

# December 6

## SAINT NICHOLAS, BISHOP OF MYRA

### 80.1 First Point

It is said of Saint Nicholas that from his earliest years he led a very mortified life. This virtue appeared when he was still fed at the breast, for on Wednesdays and Fridays, he took his nurse's milk only once a day. Accustomed to fasting this way, he continued this holy practice all the rest of his life, during which he had mortification very much at heart. He often wore a hair shirt. God likewise gave him occasions to suffer and to practice patience during the long period of banishment to which Emperor Diocletian condemned him. During this exile the saint considered himself fortunate to be able in this way to give public testimony to his faith.

An austere and penitential life is the safeguard of chastity and disposes the soul for friendship with God, for it detaches it from the body and material pleasures and enables it to devote itself to God and to receive his inspirations. It also frees the soul from all the obstacles that might prevent it from possessing the Spirit of God.

If your life is not as austere as the life of this saint, at least make it austere in another way appropriate to your state by daily mortification in something during meals with regard to the quantity, the quality, or the taste of your food, by eating with great moderation, or by leaving the table without being entirely satisfied, granting your senses only what is absolutely necessary. Are you faithful to these practices?

### 80.2   Second Point

This saint loved prayer, and it was through his prayers that he calmed a furious storm when he was on the sea to make a devotional visit to the holy places of Jerusalem. To make prayer more easily and with more devotion, he spent much time in churches and went there early in the morning. It is said that this is what led to his being chosen as bishop in a seemingly miraculous manner. Prayer also helped him a great deal to govern his diocese, for in this way he became imbued with the episcopal spirit and the divine wisdom that he needed to guide souls.

Your obligation to instruct children and to bring them up in the Christian spirit ought to make you very diligent in prayer to obtain from God the graces you need to carry out your work well and to draw down on you the light you need to know how to form Jesus Christ in the hearts of the children entrusted to your guidance[1] and how to give them the spirit of God. Realize that being filled with God as much as you ought to be in the state in which Providence has placed you obliges you to converse frequently with God.

### 80.3   Third Point

The love that Saint Nicholas had for the poor was surprising, for it led him to explore all possible ways to provide for their needs. This love led him in person, secretly during the night and on three separate occasions, to bring what was needed to provide a dowry for three young girls, whose father was ready to force them to become prostitutes because he did not have the means to get them married. This same charity led the saint to free a young man, captured by the Saracens, who was serving the king at table and invoked the saint on his feast, begging him to grant him this favor.

Because you are under the obligation to instruct the children of the poor, you must, consequently, cultivate a very special tenderness for them and procure their spiritual welfare as far as you will be able, considering them as members of Jesus Christ[2] and his well-beloved. The faith that must inspire you ought to make you honor Jesus Christ in their person[3] and prefer them to the wealthiest children on earth, because they are the living images of Jesus Christ, our divine Master. By the care you have for them, show how truly dear they are to you, and ask Saint Nicholas, their patron, to obtain for you from God some share in his love for the poor, especially a great zeal to procure purity for them, a virtue that is so difficult to preserve in an age as corrupt as ours.

---

Saint Nicholas (fourth century), bishop of Myra, Asia Minor, is known largely from legends and popular devotion as the patron of sailors in the East and of children in the West. When the Saracens took possession of Myra, his relics were brought to Bari, Italy, and he is often called Saint Nicholas of Bari. The stories recounted by De La Salle in the third point of his meditation are the probable origins of his becoming the patron of children. De La Salle manifests this devotion in *Conduite des Écoles chrétiennes* by making the feast of Saint Nicholas a special holiday for the students. In *Pratique du Réglement journallier*, he specifies that a Mass is to be offered in the saint's honor (CL 24:197; CL 25:114; see also *Letters,* 49.10). The notion of Santa Claus was brought to America, and from there to England, by Dutch Protestants. The story in De La Salle's first point, of Saint Nicholas as a baby, is taken from the Second Nocturn of the former Office in the Breviary.

---

1. Gal 4:19          2. 1 Cor 6:15          3. Mt 25:40

# December 7

## SAINT AMBROSE,
## ARCHBISHOP OF MILAN

### 81.1  First Point

While provincial governor, Saint Ambrose was elected bishop of Milan through a sort of miracle and by God's inspiration. He had come to the assembly of the bishops of the province solely to prevent the Arians, who wanted to choose a bishop belonging to their party, from causing disorder. The saint did all he could to oppose his own election, but when he did not succeed, in order to rid himself completely of the spirit of the world, he resigned all the positions he held, abandoned all he possessed in these positions, and gave his fortune to the poor and to the Church. In this he imitated the Apostles, who had left all to follow our Lord[1] and to preach his Gospel. This spirit of poverty filled the holy prelate as soon as he was promoted to the episcopal dignity and inspired him with such a love for the poor that he even sold the sacred vessels to help them in a time of public calamity.

To begin to belong entirely to God, we need to make ourselves poor. We even need to have as much affection for poverty as people of the world have for riches. This is the first step that Jesus Christ wishes us to make when we enter the way of perfection.[2] Do you have an effective love of poverty? To give proof of this, are you pleased when you lack something, even necessary things? Ask these questions often.

### 81.2  Second Point

When Saint Ambrose became a bishop, his natural eloquence became heavenly and completely divine. It served him so well in the conversion of souls that no one was able to resist him. With God's help he had the power to convert Saint Augustine from a stubborn Manichean to one of the greatest doctors of the Church. This was also the reason why the heretics feared him and did not dare challenge him, because he alone was quite able to refute all of them. He joined to his eloquence and piety a marvelous power and firmness that were reinforced by his extraordinary disinterestedness.

You do not need eloquence of this sort, but you do need to share in his apostolic zeal in order to labor usefully in your work of saving souls. Often ask God for the grace to touch hearts as he did.

This is the grace of your state, for it would be of little use to those whom you instruct if, as Saint Paul says of the Jews, their minds remained blinded and hardened after so many instructions and if, after you have announced to them so many times the truths of the holy Gospel, a veil still remained over their hearts.[3]

### 81.3 Third Point

Saint Ambrose labored with marvelous success to reestablish the discipline of the Church. He did away with several abuses that had insinuated themselves into his province. For this purpose, he carried episcopal vigor to such an eminent degree that he resisted the emperors themselves when they opposed his plans. To provide a solid foundation for the restoration of discipline, he was instrumental in having decrees voted on this matter in several councils that he attended outside his province. He did the same in several councils he held in his own diocese, which were effective in maintaining the good that he had procured by his zeal.

To make your zeal useful to others, you must first exercise it in regard to you and to your community. With this in mind and in regard to you personally, make sure that you do not pardon the slightest fault or let anything escape you that can in the least displease God, without peforming a penance that can remedy the evil. You must also, out of zeal for discipline, contribute so well to establish and maintain observance of the Rule in your community that it may become a heaven on earth, where charity and peace reign.

---

Ambrose (ca. 340–397) was born at Treves (Trier), Germany. His father was governor of the Gauls and a member of the Roman aristocracy. Ambrose was educated in Rome and became a provincial governor with headquarters in Milan. While presiding at the election of the bishop of Milan, he was nominated by acclamation, even though he was not yet a Christian, although his family was. He was forthwith baptized, ordained a priest, and consecrated a bishop. He took his assignment seriously, prayed, studied, and became a great pastoral bishop without losing his sense of the dignity and power of his office. His preaching contributed to the conversion of Saint Augustine, whom he baptized in 387. He introduced Eastern melodies into the Western Church. The Ambrosian rite is part of his influence on the liturgy.

---

1. Mt 4:22          2. Mt 19:21          3. 2 Cor 3:14–15

# December 8

## THE IMMACULATE CONCEPTION
## OF THE MOST BLESSED VIRGIN

### 82.1 First Point

From all eternity, God destined the Most Blessed Virgin to be the mother of his Son and so formed her in soul and in body that she was worthy to hold him in her womb. This is why he preserved her from anything that could be the least displeasing to him. Because it would have been a disgraceful thing for the mother of God to have had anything to do with sin, God, by an entirely special privilege, exempted her from original sin. It is true that we cannot understand how this came about; nevertheless, it would be unbecoming for us to doubt the exemption she had from sin in her conception, for this is the pious and common sentiment of the faithful, and the Church accepts it as appropriate.

Honor the Most Blessed Virgin today, then, as the purest of all creatures and the only one on earth who has been exempt from original sin. Tell her, with the whole Church, that she is all beautiful and that in her soul there is no stain of sin,[1] not even the sin that is common to all the human race. Beg her on this day, in virtue of this extraordinary grace that God gave her, to obtain for you from God to be entirely freed from the corruption of the world throughout your life.[2] Ask that there no longer be found in you any habit of sin, for this is what makes a soul unworthy of God's special graces.

### 82.2 Second Point

Not only was the Most Blessed Virgin preserved from original sin in her conception, but also she had at that instant a grace powerful enough to preserve her from all sin. This grace was so effective in her that she never did commit a single sin, which led Saint Augustine to say that when we speak of sin, we must always exclude the Most Blessed Virgin. The holy Fathers compare her to the Ark of the Covenant, which was made of incorruptible wood,[3] in order to indicate to us that from the very first instant of her being, she received the grace of innocence and original justice, which she never lost, even though, like us, she was able to do both good and evil.

Let us recognize that in the Most Blessed Virgin there was never any action that did not make her worthy of God, that her soul was always filled with him, so that he might prepare her to hold and to form within herself the body of God.

You have the happiness of often holding within you the body of this same God. Offer him, then, by your holy actions the respect you owe him. Always act in a manner that is worthy of him, so that he may desire to come to you and to reside in you. Show by your behavior that you understand how fortunate you are to possess him and that although you cannot always have his sacred body within you, you do not cease to possess his Spirit because of that.

### 82.3 Third Point

To make the Most Blessed Virgin pure at the moment of her conception, God also preserved her from concupiscence, that is, from the inclination to sin, not willing that anything connected with sin be near her. Because God is holy, he had no desire to unite himself with a creature soiled by the slightest fault.

Give thanks to God, with Mary, for the great things he has done in her.[4] Look upon her as the masterpiece from God's hands, and ask him to free you from everything that might contribute to make you fall into the least fault, especially into any of the sins to which you were inclined in the world.

———

This feast was first celebrated in the Eastern Church and was only gradually introduced into Europe during the ninth century. It was promoted by the Franciscans in the thirteenth century, and the Franciscan Pope Sixtus IV introduced it in Rome in 1477. Because Pope Clement XI extended it to the universal Church in 1708, it received a special impetus toward the end of De La Salle's life. This might have promoted a special devotion among the first Brothers and influenced this meditation by De La Salle. According to later regulations of the community of Saint Yon:

> This feast is kept with great solemnity throughout the Institute, for it was after vowing to fast on the eve of this feast every year, in addition to the Friday fast, and to celebrate the feast and its octave solemnly as far as they were able that the Brothers obtained Letters Patent from the king and the Bull of Approbation of the Institute from the Holy See. Moreover, the Lord has provided the means needed to construct the chapel and other buildings at Saint Yon and has given prosperity to this house in a seemingly miraculous manner. On this day, just as on Easter Sunday, everything that is most beautiful will be used in the chapel. There is an indulgence for the celebration and also for the exposition of the Most Blessed Sacrament. During each day of the octave, four candles are lighted at Mass, and three Brothers go to Holy Communion.

The dogma was defined as an article of faith by Pope Pius IX in 1854. In 1858 our Lady appeared to Saint Bernadette at Lourdes, declaring herself to be the Immaculate Conception.

---

1. Song 4:7
2. 2 Pt 1:4
3. Ex 25:10
4. Lk 1:49

# December 21

## SAINT THOMAS, APOSTLE

### 84.1[1] First Point

Saint Thomas, whose zeal impelled him to urge the other Apostles not to leave Jesus Christ but rather to die with him,[2] nevertheless, was not willing to believe, on the report they gave him, that Jesus had risen. He told them that he would not believe until he had seen him.[3] People criticize very much the incredulity of Saint Thomas on this occasion, and they are right, because no doubt he ought to have put faith in what he was told by the other Apostles, who had seen Jesus Christ. Still, the majority of Christians are even more unbelieving than Saint Thomas, because they do not believe in Jesus Christ.

For Jesus says in the Gospel, Blessed are the poor;[4] the majority of Christians consider them unfortunate. Jesus Christ says that it is necessary to do good to our enemies and to pray to God for them;[5] they think only of getting revenge for the outrages they imagine someone did to them and of doing harm to those who have injured them in some way. Jesus Christ says that it is necessary to carry our cross daily;[6] they seek all possible ways to escape suffering. Is that to have faith and to believe in the Gospel when they act this way?

Do not be so blinded, for you have the advantage of reading the Gospel and of meditating on the truths found in it every day, and you are responsible to teach these truths to others. Show by the way your actions conform to these holy maxims that, in fact, you do believe them by putting them into practice.

### 84.2 Second Point

Saint Thomas revived his faith as soon as Jesus Christ appeared to him and made him touch his sacred wounds. Although he was able to see only the wounds of a mortal man, he immediately cried out that the One whom he saw was truly his Lord and his God.[7] Saint

Thomas' unbelief, says Saint Gregory, is of much greater use to us than the faith of the other Apostles, who believed in the Resurrection of Jesus Christ as soon as he appeared to them. The incredulity of Saint Thomas has helped us, adds this Father, to make our own faith firmer, because although he saw only a man, he confessed that this man was his God.

By thinking of what Jesus Christ has suffered for us, we will reinspire our feeble and wavering faith and dispose ourselves to suffer for God and to practice the maxims that are the most opposed to the feelings of nature. If we truly believe and are truly convinced that Jesus Christ has suffered for us in all the parts of his body, how can we love the pleasure found in the use of creatures, knowing that Jesus Christ loved nothing in this world except suffering and that, as Saint Paul says, he bore his cross and yearned to be attached to it?[8] This example must be for you, as it was for Saint Paul, a great source of comfort and encourage you, as it did him, to be filled with joy in all your suffering.[9]

### 84.3 Third Point

Saint Thomas demonstrated his faith with distinction when he brought the Gospel to the most distant lands and sealed it with his own blood. The profession of faith of this great Apostle was so effective that there are still many Christians in the country where he died who, to show that they are descendants of those who were formed as Christians by him, call themselves the Christians of Saint Thomas.

In vain do you believe what Jesus Christ proposes to you in the holy Gospel if your actions do not give proof of your belief; in such a case, your faith is in vain.[10] Make it known by your actions that you are guide as a child of those who were instructed by the holy Apostles in the truths of the faith. Are you ready, as they were, to die to prove the good quality of your faith? Or on the contrary, might you not be disposed to lose the grace of God and heaven in order to escape suffering? How do you show that you possess the Christian spirit? Be assured that to possess it, your actions must not give the lie to the faith you profess but, instead, be a lively expression of what is written in the Gospel.

―――――――

The only reliable details about the life of Saint Thomas are those in the Gospel. His name in Syriac means twin; Didymus is the Greek equivalent. When Jesus was going to Jerusalem to raise Lazarus, some of the Apostles reminded him that his life had recently been threatened there. Then it was that Thomas said, "Let us also go that we may die with him." At the last supper, Thomas asked our Lord, "How can we know the way where you are going?" Jesus answered, "I am the way, the truth, and the life." Most memorable is the Gospel account of Thomas' doubts about the Resurrection and our Lord's special appearance to him. Tradition says that Saint Thomas suffered martyrdom in India and that part of his relics are there, at Mylapore. The Roman Martyrology mentions that some of his relics were moved to Edesa on July 3, and it is on this day that his feast is now celebrated.

1. Number 83, one of the six meditations in the *Additions,* is found at the end both of the original edition and of this edition.
2. Jn 11:16
3. Jn 20:25
4. Mt 5:3
5. Mt 5:44
6. Lk 9:23
7. Jn 20:26–28
8. Heb 12:1; Lk 12:50
9. Col 1:24
10. Jas 2:20

# December 24

## VIGIL OF THE NATIVITY OF JESUS CHRIST

### 85.1 First Point

The Emperor Augustus having issued an edict ordering a census to be taken of all the inhabitants of all the cities belonging to the Roman Empire, every person was obliged to register in his native town. This made Saint Joseph leave Nazareth, the city in Galilee where he lived, to go to Bethlehem, a town in Judea, to register there with Mary, his wife.[1] On arriving there, they looked for a house where they could stay, but no one was willing to accept them, because they were occupied by people more wealthy, more distinguished than they.

See how the world acts! People consider only what is externally apparent in a person and pay respect only if they are attracted by what fascinates the eyes of the world. If the people in Bethlehem had regarded Mary as the Mother of the Messiah, as the woman who would soon bring forth for the world God made man, who would have dared to refuse to lodge her in their home? What marks of respect would not all Judea have paid her? But because they considered her only as an ordinary person and the wife of a working-man, there was no shelter for her.

For how long has Jesus been presenting himself to you and knocking at the door of your heart to make his dwelling within you, and you have not wanted to receive him? Why? Because he only presents himself under the form of a poor man, a slave, a man of sorrows.[2]

### 85.2 Second Point

The Most Blessed Virgin, the Mother of Jesus, not finding anyone willing to offer her lodging in Bethlehem, was obliged to withdraw to a stable. While she was there, *it happened that the time of her pregnancy was completed, and she brought forth her firstborn child into the world.* This is why she found it necessary to lay Jesus Christ, her Son, in a manger for a bed.[3]

You often receive Jesus Christ in your heart, but is he not there as though in a stable, finding there only dirt and corruption, because you have affection for other things rather than for him? If you looked upon him as your Savior and your Redeemer, what honor would you not pay him? Would you not keep him company, regarding him as God by paying attention to his holy presence and as man by meditating on his sufferings and his Passion?

To find out whether you profit by the coming and dwelling in you that Jesus desires very much, consider whether you are more reserved, more recollected, and better behaved than you are on other days. On Communion days, do you watch more carefully not to lose control and give way to any ill humor or disorderly impulse?

If you wish to profit by the coming of Jesus Christ in you, let him be the master of your heart, and be docile to whatever he might require of you, often saying to him with the Prophet Samuel, Speak, Lord, for your servant is listening,[4] and with David, I will hear what the Lord God will say in me.[5]

### 85.3 Third Point

Because we know that Jesus Christ is going to come into us today and we recognize him for what he is, let us prepare for him a dwelling place worthy of him. Let us dispose our hearts to receive him in such a way that he may be pleased to make his home there! With this in view, let us apply ourselves to detach our hearts from all that is profane and earthly in them. The earthly soul, says Saint Paul, speaks with affection of the things of the earth and does not know how to speak of anything else.[6] But, the same Apostle says, *the heavenly person speaks of the things of heaven and rises above everything else.* For this purpose the Son of God has come to earth and wishes to come into our hearts: to make us share in his nature[7] and to help us become altogether heavenly people.

------

The 1718 Rule of the Brothers states that on this vigil, at 10:30 p.m., the Brothers go to the oratory, where a subject of meditation is read, and afterward go to the church to be there for the beginning of Matins. They make their prayer there until the time for Mass, at which they receive Holy Communion (CL 25:115). No doubt De La Salle wrote this meditation for that occasion. It is a good example of the Christocentric character of Lasallian spirituality. The mystery of the Incarnation is a key to the prayer of De La Salle. See also the meditation for March 25.

1. Lk 2:1, 3–5       4. 1 Sm 3:10      7. 2 Pt 1:4
2. Mt 25:44–45; Is 53:3    5. Ps 85:9
3. Lk 2:6–7           6. 1 Cor 15:47–48

# December 25

## THE NATIVITY
## OF JESUS CHRIST

### 86.1 First Point

Today Jesus Christ is born poor in a stable. The Most Blessed Virgin brings him into the world in a place where she finds no comfort or any human help and where there is no other bed for this newborn Child than a manger.[1] Behold the palace and the bed for presenting Jesus our Savior on his entry into the world! This is how he is lodged in the middle of the night in a very rigorous season. Despite his pressing needs, no one goes to any trouble to help him.

The poverty that Jesus practices so eminently at his birth ought to commit us to have great love for this virtue, for it is to make us love it that he is born in this condition. Let us not be surprised, then, when we lack something, even necessities, for at his birth, Jesus was lacking everything. This is how we must be born in the spiritual life, dispossessed and deprived of everything. Because the Son of God willed that the humanity he took on be in this condition, he also wants us to share this disposition, so that he can take entire possession of our hearts.

## 86.2 Second Point

It is not enough for Jesus to be born poor. He likewise chose lowliness as his lot[2] in this world, according to the words of the Royal Prophet. He wished to make his entry into the world in a place where he was unknown and where no attention would be paid either to him or to his holy Mother, a place where he would be abandoned by everyone. It is true that he is visited at his birth, but it is only by poor shepherds,[3] who can honor him only by their good wishes. Even so, it is necessary for an angel sent by God to notify them that this Child about to be born in Bethlehem is their Savior, whose birth would be for all the people a subject of great joy.[4]

Except for these poor shepherds, no one even thought of Jesus when he was born. It even seems that God does not want the rich and the great to find their way to him, for the angel who announces his coming gives the shepherds no other sign to recognize him than the poor and lowly circumstances where they would find him, which could only turn away those who love only what is renowned.

In choosing our state, we ought to have resolved to be as lowly as the Son of God when he became man, for this is what is most noticeable in our profession and in our work. We are poor Brothers, forgotten and little appreciated by the people of the world. Only the poor come looking for us. They have nothing to offer us but their hearts ready to accept our instructions. Let us love what is most humiliating in our profession in order to share in some way in the lowliness of Jesus Christ at his birth.

## 86.3 Third Point

*The shepherds*, says the Gospel of this day, made haste to go over to Bethlehem, where they found Mary and Joseph and the Infant lying in a manger. On seeing him, they recognized what had been told them and then went back, glorifying the Lord for all that they had seen and heard.[5]

Nothing draws souls to God more strongly than the poor and humble condition of those who wish to lead them to him. Why did the shepherds praise and bless God? Because they had seen a poor Infant lying in a manger and because on seeing him, they had recognized, thanks to an interior light with which God enlightened them, that this Infant was truly their Savior and that it was to him they must have recourse to escape the misery of their sins.

Be convinced that as long as you remain bound in your heart to poverty and to everything that can humble you, you will do good for souls. The angels of God will make you known and will inspire fathers and mothers to send you their children to be instructed. By your instructions, you will touch the hearts of these poor children, and most of them will become true Christians. But if you do not resemble the newborn Jesus by these two outstanding qualities, you will be little known and little employed, nor will you be loved or appreciated by the poor. You will never have for them the role of savior that is proper for you in your work, because you will draw them to God only insofar as you resemble them and Jesus at his birth.

———

Just as the previous meditation reflects the basic Christological orientation of De La Salle's spirituality, this meditation for Christmas stresses the ascetical response to this Christology, namely, the acceptance of poverty and lowliness in imitation of the *kenosis* of Christ. However, De La Salle is careful to show the Brothers how this spirit is wholly relevant to their educational work.

———

| | | |
|---|---|---|
| 1. Lk 2:7 | 3. Lk 2:16 | 5. Lk 2:16–20 |
| 2. Ps 22:7 | 4. Lk 2:9–11 | |

# December 26

## SAINT STEPHEN, THE FIRST MARTYR

### 87.1 First Point

It is said of Saint Stephen in the Acts of the Apostles that he was filled with faith.[1] He certainly showed this, for he always guided himself and acted by the spirit of faith.

Was he not, in fact, inspired by this spirit when he spoke with such great zeal to the Jews and when several of them who disputed with him could not resist the Holy Spirit, who was in him and inspiring his zeal?[2] After he recounted for them all the benefits with which God had honored their fathers and the little gratitude that most of them had shown,[3] he reproached them for being just like their fathers and for not observing any better than they the Law that they had received through the ministry of angels.[4]

Was he not filled with faith when, following the recommendation given by Jesus Christ, he pardoned his enemies and begged God not to impute to them the sin they were committing by putting him to death[5] and when, in the fervor of his prayer, he saw the heavens opened and the Son of God made man at the right hand of God, his Father?[6]

This is how faith ought to make you act and how you ought to make known by your conduct, as he did, that you are true disciples of Jesus Christ, having only God in view in all your actions and announcing, with as much boldness and intrepidity as he did, the maxims of the holy Gospel. In all this what must strengthen your zeal as well as your faith is the fact that you announce these truths in your position as ministers of God.[7]

### 87.2 Second Point

This saint was not satisfied to be filled with faith. He wanted to share the fullness of his faith with those of his nation by preaching to them the new religion that had just been established and by making known to them, with the testimony of Holy Scripture, Jesus Christ, whom they did not know and who had come to give them the means of salvation and to die for them. He also wanted to make them realize that they were the ones who, moved by hatred and envy of the good he had done, had him condemned to death.[8] But these Jews, with their hard and uncircumcised hearts,[9] as Saint Stephen told them, showed indeed the truth of what Saint Paul says, that all do not obey the Gospel,[10] and of what Isaiah says, Who are those who have believed what you have preached to them?[11]

You have been chosen by God to make Jesus Christ known and to proclaim him. Therefore, admire the goodness of God to you, as the same Apostle says, provided, however, that you remain firm in the state where his goodness has placed you.[12] Following the example of Saint Stephen, then, make Jesus Christ known to those whom you have to instruct. Teach them the rules of the Christian life and the means they must use to be saved. For this purpose God entrusted to you the ministry in which you are employed. Do not become unworthy of it by negligence.[13]

### 87.3 Third Point

After teaching the faith, Saint Stephen also died for the faith. The Jews could not endure the reproaches and explanations he leveled at them about their ingratitude to God and their hardness of heart. They threw him out of the city and stoned him[14] as a blasphemer. That is how they treated all the Prophets,[15] our Lord says. This saint considered himself fortunate to be treated like those who had preceded him. Saint Augustine says that he welcomed with gratitude this shower of stones that fell upon him. Faith filled his being and made him feel truly honored at being persecuted in this way, as Jesus Christ, his Master, had been.[16] All he did during this time was to look to heaven to show God his gratitude for so great a favor.

Enter into these dispositions from today on. Willingly endure all the trials you are given, and do not be troubled by any of them or complain of anything. After the example of Saint Stephen, you must by faith consider all you have to suffer from your neighbor as gifts and benefits coming from God. Only pure faith can inspire such sentiments.

———

De La Salle presents Saint Stephen to the Brothers as a model of the spirit of faith, which they had chosen under his guidance as the spirit of their Institute, not only for their own life but also as the purpose of their work with their students. This feast is of very early origin in the Church, at least as early as the fourth century.

---

1. Acts 6:5
2. Acts 6:9–10
3. Acts 7:1–50
4. Acts 7:51, 53
5. Acts 7:60
6. Acts 7:55, 56
7. 1 Cor 4:1; cf Rom 15:16
8. Acts 7:52

9. Acts 7:51
10. Rom 10:16
11. Is 53:1
12. Rom 11:22
13. 1 Cor 4:1–2
14. Acts 7:58
15. Mt 5:12
16. Jn 15:20

# December 27

## SAINT JOHN THE EVANGELIST

### 88.1  First Point

Saint John was so specially loved by Jesus Christ that he is called his well-beloved disciple above everyone else. Saint John, not wishing out of humility to name himself in his Gospel, does not call himself anything but the disciple whom Jesus loved.[1]

Here are the ways the Savior showed him his special love: he allowed Saint John to rest his head on his chest;[2] he revealed to Saint John the highest mysteries of his divinity and of his holy humanity; when dying, he chose him to take his place and to be the adoptive son of his holy Mother.[3]

Saint Jerome gives us no other reasons for such special love on the part of Jesus for Saint John except that he always remained a virgin. This is what made him so worthy of the friendship of Jesus, to whom this virtue is especially dear.

You are in a state where you need to be honored by the friendship of Jesus. Cherish especially, then, this favorite virtue of Jesus, so
that the divine Savior may love you tenderly and take pleasure in being with you, for his delight is to be with pure people. Also, frequently turn to prayer, in which Jesus will teach you secrets that remain
unknown to most people.

### 88.2 Second Point

If Saint John was much loved by Jesus, he also loved Jesus very
much. The first sign he gave of this love was that he gave up everything in order to follow him.[4]

If Saint John followed Jesus to Mount Tabor, where he manifested his glory to his Apostles,[5] he also accompanied him to Calvary,[6]
where he appeared as an object of malediction,[7] although all the other disciples had abandoned him.[8] He was, then, the only Apostle who
followed Christ even to death, for he wanted to be the witness of his
sufferings right up to the end.[9]

He was also the first to be at the tomb of Jesus Christ, to make
sure of the truth of his Resurrection[10] and to be able afterward to announce it to the others.

See what his tender love made Saint John do to respond to the
love of Jesus for him. Reflect often that because Jesus gave himself entirely to us and for us, we too must give ourselves totally to him, do
everything for him, and not seek ourselves in anything. Our whole
care ought to be to detach ourselves from all things in order to attach
ourselves to God alone, because nothing is equal to him and he is the
only one to whom we can securely give our hearts.

### 88.3 Third Point

The love Jesus had for Saint John and that Saint John had for Jesus
produced a reciprocal love of Saint John for the Blessed Virgin and of
the Blessed Virgin for Saint John. From the moment when Jesus, dying
on the cross, entrusted his holy Mother to his dear disciple and gave
him to her as her son,[11] Saint John always kept the Blessed Virgin close
to him and gave her all the marks of tenderness that a son can have for
his mother. He took care of her in all her needs, and the Blessed Virgin,
in return, honored Saint John with her protection before God.

If we have love for Jesus and are loved by him, we cannot fail to
be deeply loved by the Most Blessed Virgin. Because there is such a
very close union between Jesus and his most holy Mother, all those
who love Jesus and are specially loved by him greatly honor Mary
and are also deeply cherished by this holy Mother of God. Let us
make ourselves worthy of this tenderness of the Blessed Virgin. To

obtain what we desire from her more easily, let us address ourselves to Saint John. As her dear son, in place of Jesus, he will secure for us from her what we cannot obtain by ourselves.

---

Although this meditation does not allude to the apostolic work of the Brothers, there is a relationship with the Brothers' spirit of zeal in the meditation's focus on love for Jesus. This meditation might be considered as a companion to the previous one on Saint Stephen, which focuses on the spirit of faith, for zeal is the second element of the spirit of the Institute. This feast is of very early origin in the Church.

---

1. Jn 13:23
2. Jn 13:23, 25
3. Jn 19:26–27
4. Mt 4:22

5. Mt 17:1–2
6. Jn 19:26
7. Gal 3:13
8. Mt 26:56

9. Jn 19:35
10. Jn 20:4
11. Jn 19:26–27

# December 28

## THE HOLY INNOCENTS

### 89.1 First Point

Today let us honor the innocence of these holy children, who had the privilege of dying before knowing evil and being able to do it. How fortunate they are, for their life was consecrated to God at an age when evil had not yet taken possession of their heart. *They were snatched out of this world almost as soon as they had entered it*, and this by an altogether special grace to be preserved from the corruption[1] that is so difficult to escape in society.

We have known the misery of the world, and we know only too well through our sad experience how rare it is to preserve innocence and purity of heart there. God has done us the favor of withdrawing us from it. Let us, then, thank him every day for so great a benefit and make our life innocent by seclusion, penance, and the holiness of our actions.

To merit perseverance in so saintly a life, let us be faithful to all the smallest practices of the community and the smallest point of the Rule. In this way we will make up for the injury that the world, which we have so fortunately left, might have done to our innocence. We will also place ourselves in a sort of guarantee of not sinning any more during the rest of our life.

## 89.2 Second Point

These holy children died as martyrs because of the cruelty of an evil prince who, as a result of what the Magi had told him concerning the birth of the Messiah,[2] feared that one of them might rob him of his crown. Thus he procured for them the means to live eternally in heaven almost as soon as they had appeared on this earth. He did them more good, says Saint Augustine, by the hatred that he showed in putting them to death than he might have done for them by all the affection he could have had for them and all the benefits he could have heaped upon them in this world. They gave witness to our religion and to the divinity of Jesus Christ, not by speaking but by laying down their life in his place.

Having neither the happiness nor the opportunity to suffer martyrdom for the faith, be a martyr for the love of God through the practice of mortification. A Christian's life, says Saint Gregory, ought to be a continual martyrdom, for we are Christian only to be conformable to Jesus Christ, who suffered throughout his whole life. This sort of martyrdom is often more painful than to shed our blood, because it lasts incomparably longer and is, consequently, all the more difficult to endure. Be encouraged, then, to accept this martyrdom by the example of the saints and especially by the example of Jesus Christ, for he spent his entire life suffering for love of us.

## 89.3 Third Point

These little children died not only as martyrs but also by taking the place of Jesus Christ. Herod wanted to kill him and looked for him everywhere. Not finding him, he resolved to kill a great number of children, assuring himself[3] that Jesus Christ would be included in their number. He wanted no exception made among those who had been born from before the time the Magi had come to Jerusalem up to that moment. What fortunate children, to have lost their life in order to preserve the life of Jesus Christ!

We can have the same opportunity as they by giving our life to prevent Jesus Christ from dying in us. Sinners, says Saint Paul, crucify Jesus Christ anew.[4] If, then, we do not want him to lose his life, we must do violence to ourselves so as not to fall into sin and not to commit the slightest fault. To procure this benefit, we need great vigilance over ourselves. In this way and by dying daily[5] through continual mortification, you will give your life to avoid miserably crucifying and putting Jesus Christ to death within you.

---

Originally, this feast had a penitential character, as if in mourning for the massacre of the children. Perhaps this is why De La Salle stresses self-denial and mortification in his meditation. The feast dates back at least to the fifth century.

---

1. Wis 4:11
2. Mt 2:16

3. Mt 2:16
4. Heb 6:6

5. 1 Cor 15:31

# December 29

## WHAT WE HAVE DONE OR FAILED TO DO FOR GOD THIS YEAR

### 90.1 First Point

We are in this world only to love God and to please him. This is what we must do throughout all our life, for this is the first thing God commands of us, which includes the whole law,[1] as our Lord says. Our love for God ought to be so great that we love nothing but God or for God. We can prove our love in three ways: the first is when we have a high esteem for God; the second is when we attach ourselves to God alone; the third is when we do all our actions for God.

Has it been apparent during this year that you have esteemed God alone? Have you often considered with admiration his infinite greatness, and then have you been filled with so profound a respect at the vision of his sublime perfections that you cried out with the Royal Prophet that their excellence cannot be conceived, nor can they be adored or praised as much as they deserve? *Have you recalled that God was present with you everywhere? Have you interiorly realized your nothingness with a feeling of adoration at the thought of God's presence?* Because nothing is more pleasing for a soul who loves God than to pay attention to him, have you made this your joy,[2] as David did? Out of respect for the presence of so great a God, have you been careful to maintain an attitude of recollection appropriate and proper to his grandeur? Because God is present everywhere, have you adored him everywhere? Pay attention to all this to show God how great an esteem you have for him.

## 90.2 Second Point

Because our soul has been created by God only that we might enjoy him, all our happiness on earth consists in being attached to him alone,[3] as the Royal Prophet says very well. It would be disgraceful for a soul, says Saint Leo, who shares in the divine nature to fall so low from its original nobility as to degrade itself by taking its pleasure in creatures. To whom ought we to give ourselves if not to the One from whom we have received everything, who alone is our Lord and our Father, and who, as Saint Paul says, has given being to all things and has made us only for himself?[4] This thought and the gratitude we owe him for all his goodness to us ought to have frequently occupied our minds and touched our hearts during this year, in order to engage us to give ourselves entirely to God and to tell him, with Saint Augustine, My God, you have made us for you alone, and our hearts will never be at rest until they rest in you!

## 90.3 Third Point

If we truly love God, everything we do we must be for his glory,[5] Saint Paul says. There ought to be no other reason why you have withdrawn from the world, for it is God who must be the purpose of your actions, just as he is their source. If you seek to please anyone other than God, you would not deserve, says Saint Paul, to bear the name of servant of Jesus Christ.[6] You would not be such, because a servant must do everything for the service of his master. This was the advice that Saint Paul gave to the faithful in his day. Whether you eat, he says, whether you drink, or whatever else you do, do it all for the glory of God,[7] and again, Whatever you do, in word or in deed, do all in the name of the Lord Jesus Christ.[8] Such ought to be the whole consolation of a Christian in this life: to act for the God who made him, from whom he receives everything, and to whom he owes all the good that he can do in this life.

Have you often reflected during this year that because God gives you life and helps you perform all your actions, all of them ought to be consecrated to him and that you do him injury when you do them for any other purpose except for him? Has it been your sole aim, as it was Saint Paul's, not to live or to act any longer except for God?[9] Like him, have you been in the disposition not to make God's grace useless in you?[10] It has been useless, no doubt, every time your actions have not been done for love of him. In the future act, as Saint Paul says, in a manner that will be worthy of God, striving to please him in all things.[11]

1. Mt 22:38–40
2. Ps *passim,* especially Ps 139:6; 145:3; 139:7–14; 9:2–3
3. Ps 73:28
4. 1 Cor 8:6; see also Acts 17:28
5. 1 Cor 10:31
6. Gal 1:10
7. 1 Cor 10:31
8. Col 3:17
9. 2 Cor 5:15
10. 1 Cor 15:10
11. Col 1:10

# December 30

## HOW WE HAVE ACTED TOWARD OUR NEIGHBOR AND IN WHAT WE WERE LACKING THIS YEAR

### 91.1 First Point: Regarding Your Superiors

It is an obligation for you to act toward your superiors as toward God.[1] Such is the advice given to you by the Apostle. Because you have a body with senses and because God's interior guidance does not suffice to lead you to him, you need guides who direct you through your senses. This is why God has given you superiors, whose duty it is to hold God's place in your regard and to guide you on the way to heaven externally as God guides you internally.

How have you acted during this year toward your superiors? Have you regarded them as God's ministers who have been given to you by him and hold his place, for it is only through the authority that God has entrusted to them and shared with them that they have a right to guide and to command you?[2] Is it with this motive that you have been submissive to their guidance?

During this year, have you been as dependent on your superiors as you depend on God? With this conviction, have you felt obliged to obey them in all things and as you believe you must obey God, who has said, Who hears you, hears me?[3] Have you been firmly convinced in the depths of your heart that all they tell you is on the part of God, or to say it better, that it is God who is telling you? From this day onward, adopt these dispositions toward your superiors.

## 91.2 Second Point: Regarding Your Brothers

Perhaps you have not reflected sufficiently during this year on the obligation that you have to be completely united with your Brothers, yet this is one of the principal obligations of your state, because you are all brothers,[4] as Jesus Christ says in the holy Gospel.

The first reason why there is sometimes little union in a community is that some wish to place themselves above others on the basis of human reasoning. This is why our Lord says to his Apostles that none of them must either call himself or let himself be called teacher, because they have but one teacher, who is Jesus Christ.[5] Our Lord says that the one who is or who believes himself to be the greatest among you must consider himself and look upon himself as the least of all.[6]

Examine whether you have acted this way during the past year toward your Brothers. If you have experienced any ill feeling toward any of them, think of what Moses said to the two Israelites in his day who were giving trouble to one another and quarreling:[7] that they are our brothers and, as Saint Paul says, that we must support one another in charity.[8] Pay attention to this word, *support*, which he uses; it shows you that we must suffer from one another. This is why, in another place, he says, Bear one another's burdens.[9] Everyone has his burdens; ordinarily, it is not precisely he who has them who carries them, because he does not feel their weight; it is that of the others whose burdens he has to carry.

Everyone must carry these burdens willingly and charitably if he wishes to keep peace with all the others. This is what Saint Paul frequently exhorts us to do in his epistles.[10] Is this how you have acted during this past year? Union in a community is a precious gem, which is why our Lord so often recommended it to his Apostles before he died.[11] If we lose this, we lose everything. Preserve it with care, therefore, if you want your community to survive.

## 91.3 Third Point: Regarding Your Students

The first thing you owe your students is edification and good example. Have you earnestly practiced virtue with the intention of edifying your disciples? Have you reflected that you must be their models of the virtues you wish them to practice?

Have you acted this year as a good teacher must do? You ought to have taught them their religion; did you work sufficiently to accomplish this task during the year? Have you regarded it as your principal duty on their behalf? Do they know their religion well? If they are ignorant of it or do not know it perfectly, is this due to your negligence?

Have you been careful to teach them the maxims and practices of the holy Gospel and to see that they practice them? Have you suggested to them practices appropriate to their age and condition? All these matters of instruction ought to have often been the subject of your reflections and of your study of how to succeed with them. A teacher who has piety in his heart, says the Wise Man, will bring forth wisdom;[12] that is, he will procure wisdom for himself and at the same time he will make wise those whom he instructs.

Have you taught those under your guidance the other matters that are part of your duty, such as reading, writing, and all the rest, with all the attention possible? If that has not been the case during this year, you will give God a large account, not only for your time but also for the food and all that has been furnished for your livelihood, for that was the intention of the assignment for which your needs were provided. Take proper measures for the future on all these matters, which are important.

| | | |
|---|---|---|
| 1. Eph 6:7 | 5. Mt 23:8–10 | 9. Gal 6:2 |
| 2. Rom 13:1–4 | 6. Lk 22:26 | 10. Col 3:14–15 |
| 3. Lk 10:16 | 7. Ex 2:13 | 11. Jn 17:11; 21–23 |
| 4. Mt 23:8 | 8. Eph 4:2 | 12. Prv 10:31 |

# December 31

## HOW YOU FAILED WITH REGARD TO YOURSELVES AND TO THE OBSERVANCE OF THE RULE THIS YEAR

### 92.1 First Point

You can fail in observance of the Rule in the community, outside the community, or in school. In the house there are three ways of failing: first, in fidelity and punctuality regarding the exercises. Have you considered this point as one of the main means of salvation, as in fact it is? The reason for this is that fidelity gives you a sort of guarantee of keeping exactly the commandments of God, because he who is faithful in little things will also be in those that are great,[1] says our Lord.

Have you not sometimes quite easily dispensed yourselves during the past year from Holy Communion simply out of lack of feeling? Have you neglected interior prayer or allowed yourselves to be distracted while making it? Have you considered these two exercises as the ones that draw down the grace of God on all the others? With this in view, have you performed these two exercises with affection?

Have all your exercises been dear to you? Have you regarded them as the absolutely necessary way to reach the perfection of your state and, consequently, to make sure of your salvation?

Have you left everything at the first sound of the bell, even when you were with people from outside the community? This must always be done without fail, for it is exactly at the first sound of the bell that you hear God's will indicated to you.

Have you been strict in keeping silence? This is the first means of establishing observance of the Rule in a house; without it you must not expect there to be any order in a religious community. Consequently, because you are obliged to contribute to the good order of your house, be faithful to these two things.

By means of them, good order will be established and maintained with ease, provided that you add obedience in all things to the person responsible for the direction of the community, for obedience is the first virtue of a community and distinguishes it essentially from secular houses.

### 92.2 Second Point

It is no less important to be faithful to the Rule outside the house than in it, because we ought to edify our neighbor, which must be especially required of religious people.

The first thing we must pay attention to is great self-control.[2] Saint Paul recommends this to the faithful above all things. Let your self-control, he says, be known to everyone.[3] This is as if he said, Do not be self-controlled only when you are alone and in private, as you must be, of course, because the Lord is near you, but also act in the same way before everyone. Thus, when you are outside the house, act in such a way that all may recognize and be edified by your self-control. This is necessary because you work for the salvation of others, and you must begin by giving them good example in order to win them to God.

You must also carefully observe silence in the streets and, as your Rule prescribes, say the rosary, so as not to be distracted by what comes before your eyes. You ought, instead, to be occupied with the presence of God. Patience and silence especially are equally necessary for you when people say something insulting or that is liable to trouble you.

Have you been faithful to all these practices during this year? They are of very great importance for you if you do not want to scandalize others and to be distracted in the streets. A person consecrated to God must be easily distinguished from a secular by his exterior appearance and by the way he acts, because he owes edification not only to prudent people, as Saint Paul says, but also to those who are not such[4] and who often take scandal over everything, especially in the case of religious.

### 92.3 Third Point

School being the place where the Brothers spend most of their time during the day, where the activities they engage in are the ones in which they are most involved, and where they find the most occasions for distraction, the Brothers cannot watch too closely over themselves not to lose any of the merit they ought to draw from their work for the salvation of their souls and not to fail there in any of their duties.

Have you been exact during this year to follow the order of the lessons, to make use of the signal always, and to correct your students whenever they have made some mistake? You cannot dispense yourselves from this without failing in one of your principal duties.

Have you been exact to teach catechism every day during all the prescribed time and in the manner indicated? Have you been concerned that your disciples be instructed in their religion? This is your principal obligation, although other matters must not be neglected.

Have you at times acted in a careless and negligent way? Have you chatted with the children uselessly, asking them for news or listening willingly to the news they told you? Have you read books other than those that the children whom you are responsible to instruct were reading? Have you wasted time, in a word, which in your profession no longer belongs to you any more than servants' time belongs to them, obliged as they are to use all of it in their master's service, as you are for the benefit of your students?

Have you accepted something from them? You know that this is in no way permitted, for if you fall into this fault, your school will no longer be gratuitous, even if all you receive from them is only some tobacco. This is something that must not be done or tolerated, because the use of tobacco is forbidden to you and because you have to conduct the school gratuitously, which is essential to your Institute.

Examine whether you have fallen into these kinds of faults during this year, how frequently, and whether in that case you have confessed them exactly in the sacrament of Confession. Take proper resolutions on all these matters. Finally, strip off the old man today, and put on the new man, as Saint Paul exhorts you to do, and ask

God, following the advice of the same Apostle, to renew in you to-morrow the spirit of your state and of your profession.[5]

---

1. Lk 16:10
2. Different translations of the New Testament render this word (*modestia* in the Vulgate) differently: unselfishness (NAB), kindness (revised NAB), tolerance (Jerusalem), forebearance (RSV and Kleist), courtesy (Knox), gentleness (Gideon), gentle attitude (Good News), moderation (Image). See Glossary in Appendix A.
3. Phil 4:5
4. Rom 1:14
5. Eph 4:22–24

# Six Additional Meditations[1]

# For Certain Feasts That Occur During the Year

# February 1

## SAINT SEVER, BISHOP

### 103.1 First Point

It is recounted in the Gospel of Saint Luke, chapter 7, that Saint John's disciples came to our Lord to ask if he was the Christ or if they ought to expect another.[2] Jesus Christ, who had performed several miracles in their presence to let them know that he was indeed the Messiah, told them, in concluding his discourse, that the Good News is preached to the poor.[3] This ought to encourage greatly all the faithful to work courageously at the great enterprise of their salvation, especially those whose birth has constrained them to live in poverty and in the privation of this world's goods.

Saint Sever took full advantage of this circumstance. To earn a living, he was obliged to hire out to an infidel master, but he nourished his soul with the bread of God's word[4] and with the holy exercise of prayer, which he practiced with great fervor in spite of the numerous obstacles that might have hindered him from doing so in the course of his laborious work. God, who is pleased to hear the meek and humble of heart, granted him the entire conversion of his master to the faith of the Catholic Church.

Is it not very foolish to love this world's grandeur and its wealth, for there is nothing great or worthy of our esteem other than what is great and estimable in the sight of God? O divine Jesus, enlighten our eyes to regard all things as you consider them, so that all our affections and inclinations may be entirely conformable to yours.

### 103.2 Second Point

The virtues of Saint Sever, together with the great number of miracles that God performed through him, made him known to all. The resulting esteem for his person was the reason why he was consecrated bishop of Avranches, chosen from the group of disciples he had instructed and led to perfection in a solitary place. But after having labored to the full extent of his zeal in this position, he was compelled by his profound humility to resign the episcopal dignity, to renounce all his earthly possessions, and to go back to his beloved solitude, where he died the death of the saints[5] in the arms of those whom he had edified by the example of his saintly life.

We ought to give ourselves to exterior duties in the same way, that is, with the sole motive of the pure will of God indicated to us by obedience. As soon as we have done what we are obliged to do, we must return to our solitude to give ourselves to our spiritual exercises, fearing lest we might wound our conscience by some sin. Let us beg God, through the intercession of this great saint, to give us an ardent affection for the interior life, so that all the moments of our life may be so many steps leading us to union with him.

### 103.3 Third Point

Saint Sever's death was no less precious before God than his life had been edifying before human eyes. Hence, to prevent his sacred body from being profaned by the enemies of the Church, his remains were transported from the spot where they lay to a field where he was buried a second time. But his outstanding holiness was manifested by the miracles that took place in this spot, so that it was thought appropriate to transfer his holy relics to the Cathedral of Notre Dame in Rouen. God, wishing to increase the honor paid to this saint, permitted, as they guided this glorious burden, that at every place where they paused for the night, it remained immovable and could not be budged from that spot until a vow was made to build a church in his honor in that location.

Oh, how good it is to serve God! How abundantly he rewards those who love him and lifts them to the heights of glory! O my sovereign Creator of all that is good, give me your holy grace to apply myself to pay you all the veneration I owe you! Grant me your holy blessing in so generous and beneficial an undertaking through the intercession of Saint Sever, the patron and protector of our parish in this place!

---

1. These six meditations appear, with the short biographies of Saint Yon and Saint Cassian, at the end of CL 12 (and the original edition of the meditations). It seems quite clear from the vocabulary and style that they were not written by De La Salle (see CL 47, pp. 539–540). The numbers of the meditations are those of the 1882 edition.
2. Lk 7:20
3. Lk 7:22
4. Mt 4:4
5. Ps 116:15

# July 17

## THE DAY
## OF TRANSFER OF HOLY RELICS

*The honor we must pay to the relics of the saints*

### 184.1 First Point

God invites us to practice this devotion by the infinite number of miracles he has performed through the holy relics of his servants. We see this at the tombs of the martyrs and the holy confessors, which are, as the councils say, fountains of salvation that Jesus Christ has left us, from which flow all sorts of relief for the sick and where we can find a source of healing to cure illnesses and disperse evil sadness and temptations through the power of Jesus Christ, which remains in them. We see this happen at the transfer of the relics of Saint Stephen, the first martyr, and of various other saints, so that we cannot doubt that God, according to his word, does indeed honor the ashes and bones of his servants,[1] who were living members and active temples of his Holy Spirit.[2] For this same reason, he even sent his angels to bury the body of Saint Catherine and revealed the presence of saints' bodies by miraculous lights, so that they might not remain unknown in a common or undignified burial place and we might learn to venerate them for the welfare of our own body and soul.

If God's goodness does so much for our welfare in return for the slight service that we render to these lifeless relics, what grace he has in store for those who try to become imitators of these great souls!

### 184.2 Second Point

The veneration of holy relics was practiced in antiquity. It was approved by the councils and by the practice of the holiest people in recent centuries. The example of the great Saint Charles Borromeo is noteworthy in this regard, as we can see in the history of his life. The saints in glory rightly desire this honor, because in heaven they are the protectors of the living. We see this in the case of Saint Denis, the Apostle of France, of Saint Sebastian, of Saint Maurice, and of others who merited honorable burial. Finally, this is an excellent means to win their intercession for us. Because they have reached the state of perfect charity, they abundantly reward the services we do them.

When we honor their relics, they increase our own devotion by their prayers. They present our prayers to God[3] and invite us to be, like them, living holocausts before the face of the Lord.

Adore God, who is so admirable in his saints. Be humbled at the feet of his divine majesty, and learn to be sanctified. Woe to anyone who still allows himself thoughts of vanity after witnessing so many examples of piety!

### 184.3 Third Point

From our veneration of holy relics, we ought to draw the following benefits. First, we entertain special esteem and profound sentiments of piety and respect toward all holy relics, especially those whose transfer we celebrate today. This ought to give us great confidence in the intercession of the saints whose relics we are happy to have near us.

Second, we become piously ambitious, considering the honors that God pays to his servants. Be assured that people who do not strive to become great friends of God by fidelity to his grace and by constantly seeking only his glory and the salvation of their souls do not deserve to bear the name of Christians, much less that of religious and of people consecrated to God. What blindness it is to wish to be honored with the saints in the next life when we do not live like the saints now, when we entertain none but earthly thoughts, are unable to distinguish what is precious from what is vile, and seek the pleasures and honors of this world. Would this not be something deserving at once of astonishment and pity for us, who wish to share in the happy lot of the saints?[4]

Let us not act in this way. Let us lift our thoughts up to heaven, and may the sight of the holy relics become for us a motive to increase and enlighten in us the spirit of martyrdom, contempt for the world, and ardent love of our Lord Jesus Christ.

---

1. Ps 34:21          3. Tb 12:12          4. Wis 5:5
2. 1 Cor 6:15,19

# September 22

## SAINT YON

### 168.1 First Point

Saint Yon was fortunate to have been a disciple of Saint Denis and to share his spirit, his virtues, and the graces granted to him, both interior and exterior. Because Saint Denis had received from God, through the mediation of Saint Paul, great insights concerning the truths of the Gospel, it was his privilege to be one of the most enlightened men of his time. Because Saint Denis was so zealous for the establishment of the Church and for spreading the Christian religion, he shared his enlightenment with Saint Yon. He could not personally instruct all the people who needed instruction in the land where he was, so he made up for some of this by means of Saint Yon, one of his disciples.

How fortunate this saint was to have a teacher such as Saint Denis, under whose guidance he learned perfectly the truths of religion and the practice of Christian virtues, in which Saint Denis trained him both by his frequent instructions and by the continual and striking example he gave him. Oh, how advantageous it is to have been taught by learned teachers, both for the truths of faith and for the practice of virtue! Let us be such teachers for those we must instruct and by our actions make ourselves what we wish to see them be.

### 168.2 Second Point

Having become a priest, Saint Yon labored at preaching the Gospel in the region around Paris. Filled with the grace and spirit of God, he converted a large number of people. This would not astonish anyone, because, like his teacher, Saint Denis, he had prepared for this task by a period of seclusion and daily prayer.

He knew that it belonged to God to touch and convert hearts and that he was only the voice crying out to the people to be converted[1] and to recognize the true God. This led him often to have recourse to God, to ask him for the grace that his human word might be as effective as the word of the holy Apostles had been in such an admirable manner.

Because the people instructed by this saint were uncultured country folk, he applied himself especially to teach them catechism, to help them learn about God and the principal mysteries of religion, and to practice the commandments of God.

Let us be thankful to God for having given us as the patron of this community a saint who, at the beginning of the Church, held it an honor to fulfill the same function that we must carry out every day. He worked at the conversion of unbelievers with very ardent zeal, because all he had in view was to make them become God's people. Let us strive to imitate his zeal and to have the same intentions in the performance of our work, because it is the same as his, that is, teaching catechism to poor children, who often enough lack education.

### 168.3  Third Point

Saint Yon's zeal for the true religion and the great number of conversions brought about by his efforts so irritated the idolaters who at that time occupied this country and whose kings lived in the same blindness that they sought by all the means they could to oppose the great progress that this saint was making in souls and in his project to establish the Christian religion in these lands. But they soon saw that neither the trouble they caused Saint Yon nor their threats were able to lessen his zeal. All they could say to the people whom he was instructing was powerless to prevent them from being attentive and docile to his doctrine. For this saint taught them even more by the example of his holy life than by his words. His life was for them like a two-edged sword, which, as Saint Paul says, divided the flesh from the spirit in them.[2] So these people seized Saint Yon, had him cruelly scourged, and then cut off his head. Such was the reward on earth of this saint for all his apostolic labors.

Even if you have no reason to expect the same reward although you live in the same kingdom, because it is now inhabited by Catholics, prepare at least for the reward promised in the Gospel, namely, persecution. Consider yourself highly blessed, according to the teaching of our Lord Jesus Christ to his disciples, when people hate you and eject you from their midst, when they treat you injuriously and hold your name in horror because of the Son of Man,[3] for this is the way they treated the Prophets[4] and the preachers of the holy Gospel.

---

1. Jn 1:23
2. Heb 4:12
3. Lk 6:22–23
4. Mt 5:11–12

# October 23

## THE VIRTUES OF SAINT ROMANUS, ARCHBISHOP OF ROUEN

### 181.1 First Point

From his earliest years, Saint Romanus was a model of all the virtues. His very devout parents took care to bring him up as a Christian no less than as a nobleman, so that he might fulfill worthily the illustrious work for which he was destined. He clearly showed how well he had profited by such an education. Having become Chancellor of France, he displayed as much vigilance over himself to preserve his piety toward God as his zeal to deliver justice. He was constantly on guard not to lose his innocence in the corruption of the world. He kept himself as pure in his exalted position as if he had lived in the most hidden seclusion.

What a source of confusion for us who so easily lose in our exterior occupations the spirit of piety that we have acquired in our interior exercises! Let us learn from this saint to live and act in the world without sharing in the corruption of spirit and the maxims of the world.

### 181.2 Second Point

This great saint, after enlightening by the radiance of his virtues the people who live in the secular world, was chosen by God to be a burning torch on the chandelier[1] of the Church. Chosen archbishop of Rouen, he applied himself with tireless zeal to eliminate idolatry among the people and simony among the clergy. He strove to win as many adorers for Jesus Christ and perfect faithful for his Church as the demon tried to steal away. In this world he feared nothing but sin, and his soul was always clothed in the robe of his baptismal innocence. He did not hesitate to confront a dragon that was not only ravaging the crops of the fields but also devouring people.

Let us strive to preserve the baptismal innocence of the children who are or who will be entrusted to us. If we have been unfortunate enough to lose it, let us strive to recover it through penance proportionate to the greatness of our sins. How happy we would be if we could recover the state of original justice! To encourage ourselves in this endeavor, let us reflect on these words of Saint Ambrose: There are only two roads to heaven, innocence preserved or innocence restored by penance.

### 181.3 Third Point

Saint Romanus, having led such a pure life, merited that God revealed to him the time of his death, which was to come while he was celebrating holy Mass. This knowledge persuaded him to withdraw into solitude, where he could think only of himself. There the demon assailed him with furious temptations, but the constant thought of the eternal truths and his diligent prayer made him victorious and gave him the occasion to increase his merit.

Only by these two means can we strengthen our souls against all the attacks of the enemies of our salvation. Meditation on the truths taught by faith is a two-edged sword, as Saint Paul says, which reaches even to the division between the soul and the spirit, the sinews and the bones.[2] But it is not enough to be convinced of the truths of salvation; we must also ask God through fervent prayer to aid us in our weaknesses and to give us the grace to practice what his Holy Spirit has made us realize that he desires of us.

---

1. Jn 5:35; Mt 5:15       2. Heb 4:12

# December 15

## OCTAVE OF THE IMMACULATE CONCEPTION OF THE MOST BLESSED VIRGIN

### 83.1 First Point

If we wish to share in the spirit of the mystery of the Immaculate Conception of the Most Blessed Virgin and to draw from it the good that God asks of us by our holy participation, let us note that this divine mother, at the moment when her soul was created, resembled a beautiful star enlightened by the light of grace and endowed with reason. What mortification it must have been for this excellent creature to see herself thus captive, shut up as though in a prison for nine months and deprived of the use of her senses and her members! What a source of humiliation for her in her knowledge of so great a degradation!

Let us imitate these admirable dispositions of the most immaculate Virgin. Let us love and willingly cultivate seclusion, silence, and recollection. Let us apply ourselves to control our senses, mortifying our members, which are on the earth,[1] as Saint Paul says. Let us, so to speak, make ourselves captives for the love of God through exact obedience and by great fidelity to our Rule. This voluntary and loving submission will make us truly free with the noble and glorious liberty of God's children.[2] O agreeable and lovable subjection, exclaims the author of the *Imitation,* by which we become truly free and holy! O sacred state of religious subjection, which makes us equal to the angels, pleasing to God, frightening to the demons, and commendable to all the faithful! O service worthy to be embraced and constantly desired, by which we acquire the sovereign good and joy that knows no end!

### 83.2 Second Point

In her Immaculate Conception, the Most Blessed Virgin enjoyed from the first moment the practice of the virtues, at least those that are interior. She knew God by infused faith; she loved him by the charity of the Holy Spirit, who filled her from the first moments of her existence. She praised, blessed, thanked, and glorified God by her spiritual and interior acts more excellently than did all the angels together.

This is what we must learn to imitate; this is what is called the science of the saints.[3] We must learn the knowledge of God in prayer and by reading good spiritual books and catechisms. We must strive to set our hearts on fire with the love of God by fervently and frequently raising our hearts in short, repeated prayers. We must strive to make ourselves agreeable in the eyes of the Divine Majesty by continual acts of thanksgiving, love, and praise, as well as by the practice of the most solid virtues, especially humility, patience, and obedience, which were so dear and so familiar to the most holy Mother of God.

### 83.3 Third Point

The Most Blessed Virgin, although enclosed in the womb of Saint Ann, was prepared by the Holy Spirit to accomplish God's great designs for her. She prepared herself by her faithful cooperation, making holy use through her interior acts of the gifts and graces that heaven abundantly gave her.

The holy religious state to which God has had the goodness to call us is our mother. The novitiate is her womb, in which she spiritually conceives the novices, who are her children. She engenders them for Jesus Christ,[4] as Saint Paul expresses it, by forming them to a truly Christian and religious way of life.

You, therefore, who have the happiness of enjoying this advantage in the novitiate, this mystical and life-giving womb of the religious life, must see to it that your spiritual conception is immaculate, that is, spotless, through exemption from all deliberate sin. Develop good habits that are conformable to the maxims of the holy Gospel, and be filled with the graces of the Holy Spirit.

The Most Blessed Virgin, nine months after her most pure conception, came forth from the womb of Saint Ann full of grace and the Spirit of God,[5] ready to do great things, namely, to procure the glory of God and the salvation of souls. Also prepare in the same way to leave the novitiate filled with grace and the Spirit of God, so that you may labor solely for his glory by procuring the salvation of souls according to the spirit and the end of our Institute or by carrying out other work and assignments in the house according to the designs of divine Providence for you. You will know these assignments infallibly through the voice of holy obedience, and in them you will most certainly find your sanctification, interior peace, and salvation. Ask the Most Blessed Virgin to obtain this grace for you through her merits and in virtue of her holy and Immaculate Conception.

---

1. Col 3:5
2. Rom 8:21
3. Wis 10:10
4. 1 Cor 4:15
5. Lk 1:28

# First Sunday in October

## THE DEDICATION OF CHURCHES

### 188.1 First Point

Reflect that the custom of consecrating churches to God is very holy and very ancient; innumerable holy places were built and consecrated by the Apostles and their successors. God, who is indeed everywhere by his immensity, is, nevertheless, present in a very special way in those places where he has willed buildings to be in his honor, like so many tabernacles where he has chosen to dwell with people,[1] to be adored, and to receive their prayers. In these sacred places, God wishes the holiest of actions to be performed and the most august services of religion to be offered.

For this reason, we are commanded to attend these ceremonies with respect; destruction threatens those who profane these churches by their irreverence and misbehavior.[2] Reflect, further, that we solemnize the dedication day of churches in order to make reparation to God for all the acts of impiety and the other faults that have been committed there during the year. We also thank the Lord for all the favors we have received there and renew the devotion and veneration we owe to the church, which is called the house of God.[3]

Consider how you have acted there, with what spirit you enter the church, and with what dispositions you offer there your prayers to God. Is it with lively faith in the presence of God and genuine sentiments of respect that you owe to this infinite majesty?

### 188.2  Second Point

Reflect that Jesus Christ is truly present in the Most Blessed Sacrament reserved in churches. This is why we are still more especially bound to recognize the presence of God in these holy places. God chose them in order to be honored there with special worship and is pleased to give graces more abundantly to those who ask for them with sincere devotion.

If under the Old Law, people had to tremble with fear and respect when they entered the Tabernacle,[4] which contained the Ark of the Covenant[5] and the Tables of the Law,[6] with what reverence and thoughts of our nothingness must we not enter the place where God is, as it were, seated on a throne of love to have mercy on us and where God is constantly adored by innumerable angels, who consider it a great honor to stand in his presence and pay their homage?

### 188.3  Third Point

Consider that what ought to encourage us to have deep sentiments of respect and devotion in these holy places is the thought that this is where God is pleased to give us grace with very special generosity, goodness, and mercy. This is where the Father of mercies welcomes with open arms the prodigal,[7] where the Good Shepherd brings back to the fold the strayed sheep,[8] where the afflicted find comfort, and where the sick are healed, the weak are strengthened, and the tempted are given new power over their enemies. Finally, this is where God listens favorably to the prayers we offer and is pleased to fill with graces those who have recourse to his goodness.

Let us acknowledge all these truths, and let us resolve again to act with such respect in churches that we may be worthy to receive the divine mercy there and to experience in ourselves all its effects in us.

Let us renew the consecration of the temple of our body and our soul[9] by consecrating to God our heart and all our will after devoutly receiving Holy Communion.

---

| | | |
|---|---|---|
| 1. Rev 21:3 | 4. Lv 16:2 | 7. Lk 15:20 |
| 2. 1 Cor 3:17 | 5. Ex 40:2–3 | 8. Lk 15:4–6 |
| 3. Gn 28:17 | 6. 2 Cor 5:10 | 9. 1 Cor 6:19 |

# Life of Saint Yon, Priest and Martyr

On September 22, the Church celebrates the feast of Saint Yon, priest and martyr, who suffered in the district of Hurepoix, diocese of Paris. The history of his glorious martyrdom is related by a devout and ancient author of the ninth century who learned it from the best writers of those days.

Saint Yon lived in the early years of the infant Church. He accompanied Saint Denis, the first bishop of Paris, when the latter came to France, and he was associated with the work of this evangelical mission. The fact that the Apostle of France chose Saint Yon to help him in a ministry at once so difficult and so important allows us to presume that Saint Yon possessed all the qualities needed by an excellent Gospel worker, even by an Apostle. Thus we can judge the zeal he showed for the glory of God in spreading faith in Jesus Christ and the charity he displayed in making idolators abandon the errors and vices in which they were immersed and in procuring eternal salvation for them. Above all, we can be sure that he possessed courage and patience to overcome the obstacles and to despise dangers, insults, and threats.

The holiness of Saint Yon's life contributed no less than his preaching and his miracles to the conversion of pagans, for God had made him mighty in word and in deeds,[1] which are graces that he customarily imparts to those he sends as pioneers to bring the light of the Gospel to countries still plunged in the darkness of paganism and the shadow of death.[2]

Once he was ordained priest, Saint Yon labored mainly in the area where Saint Denis sent him to work, namely, in the section of the territory of Paris that has since received the name of Hurepoix, where the diocese of Paris adjoins those of Sens and Chartres. The main center of his mission was the little town of Chartres, on the river Orge. Having established the faith of Jesus Christ very successfully there, Saint Yon merited to see his efforts crowned by martyrdom, some years after the death of Saint Denis. He was arrested by an officer named Julian, who was following the order given to him by the governor of Paris, the same person who had Saint Lucian put to death at Beauvais and Saint Piat at Tournai.

Saint Yon was condemned by the judge to be beheaded according to the edicts of the emperors against the Christians, either the one that the Emperor Aurelian had published a few days before his death or the one that Maximian Herculeus, Diocletian's colleague, had published in Gaul at the beginning of his reign, about the year 287. Be that as it may, Saint Yon was led to execution on a neighboring hill, about a league from Chartres, where he consummated his glorious martyrdom on August 5, the day given in his Acts as the day of his martyrdom. This was already the day on which his feast was celebrated when his Acts were compiled toward the end of the ninth or the beginning of the tenth century. This is also the day on which the Church of Paris has chosen to celebrate the feast. It is not known why the authors of the Roman martyrology, where the saint is called Jonas, placed the feast on September 22.

A widespread tradition throughout the area holds that Saint Yon was beheaded near the little river Orge, which traverses the town of Chartres. The scaffold stood on a small eminence, and the saint's head tumbled down into the river. His body then walked down and retrieved the head, a sight that terrorized the executioner as well as the spectators. Once Saint Yon was dead, the faithful of Chartres came and took his body from the hill and gave it an honorable burial near the walls of their city. There it rested in great veneration, especially after peace had been restored to the Church in the time of the Emperor Constantine.

The body remained there until it was transferred to Corbeil, another town in the diocese of Paris, located on the Seine, about five or six leagues from Chartres. It seems, however, that only part of the saint's body was brought there; what remained at Chartres is kept in a silver reliquary beneath the altar, following the ancient custom. These relics are so important that the Breviary of Paris states that the body of Saint Yon is still kept in this church, saying nothing about what was transferred to Corbeil.

We do not know exactly when this transfer was effected. It is celebrated at Corbeil on the same day as the principal feast of the saint, namely, August 5. His relics are still preserved in the church of Notre Dame, which is the principal one of the locality. This is what tradition relates as certain regarding the transfer of Saint Yon's relics to Corbeil-sur-Seine. This city possesses only the holy martyr's head and got possession of it as follows:

Through the relics of Saint Yon many miracles were accomplished; his head, in particular, enjoyed this power. When the river was at flood stage and there was danger of inundation, all the citizens had to do was to bring the head of the saint close to the river bank and at once the flood subsided and the waters returned to their normal channel. On one occasion, the Seine had risen very high and threatened to submerge the entire city of Corbeil. So the clergy and the people of that city sent a deputation to the officials of Chartres, asking them to lend them the head of the saint and promising to return it with all due honor once they were delivered from the danger. This plea was granted but only on condition that hostages be given. When they heard this, the people of Corbeil thought of a stratagem to be able to keep the precious relic permanently within their walls. They dressed some little orphans in magnificent clothes and sent them over with much pomp, after which the inhabitants of Chartres delivered the head of Saint Yon and kept these children, whom they believed to be the sons of the most outstanding citizens of the city. After the precious relic made the waters recede as usual, the clergy and the people of Corbeil enthroned it in their church and resolved not to give it back to Chartres. The deputies who came to demand the return of Saint Yon's head were told instead that they could keep the children whom they had accepted as hostages. Ever since, the saint's head has remained in Corbeil, where it works many great miracles.

The hill that had witnessed the shedding of the saint's blood, although no longer possessing his holy remains, did not fail to become an object of respect and veneration on the part of the people. Their devotion and gratitude urged them to go there to honor the memory of the holy martyr on the very spot where the earth had received his blood as the seal on the truth that he had preached. A church was built there in his honor, and a monastery was founded, but in the course of time, as happened to many other monasteries, this one was reduced to a simple priory, which exists to this day, and a parish. So many people came there that an important town grew up with some fortifications around it, bearing the name of Hautefeuille. There the local lord maintained a garrison for defense in the time of Hugh Capet. Later wars devastated the locality, and there remains only a tiny village, named Saint-Yon. The local lord still retains some of his feudal rights with the title of his ancient barony.

---

1. Lk 24:19          2. Lk 1:79

# Life of Saint Cassian, Bishop and Martyr

On August 13, the Church honors the memory of Saint Cassian, one of the most illustrious martyrs of Jesus Christ, who suffered under the pagan emperors when he was the bishop of Brescia, a suffragan of the archdiocese of Milan. Out of zeal for the Christian religion, he became a schoolteacher in the city of Imola, in Italy, situated in the Romagna, which in other times was called Forum Cornelii, after its founder, Cornelius Sulla.

The poet Prudentius, who wrote an account of the saint's life in verse and later composed another in prose, found out about him when he made a devotional visit to his tomb. There he saw a painting in which the saint's martyrdom was depicted; he also learned about it from a devout cleric of the locality. Here is a summary of his account:

Saint Cassian, having been driven from his episcopal see during the persecution that occurred under the Emperor Julian the Apostate, withdrew to Imola. He thought that he could not better exercise his zeal than by instructing youth. To inspire these children with the principles of the religion and the faith taught by Jesus Christ, he taught them the basic elements of literature, that is, how to read and write. He taught them signs that express several things by a single character, so that they could write as quickly as a person could talk. This was a method widely used in those days.

The saint was reported to the city judge, who was a partisan of the passions of the apostate emperor. The judge had Cassian arrested and brought before him, intending to force him to renounce the worship of the true God and to adore the false divinities. But when Saint Cassian refused to sacrifice to the idols, the judge became angry over his constancy and declared him guilty of sacrilege against the gods and rebellion against the edicts of the emperor. The tyrant thought he could find no means more appropriate to take vengeance on Saint Cassian than to abandon him to his own students, most of whom were still pagans.

He was, therefore, brought back to his school and stripped, with his hands tied behind his back. The crowd of his students went against him for fear of offending the judge and, perhaps, also to take revenge for the just and necessary punishments they had received from him. Some broke their slates on his head; others pierced his flesh with thousands of blows by their metallic styluses, which were like engraver's tools or awls. These were used in those days to make marks on wood or on wax. Thus they caused him to die a long and drawn out death. His martyrdom was all the more cruel and painful because his young executioners could not kill him outright. He languished in the midst of torments that were constantly renewed and did not end until he had lost all his blood, drop by drop. This happened on August 13, around the year 363. All the martyrologies mention Saint Cassian.

Prudentius called upon this saint to obtain for him a fortunate and prosperous journey that he was to make to Rome. His prayer was heard, and when he returned to Spain, his native country, he composed the history of Saint Cassian's martyrdom as we have related it.

The city of Brescia recognizes him as its bishop, and the cathedral of Imola still bears the name of Saint Cassian. A very ancient tradition states that his body still rests beneath the high altar.

# PART THREE

—— ✦ ——

# Meditations
## for the Time of Retreat

For the use of all people who are engaged in the education of youth, especially for the retreat that the Brothers of the Christian Schools make during the time of vacation.

by Monsieur John Baptist de La Salle,
Doctor of Theology,
Founder of the Brothers of the Christian Schools

Rouen
Antoine Le Prévost Press
rue Saint Vivien
[1730]

# Introduction

by
Miguel Campos, FSC

Condensed with permission from the introduction to *Meditations for the Time of Retreat* (Winona, MN: Saint Mary's College Press, 1975).

# 1. Development of the Text

### History of the Text

Among all the writings of John Baptist de La Salle, *Meditations for the Time of Retreat* has had an unhappy history. His other works have enjoyed from the beginning a much greater popularity. Those dealing with the professional functions of the Brothers were the most frequently published: *Les Règles de la Bienséance, Conduite des Écoles chrétiennes, Devoirs d'un Chrétien envers Dieu, Instructions et Prières*. Similarly those dealing with the ascetical principles of the Brother's life had many editions: *Les Règles communes, L'Explication de la Méthode d'Oraison,* and *Recueil*. All these writings undoubtedly made a profound impression on the minds of the Brothers. However, it must be recognized that very often a fundamentalist understanding predominated in the interpretation and the reading of these publications, although there is no question that such an approach did not prevent an element of creativity in the history of the Institute, clearly demonstrated in the well-known variety of educational projects developed by the Brothers. This creativity, it must be admitted, was occasionally impeded by a fidelity to the letter of the text, with its limited perspectives. There was also a focus on the practical and the more observable elements of the writings and an emphasis on precise compliance, which often resulted in a loss of relevance to contemporary needs.

*Meditations for Sundays and Feasts,* however, even though the book was used almost daily and was frequently cited in the official circulars of the Institute, suffered from the routine or superficial method in which the meditations were employed. They served very often to illustrate only the spiritual thought of the present moment. The fate of *Meditations for the Time of Retreat* was even worse. Although re-edited several times and prescribed by the Rule to be read during the annual retreat, these meditations somehow remained in the dark for most Brothers. It is a fact that there is no reference to these meditations in any General Chapter from 1717 to 1901, that is, from the Chapter just before the death of the Founder up to and including the one held in 1901. Similarly, except for one volume of circulars during the generalate of Brother Joseph (1884–1897), any reference to these meditations in the official circulars of the Institute is extremely rare. Somehow, despite the great attachment of the Brothers to all the writings of De La Salle, *Meditations for the Time of Retreat* has been hardly known.

Several recent publications have led to a change of attitude regarding Lasallian studies. First there was the doctoral dissertation of Brother Michel Sauvage, *Catéchèse et Laïcat* (Paris: Ligel, 1962). Without overlooking the other writings of De La Salle, this dissertation focuses on *Meditations for the Time of Retreat* as central to Lasallian thought. Brother Michel's very systematic study of the New Testament citations in these meditations furthered a rediscovery of the depth of meaning in this work of the Founder. Another very thorough study, that of Brother Luis Varela, also throws considerable new light on the role of Holy Scripture in Lasallian spirituality (*Biblia y Espiritualidad en San J. B. de La Salle,* Salamanca: Sinite, 1966).

Through such studies *Meditations for the Time of Retreat* was rediscovered. The 1966–1967 General Chapter made several references to it; more significantly, these references, especially in *Declaration on the Brother in the World Today,* inspired the general determination of the Chapter to have the Brothers of today understand and live the charism of De La Salle. Both this understanding by the Chapter and *Meditations for the Time of Retreat* are the focus of this writer's doctoral dissertation, *L'Itinéraire Évangélique de Saint J. B. de La Salle et le recours à l' Écriture dans ses Méditations pour les Temps de la Retraite (Cahiers lasalliens* 45 and 46, 1974).

The rediscovery of these meditations coincides with the effort to rediscover the original spirit of the Founder, the task attempted by the 39th General Chapter of the Institute in response to the call of Vatican Council II for the renewal of the religious life. The Council declared that true renewal must be a return to "the original sources of all Christian life and to the original inspiration behind a given community . . . under the influence of the Holy Spirit" (*Perfectae Caritatis,* 2).

This renewal is not carried out by some kind of fidelity to the past or to a collection of citations from the writings of the Founder. It is, instead, the fidelity of a community of men seeking to hear the call of the Holy Spirit in the needs of the world and of the Church in their own times and seeking to discern the gifts of the Spirit to use them to give witness, in turn, to the good news of the kingdom of God in today's world.

A constant tradition in the Institute and a critical analysis of internal evidence leave no doubt about the authenticity and the content of these meditations. The precise date of composition has not been definitively established, but Brother Michel Sauvage has shown that De La Salle made use of a translation of the New Testament that was not available prior to 1707. There is also evidence that these meditations were composed toward the end of his life. They are the work of a mature person speaking of what he has lived through "after long experience," as is expressly stated in the introduction to the first edition.

## Sources of the Text

The literary sources of *Meditations for the Time of Retreat* have not been systematically studied. It is certain, nonetheless, that De La Salle was influenced by the concerns, the ideas, and the experiences of people of his time who were engaged in the reform of schools, especially those who were involved in the training of teachers.

Despite evidence of some limited literary influences, the amount of scriptural citations in the meditations and the altogether personal way in which Holy Scripture is cited encourage us to affirm that Holy Scripture, especially the writings of Saint Paul, is the principal source of *Meditations for the Time of Retreat*. The citations of Saint Paul are, in fact, so literal that "we must presume that the Founder worked with a New Testament constantly at hand and copied out certain passages directly" (Brother Michel Sauvage, *Cahiers lasalliens* 1:36–37).

Among the publications during the time of the Founder, one has often been proposed as a possible source because of its structure and content: *Meditations,* by Father Giry, written especially for the Sisters of the Charitable Schools of the Holy Infant Jesus for the time of their retreat and published in 1696 in Paris. The influence of this work of Giry on *Meditations for the Time of Retreat* is clear, but his citations from Saint Paul have a meaning that is entirely different from what is characteristic of De La Salle's use of Saint Paul.

There are sixteen meditations in the work by De La Salle, two for each day of the eight-day annual retreat. They present a synthesis of thought, and their style is conditioned by language that is often rigorous in its simplicity. There is nothing of the pious homily in these meditations. Their plain and direct manner has led Brother Michel Sauvage to state:

> Their language is even austere; their style, without any effort at grace. Yet in studying them, it becomes clear that they present a very coherent doctrine, well thought out over a long period of time, each word carefully chosen to carry its full weight, so that analysis is difficult and synthesis practically impossible (*Catéchèse et Laïcat,* 558–59).

It could be said that De La Salle has finally come to understand, perhaps fully and all at once, the direction that God has given to his life; God goes before him, calls him, and urges him on. Because the meditations form a work that is tightly structured, it would be a mistake to read them as an historical treatise or as a theological synthesis. The book is simply a collection of meditations, and it is for the time of retreat.

The annual retreat is a special time of the year when the Brothers consider their life in its entirety in order to get a better grasp of its meaning and its orientation before God. At this special time, the focus in the mind of De La Salle is on the *work* of the Brothers, that is, on everything that makes up the substance of their day-to-day existence. His purpose is not to provide some examination of conscience on their duties as teachers but rather to discover their spiritual, charismatic identity in the roots of their calling, which is the ultimate purpose of their life.

The main force and focus of the meditations is God, the living God, who calls, who chooses, who sends on mission. It is the God of mystery, whose saving love for everyone has been realized in Jesus Christ and is revealed visibly in the Church by an ecclesial ministry through men who are sent, like the angels, with a special charismatic gift. This gift is put to work in humble actions that must wait in patience for their full achievement. De La Salle constantly appeals to the Brothers; he continually addresses them in the second personal pronoun, *you*. This appeal is aimed at a dialogue, not with him but with the living God. When this happens, a Brother realizes that the story of his own life has meaning only in relation to the one great plan of God's saving action for all humaniy.

# 2. Content of the Meditations

Recent studies have shown us the framework for reading *Meditations for the Time of Retreat:* a Brother hears in the meditations an echo of his own life. In this introduction we will see that these meditations are, *first,* inseparable from the way of life that De La Salle chose under the influence of the Gospel, his own story; *second,* a call to the Brother to express his own life, his story; *third,* a celebration of the mystery of God's love. Finally, these meditations throw the light of the Scriptures on the way of life of the Brothers in radical relation to the work of God visible in action, in history.

## THE LIFE STORY OF JOHN BAPTIST DE LA SALLE

We cannot appreciate *Meditations for the Time of Retreat* unless we have an understanding of the interplay of the Gospel and the events of the life of De La Salle, the full human and Christian dimensions of the course he chose to follow, and the direction and quality he gave to his life in the light of his relationship with God. Only when we see the language of the meditations, in spite of its limitations, in the context of the life he lived can we begin to appreciate the rich meaning they had for him and that he intended to convey to the Brothers.

For this we must avoid any oversimplifying of the events of the Founder's life. Instead, we must enter into his itinerary and read the facts of his life in the light of certain autobiographical documents to grasp in his own language how he understood these facts (*cf. Cahiers lasalliens,* 45:77–89). We let De La Salle speak for himself and tell his own story.

A complete historical biography of De La Salle, written according to this method, would be of monumental proportions; therefore, in this introduction we restrict ourselves to four events in his life: *vocation, commitment, growth,* and *conflict.* These events are at the heart of the critical decisions that De La Salle made in favor of the teachers and the Christian Schools.

In these four key events, we can discover the convergence of previous events in his life: his doubts and hesitations, the turning point in his resolution of the conflicting issues, and the interaction between John Baptist and his Brothers, on the one hand, and with the institutions and the civil and ecclesiastical authorities he had to confront, on the other. In each case we see an option that takes shape, is affirmed, and becomes an action.

These events are not studied as four isolated, unhistorical moments but as indicators of the powerful currents in the history of a person, presented in accord with the profound significance of the Pascal mystery, the Resurrection of Jesus.

### Vocation

Through specific acts De La Salle made the decision to accept God's call to work for the Christian Schools. All his biographers cite, with more or less accuracy, a memoir written by the Founder about the first years of his new Community. This autobiographical document helps us understand God's call and De La Salle's response.

### Commitment

De La Salle made a precise and irrevocable commitment to a project that he recognized and accepted in the light of the Gospel. He vowed all his powers to the work of establishing and consolidating the Society of the Brothers of the Christian Schools. Two documents help us understand better the Gospel significance of these acts: *Memorandum on the Habit,* written to defend the garb, the existence, and the autonomy of the Community, and the *Formula of Vows* of 1691 and 1694, which shows us beyond any doubt the Paschal dimension of the commitments through which he lived and which he affirmed, celebrated, and organized in a project that responded to the needs of the world.

### Growth

De La Salle then undertook to extend and to consolidate the work of the Christian Schools (the third event), which he understood as the work of God. In this we can understand how he realized his charism in its fullness, a gift of the Spirit that he had clearly seen in the beginning (the first event) and that led him to organize a Community for a mission (the second event). The document that helps us understand the profound meaning of the acts of the third event is De La Salle's *Rules That I Have Imposed on Myself.*

### Conflict

There were conflicts that impelled the Founder to let go of his authority over the Institute and to decide, first, on a period of absence and then on a total surrender of the role of Superior, all in order to guarantee the consolidation of the work without him. There were tensions and problems provoked within the Community of the Brothers by both external and internal causes. The Christian Schools were not organized within the framework of the educational structures of the time, and certain people were proposing different forms of government for the Community. The ultimate consolidation of this work of God was not through constant victories toward a grand triumph at the end of De La Salle's life. Rather, what began in a radical incarnation, he learned, was destined to lead him to a total emptying of self *(kenosis).* The document that helps us interpret this experience is the letter of the Brothers, written to him on April 1, 1714, asking him to return from the South of France to resume his role as Superior. While not an autobiographical statement, it must have touched the heart of his experience profoundly at that time, for it led him to return to the government of the Community more determined than ever to achieve total self-effacement before his death in order to confirm the consolidation of the body of the Society.

# MEDITATIONS FOR THE TIME OF RETEAT: A CALL

*Meditations for the Time of Retreat* is a call to the Brothers to express their own personal word, their own history. These meditations are, in fact, all written in the second person, something that is not always the case with the meditations written for Sundays and feasts. They are addressed in a very special way to the Brothers, to each of the Brothers in the Community. The communitarian perspective is hardly evident at first sight, but the absence of the term *community* is only apparent. De La Salle is speaking to each of his sons, insofar as he is a part of this group of the Brothers of the Christian Schools, of this Institute, of these men associated to give themselves freely to the establishment of Christian Schools in the service of the young who are most neglected. Furthermore, the words of De La Salle are announced in an active Community assembled for its annual retreat. If it is true that the Founder presumes this communitarian reality, it remains, nonetheless, true that his challenge is addressed to each of the Brothers personally, for the Community exists only in the measure that each of its members has been taken over by God, is realizing his responsibility for the salvation of the young, and turns, then, in prayer to God, who calls him, sends him, supports him, and judges him.

*Meditations for the Time of Retreat* does not provide the Brothers with an historical summary of the origins and the formation of the Institute. It does not give the Brothers a summary of their identity in the Church or of the purpose of their ministry. It does not seek merely to build up the Brother's ego. If these meditations do succeed in making the Brothers more aware of the dignity and the value of their work, it is not because they provide any recipes for carrying out that work effectively.

These meditations go to the heart of the life of the Brothers by inviting them to consider, in the spirit of faith and zeal, the lived experience of their Institute, the experience of God discovered in their own day-to-day relations with students. When De La Salle invites the Brothers to consider their work in the Christian Schools, he is not engaging them in considerations that are historical, theological, or pedagogical. He is not urging the Brothers with abstract reasons derived from theological or pedagogical theories, nor even from the Bible. Rather, he invites the Brothers to deepen their understanding, through contemplation and prayer, of the purpose of their being Brothers, not *what* they are living for but *for whom* they exist as Brothers. The Founder is helping them both to study the substance of their daily experience in the educational service they provide and to see the Gospel dimensions of this service and of all that it demands.

At the same time that he is focusing a Brother's attention on the concrete details of his life, helping him understand better that his way of life with his students constitutes the center of his religious experience, De La Salle invites the Brother to break through space and time, and he reveals to him the mystery of God at the very heart of this way of life. This opening to the transcendent mystery, far from diminishing the concrete dimensions of the Brother's existence, allows him to see with new eyes the fullness of his being—the presence of God, where God's work is visible and effective on behalf of the children of the poor. In doing all this, De La Salle is not plunging the Brother into mere introspection, a closing in on himself. Rather, the Founder is placing the Brother at the heart of the wonderful things of God within his own existence, announcing to him what the Lord is telling him today.

## CELEBRATING THE MYSTERY

For the first Brothers, *Meditations for the Time of Retreat* spoke of events they had lived through together: the progressive establishment of the Society of the Christian Schools, founded exclusively and radically on the marvelous action of God in history, the mystery of God's love, and visibly realized in the creation of a Community to respond to the call of the poor, who were far off from God's saving grace.

These meditations constitute a contemplation of the mystery of the love of God revealing itself and acting in the existence of the Brothers for the salvation of the poor. This reference to the full dimension of the mystery breaks forth several times into an act of thanksgiving whose simplicity does not diminish the astonishment that is experienced in the face of the wonderful things of God. Such admiration and gratitude are by their very nature contagious.

These wonderful things of God are not presented as a history of salvation in the past, a doctrine that has been developed from Saint Paul. However solid the meditations may be from a doctrinal point of view, they never remain on the level of ideas. They seek, instead, to be in union with the living experience of the mystery of God, who has guided the Brothers, called them in their time, united them in a communion, and sent them to announce the good news of salvation.

De La Salle invites the Brothers to recognize in their own history this guidance by God. Free of any paternalism, he avoids acting for the Brothers, speaking their word for them. Instead, he calls on the Brothers to read, to live, and to speak their own response together in answer to the call of a mission in history that refers exclusively to the mystery of God. He does not want them simply to think again about the abstract content of some resumé of the truths that might be applicable to the externals of their position as teachers. The interpretation of *Meditations for the Time of Retreat* must be something entirely different. A recent study by this writer shows that this content consists of three major elements: the visible action of God in the Brother's history, the eschatological purpose, or destiny, of this spiritual and visible action, and the demands of the Gospel.

### The Visible Action of God in the Brother's History

The Brother is invited to become aware of the presence and the pervading action of God in his own history. The personal history of a Brother and the progressive steps of his vocation are a response to the call of children who have been left to themselves. In this history the Brother recognizes a call, a charismatic gift for the good of others. He sees himself as a minister of God (meditations 1 and 2), as a cooperator with Jesus Christ (meditations 3 and 4) whose functions are intended to make visible the hidden secret of the wisdom of God, the salvation offered to all (meditations 5 and 6).

*Meditations for the Time of Retreat* envisions a history of relationships among the Brothers and between each Brother and his students. In these relationships the Brothers and their students give themselves freely to one another, learning to leave a former way of life in order to achieve a new life through conversion and mutual education. It is a life of love and forgiveness, and in living this life, they discover and share the experience of the ever-present and generous love of God, and they live as children of God. All this implies a continual process of progressive enlightenment, of renewed life, of growing freedom— all made possible by the generous action of the Spirit of Christ, already present and striving toward a final destiny.

*Meditations for the Time of Retreat*, especially in meditations 1 through 6, calls upon and challenges the Brother's faith. The work constitutes an invitation to see, to remember that the Brother has been enlightened so that he can enlighten others, and to recognize the mystery of the work of God in the visible work of the Brother. They are workers, instruments, and cooperators in God's work.

### The Eschatological Purpose

The Brother is also invited to become aware of the purpose of this calling and of his charismatic gift. Meditations 7 through 12 especially, but not exclusively, make very clear the direction and purpose of the entire existence of the Brother. The Brother has not been given a charismatic gift for himself but for the good of children, for the building up of the Church.

In this sense De La Salle invites the Brothers to place their ministry in an historical and apostolic lineage—the Son sent by the Father, the Apostles sent by Christ, the bishops as successors of the Apostles, and the Brothers, as ministers of the Church, sharing and continuing this apostolic heritage (meditations 7 and 8). Their activities are those of ministers with and for their students. They guide them with much vigilance toward knowledge of the mysteries, toward the celebration of these mysteries sacramentally, toward initiation and growth in the Christian life. In this description we can recognize the powerful thrust of the Church following the Council of Trent, the efforts in dogma, moral, and worship. But the terms in Lasallian language, "to instruct, to teach, to guide," cannot be reduced to a strict concept of dogma, moral, and worship. These Lasallian expressions are all aimed at creating "life according to the Christian spirit," an expression that constantly returns to the Founder's pen.

This sharing of the students in the promises and the covenant, in the Body of Christ, which grows in history, involves also the relationship of Brother and student. The Brother does not free his students from the life of the flesh except insofar as he takes on the flesh-and-blood condition of their life, even to the giving of his own life. Made free together by the action of the Spirit in a fraternal union, Brother and students mutually educate one another to live the Gospel in their daily life, not only verbally but in the interaction of the words and deeds of teacher and students.

In this interaction the activities of the Brother are those of a prophet. His charismatic gift makes him see more clearly and energizes him with zeal, driving him irresistibly to neglect nothing in regard to his students, urging them to renounce any shortcomings in their former way of life, supporting them in their conversion, and encouraging them in the new life of the covenant.

In this sense just as the first six meditations end with the activities of visible angels, so the second six meditations end with the activities of the school, symbolized in the language of the seventeenth century by the words *reproof* and *correction*. De La Salle very accurately situates the religious experience of the Brother in the hard facts of his educational relationship, the interaction of the Brother with his students.

Finally, just as the first six meditations challenge the faith of the Brothers and call upon them to see the dynamic mystery of God in the concrete actions of their ministry, so the second six meditations challenge the zeal of the Brothers. They are continually renewed in their awareness that their faith is totally inseparable from the zeal that drives them to identify with their students, even to the point of laying down their life, and that such faith and zeal have no other origin than the power of the Spirit of God, of Christ, and no other purpose than the purpose of the coming of the Son of Man. This prophetic zeal of the Brother, the grace of his charismatic gift for the work of God, which is the work of the Church, constitutes the heart of the Brother's continual impulse to identify with the flesh-and-blood life of his students, the world in which they live, and the poverty of their life. At the same time, the Brother's zeal never loses its religious dimension, the awareness that all history has already been directed toward its final achievement: the total Christ, in whom all human beings and all the world will be made subject to God.

### The Demands of the Gospel

This thought leads us to the consideration of the third level of interpretation of *Meditations for the Time of Retreat,* the renewed awareness of the demands of the Gospel that are involved in the Brother's ministry. These meditations, especially, although not exclusively, the last four, put the Brothers, the whole fabric of their existence, and their activities under the judgment of the Word of God.

The tone of thanksgiving, the eucharistic tone that is characteristic of his meditations, has already been pointed out. De La Salle does not engage the Brothers in mere introspection or in a sickly closing in on self. Deeply imbued as he was with the profound meaning of the mystery and the work of God, which had revealed itself to him visibly in his own history, the Founder did not arrive at a concept of the demands of the Gospel from some doctrine or even from the Scriptures. In spite of the fact that he often expresses these demands by literal quotations from the Bible, he does not quote the Scriptures to give prescriptions or norms of behavior for the Brother's personal or professional life.

We must again note that De La Salle makes no distinction between the professional and the community life of the Brothers. This integration of professional responsibilities and the search for perfection is one of the constants of his own way of life. In this De La Salle is quite original; he goes far beyond the authors of his time when he says that the Brother renders an account of his zeal for the salvation of others before giving an account of his work for his own salvation. It is the dynamic unity of the Brother's life, of his faith and zeal in the continual drive of his calling, that is submitted to the judgment of the Word of God. Without giving a synthesis of what is subjected to the judgment, let us examine certain elements that seem important.

The judgment which is the subject of *Meditations for the Time of Retreat* is not structured around the constitutive elements of the Brother's vocation. It is, rather, an invitation to recover continually in his daily experiences, in his history with others, and especially in his efforts to respond to the call of the poor the impulse of the power of God that continually takes possession of him, calls him, sends him on mission. It is an invitation to go beyond the mediation of structures but without neglecting them. If it is preferable, we can say that the judgment will focus on the charismatic gift—the gift of instructing, of teaching, of watching, and of the faith. This judgment will not focus on things, on practices, but on the clearness of the Brother's vision, on the energy of his zeal to put his talents into action, on his ability to go beyond routine procedures without ceasing. It is in this kind of perspective that we must read the final meditations, especially the even-numbered meditations that speak of the obligations concerning particular areas of the Brother's life. The Founder does not restrict the Brother's view to structures, to the *Rule,* or to the *Conduct of the Christian Schools.* He speaks of faith and zeal and of the impulse that drives a person to discover the mystery of God in the action of his own experience and in the history of the world around him.

The judgment that is the subject of *Meditations for the Time of Retreat* is not structured around the vows. Beyond the explicit references to the formula of vows, these meditations speak of the radical gift of the Brother for the glory of God, for the salvation of the poor, or, in other words, for the glory of God made visible in the salvation of the poor. The total gift of a life is not defined by legal obligations and, in particular, does not turn the Brother back in on himself. It is, rather, a demand to identify with the flesh-and-blood reality of the students, to humble himself, and to enter fully into their life, even to giving up his own life so that they might have life.

Asceticism and ministry are here inseparable; they blend in active contemplation and contemplative action. The asceticism of *Meditations for the Time of Retreat* is, in fact, inseparable from mystical contemplation, that is, from life and growth in the Paschal mystery discerned in history and in personal experience. This asceticism is directed to service, to the gift of self to others. Never a battle against self for its own sake, it is inseparable from ministry and is understood as a total docility to the Spirit. It is fidelity to the Spirit, who calls, who sends, who is the primary witness and evidence at the judgment of the Brother. This fidelity is seen especially in its ultimate purpose: to announce the Gospel.

Because the Brother's life is ultimately related to the purpose of the coming of Jesus Christ, his whole life is subject to the judgment of the Word of God. From this fact follows the necessity to live and to help others live according to the Christian spirit, according to the maxims of the Gospel. Holy Scripture is the ultimate rule for the life of the Brother and of his students. But this announcing of the Gospel is not reduced to practices and prescriptions. It is not, for example, reduced to teaching catechism. The obligation to teach secular subjects is inseparable from the obligation to teach and instruct the students in the Christian spirit. Nor does announcing the Gospel consist only in giving good example or even in searching to give an explicit witness. Rather, it means that the Brother must become incarnate, that is, take on the flesh-and-blood reality of the students' life in an affective and effective manner, walk around in their shoes, and unite his own history to that of his students, to the whole history of salvation, and to the mystery of Christ.

Finally, as a person of hope, the Brother never settles down. In the midst of all this process of growth, he constantly keeps his eyes focused on the eschatological joy that is yet to be revealed.

## THE ROLE OF HOLY SCRIPTURE

Holy Scripture is the foundation and the substance of *Meditations for the Time of Retreat;* however, De La Salle did not restrict himself to using the Scriptures as an authority to prove something. This writer's investigation of De La Salle's recourse to the Scriptures in the meditations has shown that his approach is entirely foreign to a simplistic understanding of the Scriptures. Here we examine only the principal conclusions of that study.

### Point of Departure

The point of departure of *Meditations for the Time of Retreat*—if it is necessary to speak in these terms—is not from Holy Scripture on one side and from life on the other. De La Salle is meditating on the history that he lived with his Brothers as they realized together a *common* project that united them: to conduct the Christian Schools, to rescue the poor from their miserable condition, and to help them enter meaningfully into the history of the world and of salvation. This is where the role of Holy Scripture must be placed.

In the light of Holy Scripture, De La Salle understands and invites his Brothers also to understand this history of the Society as the history of a faithful God, who began everything, who brings his saving plan to reality every day, and who will faithfully bring it to a successful conclusion at the return of Christ.

In this connection the first and the last quotations from the Scriptures in *Meditations for the Time of Retreat* are very significant. The first quotation speaks of the saving will of the God of creation for all men and women (1 Tim 2:4). The last quotation presents the reward of the Brother (Apoc 22:14). These two quotations show, to a certain extent even in their literal meaning, that the Founder's thought is moving in the living plan of the history of salvation, from the original call of humanity up to the final completion of universal salvation through Jesus Christ in the heavenly Jerusalem.

### Three Types of Citation

It must be emphasized that for De La Salle, the Gospel, which he so often cites, is not a dead book but the good news of the present and living action of the Spirit of God, made visible in the action and the interacting relationships of teachers and students. The Founder quotes the Scriptures to refer the Brothers and their students to the transcendent totality of the history of salvation, to root them existentially, and to call them to live the Gospel in their life. Recent research helps to understand better how De La Salle used Holy Scripture.

A study of all the New Testament references in the meditations shows that the introductory formulas of these citations, as well as their meaning in the thought of the Founder, allow a classification of his recourse to the Scriptures into three categories:

Sometimes De La Salle cites the Scriptures as *a profession of faith*. This is not some proof derived from Holy Scripture as an authority. It is not an abstract, timeless truth. In these citations the Founder is reading a fact of ecclesial life today that has been part of the reality of the Brothers' life within the full history of God's plan. The reference is intended to break through the limits of space and time as they are lived by the Brothers or, better still, to open the eyes of his disciples, so that they can see what is at play in their humble tasks: the realization of the plan of God. But this openness to the transcendent aspect of their life, far from making them escape from the hard facts of life, drives them to be even more practical and more fundamental in their commitments, because what is at play has an historical and eschatological meaning that is totally beyond any superficial understanding.

Sometimes De La Salle alludes to apostolic times. It is not because he wants to reconstruct them in some archeological fashion. These citations can be called *citations of remembrance (mémoire)*, because he is reading the today of the Brothers in a remembrance of the fidelity of God, who has acted powerfully in his own history and continues to do so here and now in the concrete commitments of the

Brothers. These citations open up the historical-eschatological-sacramental dimension of life in harmony with apostolic times, and they invite the Brothers to become more and more rooted in this history, to see in themselves more and more clearly the action of the living Spirit of Jesus Christ.

More often, the Scriptures are cited without any formula of introduction and directly in reference to the Brothers. In these citations the Founder places the entire life of the Brothers under the judgment of the Word of God, not to crush them into being afraid but to invite them to renew within themselves ceaselessly the vitality of their faith and zeal, to evaluate their activities, and to verify the authenticity of their educational relationships in the light of the Gospel. These citations can be called *the citations of the call.*

This threefold manner of citing the Scriptures leads us to avoid any expression such as "De La Salle *uses* Holy Scripture." He does not use it for a rhetorical purpose, to apply some definitions to the obligations of the Brothers, or even to prove the value of their state of life or the meaning of the purpose of their Institute. In one sense Holy Scripture does not come to him from outside, but the words he cites come from a gut level, from the lived reality of the life he has lived and that he has contemplated in the light of faith.

### The Pauline Synthesis

One final observation is the place of the great Pauline synthesis on the Mystery of God and on the work of the ministry. The passage of 1 Corinthians 3:9–10 constitutes a pivotal thought in *Meditations for the Time of Retreat.* It is the work of God to which the Brother contributes, according to the gift that is given to him, the grace with which God endows him. Without trying to see in De La Salle a forerunner of modern exegesis, we can still be struck by the fact that the Founder has intuitively followed the theological itinerary of Saint Paul and, in particular, the progressive development of his reflection on the mystery of the wisdom of God, from the time of the first syntheses in 1 Thessalonians and 1 Corinthians up to the later syntheses in the epistles to the Colossians and to the Ephesians.

Especially in the first six meditations, the Pauline theme of both epistles to the Corinthians is often amplified by citations from the epistles to the Colossians and to the Ephesians and declared directly in reference to the Brothers. Far from diminishing the important role of the religious experience of the Brothers, this transcendent enlargement of the meaning of their work as the work of God serves only to heighten the value of the identity and the purpose of their ministry.

In the second six meditations, especially in the seventh, it is striking that De La Salle recalls the apostolic experience of the First Epistle to the Corinthians and the Epistle to the Galatians and understands this experience in the light of the correct apostolic theme as developed in the later synthesis of the Epistle to the Ephesians. Even more than in the first six meditations, the historical-eschatological dimension implied in these later meditations invites the Brother to look at all history from a profoundly religious point of view and to see himself as a man seized by God's Spirit and endowed with a charism that drives him with zeal for the new covenant between God and humanity. As Jesus Christ became the bridegroom of his Church and gave his life out of love, so the Brother gives himself totally to the welfare of children and is ready to lay down his life for the sake of those in his care.

Finally, in the last four meditations, whose dominant theme is the eschatological joy of the judgment, it is not surprising to find that the citations of remembrance, referring to the apostolic experience of the epistles to the Corinthians, are read at the same time in the light of the later synthesis of the First Epistle to the Ephesians and the earlier synthesis of the First Epistle to the Thessalonians, which we know has a strong emphasis on the eschatological theme. In these meditations, far from turning the Brothers in upon themselves or in upon their institutions, De La Salle calls upon them to be serious about God's prophetic judgment and to evaluate constantly their life and their activities.

# 3. *Meditations* and the Brothers Today

These meditations were originally concerned with the heart of the experiences of the first Brothers, but the cultural context of these experiences has changed radically. We must, therefore, ask ourselves whether the meditations have anything to say to us today. It is clearly not true that they are in their entirety timeless, good for all times and in all their details. In no way can they have some magical way of speaking to all of our experiences today. Here we point out some of their limitations, so that understood in that light, they can be read with greater profit.

### Limitation of Language
It is quite evident that these meditations are rooted in a particular cultural milieu. The direct influence of a similar work by Giry, the use

of the classic arguments to prove the importance of the catechetical ministry, the central place given to the mystery of the Cross and the mission of the Holy Spirit, and the presence of several pedagogical ideas—all these elements in *Meditations for the Time of Retreat* bear witness to the apostolic and cultural framework within which these meditations were written. It follows that there are definite limitations in the theological, anthropological, and even pedagogical language and thought. Good examples of such limitations are the concept of "corrupt nature," the phrase, "salvation of souls," and the references to angels and to the devil. Similar limitations of word and thought are found in the description of the child's learning process, the manner of correcting faults, even the theology of Redemption, and the opposition expressed between speculative and practical truths.

It has been shown that we can interpret Lasallian language, not in the light and language of present perspectives, which would be anachronistic, but in De La Salle's thought taken in its totality and especially in its full purpose and meaning. Nevertheless, the explicit meaning of De La Salle's language must be recognized. It would be less than honest to eliminate certain passages that seem no longer in harmony with our taste or with way of speaking.

### Limitations of Content

It would be a twisting of the thought of De La Salle to attempt to find in these meditations a synthesis of his entire thought. From a doctrinal point of view, certain basic themes in the thought of the Founder are missing in *Meditations for the Time of Retreat,* for example, community and obedience.

### Limitations of Style

These meditations are not easy reading. This is partly due to the different uses of Holy Scripture and to the unpolished style of the writing. We must remember particularly that *Meditations for the Time of Retreat* speaks of a spiritual experience that has been lived throughout the history of one man's lifetime. In any experience there is always something that cannot be communicated. The words of an historical account can only help us come near to this experience. These meditations, then, cannot tell us everything. Any writing, even the most thorough autobiography, is only an incomplete presentation, however well organized, of an experience.

For this reason *Meditations for the Time of Retreat* demands a serious effort, a realistic endeavor, to share in a spiritual way of life that has been lived by another person. This is the major problem: does this spiritual experience of De La Salle and the first Brothers have anything to say to us today?

# THE EXPERIENCE OF DE LA SALLE
# AND OUR EXPERIENCE TODAY

We cannot read *Meditations for the Time of Retreat,* even if it is one of the great texts of French spirituality of the seventeenth century, and pretend that nothing has happened between the time when De La Salle wrote his meditations and our time today.

### Our Cultural Framework

It is commonplace to observe that we are living in a world of profound and rapid change, of social and cultural transformations that seriously affect our understanding of religious experience. This cultural explosion has repercussions that are especially experienced in the life of the Brothers of the Christian Schools. The Brother looks upon his consecration to the Gospel in the service of education as a direct involvement in the construction of this world. In this his perspective is directed to the future, engaged as he is with the most sensitive element of society: youth. With the changes that are occurring, the young are called upon to learn not only the techniques for integrating themselves harmoniously into society but also how *to be* in an entirely new way to make society something new.

Similarly, we have been witnesses and agents of rapid changes in the understanding of what the Church is meant to be, with many models of the Church coming and going at the same time, often creating tension not only between different people but also within individuals. Religious education has probably been one of the major forces in developing new models of the Church, and yet, religious education has undergone rapid and profound changes within a relatively short period of time. We have experienced a transition from a so-called traditional method of catechesis—to know what must be believed, practiced, and fulfilled—to a kerygmatic method, and now to yet another, more dynamic concept based on a better understanding of anthropology and sustained by a more adequate theology of revelation.

Beyond all this, the spiritual experience of the individual Brother is rooted every day in the context of a school that is undergoing profound changes that call sometimes for total renovation. He is involved with youth who are often impatient and challenging. He is confronted with numerous efforts to discover completely new alternatives in the entire field of education.

### The Charism of the Founder Today

Fidelity to the Founder is achieved in terms that are relational and historical. The gift of the Spirit is manifested in the life and writings of John Baptist de La Salle, but this fidelity is not to be understood as a return to the past or a literal fidelity to established structures.

On the contrary, this fidelity is lived and realized only in a community effort and in the determination of people to respond to the call of the present needs of our time. Only in this way can we share in the spirit that moved the Founder in his response in his time.

Attention to the present, remembrance of the past, and hope for continuity of the project for the future all take place within the historical process by which the Brother is progressively integrated into a Community with a specific purpose. Thus the questions of identity and purpose are inseparable and are placed in a mystic perspective flowing from the charismatic gift of an ecclesial ministry, not from any abstract or general conception of the religious life.

The question, "For what purpose am I a Brother?" becomes "For whom am I a Brother?" The Brother's spiritual way of life and his recognition of a charismatic gift are not isolated products but are united in the roots of his personal history, in the spark of his original inspiration. His way of life also continues to grow with endless vigor under the power and the light of the Holy Spirit.

His way of life is open not only to others who surround him today but to historical perspectives far more extensive: the whole spiritual dynamism of the Church, which is ever open to the continually new action of the Holy Spirit. It is in view of all this that we can better appreciate the role of *Meditations for the Time of Retreat* today

### *Meditations for the Time of Retreat:* a Charismatic Gift

It can happen in the course of the school year that scholastic responsibilities and community problems lead to a loss of perspective that is experienced in such a deeply personal way that it cannot be expressed in any abstract generalizations. It is, of course, not inevitable that the school year always ends with a loss of perspective, but often enough, there occurs an absolutizing of our experiences, of structures, even of the manner of looking at educational functions. It can happen that the religious dimension of very concrete commitments is lost and that religious experience is cut off from the work of everyday living. This is not to suggest that the work of the Brothers leads inevitably to such a crisis. But without entering into the very personal and unique domain of such individual and community crises, a Brother becomes a Brother only for others, for a mission. This living synthesis that is made from one day to the next is never achieved. In times of crises (crises that are revelatory) as well as in good times, the Brothers are committed to live the Gospel as a living word, not a dead one. They must seek in community to be profoundly in harmony with the Gospel in their daily actions, with the new life that unites with and gives form to the world by the power of the Spirit of the new covenant.

*Meditations for the Time of Retreat* questions the educator at the very heart of a spiritual way of life: the fulfillment of the ecclesial charism received for the benefit of the body of Christ growing up in the world.

### *Meditations for the Time of Retreat:* Celebration of the Spirit

The Holy Spirit is ever active in the life of a minister endowed with a charismatic gift.

*Meditations for the Time of Retreat* can speak to us if we bring to our reading of them our own personal story, if we keep with us the full dimension of our personal way of life, the details of our daily existence, the people involved in these details, the words said, and the decisions made, the commitments to which we have given ourselves.

Our whole story, read in the light of these meditations, can bring us to prayer, prayer that is inseparable from our ministry, prayer that is not reduced to intervals or the powerful moments of the annual retreat. It will be a prayer that is a joyous contemplation and celebration.

• *Celebration* of a life that is lived in openness to the total Mystery of God and is developing, even by means of our most simple activities.

• *Celebration* of gratitude for the goodness of God, for his Providence, for his call, for the charismatic gift that reveals his saving action, his glory; for the mystery of Christ, who reveals himself in the saving of the young.

• *Celebration* of the joyful poverty of the minister, a poverty that comes from the very problems of the minister and his ministry, an awareness that it is God who saves, that God alone can touch hearts through the ministry of weak humans, fragile ministers; a poverty that becomes a confident beggar, asking to be filled with God's Spirit in order to be the "good news" for others.

• *Celebration* of the confidence of the minister, based on the fidelity of God, who chooses, calls, sends; confidence, because the minister is invited to place trust in the gifts of God; confidence that becomes trust in others, a commitment to affirm the best in others; confidence in the ability of the young, even the most difficult, to become free, to grow, to give themselves for the sake of others.

• *Celebration* of hope as the very origin of his commitment, as the basis for his willingness to die, as the dynamism of his tentative assurance already begun in Jesus Christ, for which the Spirit is the guarantee; hope that is also a challenge to go beyond self, to be always on the move, without compromise, challenging in himself, in his community, and in his students anything that opposes the action of the Spirit working to bring everyone to the freedom of the family of God.

• *Celebration,* then, of our own story, seen as a Paschal way of life, with its heights and its depths, as the recreating, enlightening, redeeming, freeing action of God; an action that is visible and effective in us to the degree that we are filled with the Spirit of God for others; it is a challenge to live our way of life as a continual incarnation in the flesh-and-blood world of our students, dying to ourself, a *kenosis* even to the end of our life, so that the young may have life to the full and come to the glory that is their destiny; it is a challenge to assume continually the mission of the Son of Man, of the Good Shepherd, with his power, not of authority but of service, capturing the very rhythm of the hymn to Christ in the Epistle to the Philippians, to live today the Paschal way of life, growing always in the Spirit of Christ.

Miguel Campos, FSC

# First Meditation

*That God in his Providence has established the Christian Schools*

### 193.1 First Point

God is so good that having created us, he wills that all of us come to the knowledge of the truth.[1] This truth is God and what God has desired to reveal to us through Jesus Christ, through the holy Apostles, and through his Church. This is why God wills all people to be instructed, so that their minds may be enlightened by the light of faith.

We cannot be instructed in the mysteries of our holy religion unless *we have the good fortune to hear about them,* and we cannot have this advantage unless someone preaches the word of God. For how can people believe in someone, the Apostle says, about whom they have not heard anyone speak, and how can they hear him spoken about if no one proclaims him to them?[2]

This is what God does by diffusing the fragrance of his teaching throughout the whole world by human ministers.[3] Just as he *commanded light to shine out of darkness, so he kindles a light in the hearts* of those destined to announce his word to children, so that they may be able to enlighten those children by unveiling for them the glory of God.[4]

Because God in his mercy has given you such a ministry, do not falsify his word, but gain glory before him by unveiling his truth[5] to those whom you are charged to instruct. Let this be your whole effort in the instructions you give them, looking upon yourselves as the ministers of God and the dispensers of his mysteries.[6]

### 193.2 Second Point

One of the main duties of fathers and mothers is to bring up their children in a Christian manner and to teach them their religion. But most parents are not sufficiently enlightened in these matters. Some are taken up with their daily concerns and the care of their family; others, under the constant anxiety of earning the necessities of life for themselves and their children, cannot take the time to teach their children their duties as Christians.

It is characteristic of the providence of God and of his vigilance over human conduct to substitute for fathers and mothers people who have enough knowledge and zeal to bring children to the knowledge of God and of his mysteries. *According to the grace of Jesus Christ that God has given to them, they are like good architects,* who give all possible care and attention to lay the foundation[7] of religion and Christian piety in the hearts of these children, a great number of whom would otherwise be abandoned.

You, then, whom God has called to this ministry, *work according to the grace that has been given to you to instruct by teaching and to exhort by encouraging* those who are entrusted to your care, guiding them with attention and vigilance[8] in order to fulfill toward them the principal duty of fathers and mothers toward their children.

### 193.3 Third Point

God wills not only that all come to the knowledge of truth but also that all be saved.[9] He cannot truly desire this without providing the means for it and, therefore, without giving children the teachers who will assist them in the fulfillment of his plan. This, says Saint Paul, is *the field that God cultivates, the building that he is raising,* and you are the ones whom he has chosen *to help in this work by announcing* to these children the Gospel of his Son[10] and the truths that are contained in it.

This is why you must honor your ministry and keep trying to save some of these children.[11] Because God, according to the expression of the same Apostle, *has made you his ministers in order to reconcile them to him and has entrusted to you* for this purpose *the word of reconciliation* for them, exhort them *as if God were exhorting them through you,* for you have been destined to cultivate these young plants[12] by announcing to them the truths of the Gospel[13] and to procure for them the means of salvation appropriate to their development.

Do not teach them these truths *with scholarly words, lest the cross of Christ,* source of our sanctification, become void of meaning[14] and all you say to them would produce no results in their minds or hearts. Because these children are simple and for the most part poorly brought up, those who help them save themselves must do this in so simple a manner that every word will be clear and easy for them to understand.

Be faithful to this practice, then, so that you can contribute, as far as you are able and as God requires of you, to the salvation of those whom he has entrusted to you.

---

| | | |
|---|---|---|
| 1. 1 Tim 2:4 | 6. 1 Cor 4:1 | 11. Rom 11:13-14 |
| 2. Rom 10:14-17 | 7. 1 Cor 3:10 | 12. Ps 128:3, 144:12 |
| 3. 2 Cor 2:14 | 8. Rom 12:6-8 | 13. 2 Cor 5:18-20 |
| 4. 2 Cor 4:6 | 9. 1 Tim 2:4 | 14. 1 Cor 1:17 |
| 5. 2 Cor 4:1-2 | 10. 1 Cor 3:9 | |

# Second Meditation

*The means that those responsible for the education of children must use to procure their salvation*

### 194.1 First Point

Consider that it is a practice only too common for working people and the poor to allow their children to live on their own, roaming all over like vagabonds, as long as they are unable to put them to some work. These parents have no concern to send their children to school, because their poverty does not allow them to pay teachers, or else, obliged as they are to look for work outside the home, they have to abandon their children to fend for themselves.

The results of this condition are regrettable, for these poor children, accustomed to lead an idle life for many years, have great difficulty adjusting when it comes time for them to go to work. Furthermore, through association with bad companions, they learn to commit many sins that are very difficult to stop later on because of the persistent bad habits they have contracted over such a long time.

God has had the goodness to remedy so great a misfortune by the establishment of the Christian Schools, where the teaching is offered free of charge and entirely for the glory of God, where the children are kept all day, learn reading, writing, and their religion, and are always busy, so that when their parents want them to go to work, they are prepared for employment.

Thank God, who has had the goodness to employ you to procure such an important advantage for children. Be faithful and exact to do this without any payment, so that you can say with Saint Paul, The source of my consolation is to announce the Gospel free of charge, without having it cost anything to those who hear me.[1]

### 194.2 Second Point

It is not enough that children remain in school for most of the day and be kept busy. Those who have dedicated themselves to instruct them must devote themselves especially to bring them up in the Christian spirit, which gives children the wisdom of God, which none of the princes of this world has known.[2] It is completely opposed to the spirit and wisdom of the world, for which you must inspire children with a great horror, because it serves as a cloak for sin. Children cannot be too much separated from such a great evil, for this alone can make them displeasing to God.

Let this be your primary concern, then, and the first effect of your vigilance in your work: to be ever attentive to your students to forestall any action that is bad or even the least bit improper. Help them avoid anything that has the slightest appearance of sin. It is also most important that your vigilance over your students serves to make them be self-controlled and reserved in church and at the exercises of piety that are performed in school. For piety is useful in every way,[3] and it gives a great facility for avoiding sin and for practicing other acts of virtue because of the great number of graces it brings to those who have it.

Do you act in this way with your students? Adopt these practices in the future if you have not been faithful enough in the past.

### 194.3 Third Point

To bring the children whom you instruct to take on the Christian spirit, you must teach them the practical truths of faith in Jesus Christ and the maxims of the holy Gospel with at least as much care as you teach the truths that are purely theoretical.

It is true that a number of doctrines are absolutely necessary for us to know in order to be saved, but what would it serve to know them if we did not take the trouble to practice the good to which we are bound?

Faith, Saint James says, without good works is dead.[4] Saint Paul also says, If I knew all the mysteries and had full knowledge and all the faith such that I move mountains from one place to another but have not charity (that is, sanctifying grace), I am nothing.[5]

Is your main care, then, to instruct your disciples in the maxims of the holy Gospel and the practice of the Christian virtues? Have you anything more at heart than helping them find their happiness in these practices? Do you regard the good you are trying to achieve in them as the foundation of all the good they will practice for the rest of their life? The habits of virtue that are cultivated during youth encounter less resistance in corrupt nature and form the deepest roots in the hearts of those in whom they have been formed.

If you want the instructions you give to those whom you have to instruct to be effective in drawing them to the practice of good, you must practice these truths. You must be full of zeal, so that your students may be able to receive a share in the grace that is in you for doing good and your zeal may draw down on you the Spirit of God to inspire your students in the same way.

---

1. 1 Cor 9:18
2. 1 Cor 2:7-8
3. 1 Tim 4:8
4. Jas 2:17
5. 1 Cor 13:2

# Third Meditation

*That those who teach the young are cooperators with Jesus Christ in the salvation of souls*

### 195.1 First Point

Although Jesus Christ died for everyone, the benefit of his death is, nevertheless, not effected in everyone, because all do not make the effort to apply it to themselves. The response of our will is necessary on our part in order to make it effective. Although the death of Jesus Christ was more than sufficient to wipe out the sins of all and to be a complete reparation for them, because God has reconciled us through Jesus Christ,[1] nevertheless, the grace that Jesus merited for us effects our salvation only insofar as our will is brought to correspond with it. It is up to each of us to achieve and complete the work of our own redemption.

This is what made Saint Paul say very well, speaking of himself, I accomplish what is lacking in the Passion of Christ.[2] Is there something lacking, then, in the Passion of Christ? Nothing, certainly, on the part of Jesus Christ, but on the part of this holy Apostle, as well as everyone else, what was lacking was the acceptance of his will, the union of his sufferings with those of Jesus Christ as one of his members suffering in him and for him.

Because you are obliged to help your disciples save themselves, you must engage them to unite all their actions to those of Jesus Christ, our Lord, so that their actions, made holy by his merits and by his consecration, are able to be pleasing to God and a means of salvation for them. This is how you must teach them to benefit from the death of Jesus Christ, our Lord, and to make the advantages and merits of his death effective in them.

### 195.2 Second Point

Because you are *ambassadors and ministers of Jesus Christ* in the work that you do, you must act as representing Jesus Christ. He wants your disciples to see him in you and to receive your instructions as if he were instructing them.[3] They must be convinced that your instructions are the truth of Jesus Christ, who speaks with your mouth, that it is only in his name that you teach, and that he has given you authority over them.

They must also be convinced that *they are a letter that Jesus Christ dictates to you, which you write* each day in their heart, not with ink but by the Spirit of the living God,[4] who acts in you and by you through the power of Jesus Christ. He helps you triumph over all the obstacles that oppose the salvation of these children, enlightening them in the person of Jesus Christ[5] to make them avoid all that could be displeasing to him.

To fulfill this duty with as much perfection and exactness as God requires of you, frequently appeal to the Spirit of our Lord to make you act in your work only under his influence, so that your mind may have no part in it. This Holy Spirit, then, will come upon them generously, so that they will be able to possess the Christian spirit fully.

## 195.3  Third Point

All your care for the children entrusted to you would be useless if Jesus Christ did not give the quality, the power, and the efficacy needed to make your care useful. Because the branch of the vine cannot bear fruit of itself (our Lord says) unless it remains attached to the main stem, neither can you bear fruit if you do not remain in me. This will be the glory of my Father, that you bear much fruit and become my disciples.[6]

What Jesus Christ says to his holy Apostles he also says to you, that you may understand that all the good you are able to do in your work for those entrusted to you will be true and effective only insofar as Jesus Christ gives it his blessing and you remain united with him. It is the same for you as it is for the branch of the vine, which can bear fruit only if it remains attached to the main stem and draws its sap and strength from the vine, which is also the source of all the goodness of the fruit.

Jesus Christ wants you to understand from this comparison that the more your work for the good of your disciples is given life by him and draws its power from him, the more it will produce good in them. This is why you must ask him earnestly that all your instructions be given life by his Spirit and draw all their power from him. Just as he is the one who enlightens everyone coming into the world,[7] he is also the one who enlightens the minds of your students and leads them to love and practice the good that you teach them.

---

1. 2 Cor 5:18
2. Col 1:24
3. 2 Cor 5:20
4. 2 Cor 3:3
5. 2 Cor 4:6
6. Jn 15:4-8
7. Jn 1:9

# Fourth Meditation

*What must be done to be true cooperators with Jesus Christ for the salvation of children*

## 196.1  First Point

Be convinced of what Saint Paul says, that you plant and water the seed, but it is God through Jesus Christ who makes it grow[1] and brings your work to fulfillment. So when it happens that you encounter some difficulty in the guidance of your disciples, when there are some who do not profit from your instructions and you observe a certain spirit of immorality in them, turn to God with confidence. Very insistently ask Jesus Christ to make his Spirit come alive in you, for he has chosen you to do his work.[2]

Consider Jesus Christ as the Good Shepherd of the Gospel, who seeks the lost sheep, puts it on his shoulders, and carries it back[3] to restore it to the fold. Because you are taking his place, consider that you are obliged to do the same thing. Ask him for the grace needed to procure the conversion of hearts.

You must, then, be very devoted to prayer to succeed in your ministry. You must constantly represent the needs of your disciples to Jesus Christ, explaining to him the difficulties that you have experienced in guiding them. Jesus Christ, seeing that you regard him as the one who can do everything in your work, whereas you are an instrument that must be moved only by him, will not fail to grant you what you ask of him.

### 196.2 Second Point

Jesus Christ, speaking to his Apostles, told them that he gave an example to them, so that they may do as he had done.[4] He also wanted his disciples to accompany him at all the conversions he brought about, so that seeing how he acted, they could be guided and formed by his conduct in all they would have to do to win souls to God.

This is also what you must do, because Jesus Christ has chosen you among so many others to be his cooperators[5] in the salvation of souls. In reading the Gospel, you must study the manner and the means that he used to lead his disciples to practice the truths of the Gospel.

Sometimes he proposed as *a happiness* everything that the world holds in horror, such as *poverty*, injuries, *insults, slander, and every kind of persecution for the sake of justice*, even telling his disciples that they ought to be glad and rejoice[6] when such things happen to them.

At other times he inspired horror for the sins into which people ordinarily fall, or he proposed virtues to practice, such as *gentleness*, humility,[7] and the like.

He also made them understand that unless their justice surpassed that of the scribes and the Pharisees (who bothered themselves about externals only), they would not enter the kingdom of heaven.[8]

Lastly, he wanted *the rich and those who have their pleasures in this world* to be regarded as unfortunate.[9]

It is according to these and all the other practices of Jesus Christ that you must teach the Christian youth entrusted to you.

### 196.3 Third Point

In carrying out your service to children, you will not fulfill your ministry adequately if you resemble Jesus Christ only in his guidance and conversion of souls. You must also enter into his purposes and goals. He came on earth, as he said, only that people might have life and have it to the full.[10] This is why he said, in another place, that his words are spirit and life.[11] By this he meant that his words procure the true life, which is the life of the soul, for those who hear them and who, with gladness over what they have heard, act on them with love.

This must be your goal when you instruct your disciples, that they live a Christian life and that your words become spirit and life for them. Your words will accomplish this because 1) they will be produced by the Spirit of God living in you, and 2) they will procure the Christian spirit for your disciples.

In possessing this spirit, which is the Spirit of Jesus Christ, they will live that true life which is so valuable to us because it leads surely to eternal life.

Guard against any human attitude toward your disciples; do not take pride in what you are doing. These two things are capable of spoiling all the good there is in the performance of your duties. *What have you* in this regard that has not been given to you? If it has been given to you, why are you boasting as if you had it on your own?[12]

Keep, then, the goals of your work as completely pure as those of Jesus Christ; by this means you will draw his blessings and graces upon yourselves and all your labors.

---

1. 1 Cor 3:6
2. 1 Cor 3:9
3. Lk 15:4-5
4. Jn 13:15

5. 1 Cor 3:9
6. Mt 5:3, 10-12
7. Mt 11:29
8. Mt 5:20

9. Lk 5:24
10. Jn 10:10
11. Jn 6:64
12. 1 Cor 4:7

# Fifth Meditation

*That those chosen by Providence for the education of children must fulfill the functions of Guardian Angels for them*

### 197.1  First Point

It can be said that children at birth are like a mass of flesh. Their mind does not emerge from the matter in them except with time and becomes refined only little by little. As an unavoidable consequence, those who are ordinarily instructed in the schools are not yet able by themselves to understand easily the Christian truths and maxims. They need good guides and visible angels to help them learn these things.

Angels have this advantage over us, that they are not bound to a body and to all the functions of the senses, without which ordinarily our mind rarely operates. Angels, therefore, have intelligence far superior to ours and can contribute much to our understanding, no matter how very unsullied the level of our mind might be. The angels who guide us share with us their understanding and knowledge of the true good. By this sharing of the enlightenment of the Guardian Angels, we can have a more penetrating knowledge of God, his perfections, all that is related to God, and the means of going to God.

If this is true of all of us, it is incomparably more true of children, *whose mind is more dull,* because they are less free of their senses *and of matter.* They need someone to develop the Christian truths for them in a more concrete fashion and in harmony with the limitations of their mind, for *these truths are hidden from the human mind.* If this help is not given, children often remain all their life insensitive and opposed to thoughts of God and incapable of knowing and appreciating them.[1]

For this purpose, the goodness of God has provided children with teachers who will instruct them in all these things. Admire the goodness of God in providing for all the needs of his creatures, taking the means to procure for all humanity the knowledge of the true good, that is, what concerns the salvation of their souls. Offer yourselves to God to help by assisting the children entrusted to you as much as he will require of you.

### 197.2  Second Point

To be saved, it does not suffice to be instructed in the Christian truths that are purely theoretical. As we have said already, faith without works is dead,[2] like a body without a soul; consequently, it is not sufficient to help us achieve our salvation.

It is, then, not enough to procure the Christian spirit for children and to teach them the mysteries and doctrines of our religion. You must also teach them the practical maxims that are found throughout the holy Gospel. But because they do not yet have a mind sufficiently able to understand and practice these maxims by themselves, you must serve as visible angels for them in two ways: 1) you must help them understand the maxims as set forth in the holy Gospel, and 2) you must guide their steps along the way that leads them to put these maxims into practice.

For this they need visible angels, who by their instructions and good example will encourage them to appreciate and to practice these maxims. By these two means, then, these holy maxims will make a strong impression on the mind and on the heart.

Such is the function you ought to perform for your disciples. It is your duty to act toward them as your Guardian Angels act toward you. You must win them over to practice the maxims of the holy Gospel, and to this end you must give them means that are easy and accommodated to their age. Gradually accustomed to this practice in their childhood, when older they will have acquired these maxims as a kind of habit and will practice them without great difficulty.

### 197.3  Third Point

You encounter so many obstacles to salvation in this life that it is impossible to avoid them if left up to you and your own guidance. This is why God has given you Guardian Angels to watch over you, as the Prophet says, to prevent you from falling by tripping against some stone,[3] that is, some obstacle to your salvation. Your angels inspire you and help to keep you away from the path where you might encounter an obstacle.

How much easier it is for children to fall over some precipice, because they are weak in mind as well as in body and have little understanding of what is for their own good. Therefore, they need the light of watchful guides to lead them on the path of salvation, guides who have an adequate understanding of matters concerning piety and a knowledge of the ordinary faults of young people. Thus they will be able to help them be aware of pitfalls and keep away from them.

This is what God has provided in giving children teachers whom he has charged with this care and to whom he has given the concern and the vigilance[4] not only to prevent anything whatsoever harmful to their salvation from capturing their hearts but also *to guide* the children through all the dangers they meet in the world. The result will be that the devil will not even dare approach them, because they are under the guidance of these attentive leaders and under the protection of God.

Ask God today for the grace to watch so well over the children confided to you that you will take every possible precaution to shield them from serious faults.

Ask God to be such good guides for them, through the light that you will procure for yourselves by turning to God and by the fidelity with which you do your work, that you will see clearly every obstacle to the good of their souls and keep away from the path of their salvation everything that could harm them.

This is the principal care you must have for the children entrusted to you. It is the main reason why God has entrusted you with so holy a ministry, and it is on this that God will call you to give a very exact account on the day of judgment.

---

1. 1 Cor 2:14     3. Ps 91:12     4. Rom 12:8
2. Jas 2:17

# Sixth Meditation

*How the function of Guardian Angels is fulfilled in the education of youth*

### 198.1 First Point

Because Guardian Angels are highly enlightened and know the good as it is, through them God makes known this good and the secrets of his holy will to those whom he has predestined to be his adopted children in Jesus Christ and by whom he has called them to be his heirs.[1] By the light these angels share with those who are called, they teach them the good that must be practiced and what they must do to become heirs.

This is symbolized by the ladder that Jacob saw in a dream when he was going to Mesopotamia. Angels were going up and coming down the ladder.[2] They were going up to God to make known to him the needs of those for whom he made them responsible and to receive his orders for them. They were coming down to teach those whom they were guiding the will of God concerning their salvation.

You must do the same thing for the children entrusted to your care. It is your duty to go up to God every day in prayer to learn from him all that you must teach the children and then to come down to them by accommodating them at their level in order to instruct them about what God has communicated for them to you in your prayer, as well as in Holy Scripture, which contains the truths of religion and the maxims of the holy Gospel.

For this purpose, you must not only know all these truths in general, but it is also important that you have such a grasp of all of them that you are able to expand on them sufficiently to make them understood clearly and in detail by your disciples.

Have you studied well all these truths up to the present, and have you been thoroughly committed to impress them firmly on the minds of these children? Have you regarded this responsibility as the most important one in your work?

From this moment take the steps to make it your main concern to instruct perfectly those who are entrusted to you to learn the truths of the faith and the practical maxims of the holy Gospel.

### 198.2 Second Point

The holy Guardian Angels are not satisfied with illuminating the mind of those under their guidance with the light needed to know God's will for them and to be saved. They also inspire their charges and procure for them the means to do the good that is proper to them.

God uses the angels not only to deliver *those entrusted to them from the powers of darkness and make them grow in the knowledge of God* but also *to help them lead a life worthy of God, so that they will be pleasing to him in every way and produce good works of every sort.* The angels are zealous for the good of those in their care, because of the commission they have received from *God, the Father of light and of all good.* They contribute, as far as they are able, to make those in their care worthy to share the lot of the saints.[3]

You share in the ministry of the Guardian Angels by making known to children the truths of the Gospel, which you have been chosen by God to announce.[4] You must teach them how to put these truths into practice, and you must have very great zeal to procure their accomplishment of this practice.

In imitation of the great Apostle, you must encourage them to live in a manner worthy of God, because God has called them to his kingdom and his glory.[5]

Your zeal must go so far in this that to achieve it, you are ready to give your very life, so dear to you[6] are the children entrusted to you.

It is your duty, then, *to admonish the unruly* and to do this in such a way *that they give up their former way of life;* you must rouse up those who lack courage, support the weak, and be patient toward all.[7] Your purpose is to be in a position to stop and to curb *their corrupt inclinations* and to establish them in the practice of good in such a way that they give the demon no access to themselves.[8]

Is this the guidance you have maintained toward your disciples up to now? Have you been helping them practice the good that is appropriate to their years? Have you shown concern that they practice piety, especially at prayer and in church, and that they receive the sacraments frequently?

You must watch over them a great deal to procure for them the practice of good and a horror for sin, which are two very useful ways to help them achieve their salvation.

### 198.3 Third Point

If you want *to accomplish your ministry* as Guardian Angels for the children whom you instruct, *to build up* with them the body of Christ, and to make them holy and perfect,[9] you must work to inspire them with the same sentiments and to put them in the same dispositions in which Saint Paul tried to place the Ephesians through the letter he wrote to them.

1) He urged that they *not sadden the Holy Spirit of God, with whom they have been marked* in Baptism and in Confirmation as by a seal for the day of redemption.[10]

2) You would be deserving of blame if you did not engage them *to renounce their former way of life;* you must, therefore, lead them with the same zeal to renounce lying and to speak the truth to their neighbor at all times.[11]

3) You must help them to be gentle and to have tenderness for one another, to be mutually forgiving, as God has forgiven them in Jesus Christ,[12] and to love one another even as Jesus Christ has loved them.[13]

Is this the way you have instructed your disciples up to now? Are these the maxims with which you have inspired them? Have you had enough vigilance over them? Has your zeal been ardent enough to bring them to practice these maxims?

Bring all your efforts to be faithful in this in the future.

---

1. Eph 1:5, 9, 11
2. Gn 28:12
3. Col 1:10-13
4. 1 Thes 2:4
5. 1 Thes 2:12
6. 1 Thes 2:8
7. 1 Thes 5:14
8. Eph 4:22, 27
9. Eph 4:12
10. Eph 4:30
11. Eph 4:22, 25
12. Eph 4:32
13. Eph 5:2

# Seventh Meditation

*That the care of instructing youth is one of the most necessary works in the Church*

### 199.1 First Point

God, having *chosen and destined Saint Paul*, as the Apostle says, *to preach the Gospel to the nations*, gave him such knowledge of the mysteries of Jesus Christ[1] that he was enabled, *like a good architect, to lay the foundation for the building* of the faith and of the religion *which God raised up* in the cities where Saint Paul announced the Gospel according to the grace that God had given him.[2] He was the first of all to preach in these places. That is why he says quite justly that those to whom he announced the Gospel are his work and that he has begotten them in Jesus Christ.[3]

Without comparing yourselves to this great saint (and keeping in mind the due proportion between your work and his), you can say that you are doing the same thing and fulfilling the same ministry in your profession.

You must, then, regard your work, which has been entrusted to you by pastors and by fathers and mothers, as one of the most important and necessary services in the Church.

This means that you are called to lay the foundation for the building of the Church[4] when you instruct children in the mystery of the most Holy Trinity and the mysteries accomplished by Jesus Christ when he was on earth.

For, according to Saint Paul, *without faith it is impossible to please God* and consequently be saved and enter the homeland of heaven, because faith is the foundation of the hope that we have.[5] The knowledge, then, that each must have of the faith, the instruction that must be given concerning the faith to those who are ignorant of it, is one of the most important things in our religion.

How much, then, must you consider it an honor that the Church has assigned you to such a holy and exalted work, to be chosen to procure for children the knowledge of our religion and of the Christian spirit.

Pray God that he will make you fit to fulfill such a ministry in a manner worthy of him.

### 199.2 Second Point

The importance of this ministry is seen in the fact that the holy bishops of the early Church regarded it as their main duty and even considered it an honor to instruct the catechumens and new Christians and to teach catechism to them. Saint Cyril, Patriarch of Jerusalem, and Saint Augustine have left us catechisms, which they wrote and taught and which they also caused to be taught by the priests who helped them in their pastoral duties. Saint Jerome, whose knowledge was so profound, testifies in his letter to Leta that he considered it a greater honor to teach catechism to a young child than to be a tutor to a great emperor. Gerson, the great chancellor of the University of Paris, had such high esteem for this ministry that he also practiced it.

These great saints acted this way because teaching was the first ministry Jesus Christ gave his holy Apostles, a fact Saint Luke reports when he says that as soon as Jesus had chosen his Apostles, he sent them forth to proclaim the Kingdom of God.[6] This is also what Jesus Christ requested of his Apostles very clearly just before he departed from them, telling them, Go, teach all nations, baptizing them in the name of the Father and of the Son and of the Holy Spirit.[7]

This is likewise the first thing Saint Peter did in the Temple of Jerusalem after the descent of the Holy Spirit, with the immediate result that three thousand people began to embrace the faith in Jesus Christ.[8]

This was also the special work of Saint Paul, as is evident in his discourses in the Areopagus and the ones that he gave before Felix and Festus, as reported in the Acts of the Apostles. Saint Paul testifies to the Corinthians that it would even be painful to him if he had to come to them without being useful by instructing and catechizing them.[9]

But Jesus Christ did not limit himself to entrusting to his Apostles the work of teaching catechism. He too did this work and taught the principal truths of our religion, as reported in a great number of places in his Gospel, where he tells his Apostles, I must announce the Gospel of the kingdom of God, because this is why I have been sent.[10]

Say the same thing, that this is why Jesus Christ has sent you and why the Church, whose ministers you are, employs you. Bring all the care needed, then, to fulfill this function with as much zeal and success as the saints have had in fulfilling it.

### 199.3 Third Point

There is no need to be astonished if the holy Apostles and the first bishops of the early Church had such esteem for the function of instructing the catechumens and the new Christians and if Saint Paul especially gloried *in being sent to preach the Gospel, not with learned words, for fear that the cross of Jesus Christ would be destroyed, for God turned the wisdom of the world into folly.* Saint Paul, *enlightened by God's wisdom and inspiration,* says that the world did not recognize God through its wisdom, so it pleased God, through the folly of the preaching of the Gospel, to save those who accept the faith.[11]

The reason that Saint Paul gives for this is that God's secret plan was unveiled to him. He had received the grace of unveiling to the nations the incomprehensible riches of Jesus Christ,[12] so that *those who previously were deprived of Jesus Christ and were strangers to the covenant of God, without hope in his promises,* now belong to Jesus Christ and are strangers no longer. They have become fellow citizens with the saints and servants of God's household. They are the structure that has been built on the foundation of the Apostles and raised up by Jesus Christ. They have become the sanctuary where God dwells through his Holy Spirit.[13]

Such is the result accomplished in the Church by the instructions given, after the holy Apostles, by the great bishops and pastors of the Church, who devoted themselves to instructing those who wanted to become Christians. This is why this work seemed so important to them and why they devoted themselves to it with such care.

This is also what ought to engage you to have an altogether special esteem for the Christian instruction and education of children, because it is a means to help them become true children of God and citizens of heaven. This is the very foundation and support of their piety and of all the other good that takes place in the Church.

Thank God for the grace he has given you in your work of sharing in the ministry of the holy Apostles and the principal bishops and pastors of the Church. Honor your ministry[14] by becoming, as Saint Paul says, worthy ministers of the New Testament.[15]

1. Gal 1:15-16
2. 1 Cor 3:9-10
3. 1 Cor 9:1
4. Eph 2:22
5. Heb 11:1-6
6. Lk 9:1-2
7. Mt 28:19
8. Acts 2:14-40
9. Acts 17; 24; 25; 26; 2 Cor 12:14-15
10. Lk 4:43
11. 1 Cor 1:17-21
12. Eph 3:3, 8
13. Eph 2:12, 19, 20, 22
14. Rom 11:13
15. 2 Cor 3:6

# Eighth Meditation

*What must be done to make your ministry useful to the Church*

### 200.1  First Point

Consider that because you must work in your ministry for *the building of the Church on the foundation which has been laid by the holy Apostles,* by the instruction you are giving to the children whom God has entrusted to your care and who are entering into the construction of this building,[1] you must do your work as the Apostles carried out their ministry.

As told in the Acts of the Apostles, every day, both in the Temple and in homes, they never stopped teaching and proclaiming Jesus Christ.[2] It followed that every day the Lord increased the number of faithful and the union of those who were being saved.[3]

The zeal that the holy Apostles had to announce the teaching of Jesus Christ caused the number of disciples to increase, so they chose seven deacons to distribute alms to the faithful and take care of their other needs,[4] so greatly did these holy Apostles fear to encounter any obstacles able to distract them from preaching the word of God.

If the holy Apostles acted this way, it was because Jesus Christ had given them the example, for it is said of him that he was teaching every day in the Temple, where all the people listened to him with attention,[5] and at night he would withdraw and go to pray on the Mount of Olives.[6]

You, then, who have succeeded the Apostles in their work of catechizing and instructing the poor, if you want to make your ministry as useful to the Church as it can be, you must every day teach them catechism, helping them learn the basic truths of our religion, following the example of the Apostles, which is that of Jesus Christ, who devoted himself every day to this task.

Like them you must also withdraw afterward to direct your attention to reading and to prayer, to learn thoroughly the truths and the holy maxims that you wish to teach, and throuogh prayer to draw down God's graces, which you need to do this work according to the Spirit and the intention of the Church, which entrusts it to you.

### 200.2  Second Point

It would have been of little use if the holy Apostles had instructed the first Christians in the essential truths of our religion and did not lead them to live the Christian way of life and conform to what they had lived with Jesus Christ. The Apostles were not satisfied with teaching doctrine; they had a marvelous care to bring the first Christians to practice their religion.

God blessed their care in such a way that it is said that those who first received the faith persevered in the teaching of the Apostles, in the communion of the breaking of bread, and in prayers. They continued to go to the Temple every day united in the same spirit.[7] In other words, after they were baptized, they were living in harmony with the teaching of the Apostles.

Following his conversion, Saint Paul did the same, for it is said of him that after instructing the people of Ephesus *for three months in the Jewish synagogue, he then taught* every day in the school of a man named Tyrannus and continued this practice for two years,[8] *with the result that* the disciples of that city were baptized in the name of the Lord and received the Holy Spirit through the laying on of hands.[9]

The chief care, then, of the Apostles, after instructing the first faithful, was to have them receive the sacraments, assemble for prayer together, and live according to the Christian spirit.

Above everything else, this is what you are obliged to do in your work. In imitation of the Apostles, you must take altogether special care that those whom you instruct receive the sacraments in particular and that they are made ready to receive Confirmation with the proper dispositions in order to be filled with the Holy Spirit and the graces that this sacrament produces. You must see to it that they go to Confession often after learning how to do it well. You must dispose them to receive their first Communion with holy dispositions and to receive Communion frequently thereafter in order to be able to preserve the grace they received the first time they performed this action.

Oh, if you knew the great good that you do for them by procuring the preservation and increase of grace by their frequent use of the sacraments, you would never let up instructing them about this!

### 200.3 Third Point

Saint James says, If someone says that he has the faith and that he does not have the works, of what use to him is his faith; can it save him?[10] What would it benefit you, then, to teach your disciples the truths of the faith if you do not teach them to practice good works? For faith that is not accompanied by works is dead.[11]

It will not, then, be enough for you to have instructed your disciples about the mysteries and the truths of our holy religion if you have not helped them learn the chief Christian virtues and if you have not taken an altogether special care to help them put these virtues into practice, as well as all the good of which they are capable at their age. For no matter how much faith they may have or how lively it may be, if they do not commit themselves to practice good works, their faith will be of no use to them.

You must especially teach this maxim to those whom you instruct if you want to put them on the road to heaven, so that you can say to them that you have acted in a way that is beyond reproach, and this has given consolation to us.[12]

Inspire them also with piety and self-control[13] in church and in the exercises of piety that you have them perform in the schools. Instill in them the innocence and humility[14] that our Lord recommends so strongly in the Gospel. Do not forget to help them acquire gentleness, patience,[15] love and respect for their parents,[16] and all the conduct that is proper to a Christian child, in a word, all that our religion demands of them.

---

1. Eph 2:20-22
2. Acts 5:42
3. Acts 2:47
4. Acts 6:1-4
5. Lk 19:47-48
6. Lk 21:37
7. Acts 2:41-45
8. Acts 19:8-10
9. Acts 19:5-6
10. Jas 2:14
11. Jas 2:26
12. 2 Cor 7:11-13
13. 1 Tim 6:11
14. Mt 11:29
15. Col 3:12
16. Eph 6:2

# Ninth Meditation

*The obligation of those who instruct youth to have much zeal to fulfill well so holy a work*

### 201.1 First Point

Reflect on what Saint Paul says, that it is God who has established in the Church Apostles, Prophets, and teachers,[1] and you will be convinced that he has also established you in your work. The same saint gives you another expression of this when he says *that there are diverse ministries, but there are different operations, and the Holy Spirit manifests himself in each of these gifts for the common good,* that is to say, for the good of the Church. One receives by the Spirit the gift to speak with wisdom; another, the gift of faith by the same Spirit.[2]

You must not doubt that it is a great gift of God, this grace he has given you to be entrusted with the instruction of children, *to announce the Gospel* to them and to bring them up in the spirit of religion. But in calling you to this holy ministry, God demands that you fulfill it with ardent zeal for their salvation, because this is the work of God, and he curses the one who does his work carelessly.[3]

Let it be clear, then, in *all your conduct* toward the children who are entrusted to you, that you regard yourselves *as the ministers of God, carrying out your ministry with love* and a *sincere* and true zeal, *accepting with much patience the difficulties* you have *to suffer*, willing to be *despised by men and to be persecuted, even to give your life* for Jesus in the fulfillment of your ministry.[4]

The zeal that ought to inspire you is meant to give you these dispositions, so that you recognize that it is God who has called you, who has destined you for this work, and who has sent you to labor in his vineyard.[5] Do this, then, with all the affection of your heart, working entirely for him.

### 201.2 Second Point

What ought to engage you further to have great zeal in your state is the fact that you are the ministers not only of God but also of Jesus Christ and of the Church. This is what Saint Paul says when he expresses the wish that everyone ought to regard those who announce the Gospel as ministers of Jesus Christ,[6] who write the letter that he has dictated, not with ink but with the Spirit of the living God, not on tablets of stone but on tablets of flesh, which are the hearts[7] of children.

For this reason and in this spirit, you must have the love and the glory of God as your single aim in the instruction of these children, *for the love of God ought to impel you, because Jesus Christ died for all, so that those who live might live no longer for themselves but for him who died for them.* This is what your zeal must inspire in your disciples, as if God were appealing through you, because you are ambassadors for Jesus Christ.[8]

You must also show the Church what love you have for her[9] and give her proof of your zeal, *because it is for the Church (which is the body of Jesus Christ)* that you work. You have become her ministers, according to the order that God has given you to dispense his word.[10]

Because the Church has great zeal for the sanctification of her children, it is your duty to share in her zeal, so that you can say to God, as the holy King David said, The zeal of your house has consumed me.[11] For this house is none other than the Church, because the faithful form this building that has been built on the foundation of the Apostles and raised up by Jesus Christ, the main cornerstone.[12]

Act in such a way through your zeal that you give tangible proof that you love those whom God has entrusted to you, just as Jesus Christ has loved his Church. Help them enter truly into the structure of this building and be in a condition to appear one day before Jesus Christ full of glory: without stain, without wrinkle, without blemish.[13] This will make known to future ages the abundant riches of the grace that God has given them[14] by procuring for them the help of instruction and that God has given you to instruct and educate them, so that they may one day become heirs of the kingdom of God and of Jesus Christ, our Lord.[15]

### 201.3 Third Point

Because your ministry has for its purpose to procure the salvation of souls, the first concern you ought to have is to procure this goal as far as you are able. You must in this *imitate God* to some extent, for he so loved the souls he created[16] that when he saw them involved in sin and unable to be freed from sin by themselves, the zeal and affection that he had for their salvation led him to send his own Son to rescue them from their miserable condition. This is what made Jesus Christ say that God so loved the world that he gave his only Son, so that whoever believes in him may not die but may have eternal life.[17]

See what God and Jesus Christ have done to restore souls to the grace they had lost. What must you not do for them in your ministry if you have zeal for their salvation! How much you must be disposed toward them as Saint Paul was toward those to whom he preached the Gospel, to whom he wrote that he was not seeking anything they had but was seeking only their souls.[18]

The zeal you are obliged to have in your work must be so active and so alive that you can tell the parents of the children entrusted to your care what is said in Holy Scripture: Give us their souls; keep everything else for yourselves,[19] that is, what we have undertaken is to work for the salvation of their souls. It is also the only reason you have committed yourselves to take the responsibility to guide and to instruct them.

Tell the parents also what Jesus Christ said about the sheep of which he is the shepherd and which must be saved by him: *I came,* he said, *that they might have life and have it to the full.*[20] For this had to have been the kind of ardent zeal you felt for the salvation of those you must instruct when you were led to sacrifice yourselves and to spend your whole life to give these children a Christian education and to procure for them the life of grace in this world and eternal life in the next.

---

| | | |
|---|---|---|
| 1. 1 Cor 12:28 | 8. 2 Cor 5:14-15, 20 | 15. Rom 8:17 |
| 2. 1 Cor 12:5-9 | 9. 2 Cor 8:24 | 16. Eph 5:1-2 |
| 3. Jer 48:10 | 10. Col 1:24-25 | 17. Jn 3:16 |
| 4. 2 Cor 6:3-9 | 11. Ps 69:10 | 18. 2 Cor 12:14 |
| 5. Mt 20:3 | 12. Eph 2:20-22 | 19. Gn 14:21 |
| 6. 1 Cor 4:1 | 13. Eph 5:25-27 | 20. Jn 10:10 |
| 7. 2 Cor 3:3 | 14. Eph 2:7 | |

# Tenth Meditation

*How a Brother of the Christian Schools ought to show zeal in his work*

### 202.1 First Point

Consider that the purpose of the coming of the Son of God into this world was to destroy sin. This must also be the main purpose of the establishment of the Christian Schools and, therefore, the first object of your zeal. It must lead you to allow nothing in the children under your guidance that could displease God. If you observe in them something that offends God, you must immediately do all that you are able to remedy the problem.

That is why, following the example of the Prophet Elias, you must show your zeal for the glory of God and the salvation of your disciples. I have been roused with a very great zeal for the Lord God of hosts, he says, because the children of Israel have broken the covenant that they had made with God.[1]

If you have zeal for the children for whom you are responsible and have committed yourselves to keep them from sin, which is your duty, you must take on this spirit of the Prophet Elias when they fall into some fault. Driven by this same holy ardor that roused this Prophet, you must say to your disciples, I am so zealous for the glory of my God that I cannot see you renounce the covenant you made with him in Baptism and the dignity of children of God, which you received in that sacrament.

Often urge your disciples to avoid sin with as much speed as they would flee the presence of a snake. Let your first attention be given especially to inspire them with a horror for *impurity*, lack of reverence in church and at prayer, *stealing, lying, disobedience, lack of respect for their parents,* and *other faults in regard to their compan-*

*ions.* Help them understand that those who fall into these kinds of sins will not possess the kingdom of heaven.[2]

### 202.2 Second Point

You must not be satisfied with keeping the children in your care from doing evil. You must also lead them to practice well all the good of which they are capable. Take care of this, then, and see to it that they always speak the truth and that when they want to affirm something, they limit themselves to saying that it is or is not so.[3] Help them understand that they will be believed more readily when they use few words than when they swear great oaths, because people will consider that it is in a Christian spirit that they do not use more words.

Help them put into practice what our Lord says when he commands us to love our enemies, to do good to those who do evil to us and who persecute us and speak unjustly against us.[4] Help them completely avoid rendering evil for evil, injury for injury, and taking revenge.

You must encourage them, in accord with the teaching of Jesus Christ, not only to be satisfied with doing good actions but also to *avoid doing them before others in order to be esteemed and honored,* because those who act this way have already received their reward.[5]

It is important that you teach them to pray to God, as our Lord taught those who followed him, *and to pray* with much piety and in secret,[6] that is, with much recollection, getting rid of all thoughts that could distract their minds during the time of prayer, so that they will be occupied solely with God and easily obtain what they ask of him.

Because the majority of your disciples are born poor, you must encourage them to despise riches and to love poverty, because our Lord was born poor and loved the poor, with whom he was also glad to be present. He even said that the poor are blessed, because the kingdom of heaven belongs to them.[7]

These are the kinds of maxims and practices you must continually inspire in your disciples if you have any zeal for their salvation. This will be the way you will show how zealous you are for the glory of God. Because these maxims can come only from God (being contrary to human inclination), it is a mark of zeal for the honor and glory of God to inspire children to put them into practice.

### 202.3 Third Point

Your zeal for the children you instruct would not go very far and would not have much of a result or success if it were limited only to words. To make it effective, your example must support your instructions, and this is one of the main signs of your zeal.

Saint Paul, speaking to the Philippians after teaching them different maxims, adds, Act according to the same maxims, and so be imitators of me. Look to those who live according to the example that I have given you.[8] Do the things I have taught you, what I have said to you, what I have written to you, and of which I have given you the example.[9] So, the ardent zeal of this great saint for the salvation of souls was to have them observe what he practiced.

This is also the way that our Lord acted, of whom it is said that he began *to do* and then to teach.[10] Speaking to his Apostles after he had washed their feet, he says, I have given you an example, so that you may do as I have done to you.[11]

It is easy to conclude from these examples that your zeal for the children who are under your guidance would be very imperfect if you exercised it only by instructing them. It will only become perfect if you practice what you are teaching them. Example makes a much greater impression on the mind and the heart than words, especially for children, for they do not yet have a mind sufficiently able to reflect, and they ordinarily model themselves on the example of their teachers. They are led more readily to do what they see done for them than what they hear told to them, above all when the teachers' words are not in harmony with the teachers' actions.

---

| | | |
|---|---|---|
| 1. 1 Kgs 19:14 | 5. Mt 6:1, 5 | 9. Phil 4:9 |
| 2. Gal 5:21 | 6. Mt 6:6 | 10. Acts 1:1 |
| 3. Mt 5:37 | 7. Mt 5:3 | 11. Jn 13:15 |
| 4. Mt 5:44 | 8. Phil 3:16-17 | |

# Eleventh Meditation

*The obligation of the Brothers of the Christian Schools to reprove and to orrect the faults committed by those whom they are charged to instruct*

### 203.1 First Point

One of the characteristics and one of the effects of the zeal people have for the well-being and salvation of souls is to reprove and correct those in their care when they fall into some fault. This is how Jesus Christ often made his zeal for the Jews manifest in the Temple, when he went there and drove out those who were buying and selling[1] the things needed for the sacrifices. At the time, he made a whip of cords that he used to chase them.[2]

Jesus acted similarly toward the Pharisees, because he could not tolerate their hypocrisy and false piety,[3] much less their pride, which led them to esteem and praise their own actions[4] while belittling and blaming the behavior of others.[5] He condemned all their conduct, because they satisfied themselves with teaching others but took no pains to practice what they taught.[6] In all these encounters, Jesus Christ rebuked and blamed them publicly. See what Jesus Christ did not only to the Pharisees but also to others on several occasions.

Saint Paul, with similar freedom, reproved the Corinthians for tolerating an incestuous person among them, telling them that they ought to have handed him over to the devil to be tormented in his body, so that his soul might be saved.[7]

You too must reprove and correct your disciples when they commit some fault, the more so because it is typical of children often to make mistakes by doing many things without thinking. The reproofs and corrections give them time to reflect on what they have to do and cause them to watch over themselves in order not to keep making the same mistakes.

Be exact, then, not to allow considerable faults in them without providing this remedy for them.

### 203.2 Second Point

People are naturally so inclined to sin that they seem to find no other pleasure than committing it. This is seen especially in children, because their minds have not developed yet and they are not capable of much serious reflection. They seem to have no other inclination than to please their passions and their senses and to satisfy their nature.

This is why the Holy Spirit says that it is as if folly is tied to the neck of children, and correction is the only way to cure them.[8] The way to free the souls of children from hell, then, is to make use of this remedy, which will procure wisdom for them. Otherwise, if they are abandoned to their own will, they will run the risk of ruining themselves and causing much sorrow to their parents. The reason for this is because the faults turn into a habit, which will be very difficult to correct. The good and bad habits contracted in childhood and maintained over a period of time ordinarily become part of nature.

This is why those who guide young children must reprove them, as Saint Paul says, with all the force of authority, to make them return from their wandering and rescue them from the snares of the demon, who holds them captive to his will.[9] In effect it can be said with reason that a child who has acquired a habit of sin has, in some sense, lost his freedom and has made himself a miserable captive, according to what Jesus Christ says, The one who commits sin is the slave of sin.[10]

You, who are teachers of those you guide, must take all possible care to bring those under your guidance into the liberty of the children of God, which Jesus Christ obtained for us[11] by dying for us. To do this, you need to have two qualities in your relationship with them. The first is *gentleness* and *patience*. The second is *prudence* in your reproofs and corrections.

### 203.3 Third Point

What ought to inspire you even more to reprove and correct the faults of your disciples is the fact that if you fail in this, you will be reprehensible before God, who will punish you for your weakness and neglect in this matter.

Because you are substitutes for their fathers and mothers and their pastors, you are obliged to keep watch over these children as the ones accountable for their souls.[12] So, if you do not watch over their conduct, you must realize that because these children are not able to guide themselves, you will render an account to God for the faults they commit, just as if you had committed them.

The high priest Eli is a very clear example, and a frightening one, of this truth. Because he allowed bad behavior in his children, God announced to him, through Samuel, that he was condemning his house for all eternity because of his sin[13] and because, although knowing that his sons were behaving in an unworthy manner, he did not correct them. As a result, God swore that this fault could not be expiated by sacrifices or offerings to the Lord, so great was the sin considered by God.

You who hold the place of parents and pastors of souls, fear that God will act the same way toward you if you neglect to reprove and correct your disciples when it is needed, for you would have neglected the service with which God honored you when he put you in charge of guiding these children.

He has entrusted you especially with the care of their souls, which is what God had most at heart when he made you the guides and guardians of these young children.

Fear that your negligence may not be pardoned, any more than that of the high priest Eli, if you have not been sufficiently faithful to God in your work of striving to preserve in the grace of God these souls entrusted to your guidance.

1. Lk 19:45-46
2. Jn 2:15
3. Mt 6:2-5
4. Lk 18:9-14
5. Mt 9:11; 12:2

6. Mt 23:3
7. 1 Cor 5:5
8. Prv 22:15
9. 2 Tim 2:25-26
10. Jn 8:34

11. Gal 4:31
12. Heb 13:17
13. 1 Sm 3:13-14

# Twelfth Meditation

*The way in which we must reprove and correct the faults of those whom we are guiding*

### 204.1  First Point

It would be of little value to make reproofs and corrections if those who make them did not take the right steps to make them well. The first thing to which we must pay attention is not to undertake reproofs and corrections except under the guidance of the Spirit of God. This is why, before undertaking them, it is proper to become interiorly recollected, to give ourselves up to God's Spirit, and to be disposed to make the reproof or undertake the correction with the greatest possible wisdom and in a manner best suited to make it useful to the one whom we intend to correct.

For people, including children, are endowed with reason and must not be corrected like animals but like reasonable people.

We must reprove and correct with justice by helping the children recognize the wrong they have done and what correction the fault they have committed deserves, and we must try to have them accept it.

Also, because they are Christians, we must be disposed to make the reproof or correction in such a way that God may be pleased with it and that the children accept it as a remedy for their fault and a means of becoming more wise. For this is the result that the Holy Spirit says correction must produce[1] in children.

It is proper also to consider before God what sort of correction the fault deserves, whether the one at fault is truly determined to receive it with submission or whether it is necessary to try to dispose him to be submissive.

There is no need to fear that corrections will have a bad result if we have acted prudently in making them. On the contrary, teachers who reprove and correct those who commit faults draw upon themselves the praise of people, the blessing of God, and the gratitude of those who have been corrected. For you will have done them more good in that way than if you had flattered them with beautiful words,[2] which only serve to deceive and maintain them in their faults and disorderly conduct.

Have you up to the present paid attention so that you correct your disciples only with God in view? Have you not corrected them with exaggerated zeal, perhaps with impatience and in anger? Was that to help them change their conduct, or was it not rather to punish them for some annoyance they caused you? Has charity guided you in this behavior, or have you acted instead to vent your bad humor on them?

Pay close attention to this in the future, so that your conduct in this important matter will be motivated only by the desire to please God.

### 204.2 Second Point

Although Saint Paul warned his disciple Titus to admonish with vigor those who live without obedience, lest they corrupt their faith,[3] and he also told Timothy to do the same thing, to cause fear in others,[4] he wrote to him at the same time that he ought to be patient and moderate in correcting those who offer resistance, because perhaps God will give them the spirit of repentance.[5] This is one of the best ways to win and to touch the hearts of those who have fallen into a fault and to dispose them to be converted.

This is the way the Prophet Nathan went about it when he was sent by God to King David to get David to enter into himself and become aware of the two sins, adultery and murder, that he had committed. The Prophet began by telling him a parable about a rich man who had a great number of sheep and stole the only sheep owned by a poor man. This simple story of terrible injustice, as told by Nathan, aroused the anger of David against the guilty man and made him say that he was deserving of death and that he would not grant him any pardon. At this Nathan answered him, You are that very man![6] He immediately applied his story to the two crimes that David had committed, representing to him in God's name the graces that God had given him and how he had abused them.

This is the sort of method you must use with those you instruct when they fall into some fault and you have to correct them. If it happens that you have been aroused by some passion, avoid making any correction while you experience this emotion, because then the correction would be very harmful to your disciples as well as to you. In those situations focus within, and allow the time of anger to pass without showing it exteriorly. Then, when you feel that you are completely free of passion, you will be able to surrender to God's Spirit and to make the correction you planned with all the moderation of which you are capable.

Have you acted this way in the past? Pray God never to allow you to be carried away by any outburst of anger when you have to punish any of your disciples.

### 204.3 Third Point

The result that the wise reproof of Nathan produced in David ought to make you realize how much good the corrections you give your disciples will profit them when they are given with gentleness and charity. David became angry at the man Nathan described in his parable, and when he realized that he was the one for whom the parable was told, he had no other response but the words, I have sinned;[7] at once he took on a severe penance. When the child born of his adultery died, David adored God and made it clear that he accepted his holy will. This is how the wise and restrained manner of the Prophet toward the sinful David softened the king's heart: he acknowledged his two sins, asked God's pardon for them, and was truly sorry.

The result of a wise correction is that those receiving it are disposed to correct their faults, whereas when correction is administered through passion and without God in view, it serves only to turn the disciple against his teacher and to arouse in him feelings of revenge and ill will, which sometimes last a long time, because results are generally related and similar to the cause that produces them.

If, then, you want your corrections to have the results they ought to have, administer them in a way that can please God and those who receive them. Take care, above all, that it be charity and zeal for the salvation of the souls of your students that lead you to correct them. Show them so much kindness when you give corrections that although you might cause them pain, they will not be angry at you but will show you gratitude for the good you have done for them, great regret for their faults, and a firm intention not to commit them again. From this very moment, be disposed to use the means needed to carry out this resolution.

---

| | | |
|---|---|---|
| 1. Prv 12:1 | 4. 1 Tim 5:20 | 7. 2 Sm 12:13-22 |
| 2. Prv 28:23 | 5. 2 Tim 2:24-25 | |
| 3. Ti 1:10-13 | 6. 2 Sm 12:1-12 | |

# Thirteenth Meditation

*That as a teacher, you must give an account to God of the way you have done your work*

### 205.1 First Point

*You cooperate with God in his work*, says Saint Paul, and the souls of the children whom you teach are the field that God cultivates through you.[1] Because he is the One who has given you the ministry you exercise, when all of you appear before the judgment seat of Jesus Christ, each will give his own account to God of what he has done as a minister of God and as a dispenser of his mysteries[2] for children.

Jesus Christ, having been appointed by God to be your judge, will say to you, as the owner said to his manager, Give me an account of your administration.[3] He will then look into the very depths of your heart to examine whether you have been faithful managers of the wealth he has entrusted to you and the talents he has given you to work in his service. The good or the bad use you have made of these gifts will then become clear, for the Lord, who judges you, will unveil what is most hidden and most secret in the depths of your heart.[4]

If you want to prevent the account that you must give from becoming heavier with the passage of time, make one every day to yourself. Examine before God how you are conducting your work and whether you are failing in any of your duties.

Come to see clearly who you are. Find fault accurately and unsparingly, so that when Jesus Christ comes to judge you, you will be able to face his judgment without being afraid. For when he comes, he will find nothing to condemn in you, because you will have anticipated his judgment, regarding not only your own person but also the talents and the graces you have received from God to fulfill well the service that he assigned to you.

For he has made you the guardians and guides of children, who belong to him and over whom he has acquired the right of father, not only by creation but also by holy Baptism, whereby they are all consecrated to him.

### 205.2 Second Point

Consider that the account you will have to give to God will not be inconsequential, because it concerns the salvation of the souls of children whom God has entrusted to your care, for on the day of judgment, you will answer for them as much as for yourself.

You must be convinced of this, that God will begin by making you give an account of their souls before making you give an account of your own. When you took responsibility for them, you became committed at the same time to procure their salvation with as much diligence as your own, for you engaged to work entirely for the salvation of their souls.

This is what Saint Paul brings to your attention when he says that *those who have been put in charge of others must render an account of them to God.* He does not say that they will render an account of their own souls but of the souls of those for whom they are responsible. It is over those souls that they must watch, because they are obliged to render an account to God for them.[5]

The basic reason for this is that when they carry out well the service of guides and leaders of the souls entrusted to them, they fulfill at the same time their own duties before God. God will fill them with so much grace that they will be made holy while they are contributing as far as they are able to the salvation of others.

Have you up to the present regarded the salvation of your students as your personal responsibility during the entire time they are under your guidance? You have exercises that are arranged for your own sanctification, but if you have an ardent zeal for the salvation of those whom you are called to instruct, you will not fail to perform them and to relate them to this intention. In doing this you will draw down on your students the graces needed to contribute to their salvation. You can be assured that if you act this way for their salvation, God will assume the responsibility for yours. Take on this spirit for the future.

### 205.3 Third Point

In making you responsible for the instruction of children and their formation in piety, Jesus Christ entrusted to you the task of building up his body, which is the Church.[6] You are likewise responsible, as far as you are able, to make her holy and to purify her by the word of life, so that she may be able to appear before him full of glory, without stain, without wrinkle, without any defect, but completely pure and beautiful.[7] For this he wants you to give him an exact account when he calls for it, because he holds this responsibility very much at heart, *having loved his Church so much that he gave himself up for her.*

Because children are the most innocent part of the Church and usually the best disposed to receive the impressions of grace, Jesus Christ desires that you fulfill so well your task of making them holy *that all of them will come to the age of the perfect man and the fullness of Jesus Christ, so that they are no longer like children tossed here and there, no longer turned around by every wind of doctrine, by deceit, and by trickery,* whether by companions with whom they associate *or by men leading them into falsehood* by their evil proposals.

Rather, in all things they are growing up in Jesus Christ, who is their head and through whom the whole body of the Church holds its structure and its union, so that they may always be so united with the Church and in her that by the hidden power that Jesus Christ furnishes to all his members,[8] they will share in the promises of God in Jesus Christ.[9]

Be, then, in a position to be able, when he questions you, to tell him that you have performed all these duties well. Be assured that the best way to do this and to be pleasing to Jesus Christ when he judges you will be to present to him all those children whom you have instructed *as part of the building of the Church and have brought* by your care into its structure to become the sanctuary where God dwells by the Holy Spirit.[10]

This is how you will show Jesus Christ that you have truly fulfilled your ministry and that you have worked effectively to build up and sustain the Church, as Jesus Christ has engaged you to do.

---

| | | |
|---|---|---|
| 1. 1 Cor 3:9 | 5. Heb 13:17 | 9. Eph 3:6 |
| 2. 1 Cor 4:1 | 6. Eph 4:12 | 10. Eph 2:22 |
| 3. Lk 16:2 | 7. Eph 5:25-27 | |
| 4. 1 Cor 4:5 | 8. Eph 4:12-16 | |

# Fourteenth Meditation

*Matters related to his work on which a Brother of the Christian Schools must give an account to God*

### 206.1  First Point

Because God has called you to your ministry in order to procure his glory *and to give* children the spirit of wisdom and the insight to know him and to enlighten the eyes of their hearts,[1] you will give an account of how well you have instructed those who have been under your guidance. This is an inescapable obligation for you, and you will be punished for their ignorance in these matters (if it is your fault), just as if you had been ignorant of them.

You will give an account to God whether you were exact to teach catechism and to do so on all the days and for all the time prescribed for you; whether you taught your disciples the subjects in the catechism that they must know according to their age and ability; whether you neglected some students because they were the slowest, perhaps also the poorest, and whether you showed favoritism toward others because they were rich, pleasant, or naturally possessed more lovable qualities than the others did.

You will give an account whether you instructed them well how to assist at Holy Mass and to confess their sins; whether you preferred to teach secular subjects, such as reading, writing, and arithmetic, although you must not neglect these, for they are strictly required of you, but the lessons that contribute to the support of religion are of much greater importance; whether during all the time available for your assignments, you wasted some on useless activities or even on useful ones that were not your duty; finally, whether you took care to learn (during the time assigned to you for this) the subjects you are obliged to teach to those for whom you are responsible.

Are your accounts in good order, and are you ready to give them? If that is not the case, put them in order without delay, and examine seriously what your conduct has been in this regard. If there has been any negligence in your conduct, make a firm resolution to correct it. Before God be determined to do better in the future, so that death will not surprise you in such an unfortunate condition.

### 206.2 Second Point

When you appear before God, it will not be sufficient for you to have instructed the children entrusted to you, but you will be found guilty if you have not watched over their conduct. For it is your duty *to watch over them* exactly, being obliged to give an account to God for their souls.[2] Have you considered carefully what it means to give an account to God for the salvation of a soul that is damned because you did not take care to lead it to what is right and to assist it to live accordingly?

Are you convinced that you are obliged to take care of your disciples during all the time they are in church, as much as when they are in school, in order to prevent them from doing anything even the least displeasing to God? Is it not also your responsibility to be attentive during the prayers you have them say, so that they do so with great piety, decorum, and respect as speaking to God?

Do you believe, perhaps, that you are responsible for your disciples only during the time of school, that your vigilance need not extend to their behavior outside of school in order to help them, as far as you are able, to live everywhere in a Christian manner and not associate with bad companions during the entire time they are under your guidance?

To give an account for their souls means to give an account of everything that concerns their salvation; to watch exactly means to watch over everything with diligence, omitting and neglecting nothing.

If you have not been diligent in all these matters, consider that you are guilty before God, and have a great fear to appear before God at the moment of your death after you have lived in such negligence of all that concerns his service.

### 206.3 Third Point

What you say and do need not be as great a concern in the account you will have to render to God as the intention and the manner of these actions. For the faults of speaking and acting are usually more tangible and come more readily to your mind. Of intention Saint Paul says that whether we speak or whether we act,[3] we must do all things in the name of our Lord Jesus Christ, not in order to please men but to please God.[4] This is the purpose you must have and the sole motive that God wants you to have in your work.

Is it not true that often you have hardly thought of this at all, that usually you have had no intention whatsoever or, if you have had one, that it was purely natural and human? This single fault, then, would have corrupted all that you did, however good it might have been, and would have blocked God's blessing on your action.

You will give God no less an account concerning your ministry: whether you have worked with wisdom and seriousness and without undue familiarity with those whom you teach. This *seriousness* is what Saint Paul recommended so strongly to Titus, his disciple, as *a minister of the Gospel* and what he believed to be more necessary for him than any other good quality. After zeal for instruction and purity of morals,[5] this serious self-control is one of the most useful virtues for those who are responsible for instructing youth.

Nevertheless, do not overlook the account you will have to give of your patience and the control of your passions.[6] This, again, is a very important point to which you must be very attentive, especially when the children in your care do something out of order and you are required to reprove or correct them. There is nothing you must be more on your guard against than somehow allowing your passions to run away with you.

This must be one of the main points of the examination you ought to make regarding the account that God will ask of you concerning your work. Consider this very seriously.

---

1. Eph 1:17-18    3. Col 3:17    5. Ti 2:7
2. Heb 13:17    4. 1 Thes 2:4    6. 2 Tm 2:24-25

# Fifteenth Meditation

*The reward that those can expect even in this life who have instructed children and have fulfilled this duty well*

### 207.1 First Point

God is so good that he does not leave unrewarded the good work that is for him and the service that is rendered to him, especially for the salvation of souls. If it is true that God rewards so generously even in this world those who have left all things for him, that they receive a hundredfold in this life,[1] with how much more reason will God reward even in this present time those who have devoted themselves with zeal to spread his kingdom!

To reward so great a good work and a service that he regards so highly, God gives two kinds of reward in this world to those who commit themselves untiringly to the work of the salvation of souls. First, he gives them an abundance of grace; second, he gives them a more extended ministry and a greater ability to procure the conversion of souls.

The first of these rewards is set forth in the parable of the man who distributes his funds to his servants and gives one of them five talents in order to make a profit from them. When he learns later from that servant that he has made another five, in order to reward him, he orders *that the one talent given to the servant* who has not made any profit be taken away and given to the one who now has ten. For those who have will be given more, the Savior says, and they will be given riches in abundance.[2]

Saint Luke expresses well the second kind of reward, the larger field of ministry, in the parable of the lord taking account of the money that he has given his servants. He rewards *the first servant,* who told him that his money had increased tenfold, by giving him the government of ten villages.[3]

Oh, how fortunate you ought to consider it to be working in the field of the Lord, for our Lord says that the reaper will infallibly receive his reward![4]

For the future, then, be devoted with zeal and affection to your work, because it will be one of the most helpful ways to assure your salvation.

### 207.2 Second Point

Another reward in this life that those who work for the salvation of souls receive is their consolation in seeing God served well by those whom they have instructed and in realizing that their work has not been useless but has served to save those whom they were called upon to instruct.

In this spirit Saint Paul writes to the Corinthians, to whom he preached the Gospel, that he has begotten them in Jesus Christ[5] and that they are his work in our Lord.[6] Similarly, he finds joy to learn of their goodwill. This is what makes him boast about them, because many people have been stirred by their zeal.[7] He adds his hope that the increase of their faith will attain so much glory that it will extend farther and farther to win souls through the proclamation of the Gospel. Yet, it is in our Lord that he boasts. It is only in Jesus Christ, he says, that I lay hold to some glory for what I have done for God.[8]

The spread of God's glory, then, by preaching the Gospel made up all the consolation of this great Apostle. This must also be yours, to make God and his Son, Jesus Christ, known to the flock confided to you. Oh, what glory for you to have this resemblance to that chosen vessel of election![9] With joy, then, say as he does that the greatest cause of your joy in this life is to proclaim the Gospel free of charge, without having it cost anything to those who hear it.[10] It is indeed a great glory for you to instruct your disciples about the truths of the Gospel solely for the love of God. This thought made the Teacher of the Nations always find consolation and, according to the testimony he has given, filled him with overflowing joy in the midst of his afflictions.[11] You too must consider it a great personal reward, this consolation that you feel at the bottom of your heart, that the children whom you instruct behave well, know their religion thorooughly, and live a life of piety. Thank God with all your heart for all these kinds of rewards that he gives you in advance in this life.

### 207.3 Third Point

You can expect yet another reward, which God will give you in advance in this life if you are generously devoted to your duty and if, through zeal and the grace of your state, you have known well how to give your disciples a foundation in the Christian spirit. This is the very special satisfaction you will have when they grow up and you see them living with justice and piety,[12] keeping free from evil associates, and performing good deeds.

For the instructions you have given them *have not consisted in words only but have been accompanied by a great abundance of grace* for those who have profited from them, which will maintain them in the practice of good. Their perseverance in piety will be a great cause of consolation for you *when you call to mind the result of their faith* and of your instruction, knowing that this makes them dear to God and places them in the number of his elect.[13]

What a joy it will be to see *that they have received the word of* God in your catechism lessons, not as the word of men but as the word of God, which is powerfully at work in them,[14] as will be clearly apparent in the virtuous life they continue to live. For this reason, in the consolation you have to see *their perseverance* in piety, you will be able to say that they are your hope, your joy, and your crown of glory before our Lord Jesus Christ.[15]

Look upon this, then, as a considerable reward that God gives you, even in this world, to see that religion and piety are increased among the faithful, especially among the working class and the poor, by means of the establishment of the schools that have been placed by God under your guidance.

Thank God every day[16] through Jesus Christ, our Lord, that he has been pleased to establish this benefit and to give this support to the Church. Ask him fervently too that he will be pleased to make your Institute grow and produce good day by day, so that, as Saint Paul says, the hearts of the faithful may be strengthened in holiness and in justice.[17]

---

1. Mt 19:27-29
2. Mt 25:28-29
3. Lk 19:16-17
4. Jn 4:36
5. 1 Cor 4:15
6. 1 Cor 9:1
7. 2 Cor 9:2
8. 2 Cor 10:15-17
9. Acts 9:15
10. 1 Cor 9:18
11. 2 Cor 2:7:4
12. Ti 2:12
13. 1 Thes 1: 2-5
14. 1 Thes 2:13
15. 1 Thes 2:19
16. 1 Thes 1:2
17. 1 Thes 3:13

# Sixteenth Meditation

*The reward that a Brother of the Christian Schools ought to expect in heaven if he is faithful in his work*

### 208.1 First Point

Saint Paul complained because some of the Corinthians said that *they belonged to Paul, while others said that they belonged to Apollo.* He told them that each of them would receive his reward in proportion to his labor.[1] This ought to make you realize that your happiness in heaven will be greater than what will be enjoyed by those who have worked only for their own salvation, and it will be much greater in proportion to the number of children you have instructed and won over to God.

*The work of each one*, that is, of those who have labored on the building of the Church, says the Apostle, will be made known on the day of the Lord, because fire will be the test of the work of each one[2] (especially those who have instructed children and formed them to piety). Those who have formed them in the Christian spirit and those who have procured for them a solid piety will be seen. Such teachers will easily be distinguished from others who will not have trained their disciples in any good practice and will have been negligent in guiding them. The one whose work will survive, says the Apostle, that is, the one whose disciples will have acquired a strong piety through the teacher's effort and concern, will be rewarded in proportion to his work.[3]

Consider, then, that your reward in heaven will be all the greater inasmuch as you will have accomplished more good in the souls of the children entrusted to your care. In this spirit Saint Paul told the Corinthians, You will be our glory in the time to come on the day of our Lord Jesus Christ.[4]

You can say the same thing of your disciples, namely, that on the day of judgment, they will be your glory if you have instructed them well and if they have profited from your instructions, because the lessons you have given them and the profit they have made from them will be unveiled before the whole world. Not only on that day but throughout all eternity, you will receive the glory of having instructed them well, because the glory that you have procured for them will reflect on you.

Fulfill the duties of your work so well, then, that you may be able to enjoy this blessing.

### 208.2 Second Point

What a consolation for those who have procured the salvation of souls: to see in heaven a great number whom they have helped to obtain the advantage of enjoying so great a happiness! This will happen to those who have instructed many people about the truths of religion, as an angel said to the Prophet Daniel: *Those who instruct many people* in Christian justice will shine like stars throughout all eternity.[5] They will shine, indeed, in the midst of those whom they have instructed, who will eternally bear witness to the great gratitude they have for so many instructions they received from their teachers, whom they will regard as the cause, after God, of their salvation.

Oh, what joy a Brother of the Christian Schools will have when he sees a great number of his students in possession of eternal happiness, for which they are indebted to him by the grace of Jesus Christ! What a sharing of joy there will be between the teacher and his disciples! What a special union with one another there will be in the presence of God! It will be for them a great satisfaction, sharing together the blessings for which the call of God had given them hope, the wealth of the glorious heritage of God in the dwelling of the saints.[6]

Reach such a position in the future by fidelity to your duty, so that at the moment of your death, you will possess such a great happiness and be able to see your disciples, likewise, after they have ended their days, possess this happiness along with you.

### 208.3 Third Point

The holy King David says that he will be filled with gladness when God will grant him the grace to see him and to enjoy the glory of heaven.[7] For the sight of God fills all the powers of a person's soul in such a way that all consciousness of self is lost, so to speak. The person is entirely present within the divinity and totally penetrated with God. This is the happiness that will be possessed in heaven by those who have procured the salvation of souls, who have done this in a way that has been useful to the good of the Church, who have by their care restored the robe of innocence to a great number of their disciples, who might have lost it through sin, and who have helped preserve the innocence of many others who have never lost it.

This will happen to those who have carried out the role of Guardian Angels for the children whom Providence has entrusted to them and who have had ardent zeal in their work, practiced this zeal continually, and saved a great number of these children.

Oh, what a thrill of joy you will have when you hear the voices of those whom you have led, as if by the hand, into heaven, who will say to you on the day of judgment as well as in heaven what the girl delivered from the devil by Saint Paul said to the Apostle and those who were with him: These men are servants of the great God who have proclaimed to us the way of salvation.[8] Then they will represent the good you have done among them. Some will represent to Jesus Christ on the day of judgment the robe of innocence that you helped them keep in all its purity. Others who have committed sin and who with your help have washed away their sins in the blood of the Lamb[9] will represent to him the trouble you took to lead them back on the path of salvation.

All of them will join their voices to obtain for you a favorable judgment from Jesus Christ, praying him not to delay putting you in possession of the happiness you procured for them by your work and your concern. Oh, what glory there will be for those people who have instructed youth, when their zeal and devotion to procure the salvation of children will be made public before all people! All heaven will resound with the thanksgiving that these blessed children will render to those who have taught them the road to heaven!

Act, then, in such a way by your good and wise guidance of those who are entrusted to you that you will receive all these blessings and all this glory.

---

1. 1 Cor 3:4-8
2. 1 Cor 3:13
3. 1 Cor 3:14
4. 2 Cor 1:14
5. Dan 12:3
6. Eph 1:18
7. Ps 17:15
8. Acts 16:17
9. Rev 7:14

# APPENDICES

———— ✦ ————

# Appendix A

## Original Introductions
to *Meditations*

### Introduction to the first edition of
### *Meditations for Sundays*
### *and Principal Feasts of the Year* (CL 12)
### (probably written by Brother Timothée, Superior General)

The favorable reception accorded to the publication of *Meditations for the Time of Retreat,* written by Monsieur de La Salle, when they were sent to the houses of the Institute, the holy eagerness with which everyone at the following retreat was inspired to listen to them with unusual attention in order to be spiritually nourished, and the recent urging from several Brothers led us to work with added enthusiasm for the publication of the meditations that this holy priest also wrote for the Sundays and the principal feasts of the year, which are contained in the two sections of this book, in order to circulate them more easily to all the houses of the Society to procure thereby with blessing the results that this holy man proposed in devoting himself to this work during the last years of his life, spending a great deal of time for this purpose.

A person of learning and considerable wisdom, who has been willing to devote his time to examine the entire manuscript of these meditations before having them printed, was filled with admiration and astonishment over the ardent zeal of this apostolic man in his writing, so simple and full of candor, without any artifice or display of human eloquence, and which in every way is the expression of the Spirit of God coming from the maxims and truths of the Gospel and founded on the example of Jesus Christ and the saints.

This holy priest, without realizing it, has expressed in this book the very spirit that inspired him and served as a guide for all his actions. This is also the spirit that he always tried to impress on the minds and hearts of those whom divine Providence entrusted to his care. This ought to be, therefore, the special application of all those who have the good fortune and the advantage of reading or of hearing read these holy instructions, rather than imitating the Israelites who at first received with joy and admiration the manna given to them by God through the ministry of angels but then gradually became disgusted with it, although this heavenly nourishment contained in it all kinds of wonderful taste. To avoid falling into such a disorder, we must look on these holy teachings as heavenly bread given by God, not by the angels of heaven but by the ministry of a father (who led an angelic life on earth) and given to nourish his children, whom he had born to Jesus Christ by grace. We must imitate those generous and courageous Rechabites, spoken of in Holy Scripture, who, when invited on behalf of God by the Prophet Jeremiah to act against the words and wishes of their ancestor, Rechab, replied that they could not break any of the commands that their ancestor had given them. By a similar practice and obedience, we will be true children of such a zealous and charitable father and very worthy founder.

---- ✦ ----

### Introduction to the first edition of *Meditations for the Time of Retreat* (CL 13), adapted with permission from the translation published by Saint Mary's College Press, Winona, MN, 1975 (probably written by Brother Timothée, Superior General)

This little book of meditations contains reflections on the main duties of those who are generously devoted to the Christian education of youth, composed by Monsieur de La Salle and intended to help a person become deeply committed to these important duties during a time of spiritual renewal.

For that purpose, the author considered it fitting that the Brothers of the Institute of the Christian Schools make use of these meditations for their prayer in the afternoons on the eight days of retreat that they make each year during the time of vacation. He wanted to help them appreciate the greatness of their profession as teachers and the necessity of fulfilling so holy a ministry with great fidelity to all its responsibilities.

He divided his little work into sixteen meditations, two for each day of the retreat, so that one of the two could take the place of public or private reading and serve as material for a conference or exhortation in the evening.

Care has been taken, before sending these meditations to the press, to have them examined by a person of learning and sound doctrine, who corrected a large number of errors that had slipped in through the carelessness and negligence of those who had copied from the original.

Out of respect for the author, it was thought proper to leave the meditations just as they were, although they were written more in the style of instructions, exhortations, and regulations than of meditations. They are without expressions of fervent desire, feelings of tenderness, or resolutions customary in similar meditations, but this is not surprising; the author did this intentionally, as in the meditations he wrote for all the Sundays and feasts of the year. His purpose was to instruct and exhort the Brothers rather than to teach them how to express their desires, emotions, and intimate conversation with God.

He had provided for this training by giving the Brothers a method of interior prayer, in which he taught them very clearly how to express their desires, feelings, and resolutions with facility and effectiveness. Holy man that he was, he held as a practical truth that the acts of prayer that come from a person's own heart are incomparably more important than those that come from the expression of desires or feelings in someone else's meditations, although he was far from disapproving of these.

There is a great deal of repetition of the same ideas in several of the meditations, but this ought not to be surprising, for it was the usual practice of our Lord, recorded in several places of the Gospel, and also of Saint Paul, Saint John the Evangelist, and many other saints, both of the Old and the New Testament. Such a method has been inspired by the Holy Spirit in order to impress more deeply on the mind and heart the holy truths being taught.

The simplicity and candor of the style of these meditations might suggest that the art of persuasion, although present, is lacking its full measure, but the use of these meditations has always made it clear how effective they are. After all, throughout the meditations there is the deep faith that was so characteristic of this holy priest and the ardent zeal for the instruction of children that was so much a part of his life.

Finally, we need not be surprised that this apostolic man set forth so strongly the dignity and merits of the profession and functions of people who have dedicated themselves to the Christian instruction of children or that he would use for this purpose so many passages of Holy Scripture to confirm what he states, especially from the Epistles of Saint Paul, which he had mastered perfectly and on whose authority he grounded himself. He knew from long experience and even more from the enlightenment he gained from God how valuable and important in the eyes of the divine majesty is the instruction of youth. This led him to inspire the same sentiments in those to whom he spoke.

He was also convinced that many people regarded this ministry as very unimportant, contrary to the practice and thought of Jesus Christ and of many saints and distinguished people, who considered it a very great vocation and worked at it themselves with surprising zeal. Saint Jerome and Saint Gregory are among this number, as are many, many others spoken of in the history of the Church. Saint Protogenes is an admirable example of this. He was bishop of Edessa, exiled by the Arian Emperor Valens to the city of Antinous in Egypt, a city populated by many who practiced idolatry. There he devoted himself to conduct a school with marvelous success, eliminating paganism almost entirely.

Saint Cassian did the same thing in the city of Imola in Italy and won the crown of martyrdom when he was given over by a sentence of the judge to the vengeance of the children he taught, some of whom were still pagans. Finally, the admirable example of the great and devout Gerson, Chancellor of the University of Paris, is a sufficient proof of this truth. He retired to Lyons and did not think it beneath his dignity to dedicate himself to conduct a school for children and to devote himself to freeing them from evil. To those who begged him to use his talents for more brilliant services, he said that they would possibly be more glorious but not more useful.

# Appendix B

## Glossary of Words in *Meditations*

The following glossary has been prepared, in part, to explain how individual French words are translated in the meditations but also to comment on certain other expressions that are typical of De La Salle.

*s'abandonner:* abandon, to abandon the self. The attitude of total trust in God is a key element in the spirituality of De La Salle and in the spirituality of his time.

*âme(s):* soul(s). This expression is regularly translated as soul(s), although today we are inclined in certain contexts to use words such as *person(s), being,* or *self* when De La Salle and his contemporaries use the word in such expressions as the salvation, conversion, care, depth, or peace of a person.

*détachement:* detachment. This word embodies a key element in the spirituality of De La Salle and his time: an interior disposition to become independent of all created things in order to be totally given to God and the things of God.

*disciple:* disciple. De La Salle often uses this word in the meditations when he is referring to the students of the Brothers. He no doubt wants the Brothers to consider that their relation to the students is similar to that of Christ to his followers. More commonly, De La Salle uses the word *enfants (children)* when he means the students of the Brothers. He uses the word *élèves (students)* only rarely.

*dissipation:* dissipation. This French word is usually translated by the words *distraction, thoughtlessness,* or some other equivalent. For De La Salle, it means a lack of recollection or of interiority and refers to any activities of the Brothers that would interfere with prayerfulness or attention to their duties.

*emploi:* employ. This word usually refers to the Brothers' task of teaching, their employment. It is generally translated by the word *work*. De La Salle also uses the words *ministère* and *fonction* to speak of the Brothers' work, but less often than the word *emploi*.

*esprit:* spirit, mind. As with the Latin word *animus,* this word can mean either spirit or mind. More often than not in the meditations, De La Salle means mind rather than spirit, except when speaking of the broader sense of the Christian spirit or the spirit of faith.

*état:* state. De La Salle uses this word more often than *profession* or *vocation* to refer to the Brothers' state of life.

*exercice(s):* exercise(s). In the singular this word generally means practice, as in the practice of obedience. In the plural it usually refers to such practices of the religious life as prayer, spiritual reading, and other parts of the daily schedule; in these instances it is translated simply as exercises, part of the terminology of the time.

*hommes:* men. When De La Salle uses this word to express the human race generally, it is translated by an inclusive word, such as *people,* or by an appropriate form of the first person plural pronoun, which is what De La Salle has in mind. This will also be done in some instances of the French impersonal *on;* otherwise, there is no effort to use inclusive language in the text, for De La Salle is writing for an exclusively male readership.

*instruire:* to instruct. De La Salle uses this word or the related noun when he is speaking of religious instruction; *instruct* is the translation throughout the meditations. The verbs *enseigner* and, sometimes, *apprendre* are used for the more general idea of teaching. (Cf. *Catéchèse et laïcat,* by Michel Sauvage, pp. 162–164).

*libertinage.* This word is translated as *wayward conduct* or some similar expression when it refers to the misbehavior of children, although there are a few occasions when *immorality* is used to express what De La Salle has in mind. In any case the literal translation does not seem appropriate.

*modestie.* This word is a key word for De La Salle, but most of the time, if at all, it cannot be translated literally in the meditations as modesty. Examination of the use that De La Salle makes of this word in *Recueil, Règles de la bienséance,* and the chapter on *Modestie* in the Rule of the Brothers leads to the conclusion that the idea of *modestie,* for De La Salle, means the exercise of self-control, or proper behavior, in regard to all parts of the body. Words such as *reserve* or *decorum* are often good translations. The word *modestie* refers to proper behavior when alone, with others, in church, or at prayer. It is an element of the stylized behavior of the bourgeois society of the time. De La Salle is careful to motivate such behavior by the sentiments of faith, especially in *Règles de la bienséance*. For the numerous ways the Latin word *modestia* has been translated in the well-known passage of Saint Paul, see the footnote on MDF 92.2, for December 31.

*monde:* the world. De La Salle often uses this word to express the spirit of the world as opposed to the spirit of the Gospel or of the spiritual life. It is translated literally when he uses the word in that sense.

*mouvement:* movement. De La Salle often uses this word to express the action of the Holy Spirit in a person, or it can mean the person's own experience of this action, such as inspirations. In these instances the word is usually translated literally.

*oraison:* prayer. There is no English word to distinguish this French word from the other French word, *prière*. Both words can be translated by the English word *prayer*. When De La Salle uses the word *oraison,* it is clear from the context that he is not referring to vocal prayer but to prayer of the heart, whether it be meditation, contemplation, or some other similar form of prayer. The word *oraison* is translated as prayer or as interior prayer.

*piété:* piety. For De La Salle this word has a much broader meaning than the word *piety* in English. It can mean the faithful practice of religion or of some aspect of it, such as religious conversation, acts of devotion, or other practices of spirituality. Because it is a key word for De La Salle in both his spiritual and his educational thought, it is translated literally throughout the meditations.

*pureté:* purity. When De La Salle uses this word, he is most often referring to innocence or to purity of heart, although there are occasions when he uses the word in the more specific sense of chastity. On one occasion in the meditations, he uses it to refer to the vow of chastity.

*régularité:* regularity. This is a key word in De La Salle's thinking about community life. It means faithful observance of the Brothers' Rule and other regulations. Because the literal translation is no longer used in this sense, the word and related words are translated as *observance of the Rule, fidelity to the Rule,* and similar expressions.

*retirer:* to withdraw. De La Salle uses this verb and its related forms to describe the action of a person who leaves day-to-day activities in order to devote time to prayer and to other actions focused on God.

*retraite:* seclusion, withdrawal, spiritual retreat. This word also embodies the idea of withdrawing from day-to-day activities in order to be devoted to thoughts about God. It has almost the same meaning as the French word *solitude,* which is translated literally. The word *retraite* is usually translated as seclusion or withdrawal.

# Appendix C

## Arrangement and Content
## of *Meditations*

*Méditations pour les Dimanches et les principales Fêtes de l'année* (MDF) was published in a single volume divided into two sections. The first contains 77 meditations for Sundays; the second, 108 meditations for the feasts of the Church's liturgical year. Each meditation has three points, or parts, the customary arrangement for books of meditations in seventeenth-century France.

In the first edition of the meditations, the Gospel for the Sunday or the feast is printed at the head of each meditation, which begins with a kind of exegesis on this Gospel, written by De La Salle for the Brothers. These meditations aim at teaching the Brothers fundamental doctrine of the Christian life for their own spirituality and for the education of their students. For this purpose, the Founder invites the Brothers to consider and to incorporate into their life and ministry the spirit and the teaching of the life of Jesus Christ.

There are eleven meditations on the various aspects of religious obedience.[1] De La Salle stresses community as an important factor for achieving success in mission. The meditations developing this topic are numbers 30, 60, 65, 68, and 72–77. For De La Salle, the Community of the Brothers is the Church of Jesus Christ, where the Spirit manifests his presence (MDF 169.3). In the four meditations for Rogation Days (MDF 36–39), De La Salle examines the importance of prayer and the way to encounter God and obtain his grace. The feast of Pentecost gives De La Salle the opportunity to explain the benefits of the presence of the Holy Spirit residing within us (MDF 42–45). The work of the school holds a significant place in all the meditations: four of them focus on the Brothers' duties in their educational ministry (MDF 2, 3, 56, and 61).

Several other topics dealing with the conduct of the Brothers are treated in these meditations. Allusions to asceticism and the acceptance of suffering are numerous (MDF 16, 23, 24, 25, 27, 28, and 59). In the matter of consolations (MDF 18) or of interior and exterior trials (MDF 35 and 71), De La Salle makes but one recommendation: have only God in view. The interior peace (MDF 31) desired by Jesus for his disciples after the Resurrection is the effect of the love of God, which unites us to Jesus Christ. Faith (MDF 32), abandonment to God (MDF 20, 67), love of seclusion (MDF 6), humility (MDF 63), and poverty (MDF 34) are subjects that De La Salle recalls to his disciples continually.

De La Salle also reflects on the great mysteries of the liturgical year: the Most Holy Trinity (MDF 46), the Passion and death of Jesus (MDF 23–28), the Resurrection and Ascension (MDF 29 and 40), Pentecost (MDF 43), and the Eucharist (MDF 26 and 47–55).

The second section of MDF includes 108 meditations on the feasts of the saints. In the first edition, they are arranged in the order of the civil calendar.[2] In these meditations De La Salle presents the same themes found in the meditations for Sundays but developed in reference to the actions and virtues of individual saints. De La Salle's choice of the saints for these meditations is based on criteria that he identifies in his little book, *Recueil de différents petits traités*, which deals with various aspects of the Brothers' life.[3]

In the first edition, six meditations were added as an appendix and are grouped under the title, *Six Additional Meditations for Certain Feasts That Occur During the Year*. De La Salle's authorship of these six meditations was the subject of considerable controversy for some time. That they are not his work is clear now, partly from a study of their subject matter, format, sources, and titles and partly from the fact that they were originally added as an appendix (cf. CL 47:539–556). Their author is still unknown. The appendix also includes accounts of the life of Saint Yon, the titular saint of the Brothers' house in Rouen, and of Saint Cassian, whom De La Salle chose as one of the patrons of the Institute (CL 8:493).

The sixteen *Meditations for the Time of Retreat* (MTR) were written by De La Salle toward the end of his life.[4] Here he invites the Brothers to reflect before God on the purpose of their work and on their day-to-day life on behalf of their students. These meditations were for a long time ignored by the Institute, but they have been brought to light and recognized for their great value by the thorough research and doctoral dissertations of Brother Michel Sauvage[5] and Brother Miguel Campos.[6]

# French Editions

There is no documentary evidence that De La Salle ever intended his reflections, as he called them (MDF 70.1), to be published outside the Institute. Although the preface to the first edition of MDF is not signed, it seems clear that it was written by Brother Timothée, second Superior General, and that he was encouraged to publish MDF by the favorable comments people made about MTR (CL 12 *Avant Propos*). The first editions of MDF and MTR, unfortunately, do not have a date of publication, but the Archives of the Generalate has a first edition of MDF with an inscription written on the title page, "To the Brothers of Nogent-le-Rotrou, 1731." Because MTR was printed before MDF, the date of 1730 is ascribed to MTR and 1731 to MDF.

The meditations were not reprinted during the eighteenth century. After the restoration of the Institute in 1805 under Brother Frumence, Vicar General, a plan to reprint the writings of De La Salle was initiated by Brother Paulien, the Director of Novices at Langres.[7] Because *Explication de la Méthode d'Oraison*, a work De La Salle had written to help the Brothers profit from their time of meditation, was published in 1816 by Laurent-Bournot, we might presume that MDF and MTR, issued by the same printer but without a date, were also published in 1816. In these second editions, there is no change in the text, but the typography is updated and an index is added.

The third edition of MTR was printed in 1853, and five years later, MDF.[8] Under the impression that these meditations were not written by De La Salle but were composed from notes taken by the first Brothers, the editor of this third edition substantially altered the wording of the text.[9] As a result, De La Salle's thought lost not only its original force but even its meaning. In addition seventeen meditations were suppressed.[10] How did this happen to writings that up to this time were attributed without question to De La Salle?

In 1842 the Congregation of Rites began the examination of the writings of De La Salle as part of the process for his beatification and canonization. Because it was impossible to verify the absolute authenticity of the writings that were not in manuscript form, the theologians investigating the writings of the Founder raised many questions. The only texts that they considered favorably were *Recueil*, *Explication*, and MTR. The Vatican defenders of the cause suggested that the Brother Postulator, who was advancing the beatification process, ought to abandon efforts to prove that De La Salle had written MDF and the other works that had been attributed to him. As a result, the 1852 decree by the Congregation of Rites states that except for the manuscript letters of De La Salle, the other writings attributed to him cannot be recognized as authentic. Rayez has characterized this move as the 1849 mishap by the Congregation of Rites.[11]

This judgment of the Congregation of Rites on the meditations led to confusion and disagreement among the Brothers. On the occasion of the bicentenary of the founding of the Institute, in 1880, Brother Superior Irlide published the seventeen meditations suppressed in 1858 as an appendix to an edition of *Résumés of the Meditations for Sundays and Principal Feasts of the Year.*[12]

Two years later, the fourth edition of the meditations appeared. According to the editor, this edition conforms absolutely to the first edition, except that the mistakes of style that were most obvious were corrected just as the author would have done had he been able to correct his work in the printing process.[13]

In this fourth edition, MDF and MTR are included in the same volume for the first time. Also, the six meditations of the original appendix are inserted among the meditations for feasts; all the meditations are numbered in chronological order. A passage of Holy Scripture introduces each meditation, and a result and a spiritual bouquet are put at the end. The liturgical calendar is adopted for the order of the feasts, and a table of contents and an index are included.

In 1890 during the time Brother Joseph was Superior General, a special edition of MTR was published, to which were added from MDF other thoughts of De La Salle on the education of the young.

The fifth edition, combining MDF and MTR, appeared in 1922, during the time of Brother Superior Imier de Jésus. The introduction declares that the editors made every effort to reproduce the first edition as exactly as possible.[14] It was admitted, however, that certain changes in the text were made to make it easier to understand the thought being expressed by De La Salle. There are two other changes in this edition: references for the scriptural citations are added, and résumés are placed at the beginning rather than at the end of the meditations.

Despite the fact that the editors of the fourth and fifth editions of the meditations intended to reproduce the first edition, significant changes were introduced into the texts.

The sixth edition differs from its predecessors.[15] It reproduces without any change the text of the first edition. Only the scriptural references are inserted; they are, in fact, increased as a result of the research of Brother Michel Sauvage and Brother Luis Varela (cf. note 7 of the introduction).

# English Editions

In 1882 Brother Noah published the first English translation of MDF, in two volumes.[16] He also translated the *Résumés* that Brother Irlide had published in 1880 and had them printed at the head of each of the meditations. In addition he used the introduction of Brother Irlide's 1880 text for this first English edition. It was unfortunate that Brother Noah was not able to use the new 1882 French edition of MDF; except for the 17 meditations that were printed as an appendix to the *Résumés*, he based his translation on the seriously modified edition of 1858.

In 1884 Brother Noah published MTR, fortunately based on Brother Irlide's edition and using the introduction of the Superior General, dated April 30, 1882.[17]

In 1925 Brother Benezet Thomas, Assistant Superior General for the English-speaking Districts, was responsible for the translation into English of the *Résumés des Méditations,* which had been published in 1916 under the aegis of Brother Imier de Jésus, Superior General.[18]

It is regrettable that for more than half a century, the translation of MDF that carried the spiritual message of their Founder to the English-speaking Brothers was based on the altered texts of nineteenth-century French editions. Brother Clair Stanislas Battersby took the initiative to remedy this situation.[19] In 1953 he published the second English edition of MDF and MTR, in one volume, basing his translation on the first editions of these works. Out of concern for exactness in the scriptural citations, Battersby replaced the original words of De La Salle with texts of a more recent English translation of the Bible, that of Ronald Knox.

Battersby did not number the meditations as had been done since 1882. He numbered feasts to follow the order of the civil calendar; the six meditations of the appendix of the first edition were again relegated to an appendix, and an index of names and topics completed the edition. In 1964 Battersby republished the text of the meditations, this time omitting MTR and numbering the meditations according to their sequence in the liturgical calendar.

In 1975 a new translation of MTR was produced by Brother Augustine Loes.[20] It was based on the first edition as published in *Cahiers Lasalliens* 13 and had the benefit of the research of Brother Michel Sauvage and Brother Miguel Campos. Campos wrote the introduction, which gives a fairly extensive summary of his research on MTR. A condensed form of this introduction is used to introduce these meditations in this present volume.

# Editions in Other Languages

In the course of the twentieth century, there has been a remarkable growth of the Institute outside France. Many different cultures and languages have undertaken the work inaugurated by De La Salle. The translation of the educational and spiritual writings of the Founder was essential to this development, and during the past 50 years that work has been undertaken. In 1930 MDF and MTR were translated into Spanish; subsequent Spanish editions appeared in 1970 and 1986. A German translation was published in 1932; one in Slovak, in 1934; in Japanese, in 1955, and in Italian, in 1989.

MTR has been published in separate editions in Spanish in 1951 and 1978, in Flemish in 1926, in Italian in 1934 and 1973, in Arabic in 1959, in Maltese in 1950, and in Thai in 1988.

# Sources of MDF and MTR

MTR was the first text to receive the benefit of contemporary research. The creation of the *Cahiers lasalliens* in 1959 under the leadership of Brother Maurice-Auguste Hermans became the vehicle for communicating this research worldwide.[21] The first volume of the *Cahiers* is the work of Brother Michel Sauvage, entitled, *The New Testament Citations in MTR* (cf. note 7 of the introduction). After careful analysis of these citations, Sauvage concludes that De La Salle had used Amelote's French translation of the New Testament, published in 1707.[22]

This confirmed Sauvage's thesis that these meditations are the work of De La Salle at the end of his life, based on his long experience of the guidance of God. In his preface Sauvage states, "The text is firmly fashioned, and the teaching is thorough, fully developed, placing the mission of the Brother in the plan of God and in the mystery of Christ and the Church."

To what extent is MTR dependent on the meditations that François Giry composed for the Sisters of the Charitable Schools?[23] Georges Rigault states that without doubt De La Salle read these meditations and borrowed some general ideas and scriptural quotations from them.[24] Sauvage shows that the Founder used 181 quotations from the New Testament (CL 1:97–99). In Appendix A he shows that only 16 of the 58 passages of the New Testament in Giry are used in

MTR, and in some of these instances, the context is not the same. It is interesting also that Giry makes fewer references to the Old Testament (8) than De La Salle does (14). Rigault, Sauvage, and Campos agree that De La Salle's use of Holy Scripture is clearly superior in both soundness of doctrine and depth of thought.[25]

More recently, a study of the sources of the meditations for the principal feasts has been published as volume 47 of the *Cahiers lasalliens* (see note 8 of the introduction). The author, Brother Jean-Guy Rodrigue, identifies most of the sources that De La Salle used in preparing these meditations. From this research it is possible also to identify some of the books in De La Salle's library or the Brothers' library at Saint Yon. Of special interest also are the different ways De La Salle used his sources, his method of work, and the major elements of his spirituality.

Rather regularly, De La Salle gave spiritual talks to the young people with whom he lived, especially to the novices. Sundays and feast days were prime occasions.[26] On Sundays he would use the Gospel of the Mass to develop a topic on the spirituality, the professional work, or the community life of the Brothers. His own library, which according to his early biographer was well furnished (CL 8:121; 4:61; 51:23), became one source for his reflections on the saints.

For his meditations on the feasts of the Church, De La Salle regularly used *Martyrologe,* by François Paris,[27] *Les Fleurs de la vie des Saints,* by Pierre de Ribadeneira, SJ,[28] and *Bréviaire romain,* which he read every day.

De La Salle's preference for the short accounts of the saints by Paris is evident. There are one or more similarities to the Paris work in 56 of his meditations on the saints, 21 of which reflect Paris in all three of the meditation points (CL 47:538).

Ribadeneira's work is the second source used most frequently by De La Salle. This is a voluminous work in two folio-size books, each of 600 pages, full of details on all the saints celebrated during the liturgical year. Similar details appear in 46 meditations of De La Salle, in 12 of which they are in all three points. Brother Louis-Marie Aroz has discovered that a copy of Ribadeneira's work was in the library that De La Salle inherited from his father, Louis de La Salle.[29]

*Bréviaire romain* is used by De La Salle at least once in 35 meditations, usually to introduce a patristic quotation. These citations from *Bréviaire* occur most often in meditations for the months of August (8 of 14 meditations) and December (7 of 13 meditations) (CL 47:538).

De La Salle borrows from his sources for the beginning of each of the three points in his meditations. Here he singles out a fact or a particular virtue from the saint's life that will be especially helpful to the Brothers in their own daily life. In the second portion of each point, De La Salle speaks directly to the Brothers. Basing his comments on the details of the life of the saint, he shows that the example of the saint relates to the Brothers' life. Here the thought of the Founder appears, a conviction developed through his own religious experience, which he asks the Brothers to apply to their vocation and ministry.

The New Testament references in any historical work are often a clue to the date of the work. This is true, as already mentioned, of MTR (see note 7 of the introduction). Similarly, research on the meditations on the saints has revealed some striking similarities between the texts of De La Salle and two editions of the New Testament, Amelote's of 1688 and Mons' of 1668 (CL 47:16–22). However, the state of this research is not conclusive, and a more thorough study of other editions of the New Testament is needed.

Research on the sources of the meditations for Sundays has not yet been undertaken, although a preliminary study has thrown some light on De La Salle's meditations on obedience (MDF 7–15) and on the Eucharist (MDF 47–55). In 1967 Brother Secondino Scaglione demonstrated that a probable source for the meditations on obedience[30] is the writing of Modeste of Saint-Amable, a discalced Carmelite.[31] As for the meditations on the Eucharist, only a preliminary observation has been made about meditation 55; Cardinal Gousset observed in his written testimony during the process of beatification that a work of the Jesuit, Crasset, is a probable source.[32]

---

1. These are the meditations for the Sundays after Epiphany and before the time of Lent (7–15); meditations 21 and 57 are on the same theme.
2. Since the 1882 edition, the order of the liturgical calendar has been adopted for the meditations. The 1882 edition also numbers the meditations from 1 to 192, including the six meditations that were originally in the appendix and meditation 94, on the Holy Name of Jesus, composed by Brother Irlide, Superior General; this was replaced in 1922 by a text made up of excerpts from *L'Explication de la Méthode d'Oraison* and then suppressed in the edition of 1982.
3. *Recueil de différents petits traités*, CL 15, pp. 62–63. For the sources of this text, see CL 16, p. 37, and CL 47, pp. 26–27. The English edition, *A Collection of Various Short Treatises for the Use of the Brothers of the Christian Schools*, was published in 1932 by the La Salle Bureau, New York; revised edition by W. J. Battersby, Saint Mary's College Press, Winona, MN, 1965. In 1993 Lasallian Publications issued a new edition of Battersby's translation, edited by Brother Daniel Burke, FSC, and published by the Christian Brothers Conference, Landover, MD.
4. Cf. *Méditations pour le Temps de la retraite*, Rome, 1976, pp. 7–8; also CL 1 p. xxxv.
5. Sauvage, *Catéchèse et laïcat*.
6. Campos, *Itinéraire évangelique* . . . , CL 45–46.

7. Brother Paulien, Antoine Boudoul (1749–1820), made his perpetual profession in 1783. At the time of the Revolution, he was Director of Novices at Avignon. After the restoration of the Institute, he participated in the General Chapter of 1810, at which Brother Gerbaud was elected Superior General. He was then appointed Director of Novices at Langres and later in Paris. (Cf. Rigault, *Histoire générale de l'Institut des FÉC,* Vol. III, p. 493, and Vol. IV, p. 465; *Circulaires instructives et administratives* (CIA), No. 112, pp. 96–97; No. 137, pp. 169 and 176; No. 234, p. 63; Lucard, *Annales,* pp. 702 ff).

8. Even the titles of the books were changed: *Méditations pour le Temps de la Retraite propre aux Frères des Écoles chrétiennes et autres personnes vouées a l'enseignement de la jeunesse* and *Méditations dites du Venerable Jean-Baptiste de La Salle sur les Évangiles de tous les dimanches et sur les principales Fêtes de l'année.*

9. Cf. edition of 1858, preface, V-VI.

10. These are the meditations on Saints Sulpice, Severus, Peter Martyr, Catherine of Siena, the Martyrdom of John the Evangelist, Michael the Archangel, Peter Celestine, Mary Magdalen of Pazzi, Germain, Margaret, Basil, Cajetan, Cyprian, Romanus, Marcellinus, Elizabeth of Hungary, and Catherine. In his study of the writings of De La Salle, Brother Pamphile explains the suppression of these meditations by the fact that they relate to feasts that are little known (CIA No. 234, p. 70).

11. A. Rayez, *Études lasalliennes,* in *Revue d'ascétique et de mystique,* RAM, No. 109, p. 37.

12. *Méditations du venerable Jean-Baptiste de La Salle . . . Résumés par le T. H. Frère Irlide, Supérieur Général,* Versailles, L. Ronce, 1880.

13. *Méditations du venerable Jean-Baptiste de La Salle . . . ,* Versailles, L. Ronce, 1882, introduction, VIII.

14. *Méditations de Saint Jean-Baptiste de La Salle à l'usage des Frères des Écoles chrétiennes,* Paris, Procure générale, 1922, preface, V.

15. *Saint Jean-Baptiste de La Salle. Méditations,* Paris, Region France, 1982. The preface is signed by Brother Michel Sauvage, FSC.

16. Brother Noah, Francis Curran (1845–1897), was born in Montreal, where he also made his novitiate. He taught for several years in Quebec before several assignments as teacher or director of schools in the United States, England, and France. He also worked on a translation of *Conduite des Écoles chrétiennes.*

17. The 1884 MTR edition is entitled *Meditations on School . . .* and published by De La Salle Institute, 48 Second Street, New York.

18. Brother Benezet Thomas, Roderick William Kane (1848–1928), was born in Dublin. At the age of 20, after completing his studies in engineering, he went to the United States. Two years later, he entered the novitiate in San Francisco. He became President of Saint Mary's College, of Manhattan College, and then of Waterford College, Ireland. In 1911 he was named Assistant Superior General, an assignment he held for twelve years. He died at Lembecq-Lez-Hal, Belgium, at the age of 80.

19. Brother Clair Stanislas, William Battersby (1904–1976), was born in Gosport, England. He made his perpetual profession in 1929 and earned his doctorate from London University in 1947, subsequently publishing the material of his thesis in a volume on De La Salle's innovative work in education. In all he published a dozen books on the Founder and different Brothers of the Institute. He spent his last years in the United States at Christian Brothers College, Memphis, Tennessee.

20. *Meditations for the Time of Retreat by John Baptist de La Salle*, Saint Mary's College Press, Winona, MN, 1975.

21. Brother Maurice-Auguste Hermans was Director of the *Cahiers lasalliens* (CL) series from its beginning in 1959 until his death in 1987. MDF is No. 12; MTR is No. 13; they were published in 1962 and 1963, respectively.

22. *Le Nouveau Testament de Notre-Seigneur Jesus-Christ—Traduit sur l'ancienne Édition Latine, corrigée par le commandement du Pape Sixte V. et publiée par l'autorité de Pape Clement VIII. Par R. P. D. Amelote, prestre de l'Oratoire, Docteur en Théologie, Avec permission de son Éminence Monseigneur le Cardinal de Noailles, archevesque de Paris. Nouvelle Edition, revue et corrigée.* Paris, chez Michel David, 1707. Comparisons of the citations in the meditations were made with the editions of Bouhours (1697–1703), de Hure (1702), Trevoux (1702), and Amelote (1683, 1694).

23. *Méditations pour les soeurs maîtresses des écoles charitables du saint Enfant Jésus, de l'Institut des Soeurs de feu R. P. Barré, minime, principalement au temps de leurs retraites et de leurs exercices spirituels, sur les principaux devoirs de leur état; . . . Par le R. P. F. Giry, exprovincial des minimes, et Directeur du même Institute.* Paris, 1687.

24. Rigault, *Histoire générale de l'Institut*, Vol. I, p. 493.

25. Rigault, op. cit., p. 493; Sauvage, op. cit., CL 1:102. Campos demonstrates the depth of the spirituality of MTR in his doctoral dissertation (CL 45 and 46).

26. J. B. Blain, *Vie de M. Jean-Baptiste de La Salle.* (CL 8:121, 165).

27. *Martyrologe, ou idée générale de la vie des saints, de leurs vertus et de leurs principals actions*, Paris, Hortemels, 1691. François Paris was born in Chatillon, near Paris. The date of his birth is not known. He became a friend of Arnauld and Nicole of Port-Royal. He died in Paris in 1718 at an advancedage. Besides *Martyrologe,* he wrote several books on the sacraments, the Psalms, the Gospels of Sundays and feasts of the year, and a translation of *Imitation of Christ* (Cf. Moreri, *Le grand dictionnaire historique* . . . , Paris, 1740, Vol. 8, pp. 84–85).

28. The first edition of this work was written in Spanish and is dated 1599. The French translation was published ten years later. Pierre de Ribadeneira was born in Toledo in 1527 and entered the Society of Jesus at the age of thirteen. His mission was to establish the Society in Belgium and the Netherlands. He was also provincial in Italy, Sicily, and Rome. Around 1574, he returned to his native country, where he spent his time writing. He wrote the life of Saint Ignatius, of Saint Francis Borgia, and of Diego Laynez. He died in 1611.

29. Louis-Marie Aroz, FSC, *Jean-Baptiste de La Salle, exécuteur testamentaire de feu Louis de La Salle, son père.* Rome, 1989. (CL 51:203)

30. Secondino Scaglione, FSC, *Le citazioni dei Padri e degli Scrittori sacri nelle Méditations*, in *Rivista Lasalliana*. No. 1, 1967, pp. 33–34.

31. *L'idée du Parfait Inférieur ou l'Art d'obéir*, Clermont, Jacquard, 1671.

32. *Considérations chrétiennes pour tous les jours de l'année* . . . , Paris, E. Michallet, 01683, 3 Vols.

# Appendix D

## List of Feasts in Alphabetical Order

The numbering here is that of the meditations in this edition. The numbering of the meditations for Sundays is from 1 to 77. The numbering of the feasts begins with number 93 and runs to 192; at that point the feasts continue with number 78 and run to 89. The meditations for the end of the year, December 29, 30, and 31, follow as numbers 90, 91, and 92. Six meditations are in *Additions*, as indicated in this list.

# Appendix E

## Index of Topics

Note: This Index has been borrowed from the edition of *Méditations* published by the Brothers of the French Region in 1982, pp. 635–647. The first number is the meditation; the second number is the point.

Heaven: 5.2; 29.3; 40; 73.3; 77.1; 99.1,2; 122.3; 139.2; 156.3; 167.3; 169.2,3; 172.1,2; 175.1; 177.3; 183.1; 196.2; 200.3; 207.3; 208

Holiness: 3.3; 7.2; 39.2; 43.3; 50.2; 53.1; 57.2,3; 60; 73.3; 75.3; 77.1; 83.3; 85.3; 93.3; 97.3; 110.1; 119.2; 127; 128.3; 131.1; 135.3; 138.1; 141.2; 158.3; 162.1; 163.1; 165.2; 166.1; 171.2; 173; 174.1,3; 175.1,2; 176; 177.1; 184.2; 186.2,3; 195.1; 201.2; 205.2,3

Holy Spirit; Action of the Holy Spirit: 3.2,3; 4.3; 30.3; 35.1,3; 42 to 45; 62.2,3; 77.3; 83.3; 87.1; 90.3; 107.1; 115.2; 124.2; 134.3; 136.2; 139.3; 141.3; 142.2; 151.2; 156.2; 163.1,2; 167.2; 170.3; 171.1; 172.1; 189.1,2; 191.2,3; 195.2; 196.1; 198.3; 199.2,3; 200.2; 201.1; 205.3; 206.1

Hope: 12.1; 22.3; 40.3; 180.2; 199.3

Humility, Humiliation, Humble: 3.1; 9.1; 12.2; 16.2; 19.2; 21.2; 38.3; 46.1; 52.3; 63.2,3; 65.2; 71.2; 79.2; 81.1; 83.1; 86; 88.1; 91.2; 93.1,2; 100.2; 101.2; 104.1; 108.3; 109.3; 112.1; 113.1; 117.3; 127.2; 142.2,3; 148.3; 151.1,2; 159.1; 160.2; 161.3; 166.1,2; 170.2,3; 176.1; 180.1; 190.3; 196.2; 200.3

Ignorance: 5.1; 37.2; 60.3; 100.2; 153.1; 159.2

Imitation, of God, of Christ: 10.3; 63.2; 95.3; 130.3; 152.1; 165.2; 173.1; 175.3; 182.3; 183.2; 196.1,2; 201.3

Inspirations: 64.1; 78.1; 96.1; 97.1; 99.3; 115.2; 123.1; 125.2,3; 136.2; 141.1; 174.1; 175.1; 202.2

Institute: 127.1; 130.2; 143.2; 148.3; 207.1,3

Instruct, Instruction: 3.1; 33.1,3; 37.2,3; 39.1; 56.3; 60.3; 61.2; 78.2,3; 79.2,3; 80.2,3; 81.2; 86.3; 91.3; 98.3; 99.1,3; 113.3; 114.3; 115.3; 120.1; 131.3; 133.2; 134.2; 136.1; 137.3; 140.1; 143.2; 145.2; 146.2; 148.3; 150.3; 153.1; 155.1,3; 160.3; 166.2; 173.1; 193.1,2; 194; 195.3; 196.1; 197; 198; 199; 201.2; 205.1; 206.1; 207.3; 208

Interior, Interiority: 16.2; 58.1; 62.3; 137.1; 180.2

Jesus: (See also Mysteries of Jesus)
  Following of Jesus: 59.1; 88.2; 97.2; 144.2; 145.1
  Incarnation: 112; 201.3
  Mediation: 62; 112
  Nativity: 85; 86; 93; 94; 96
  Passion: 23 to 28; 104; 121; 129; 145; 152; 165; 195.1
  Resurrection: 29 to 32; 40; 144.3
  Transfiguration: 152

**Zeal**: 46.3; 60.3; 67.1; 78.2; 79.3; 81.2,3; 87.2,3; 93.3; 96.3; 97.3; 98.3; 99.1,2; 100.3; 101.3; 102.1; 106.1; 108.1; 109.3; 114.2; 116.3; 117.2; 119.2,3; 120.3; 121.1; 125.1; 126.2; 128; 129.1; 131.1,2; 134.2; 135.2; 136.3; 140.1; 145.3; 148.2,3; 150.2; 153.1; 155.1,2; 157.1; 160.3; 161.1,3; 162.2,3; 166.2; 167.3; 168.3; 169.2,3; 171.2,3; 175.2,3; 180.1,3; 182.2; 186.2,3; 187; 189.2,3; 193.2,3; 200; 201; 202; 203.1,2; 204.3; 205.2; 206.2,3; 207; 208.3